A Sailor's Log

CLASSICS OF NAVAL LITERATURE

JACK SWEETMAN, SERIES EDITOR

This series makes available new editions of classic works of naval history, biography, and fiction. Each volume is complete and unabridged and includes an authoritative introduction written specifically for Classics of Naval Literature. A list of titles published or currently in preparation appears at the end of this volume.

A Sailor's Log

Recollections of Forty Years
of Naval Life

by Rear Adm. Robley D. Evans, USN

With an Introduction and Notes by
Benjamin Franklin Cooling

NAVAL INSTITUTE PRESS
Annapolis, Maryland

This book was originally published in 1901 by D.
Appleton and Company, New York, New York.

Introduction and Notes copyright © 1994 by the United
States Naval Institute, Annapolis, Maryland. All rights
reserved.

Library of Congress Cataloging-in-Publication Data

Evans, Robley D. (Robley Dunglison), 1846–1912.
    A sailor's log : recollections of forty years of naval life / by
Robley D. Evans : with an introduction and notes by Benjamin
Franklin Cooling.
        p.   cm.—(Classics of naval literature)
    Originally published: New York : D. Appleton, 1901. With new
introd.
    Includes bibliographical references
    ISBN 0-87021-587-6 (alk. paper)
    1. Evans, Robley D. (Robley Dunglison), 1846–1912—Diaries.
2. United States—History. Naval—To 1900.   3. United States—
History—Civil War,   1861–1865—Naval operations.   4. Chile—
History—Revolution, 1891.   5. Spanish-American War, 1898—Naval
operations, American.   6. Seamen—United States—Diaries. 7. United
States. Navy—Biography. I. Cooling, B. Franklin. II. Title.
III. Series.
E182.E92   1993
359'.0092—dc20
[B]   93-31160

Printed in the United States of America on acid-free paper ∞

9 8 7 6 5 4 3 2
First printing

Contents

Illustrations

Acknowledgments

For their assistance in the preparation of the introduction and notes to Robley Evans's story, it is a pleasure to thank the following:

Alaska State Library and Archives (India M. Spartz, Librarian)

Colorado Historical Society (Patrick J. Fraker, Reference Librarian)

The George Washington Masonic National Memorial Association (Stephen E. Patrick, Curator)

Keith Hammond, Bardsey, England

Jefferson County Historical Society, Port Townsend, Washington (Betty Pfouts, Research Librarian)

Kansas State Historical Society (Dan Fitzgerald, Local Records Archivist)

Maryland Historical Society (Isabelle W. Athey, Library Assistant)

Missouri State Historical Society (Elizabeth Bailey, Reference Specialist)

The National Army Museum, Great Britain (Dr. Linda Washington, Head of Department of Printed Books)

National Maritime Museum, Great Britain (D. J. Mason, Head of Enquiry Services)

Nebraska State Historical Society (Staff)

The New York Historical Society (Mariam Touba, Reference Librarian)

North Carolina Department of Cultural Resources (J. R. Lankford, Jr., Assistant State Archivist)

The Historical Society of Pennsylvania (Marion Egge, Associate Librarian)

Rutgers University Libraries (Benjamin R. Beede)

Service historique de la Marine, France (Pierre Waksman, Conservateur en Chef)

South African Library, South Africa (A. Fanarof, Director)

Smithsonian Institution Libraries (Bridget Burke Mathews, Reference Librarian)

U.S. Marine Corps Historical Center (Danny J. Crawford, Head, Reference Section, History and Museums Division)

U.S. Military Academy Library (Alan C. Aimone, Assistant Librarian for Special Collections)

U.S. Naval Academy Library (Jane H. Price, Assistant Archivist)

U.S. Naval Historical Center (Dr. William S. Dudley, Head, Early History Branch; Stanley Kalkus, Director, Navy Department Library)

U.S. Department of State (Nancy Barwick and David H. Herschler, Records Historians, Office of the Historian)

University of Virginia Library (Jeanne C. Pardee, Archives Assistant)

Utah State Historical Society (Gary Topping, Curator of Manuscripts)

Virginia Historical Society (Frances S. Pollard, Reference Librarian)

The Historical Society of Washington, D.C. (Jack D. Brewer, Collections Assistant)

The Washington State Historical Society (Frank L. Green, Librarian)

The State Historical Society of Wisconsin (Geraldine Strey, Reference Librarian)

Wyoming Department of Commerce (Ann Nelson, Historian)

I would be remiss in not acknowledging the aid of the series editor, Professor Jack Sweetman of the U.S. Naval Academy, Linda W. O'Doughda, manuscript editor at the Naval Institute Press, and my wife, Mary Anne, who provided patient hours with the word processing chores.

Introduction

They called him "Fighting Bob." He ducked the nickname, yet it stuck, and, next to George Dewey, Robley Dunglison Evans may have been the most popular naval personality in America at the turn of the century. He was a man of his Age, an epoch that stretched from the young America of the expansionist 1840s through the internationalism of the Progressive Era. Born during the first year of the war with Mexico, Evans died in the election year of 1912—the pinnacle of a period surely he and Theodore Roosevelt best personified as men of action. Both figures were aggressive and opinionated but supremely confident of themselves and their mission. Evans and Roosevelt were associates in the rambunctious America of the beginning of the twentieth century.[1]

---

1. Modern biographies of Evans include the dated and highly favorable Edward A. Falk, *Fighting Bob Evans* (New York: J. Cake and H. Smith, 1931) as well as shorter, more balanced recent appraisals by Philip Y. Nicholson, "Robley Dunglison Evans," in Roger J. Spiller, ed., *Dictionary of American Military Biography* (Westport, CT: Greenwood, 1984), 310–11, and Richard W. Turk, "Robley D. Evans: Master of Pugnac-

Evans went down to the sea in 1860 and built a career upon service in the U.S. Navy. He ably served his country from 1860 to 1908 and reflected the navy's glorious role in helping the republic pass from continental to world-class power and prestige. This was a time of energy and stress for industrializing countries and their navies, and America shared that experience. Evans's career spanned a time when steam propulsion and steel construction first supplanted, then replaced, hearts of oak and Nelsonian fleets of sail. As the U.S. Navy modernized and expanded along with the boisterous nation it served, so Evans found new challenges testing his flair and abilities. All of this can be sensed innately in the words of his memoir, published in two parts commencing in 1901.[2]

Evans's *A Sailor's Log* was published the very year that an assassin's bullet put Theodore Roosevelt in the White House. Its sequel, *An Admiral's Log,* appeared nine years later. The first volume remains by far the more zestful and informative of the two. The second shows too well the pontifications of an aging admiral. Still, taken together, the two books capture Evans's eye for publicity and a good yarn. They remain among the few published memoirs left by admirals of the new steel navy.[3] Moreover, they portray Evans as a dedicated

---

ity," in James C. Bradford, ed., *Admirals of the New Steel Navy: 1880–1930* [Makers of the American Naval Tradition] (Annapolis, MD: Naval Institute Press, 1990), 73–96.

2. *A Sailor's Log: Recollections of Forty Years of Naval Life* (New York: D. Appleton and Company, 1901), and *An Admiral's Log: Being Continued Reflections of Naval Life* (New York: D. Appleton and Co., 1910).

3. In addition to Evans's memoirs, see Charles E. Clark, *My Fifty Years in the Navy* (Boston: Little, Brown, 1917 and 1984 reprint); George Dewey, *Autobiography of George Dewey* (New York: Scribner's, 1913 and reprinted in "Classics of Naval Literature" series, with an introduction and notes by Eric McAllister Smith [Annapolis, MD: Naval Institute Press, 1987]); Bradley A. Fiske, *From Midshipman to Rear Admiral* (New York: Century, 1919); Caspar F. Goodrich, *Rope Yarns from the Old Navy*

public official, devoted to duty, honor, and his country. If he relished the limelight (his disclaimers to the contrary aside), it was not because of some ulterior desire to strut upon the world's stage. Rather, Evans's talisman was success—his own, that of his crew, his ship, and his navy. And he liked to talk about such success.

Readers will perceive the essence of Robley Evans from the moment they open to the title page of *A Sailor's Log*. Opposite, Evans appears on the frontispiece as the captain of the battleship *Iowa*. Jaw squared, eyebrows slightly cocked, Evans emits energy and determination. His dress is natty: his white duck trousers and white shoes epitomize the trim naval service of an era that painted its warships hues of buff and white in peacetime. Contrast this photograph with others in the volume that show Evans aged and pained from wounds left from the Civil War and aggravated by four decades of service afloat. Evans, despite periodic tours on the beach, will ever symbolize the seagoing sailor, most comfortable on the bridge of his ship.

If the frontispiece captures that image of Evans for posterity, his words play out the central themes of his life. His origins were humble. Born on 18 August 1846 to a rural doctor's family in the piedmont section of Floyd County, Virginia, Evans was the first of four children. He learned early in life the tenets of agrarian self-sufficiency tempered by sibling teamwork. He acquired the mores of a Virginia slaveholding family (although his father owned but several slaves), and his subsequent passages about Black Americans and foreigners other than of Anglo-Saxon stock seem typical of his heritage.

(New York: Naval History Society, 1931); Alfred Thayer Mahan, *From Sail to Steam: Recollections of Naval Life* (New York: Harper and Brothers, 1908); and Winfield Scott Schley, *Forty-Five Years Under the Flag* (New York: D. Appleton and Co., 1904). Readers should also consult William B. Cogar, *Dictionary of Admirals of the U.S. Navy, Volume I, 1862–1900* (Annapolis, MD: Naval Institute Press, 1989).

After his father's death and the removal of his family to northern Virginia, Evans took up residence with an uncle in Washington, a national capital in an emerging nation on the eve of civil war. His uncle was well placed for the warp and woof of Washington politics, but the thirteen-year-old Robley's attention was captured more by action on the little city's bustling waterfront. He tells us that this scene cultivated his desire for a life at sea. One of his uncle's acquaintances—Utah territorial representative William H. Hooper—suggested an appropriate avenue to that life. He told the teenager that if he could establish residence in that Mormon land to the west, then Hooper himself would see to his appointment to the inchoate Naval Academy at Annapolis. Evans could become a naval officer and make a career of the navy.

So Robley Evans went west in 1859, and his experiences there are a vibrant part of his memoir. Robley had not been given to schoolbooks, nor was he particularly aware of the tremendous intersectional drama playing out in the halls of Congress at the end of the 1850s. Booted out of a private school for fighting, his instruction at a parochial high school in the capital in preparation for Georgetown College seemed his destiny until Hooper's suggestion. How fortuitous it was, for Evans delights in the rough trek westward, his experiences fighting hostile Indians, and facing the challenges of an alien environment. He learns more from encounters with frontiersmen, Washakie, a Shoshoni chief, and the great Mormon patriarch Brigham Young than he would have from schoolbooks. His preparation for the Naval Academy came from real-life experience. How many of his young colleagues among the midshipmen of 1860 could boast of similar training?

The fourteen-year-old Evans and his comrades would have had a much more prosaic stay at the academy had it not been for the onset of the Civil War. Evans's memoirs recount the predictable midshipman's life of hazing and the character-building tutelage of instructors and senior officers, with but little mention of classroom education. Evans got into another scrape and feared dismissal. This too passed, but one is left with the impression that the young man most enjoyed duty on board the venerable holy relic of the navy (then a training ship), the USS *Constitution,* for as he noted: "We grew into ship life gradually and naturally, and our knowledge of the ship and all her parts was complete; such knowledge can be acquired in no other way, and while many able officers hold that this is not a matter of importance on this point, I have also still to be convinced of the soundness of their reasoning." Evans's true love would always be life on board ship; his goal would always be to train his crews to peak performance. His professional life was henceforth couched in those terms and no others.

Still, it was the Civil War that most personally affected Robley Evans. Together, he and his classmates helped save the Naval Academy from possible secessionist capture in the spring of 1861. A native Virginian, Evans might have been expected to go south with many of his friends to fight for the Confederacy. Certainly his mother expected him to do so, and another of her sons fought nobly for the Old Dominion and its way of life. But Robley Evans did not resign from U.S. service, although it is not altogether clear why he did not. Most probably, the persuasive talents of the respected commandant of midshipmen, Commander C.R.P. Rodgers, kept him loyal.

At any rate, Evans's decision proved momentous, for as a Union naval officer he gained his first sea experience on board the steam frigate USS *Powhatan,* chasing rebel blockade runners, and suffered his first grievous wounds during the amphibious operations against Fort Fisher, North Carolina. His action-packed account of the latter event clearly drives home the impression of an impetuous, aggressive young naval officer in the full bloom of youth. His graphic description of defying doctors who sought to amputate his shattered limbs may well seem embellished by years of subsequent retelling, but they reflect Evans's grit and determination not to be invalided out of the service to life as a hopeless cripple. The strategic importance of the Fort Fisher victory for the ultimate Union success in the war passes virtually unnoticed in Evans's memoir. His theme is action and drama as it affected him, not the greater cause of national survival.

Having survived a medical board attempt to retire him, Evans was ready for service in the navy of Reconstruction and the Gilded Age. Promoted to the rank of lieutenant in 1864 and lieutenant commander two years later, Evans passed through a frustrating era, viewed traditionally as the "dark ages" by naval reformers. Seen as a period of redundant duty on board rotting ships in a service held captive by a penurious Congress, the U.S. Navy of the period has been recently reinterpreted as sufficient for a nation with another agenda: namely, binding up internal wounds, completing the conquest of the continent, and slowly expanding commercial intercourse abroad.[4] The passages in Evans's book reflect the thoughts of a naval officer doing his duty, not the bleats of some gold-braided reformer contemplating greater vistas for the navy. The sights and sounds of Evans's life at this point

---

4. Traditional accounts of the navy of this period appear, for instance, in Harold and Margaret Sprout, *The Rise of American Naval Power 1776–1918* (Princeton: Princeton University Press, 1939 and reprinted in "Classics of Naval Literature" series, with an introduction by Kenneth J. Hagan and Charles Conrad Campbell [Annapolis, MD: Naval Institute Press, 1990]), and Walter R. Herrick, Jr., *The American Naval Revolution* (Baton Rouge: Louisiana State University Press, 1966). Revisionist views are set forth in Kenneth J. Hagan, *American Gunboat Diplomacy and the Old Navy, 1877–1889* (Westport, CT: Greenwood, 1973); Lance C. Buhl, "Mariners and Machines: Resistance to Technological Change in the American Navy 1865–1869," *Journal of American History* (December 1974), 703–27; and "Maintaining 'An American Navy,' 1865–1889," in Kenneth J. Hagan, ed., *In Peace and War: Interpretations of American Naval History 1775–1978* (Westport, CT: Greenwood, 1978), 145–73.

can be sensed as he cruised the Orient on board the USS *Piscataqua*, the Mediterranean while navigation officer of the sloop-of-war USS *Shenandoah*, and as the executive officer of the screw sloop USS *Congress*. He occasionally alludes to the obsolescent fleet, but his stories exude more about showing the flag, ensuring respect for American interests in the third world, and completing his education as a professional sailor. For Evans, then, it was all part of on-the-job training. Whether helping ensure the Open Door in the Far East, blunting Spanish belligerence in the *Virginius* affair, or protecting American missionaries from African cannibalism, Evans's navy accomplished as much as was expected of it by the administration and the people. Evans might bridle in private about public neglect, but he concentrated on teaching those around him to do their tasks with proficiency. Some of his most satisfying duty, he suggests, came in enlisting and training the Jack-Tars of the fleet in that period. As commander of the training ship USS *Saratoga* from 1878 to 1881, he was given that opportunity, and he spent much of his career focusing on such issues, both afloat and ashore.

Not that Evans wasn't periodically stuck with obligatory shore duty, where he encountered national domestic issues, but his memoir tells us little about them. Rather, his two-year tour as instructor at the Naval Academy in the early 1870s reveals much about his racial prejudice, which merely reflected the country as a whole. Evans's feelings carry over to comments about Black diplomats and African and South American senior officials, and project a less-than-pleasant side to the American naval officer corps of the period. His brief duty as inspector and disbursing officer for the Fifth Lighthouse District in Baltimore in 1882 may have stifled the active Evans, but it also taught him much about political patronage power in an era of veterans' privilege. As equipment officer at the Washington Navy Yard and registrar of the Naval Advisory Board in that city from 1880 to 1882, however, Evans had a chance to contribute more meaningfully to a naval renaissance. Regrettably, he does not tell us more about that period in his career.

The Naval Advisory Board under Admiral John Rodgers was charged with recommending a rebuilding program for the disintegrating American Navy.[5] Evans claimed to have advanced the idea of reconstructing in steel rather than wood or iron by arguing that the country's honor and the prestige and patronage of the young steel industry demanded that approach by the government. His persuasive talents may have carried the day, although other board members were also convinced of this necessity as they deliberated the issue. Evans subsequently became chief steel inspector for the Navy Department under Secretary William C. Whitney in the mid-1880s. He tried to persuade Carnegie, Phipps and Company management to enter into partnership with the government to produce steel plating, and at one point Evans went to Pittsburgh, Pennsylvania, ostensibly on loan to the Baltimore and Ohio Railroad as steel inspector for some bridging material. "I shall always feel proud of the work, small though it was, that I did in connection with the Advisory Board," he noted. That work, and supervising the final touches of construction of some of the navy's new steel ships during the administration of President Grover Cleveland, ultimately led to the modernized navy in which Evans fought during the Spanish-American War. Still, Evans had his faults, for despite dabbling personally with signaling devices during his career, he never sanctioned the inventor-in-uniform Bradley Fiske's gunnery sighting experiments on board his own ships, like the USS *Yorktown*. Perhaps Fiske was simply too iconoclastic for a line officer of Evans's stripe!

The *Yorktown* was not Evans's first command when he became her captain in April 1891. She would, however, pro-

5. See Benjamin Franklin Cooling, *Gray Steel and Blue Water Navy: The Formative Years of America's Military-Industrial Complex, 1881–1917* (Hamden, CT: Archon, 1979), especially 28–31.

vide the vehicle for change in Evans's life and career, and the platform for his ascendancy to the naval hall of fame as a fighting sailor. Evans and the gunboat *Yorktown* went to bolster American naval presence in Chilean waters. A diplomatic imbroglio had been touched off by the murder of two and injury of eighteen other American seamen from the USS *Baltimore* at Valparaiso, and there had been other trouble about giving political asylum to refugees in the American legation. Local representative Patrick Egan, and the *Baltimore*'s captain, Winfield Scott Schley, had, in many minds (Evans's included), badly handled the situation.

Evans thus set out to rectify the situation. By standing up to local Chilean authorities, retaining tight control over his own crew, and working closely by telegraph with Washington officials such as arch-nationalist and navalist Secretary of the Navy Benjamin F. Tracy (and his equally pugnacious President Benjamin Harrison), Evans managed to contain the crisis. His own account details how he skillfully handled the situation, blustering before a Chilean squadron overwhelmingly superior in numbers and—possibly—quality, and thereby earned the appellation "Fighting Bob" in the public press. Such jingoism baffled Evans on the scene. "I wish the newspapers would let me alone," he complained, perhaps only half seriously. Why should they call him "Fighting Bob," he asked, citing numerous congratulatory letters, when he thought he was merely doing his duty in maintaining "a dignified and resolute position"? Of course, he could have stirred up a war, he admitted, "and it may be that people would have justified me." But, he concluded, "I could not justify myself."

Still, "Fighting Bob" caught the public eye, and the eye of the administration. President Harrison dispatched the nononsense Evans to command a joint Navy-Revenue Marine force that was patrolling the sealing areas of the North Pacific and Bering Sea. By 1891, the old enmity between Great Britain and the United States (not helped by covert English

support of the Confederacy during the Civil War) had abated
somewhat. The two countries reached an agreement that out-
lawed pelagic sealing, and Evans was to enforce the law
amidst Canadian and American poachers. This arduous six-
month assignment in fog-shrouded, uncharted, icy waters
once more reflected Evans's style. Firmness and adherence to
orders were tempered by tact as Evans approached the sealers.
His flotilla logged more than 25,000 miles and claimed to
supervise inspection of every sealer afloat in the region. The
government appreciated "the judgment, energy, and skill
with which Commander Evans performed the difficult duties
assigned to him in command of the United States naval force
in [the] Bering Sea," recorded Tracy in his 1892 annual
report.[6]

Why does Evans devote seemingly disproportionate space
in his reminiscences to what we, as modern readers, view as
a less-than-critical mission? He may have felt that he was
merely recounting a phase of service that would interest contemporaries, since Alaska was exotic and fairly unknown to
most Americans. Adventure, manly stories of the outdoors,
the robustness of Theodore Roosevelt's own escapades—these
were the things upon which Americans of Evans's generation
thrived. Here again, Evans may have been seeking publicity.
The novelty of operating in Arctic waters would have attracted the notice of his naval peers, and Evans surely sensed
that he and his ships were part of some larger governmental
purpose of projecting the hemispheric power of the United
States.

Expansionist diplomacy and naval rearmament were in
vogue by the 1890s.[7] The Harrison administration set the

6. U.S. Navy Department, *Annual Report of the Secretary of the Navy, 1892*
(Washington, D.C.: Government Printing Office, 1893), 40.
7. On Harrison expansionism, see Herrick, *American Naval Revolution,*
chapters 4 through 7, and Cooling, *Benjamin Franklin Tracy: Father of the
Modern American Fighting Navy* (Hamden, CT: Archon, 1973), especially
chapters 4 through 7.

pace for both, as statesmen like Harrison, Tracy, and Secretary of State James G. Blaine were clearly bent upon establishing U.S. hegemony in the Western hemisphere. Washington wanted respect from the era's superpower, Great Britain. Accommodation of the Bering Sea business was one means of solidifying the northern flank for more strenuous operations in the warmer climes of the Caribbean. As the Harrison administration forged a truly fighting navy—battleships and heavy cruisers, not merely coast defense ironclads and patrol gunboats—capable and activist naval officers like Evans had a role to play in fulfilling the goals of armed diplomacy. Evans's contemporaries such as Stephen B. Luce and Alfred Thayer Mahan might be the "thinkers" for the new steel navy, but "doers" like Evans were the men to drive the new ships and implement policy on the high seas.

Evans soon received his reward for services in Chilean and northern waters. Promoted to captain in 1893, he was assigned command of the splendid new armored cruiser USS *New York* the following summer. This was quite a plum, considering that he was still a junior captain. The *New York* epitomized the state of the art for warships of the time.[8]

Built by William Cramp and Sons of Philadelphia, she had been authorized on 7 September 1888 and took five years to complete and commission. With a length of 380 feet and displacement of 8,200 tons, she was the largest American warship at the time. Heavily armed with a main battery of six 8-inch steel-rifled cannon (four mounted forward and aft in a pair of cylindrical turrets, with two amidships in single traditional open mounts), her secondary battery included

8. Anyone searching for both visual and textual interpretation of the American Navy of the Progressive Era can find both in John D. Alden, *The American Steel Navy: A Photographic History of the U.S. Navy from the Introduction of the Steel Hull in 1883 to the Cruise of the Great White Fleet, 1907–1909* (Annapolis, MD: Naval Institute Press, 1972 and 1989 reprint), with details about the *New York* on pages *viii*, 64, 65, 66, 72, 75, 234, 257, 280, 282, 283, 286, 317, 322, 326, 367, 383.

twelve 4-inch rapid-fire guns, eight 6-pounders, four 1-pounders, four Gatling guns, and three 18-inch above-surface torpedo tubes. Propelled by twin screws linked to four vertical triple-expansion engines providing 17,401 horsepower, she could steam at 21 knots. Girded by 4-inch side and 5.6-inch turret armor, with a protective 6-inch deck, her complement of 40 officers and 526 men marveled at the generous 1,290-ton coal capacity that gave her a cruising range of more than 10,000 miles. Of a type originated by the French Navy, America's *New York* equaled the best the world had to offer in competition.

Although the *New York* still reflected the traditional American naval policy of commerce raiding, that detracted little from her fame. Evans's ship was quite popular with both U.S. and foreign naval communities, who saw her as the pinnacle of late nineteenth-century American design. Largely because of this, Evans was commissioned to display her at the opening of the North Sea canal at Kiel, Germany, in 1895. Here Evans found himself swept into the whirl of European posturings. At first he seemed more impressed with his reception in London on the way over. New friends "made as much fuss over me as if I were named Mahan," he beamed. But going on to Kiel produced new associations even more important, as Evans mixed with German royalty and developed an admiration for Imperial Germany which gave no hint of any foreboding that this other expansionist power might one day provide a naval challenge to the United States.

Evans returned from Kiel to finish and then command America's first true battleship, the USS *Indiana*. The tour lasted hardly a year, however, for Evans was appointed to the Navy Department's Personnel Board in early 1897. Working closely with Assistant Secretary of the Navy Theodore Roosevelt, Evans and his colleagues helped ameliorate classic differences in rank and pay between staff and line; institute new retirement policies to speed promotions; improve conditions and pay for warrant officers and seamen; and also reorganize and enlarge the Marine Corps. Clearly, Evans enjoyed coming in close contact with Roosevelt, with whom he claimed to develop an affinity on the eve of the Spanish-American conflict. Yet, in the end, Evans once more yearned for sea command.

Evans counseled both Roosevelt and his chief, Secretary of the Navy John D. Long, about Spanish torpedo boat capabilities, as well as the war fever he had discerned while making a survey of lighthouses along the southern coast of the United States. Again, Evans was rewarded for his services with command of the newest battlewagon, the USS *Iowa*. Evans would fight this ship in the coming war with Spain. From his cabin, he would chafe at an administration policy that prevented a bombardment of Havana, Cuba, by the North Atlantic Squadron. He would storm the bridge in disgust at Schley's tepid employment of the so-called "Flying Squadron" as it searched for the Spanish fleet of Admiral Pascual Cervera.

Evans would be at his best on the morning of 3 July 1898, when he took his ship against the Spanish fleet making its sortie for freedom from Santiago Harbor. One can almost sense the electricity as "Fighting Bob" forgets his wounds of old, as the battle is joined. Here was the supreme test for his generation of American naval officers, the challenge for the iron men in steel ships—like the *Iowa*—of the new navy. Evans's son, Franck Taylor Evans, a naval cadet from a sister battleship, stood at his side, and together they witnessed the destruction of an Old World fleet at the hands of one from the new. One senses from Evans's memoir that here, amidst the din of battle, Robley Dunglison Evans found his true calling and his ultimate home.

A Sailor's Log concludes with the triumphal return after Santiago. Evans left the *Iowa* in October 1898 and returned to sea duty four years later as commander of the cruiser division of the Asiatic Fleet. Promoted to Rear Admiral in February 1901, he now numbered among the senior leaders of the navy. Evans took great pride in serving as escort for his old friend Prince Henry of Germany as his personal contribution to restoring harmonious relations between their two countries after the standoff in the Philippines following Commodore George Dewey's victory at Manila Bay. Yet, once more, Evans fails to evidence any concern about German rivalry in the future. He may have felt it, but he said nothing about it in his autobiography.

Evans commanded the Asiatic Fleet from 1902 to 1905, and the North Atlantic Fleet from 1905 to 1907, at which time Roosevelt selected his friend to take the cream of the U.S. Navy's battle fleet on a world-encircling cruise as a symbol of American power. Evans would never complete the mission. Ill health denied him one last chance for glory. By the time the Great White Fleet returned to Hampton Roads, Virginia, on 22 February 1909, Evans had retired from the navy. Gout, war wounds, and four decades of naval life had taken their toll on "Fighting Bob."

Evans devoted his remaining years to occasional articles, a second memoir, and random services to the Navy Department, as in 1909, when he participated on a departmental reorganization board. His strong defense of warship design displeased insurgent reformers in the service, but Evans endorsed other proposals to streamline and modernize bureaucratic administration of the navy. Residing quietly with his wife, Charlotte (sister to his academy classmate Henry G. Taylor), at 324 Indiana Avenue near the capitol in Washington, "Fighting Bob" was not far from the navy yard where he had spent several tours helping to develop what would become "the New Steel Navy." He succumbed to a heart attack on 3 January 1912.

Robley Dunglison Evans bequeathed two memoirs to posterity. The first, A Sailor's Log, captures best this man of action. Evans divided his work proportionally, ostensibly as he viewed his life. He devoted three chapters (34 pages) to his early life, five chapters (71 pages) to the Civil War experience, and nine chapters (136 pages) to tours afloat during Reconstruction and the Gilded Age. The imbroglio with Chile receives four chapters (61 pages), coverage of the Bering Sea duty required five chapters (56 pages), and development of the new navy covers five chapters (41 pages). Finally, Evans devoted seven full chapters (58 pages) to his view of the Spanish-American War.

Yet, in sum, we gain a full measure of Evans only by reading all of the work closely. He suffered severe and painful wounds while leading a Marine and sailor detachment against Fort Fisher in the Civil War. He helped establish standards and specifications for the new steel navy, and as a fleet captain, he continuously strove to build a fighting navy through hard training and drill. Never an intellectual, Evans was a sea dog, fighting the elements in the Bering Sea as well as the Spaniards at Santiago. The consummate outdoorsman, he enjoyed the challenge of a sea breeze and brine in his face, and the throbbing engines of steam beneath his feet. Never completely comfortable ashore, Robley Evans was at his best projecting stamina and pugnacity afloat.

Evans's friend Theodore Roosevelt provides some of the most quotable tributes to "Fighting Bob." He wrote Evans upon reading *A Sailor's Log,* "It is not only that I think your book interesting. I feel that in addition it half unconsciously portrays the spirit which makes those of us who have the honor of the country very deeply at heart feel an undying faith in the United States navy."[9] Later, in his eulogy to Evans, Roosevelt cited the naval officer's "touch of brilliant picturesqueness" which placed him with the great naval characters "from the days of Benbow to the days of Nelson, and from the days of Nelson to those of Farragut." Roosevelt pronounced that the American Navy had perhaps never had any

9. Elting E. Morison and John M. Blum, eds., *Letters of Theodore Roosevelt,* III, 99, as quoted in Turk, "Evans," 94, fn4.

man "who more thoroughly and joyously welcomed a fight." [10] Certainly, the public press and even Evans himself cultivated that image as, when he told a San Francisco audience in May 1908, "If you wish to preserve the peace of the world, give us more battleships and fewer statesmen." [11] We are left to wonder whether Evans found it gratifying simply to live out the role that others created for him by interpreting his actions and feelings. *A Sailor's Log* reinforces the conclusion that at times he did so.

The most revealing words of Evans may well come in the final passages of his memoir. Writing how one elderly Cincinnatian had confronted him during a stopover in that Ohio River city, Evans cited the man's remark. "Captain, I want to know how it feels when you are sure that there are seventy millions of people, each of whom would like to look into your eyes and say, 'God bless you!' " Evans recalled that he could have told the kindly old man "that it made me feel that fighting by day and watching by night, that danger in storm and suffering in tropic calm, were but 'reasonable service' to such a country and such fellow-countrymen as I am bound to by every feeling of my heart." Here was a simpler Robley Dunglison Evans—a man of integrity and service to his country. Here, too, was a professional sailor, happier afloat than ashore, whose nearly half-century of duty had successfully bridged the fighting navy of wooden ships to one forged from steel and powered by steam.

BENJAMIN FRANKLIN COOLING

10. Theodore Roosevelt, "Admiral Evans," *The Outlook,* 100 (13 January 1912), 55.
11. Quoted in Peter Karsten, *The Naval Aristocracy: The Golden Age of Annapolis and the Emergence of Modern American Navalism* (New York, The Free Press, 1972), 219.

A Sailor's Log

ROBLEY D. EVANS
From a photograph taken on the bridge of the battleship Iowa

To

my wife,

without whose inspiration and assistance

it would not have been written,

this book is dedicated.

Contents

CHAPTER I

Life in Virginia Before the War

BEFORE spinning the yarn of my forty years in the navy, it seems only proper that I should give a short history of my life before entering the service.

I was born in Floyd County, Virginia, August 18, 1846.

My father, Samuel Andrew Jackson Evans, M. D.,[1] was a graduate of the University of Virginia, and named me, his first son, after Doctor Robley Dunglison,[2] who had been his

1. An educated man of the old type, Dr. Evans owned a large farm near Spangler's Mill in Floyd County, Virginia. He held some slaves, conducted a county-wide practice, and reputedly represented Floyd County in the state legislature. He married Sallie Jackson and the couple raised four children, of whom Robley Dunglison was the eldest. Sallie M. became a popular schoolteacher of the county and the wife of local physician Dr. Brainard W. Hines. Samuel T. became a prominent Tennessee physician. William M. was a lawyer in Portland, Oregon. Four years before Dr. Evans's death in 1856, the family moved to the hamlet of Jacksonville, where Dr. Evans served as an elder in the local Presbyterian church.

2. A teacher and author of great ability, Dr. Dunglison was born in Keswick, England in 1798. He received his medical degree in London in 1819, studied at the University of Erlangen, in Germany, in 1833, and returned to the practice of medicine and medical writing in London.

instructor and dear friend. The home of my parents was in the mountains of Virginia, which, at the time of my birth, were almost as wild and rough as the partially settled mountains of the West. We did not have savage Indians to contend with, but we did have their savage white brothers.

As a means of livelihood my father followed his profession of medicine, and he was the only doctor in a circuit of twenty or thirty miles. For pleasure he owned slaves and farmed, and when requested to do so, represented his constituents in the State Legislature. The life of a doctor under such conditions was a very hard one, particularly in the winter season. Frequently he had to be in the saddle all night, facing the storms of snow and rain, to help some sufferer who could only offer his thanks as pay, for most of the people were very poor. It was this exposure that finally cost my father his life in the prime of his manhood and usefulness.

My first distinct memory of myself is when I was about four years old. I had rather long, light-coloured curls, was sturdy in health, and wore a blue velvet suit, with a feather in my cap for ornament. On hiring day, when the slaves were assembled at the courthouse to find employers for the next year, I wandered about the village streets and considered myself of importance. At this time I rode from my home to the schoolhouse every day, a distance of five miles; and while I

Summoned by Thomas Jefferson to take the professorship of Medicine at the University of Virginia, he remained at Charlottesville until 1833 as first secretary of its faculty and its second chairman. He moved to the University of Maryland in Baltimore in 1833 as chair of Materia Medica and Therapeutics, then became professor of the Institutes of Medicine in Jefferson Medical College of Philadelphia in 1836. Under his tutelage as dean of the faculty, this institution made notable progress. Dr. Dunglison served as vice president of the Philadelphia Institution for the Blind and promoted the printing of books in embossed letters for the blind. In 1825 he received an honorary Doctor of Medicine degree from Yale and was granted the degree of Doctor of Laws elsewhere. Author of numerous medical works, his most important was *Human Physiology,* which was designed as a textbook for students. Dr. Dunglison died in 1869.

can recall the way the teacher used to thrash the boys, first sending them to cut the birches, I can not recall that I ever learned anything.

When I was six years old I was the happy possessor of a gun, a pony, and a negro boy. The first I learned to handle with considerable skill, was devoted to its use, and in all my life since have found both health and pleasure from the hunting habit formed at that early age. The pony, as I now recollect him, seemed bent on breaking my neck; and the coloured lad, my constant companion, taught me, among other things, to smoke and chew tobacco. He impressed on my mind many superstitions and dreadful ghost stories, some of which I remember to this day. The pony had one marked characteristic which I can also recall. He would go beautifully as long as I was going his way, but any attempt to send him over a road he did not wish to travel led to trouble. He would turn round and round and buck a few times, to rid himself of his mount, and, failing in this, lie down in the road and roll over. I managed, however, to get to the courthouse on most days, and had much pleasure and comfort from his ownership.

Like most Southern children, I was brought up and cared for by a "black mammy," and I certainly loved her dearly. She was a short, thickset, very black woman, much the shape of a flour barrel. In addition to the care of four of us, she had had eighteen children of her own; but with it all she always had time to comfort me when I was in trouble, which I must say was frequently the case. No matter how busy she might be, she could make the time to coddle her young master and comfort him in a way that no other could. The memory of her corn bread and fried chicken lingers with me after all these years. She was freed in the early days of the civil war, and spent the rest of her life in the city of Washington. She died in the Howard Hospital[3] at the good old age of one

3. Evans presumably refers to Freedman's Hospital, which was located

hundred and two years, and it was my great pleasure to know that in her last years I had given her every comfort that she could desire, and so paid off a small portion of the debt I owed her. My grandmother had given her to my mother as a marriage portion, and the faithful old soul had lived her life in our family connection.

Life in the mountains of Virginia in my early boyhood days was very different from any I have ever known since. The country was thinly settled, and the people were as a rule poor, but what they had they freely shared with their neighbours. Their hospitality was great and sincere. They were honest, hard-working people, who insisted on straight dealing, and they sometimes took the law into their own hands to enforce their ideas. There were two things one must not do—steal horses or interfere with his neighbours' slaves. Churches and schools were few and widely distributed. In place of the former we had the "circuit rider," who came and made himself at home almost as a member of the family, until his duties were performed, when he passed on to some other farmhouse, and so in turn visited the whole section. In the summer time camp meetings were organized, and then the horsemen and horsewomen gathered from all the surrounding mountains and enjoyed themselves in a very sensible way. Most of them prayed and sang until they were tired, and then withdrew to their tents and ate and drank the good things that had been prepared for them. Wheeled vehicles were not in use to any general extent for pleasure purposes, as the few roads we had were mere trails fit only for horses. Sometimes the camp would be made near a smooth stretch of road, and after the ministers and the shouters had done their work the young men would have their innings and speed

---

after the Civil War between 5th and 7th streets and Boundary (Florida Avenue) and Pomery streets, N.W., near the present Howard University Hospital site. (Howard University for Black Americans was founded in 1867 in this area of Washington, D.C.)

their favourite horses; certainly there could not have been found a more healthful recreation or a happier way of passing a week during the heat of the summer.

In the fall of the year, when the tobacco had been cured and the apple crop gathered, the overseer on my father's farm usually fitted out an expedition for Lynchburg.[4] This consisted of a number of six-horse wagons, sufficient to carry the tobacco and such other things as were to be sold. When all was ready the start was made, and this starting was quite an occasion. Every man, woman, and child wanted something from town, and the list was never completed until the train was some miles on its way. I can recall now the joy with which I made one of these trips. I had a comfortable place in one of the wagons when I wanted to ride there, or I could mount my own pony. At night we camped by the roadside, and after supper listened to the songs of the teamsters and helpers until bedtime. Early daylight found us under way after a breakfast of fried bacon and chicken, and such corn bread as one can never have now, because such corn meal as we ate in those days is no longer made. When we arrived at our destination the tobacco was soon weighed into the warehouse, the apples and chickens and bacon sold, and then we enjoyed the shopping until our money was gone. My wants were few—a pair of high winter boots with red tops, a saddle for my pony, and a few pounds of powder and shot and half a dozen boxes of caps. Then we came home with our long list of things for the winter—everything from the family groceries to the Christmas presents for the slaves, down to the last pickaninny of them all.

I remember well what a great joy the harvest season was to me as a youngster. After following the cradlers, splendid great black fellows, giants in physique, until noon, the cradles were laid aside and the men gathered under the shade

4. This prominent commercial and rail city in Amherst County, Virginia, was the scene of a Civil War battle on 16–18 June 1864.

trees for their midday meal. Then the man who had led the gang had an extra glass of apple-jack to encourage him for the afternoon's work, also a few kindly words of encouragement from my father, if he happened to be present. That leader seemed to me one of the greatest men in the world! My particular duty and pleasure during these harvest days was to carry a basket lined with raw cotton in which I gathered the eggs of the Bob White. As the nests were cut over by the cradlers, the mother birds left, never to return, and I at once gathered the eggs and put them under sitting hens to be hatched out. There was one particular clover field which was the favourite nesting place of these birds, and of course my particular delight. I once gathered one hundred and twenty eggs in this field, and succeeded in hatching most of them under a hen in the barn. When the small birds had got rid of their shells, it was interesting to see the old hen try to manage her unnatural brood. At the least bit of noise the whole lot would disappear, and you might search to your heart's content without finding one. The old hen would cluck and scratch with great energy, but the young birds remained in hiding until all danger was passed. As winter came on, I fed these birds in the barnyard, and they remained there until the spring came, when they disappeared in the grain fields.

The winters were very severe, and, of course, life was mostly indoors. When the river was in condition for such sport, we spent much time in sleighing on it. My father had brought from the East a two-horse sleigh, and in this the family had many jolly rides, particularly on moonlight nights. For myself, I think I preferred to stay in the house, where it was warm, or run away with black mammy to the quarters and hear the negroes sing and see them dance. I don't remember ever having much pleasure in the winter either in my boyhood or since; the mere fact of cold weather is enough to take the pleasure out of life for me. We usually had the house full of company both winter and summer, as we had connections who lived far enough North to enjoy the winters, and others living far enough South to enjoy the summers.

Slaves were not owned in large numbers in the mountain regions of Virginia. There was no necessity for their labour. The amount of tobacco grown was small, and the country was thinly settled. Above all, the people as a rule were poor and did their own farm work. I don't remember how many my father owned. I can recall a dozen or more, and they certainly were a happy lot. I never saw but one slave whipped, and he was struck a single blow with a rawhide on his bare back for having ill treated a riding horse. My father never sold one of his slaves, yet stories were frequently circulated that he was going to do so, and this led to no end of trouble. One winter night we were sitting in the parlour eating apples and black walnuts, which was the habit of all Virginia children in that day, before retiring. There came a knock at the door, and when it was opened one of the negro men named Sambo presented himself covered with blood. He told my father that a robber had thrown a hatchet at him and cut him badly. On examination it was found that Sambo's left hand was in bad shape—two fingers entirely cut off and two others hanging by small bits of skin. His hand was dressed and he was sent off to his cabin; but the next day blood marks on the snow showed his trail, and we soon found a stump on the bank of the river a mile or so from the house, where he had cut his own fingers off. He had missed his hand at the first blow in the dark, but the second time he succeeded. The axe with which the cutting was done was found near by, where he had thrown it. When confronted with the evidence he at once admitted his guilt, and pleaded as excuse that he believed my father meant to send him away from his family; that he had been so informed, and he knew that no one would buy him if he had only one hand. The poor chap learned to chop wood with one hand, and that was his sole occupation as long as I knew anything about him. After my father's death he was sold with the rest of the property, and brought seventy-five dollars.

Of course, no one can defend slavery as it existed in our Southern States, nor indeed in any form; but we must admit that in some ways the results were not wholly bad. No one can deny that in many cases slaves were cruelly treated, but this was not the general rule; it was not the business way of looking out for valuable property, to place it on no higher plane. Slaves, as a rule, were too valuable to be ill treated or neglected. The curse of slavery was to the white race and not the black. The bad effects were felt by the growing generation of whites; but as for the blacks, I am sure their lives were easier and happier then than since they were given their freedom. The slaves on my father's farm did not come themselves from Africa, but I have no doubt their parents, or certainly their grandparents, did. It has been my fortune to see something of the Africans in their own country, and when I compare them, with their brutal habits in their unlimited freedom and self-government, with the black people who were slaves in this country, I must conclude that slavery was not all bad. There was something about it that produced honesty and faithfulness and a race of men who, when their masters were away fighting to keep them slaves, took the same care of the women and children as the masters would have taken of them themselves. Their record in this respect is certainly as fine as anything in history. I believe there is not an authentic case of slaves having ill treated the women and children of their masters during the entire civil war. Imagine what would have been the result if these women and children had been left in the care of native Africans under such conditions!

My father died when I was ten years old, and I found myself the head of the family. In order that we might be near good schools, my mother moved at once to Fairfax

Courthouse.[5] There my schooling really began, but only continued for a short time. It was in Fairfax that the farmer said to his Northern friend who was congratulating him on the large size of his farm: "I am not as poor as you seem to think. I don't own *all* that land!" The county was always rich in lawsuits, averaging probably one or two to the acre, and since the civil war it is rich in historical incidents.

5. A quaint little northern Virginia village some twenty miles from Washington, Fairfax Courthouse had been the Fairfax County seat since 1800. The Little River Turnpike that traversed the town was a major trade route for farmers carrying their wares to market in Alexandria and Washington, D.C. Apparently, Sallie Jackson Evans was sister to Captain James W. Jackson in whose Alexandria hotel Colonel Elmer Ellsworth was shot in 1861, when he hauled down a rebel flag. The family's move from Floyd County in 1858 may have been occasioned by Mrs. Evans's desire to be closer to kinsmen following her husband's death.

CHAPTER 2

With the Indians and Buffalo

IN the year 1857 I was invited to make my home with my uncle, Mr. A.H. Evans, [1] in Washington, which I gladly did, that I might have the advantage of good schools. I found this new home a real home, and from my uncle and aunt I received all the loving-kindness and attention that I could have had from my own parents; they treated me as one of their own children, except that they were never as severe with my small faults as they were with theirs. To my dear aunt I owe a deep debt of gratitude for her unfailing love and sympathy, and to my good uncle I owe my position in the navy. He was a lawyer by profession, but at the time of which I write was clerk of the House Committee on Claims and a busy newspaper man.

Soon after reaching Washington I was fortunate enough to be admitted to the public school presided over by Mr. John

1. Alexander H. Evans is listed in the 1858 Washington, D.C., directory as an attorney, residing at 411 (old numbering system: between G and H streets on the west side) 11th Street, N.W.

W. Thompson,[2] who was undoubtedly one of the best teachers Washington has ever known. I think I could have learned a great many things from this good man, but my career in his school was very short. One day, after a smart rainstorm, I was trying to sail a toy boat in a pond in the school yard when one of the larger boys smashed my boat with a stone. I immediately smashed him with another, and he was carried home on a door. I was soon at my home with my books and belongings, and thus ended my public-school life. After a few weeks I was entered at Gonzaga College,[3] preparatory to Georgetown College,[4] and here I was lucky enough to remain until my school days in civil life were ended. In this excellent school I learned, or was supposed to learn, much Greek, Latin, and other things. Afterward, when I went to Athens on a vessel of war, I tried to practise some of my Greek, but only met with indifferent success; the people to whom I spoke were at a loss to know even what language I was trying to speak.

Much of my spare time was spent about the committee rooms of the Capitol, and on the floor of the House, where I made the acquaintance of some of the men who afterward became so prominent in the history of the country; among

2. Mr. Thompson is listed in the 1858 city directory as the principal of a school at 14th and G streets, residing at 424 (between H & I streets on the east side) 14th Street, N.W.
3. In the 1850s Gonzaga College was on the north side of F Street between 9th and 10th streets, N.W. Founded in 1821 as a Roman Catholic high school, it continues today at a North Capitol Street, N.W., location.
4. Founded in 1789 and opened by act of Congress in 1791, Georgetown College (now University) is the oldest Roman Catholic college in the United States. On 1 March 1815, Congress granted it the right to confer degrees; in 1833, the Holy See empowered it to confer degrees in philosophy and theology. Formal incorporation took place in 1844, followed by the opening of the School of Medicine in 1851 and the School of Law in 1870. "Legally" the school became a university in 1966.

them I remember particularly John A. Logan[5] and Mr. Maynard,[6] of Tennessee. I also passed many happy hours on the
water front, watching the various sailing craft as they came
and went. I had never seen salt water, and I don't think I
knew a single naval officer; but somehow it came to me that
I should like a sea life, and from this time on the idea was
never out of my mind. I had about decided to run away to
sea, when I made the acquaintance of Mr. Hooper,[7] the delegate in Congress from the Territory of Utah, with whom my
uncle was in some way associated. He asked me if I would
like an appointment to Annapolis, to which I very promptly
replied that nothing in the world would please me so much.
In order to have the appointment, however, it was necessary
that I should go to Salt Lake City[8] and become a resident. I
had four days in which to prepare for what was, at that time,

5. John Alexander Logan (1826–86), an Illinois politician and Union
general, served in the House of Representatives, 1867–71, and the U.S.
Senate, 1871–72.
6. Horace Maynard (1814–82) was a Representative from Tennessee,
1857–63 and 1866–75, a presidential elector, minister to Turkey, and
Postmaster General, 1880–81.
7. William Henry Hooper (1813–82) was a delegate from the Utah Territory, 1859–61 and 1865–73. Utah's second delegate to Congress, he
was born in Dorchester County, Maryland, and was a merchant there on
the Eastern Shore and in Baltimore before emigrating to Illinois, where
he became a steamboat captain on the Mississippi. He moved to Utah in
1850, was elected to the Utah legislature, and served as a secretary of the
territory. He became a U.S. Senator in 1862. In the House of Representatives, he defended polygamy, although he did not practice such himself.
He was a well-known banker and mercantilist of Salt Lake City.
8. According to an 1860 census, Salt Lake City had a population of
8,256 people and was the most important settlement in the territory.
Prosperity had arrived with the gold rush, as emigrants used the city as
a supply point and U.S. government troops began trading there in 1858.
The town's appearance was still unimpressive in this period, with muddy
streets and a lack of imposing buildings. The modern urban appearance
awaited the arrival of the railroad and the great non-Mormon mining
fortunes of the 1870s.

a very long and dangerous journey; but the end of the fourth day found me ready for the start.

When I left Washington, in 1859, by the Baltimore and Ohio Railroad,[9] I carried all my worldly goods in a large, old-fashioned grip sack. It contained, among other things, a navy revolver, which was about half as long as I was, and the ammunition for this weapon. On my person in a money belt I carried two hundred and fifty dollars in gold, and in my pocket a ticket to St. Joseph, Missouri.[10] I can recall after all these years the feeling of loneliness that came over me when I changed cars at the Relay House[11] and headed for the West. The job that I had cut out for myself came to me then with full force, and I felt that the chance of my ever coming back was very small. But youth and health are great things, and I was soon comfortably asleep on one of the seats, happily oblivious of my surroundings. In those days sleepers and dining cars were undiscovered luxuries. Passengers slept as best they could, and snatched their meals from designated stations along the road. Everything went well with me until we reached Davis, in the State of Missouri,[12] where we were to spend the night, as there was no connection on to St. Joseph. Upon reaching the nearest tavern I deposited my travelling bag with the clerk in the office and retired, very sleepy and

9. The nation's oldest railroad, the Baltimore and Ohio Railroad was chartered in 1828 to link tidewater Baltimore, Maryland, with the Ohio River trade. The line became a vital strategic artery for the Union in the Civil War.

10. Located on the western border of Missouri, St. Joseph was a favorite gathering point for emigrants moving west.

11. Relay House, Maryland, was a prominent point on the Baltimore and Ohio Railroad line in the Patapsco River valley, where lines converged from Washington and Baltimore before heading westward to Ohio.

12. It is unclear precisely what Evans is referring to. Davis may have been a hamlet of Daviess in Daviess County, north of the Hanibal and St. Joseph Railroad (the first railroad across northern Missouri, completed in February 1859).

used up. When I awoke in the early morning I went to the
office to get some necessary articles from my bag, but upon
trying the key found to my dismay that it would not unlock
the valise given me, though it seemed from appearances to
be mine. Investigation soon disclosed the fact that an old
gentleman who had gone East on a train at two o'clock in the
morning had taken my bag and left me his. The proprietor of
the hotel wired for the lost article, but without success; so,
after waiting over one train, I broke open the bag and found,
among other things, half a dozen beautiful fine white linen
ruffled shirts—any one of them large enough to make two or
three garments for me. Quite a crowd had gathered in the
office of the hotel, all hands fully of sympathy for the small
kid who had lost his outfit. After overhauling the bag, I
mounted a chair and disposed of the articles at auction, and
realized a sum quite sufficient to replace the things I had
lost.

At St. Joseph I met friends to whom I was consigned, and
they assisted me in finding a suitable party going my way,
and in arranging the outfit. We were a party of six—five for
California and one for Salt Lake City. Our wagons were soon
purchased and stocked with the necessary provisions, blankets, etc. Then we bought the horses and arms, and in a few
days we were ready to start. My riding animal was a rather
large gray Mexican mule, which, as it afterward turned out,
could smell an Indian farther, and, under the influence of his
scent, run faster than any animal in the outfit. I was, of
course, a very light weight, and it was all I could do at first
to manage the beast. He could outbite and outkick anything
that ever came my way. Without intending to do so, I delayed our start one day, and came very near delaying it for
all time, as far as I personally was concerned. I had gone to
a gymnasium with some other boys of my own age, when
one of them did a trick on the horizontal bar which I was
invited to imitate. I tried, but brought up squarely on top
of my head on the floor. Slight concussion of the brain was

the result, and the doctor had me in hand that night and part of the next day.

We finally ferried over the Missouri River and pulled out for our long trip over the prairies. Each member of the party had his particular duty and work to do, and each one had to do it to the satisfaction of the guide in charge, one Bromley by name. As I was very young and small, I was assigned to assist the cook in preparing meals, and was sometimes sent out after game, but was excused from standing watch at night. Each one had to look after his own animals, arms, etc.

Our journey for the first few days was through the Kickapoo Indian[13] country. We passed through several of their villages, the leading feature of which was the great number of wolfish-looking dogs they had; they were barking and snapping at our horses continually from the time we sighted the villages until we were a mile or so beyond them. These Indians seemed friendly, and, like all others that I saw, lazy and dirty, but picturesque.

After the first week we headed for the South Platte River,[14] and were soon among the buffalo. We found them in scattered herds, and then in a solid mass—the whole country covered with them as far as the eye could reach, literally untold thousands of them. At one time we drove through a herd for three days without ever being out of gunshot of these magnificent animals. Frequently we had to stop and put all our own animals between the wagons to prevent their being run over and stampeded. I noticed one curious trait of the buffalo: they would trot alongside of our outfit for miles, and

13. Kickapoo Indians were a tribe of the Algonquian group, forming a division with the Sauk and Fox. By Evans's time they had been forced southwestward from the Lake Superior area of Minnesota to Missouri and Kansas.

14. In northeast Colorado the river flows past Fort Collins, Fort Morgan, Fort Sedgwick and Fort McPherson to the junction with the North Platte River in southwest Nebraska. The Overland Trail followed the river before heading north into southeast Wyoming.

then suddenly forge ahead and cross our track! They never
seemed to care to cross behind us. When the herd was making for water, they seemed to travel in single file, with a fine
full-grown bull in the lead. The straight, narrow paths they
made led over the top of any small hill or roll in the prairie;
and we often saw the leader some distance ahead of the others, standing like a statue on an elevation, looking apparently
for signs of danger. We shot many of them, of course, but
in most cases only removed their tongues, leaving the rest
for the wolves, which in large numbers hung on to the edges
of the herd. The usual way of killing them was to ride up
fairly close and empty a revolver into the one selected, aiming to strike behind the point of the shoulder blade. In most
cases two or three shots were required before blood appeared
at the mouth, which was a sure sign that the animal was
done for. I used a Colt's revolving rifle,[15] a five-shooter, and
with this I was not required to get to such close quarters, a
proceeding that my mule always objected to.

In this beautiful valley of the South Platte we passed many
emigrant trains bound to the West and Northwest. They
were coralled generally, sometimes as many as fifty wagons
in one corral, the horses feeding about over the plains during
the daytime, but carefully guarded at night, for fear of Indians, who were generally to be found looking for something
to steal. The wagons had the canvas covers taken off, and the
exposed frames were used for "jerking" buffalo meat. Hundreds of buffalo were killed, the hides removed, and the meat

15. The Colt Revolving Rifle was the long-arm version of Samuel Colt's
famous percussion cap, revolving-cylinder pistol made at Hartford, Connecticut, as early as 1836. Improvements were added in 1840, 1842, and
1855, when the .56-caliber model held five cartridges. Government records indicate a few were purchased in 1857, seeming to prove that the
Colt rifle was the first repeater adopted and used by the U.S. Army.
These rifles were the wonders of the age due to their rate of fire and
legendary accuracy.

cut into thin strips and hung on the wagon frames, where it slowly dried in the sun. Owing to the pureness of the air, no salt was required to preserve it, and meat thus treated would last the emigrants all the way out to the Pacific coast. Our party did not care for "jerked" meat, but we did enjoy many antelope hams, which were cured by simply putting them on the end of a pole fifteen or twenty feet long and exposing them to the sun for a day or two.

All the way up the Platte Valley we met with the buffalo in such vast numbers that the idea of exterminating them would have seemed absurd, if such a thought had entered any one's mind; though they were killed by the thousand, it seemed to make no difference in the size of the herds; but this was only because no careful estimate of the number was made from year to year. As we drove or rode along over the prairie the carcasses of the buffalo covered the ground in every direction as far as the eye could reach. Immense numbers of piles of white bones showed where the animals had fallen in past years, and the thick brown spots indicated this season's work of destruction. In most cases the tongue was cut out, and the rest left to decay or be eaten by the wolves— the hide was not even removed. I came back over this same route in 1892, and was amazed to find that all these bones had been carefully gathered up, sent East, and sold. Where there had been millions of buffalo not a single herd of the magnificent game animals remained; all of them had been destroyed, and in a great measure wantonly.

We crossed the Platte at Thompson's Ford, [16] a hundred or so miles east of Pike's Peak, [17] and struck off to the northwest

16. Evans's geography becomes imprecise at this point, but it may be surmised that his party crossed the South Platte at one of three fords in southwest Nebraska, southeast of Chimney Rock.
17. The famous 14,110-foot mountain in the Front Range of central Colorado.

toward Chimney Rock[18] and Fort Laramie.[19] The trail was
fairly good, and our journey most comfortable. We usually
made an early start, and, halting for a rest in the middle of
the day, brought up in the afternoon in time to make ourselves comfortable before dark—this programme depending
somewhat upon the water, which was a question of vital importance. Having reached the water, our tent was soon up,
the wagons arranged so as to give as much protection and
shelter as possible, and the horses secured near by to feed on
the luxuriant grass. Then my part of the work was soon done:
coffee, bread, and bacon or game were served, and after the
guard for the night was arranged we turned in and were soon
sound asleep. I was small enough to sleep comfortably in the
body of one of the wagons, and this was my usual place.
Sometimes I would vary the monotony by rolling up in my
blanket and turning in on the grass under the wagon. When
we reached the rattlesnake ground I broke myself very
quickly of this habit, and always slept in the wagon.

Fort Laramie was reached in due time, and, after replen-
ishing some of our stores, we continued on our way. I think
it was the second day out from this post that we had our first
serious trouble. In trying to cross a small stream in a marshy
place late in the afternoon our leading wagon stuck in the
mud, and the united efforts of all hands failed to pull it out.
We concluded to sleep over it, and so turned in for the
night. At early daylight we found ourselves surrounded by
hostile Indians, and they soon relieved us of all further bother
about our outfit by chasing us away, taking what they

18. In their letters and diaries, many emigrants commented upon Chimney Rock (in western Nebraska) as their first encounter with the geo-
graphical features of the West. They climbed high up on the rock to
carve their names there for posterity.
19. A private fur-trading post on the edge of the eastern Wyoming prairies from 1834 to 1849, Fort Laramie became a military post thereafter,
growing into a sprawling reservation in the Indian wars, and the major
trading center in the Rockies.

wanted and burning the wagons. We saved some food, all our arms, powder, etc., and all the animals. The Indians made it very interesting for us for ten or twelve hours until we found cover, when we returned the compliment with interest. My old mule with his light mount was easily the fastest animal in that outfit. After standing the Pawnees[20] off for some time and killing a good many of them, we made our way back to Fort Laramie, where we managed to secure one wagon and some pack animals, bought a fresh lot of supplies, and continued on our way.

We had frequent trouble with Indians until after passing Fort Bridger,[21] where, owing to the absence of the buffalo herds, we were comparatively free from them. Once we were ambushed by the Blackfeet,[22] a tribe supposed to be peaceable; but a hunting party of them thought it an easy way to get some fine animals, and so laid a trap for us. We marched into their trap just after daylight in the morning, but as they had no guns, we soon got clear of them, after a hard tussle at close quarters. I was unfortunate enough to get an arrow through the tendon of my left ankle, which penetrated also the ribs of my mule, and made him perform many new tricks, much to my discomfort. After we had ridden a few

20. A confederation of Caddoan peoples that in recent centuries had moved up the western branch of the Mississippi and Missouri rivers to Nebraska and beyond. The Pawnee were farmer-hunter plains Indians.
21. Fort Bridger was a trading post in the valley of Black's Fork of the Green River, on a site in the southwest corner of Wyoming. Named for Jim Bridger, an early trapper, its convenient location on the overland route destined it to be the second most important outfitting point for emigrants between the Missouri River and the Pacific Coast. Fort Laramie was first; Fort Hall, Idaho, the third important post.
22. Blackfeet Indians were a Northern Plains, Algonquian or Siksika people. Implaccable enemies of American trappers, the Blackfeet were the most powerful nation north of the Missouri River. They were a restless, aggressive, predatory people who roamed from northern Saskatchewan to the southern headstream of the Missouri in Montana, and from about 105 degrees longitude to the base of the Rocky Mountains.

miles over very rough ground and had sent the Indians on their way much reduced in numbers, we stopped to take account of stock. Bromley, the guide, was the only one besides myself who had been struck; he had an arrow through the skin over his stomach, which at first looked as if it had gone clear through him from side to side. My mule had only three arrows in him, but some of the animals resembled the "fretful porcupine," being struck thickly all over. To get me out of the saddle was something of a job, as the arrow was driven through the buffalo hide of my stirrup and into a rib of the mule. Any approach toward him was enough to make him dance on his hind feet in true circus fashion. A lasso around both of his forelegs finally brought him to terms, and then, the arrow being cut between my leg and his side, I was released from my unpleasant seat. The wound was not serious, having been made with a hunting arrow; but I rode mostly with one foot for a week afterward. A few days later, or rather a few nights, this same gang came very near getting us. We were camped in a grove of cottonwood trees, and had no idea that Indians were after us, though we were on the lookout for them. In the middle of the night a man rode into our camp at full speed and told us of our danger. He was a pony-express rider, and in passing the red devils one of them had struck at him with some sharp weapon and nearly cut his foot in two. His accident saved us from a hot fight, no doubt, and he remained with us until we reached the next express station.

At Fort Bridger we were most kindly received by the officers and men of the Second Dragoons[23] stationed there. We

23. The Second U.S. Dragoons were constituted on 23 May 1836 and organized during June and July at Jefferson Barracks, Missouri, with Colonel David E. Twiggs commanding. Redesignated on 5 March 1843 as the 2d Regiment of Riflemen, and concurrently dismounted, they were remounted and redesignated the 2d Regiment of Dragoons on 4 April 1844. Redesignated on 3 August 1861 as the 2d Cavalry, they participated in the Mexican War, Indian campaigns, and Mormon expedition.

remained several days, to get in good shape for the final lap that was to land us in Salt Lake City. There was a beautiful trout stream running through the fort, and I amused myself by trying to catch fish. I don't recall that I was very success-ful, though I perfectly remember seeing an Indian catch trout by snaring them. He sat on the bank of the stream, mo-tionless as a statue; in his right hand he held a short rod or stick, from the end of which depended a fine copper wire with a loop in the lower end. He would watch a fish swim-ming slowly near him and slip the noose over its head and throw it out on the bank. This kind of sport required just the crafty, sneaking traits of an Indian.

From Fort Bridger we made our way to Robinson's Ferry[24] on Green River, where we were destined to make quite a stay. Robinson was a Frenchman, and kept a trading post and ran the ferry over the river. His storehouses contained a vast stock of furs ready for shipment East, and in addition all the articles usually dealt in by Indians and emigrants. Whisky, I think, was the leading article in demand by all parties, and this he had—very bad and in large quantities. Shortly after our arrival we placed all our horses in a corral near the storehouse, and were glad to think they were safe for the time. In the afternoon a party of Bannocks[25] rode up and wanted to swap horses. One of our party went with them to the inclosure to let them examine our stock, but they had scarcely entered before they set up a yell, and away they went down the river, horses and all. The last we saw of them, my old mule was leading, and setting a hot pace for the rest. The Bannocks were too strong for us to think of following them, so we decided to remain where we were until some

24. This ferry carried the Overland Trail across the Green River east of Fort Bridger in southwestern Wyoming.
25. The Bannock were a Shoshonean, roving tribe, and a branch of the Paiutes who lived in Great Basin, Idaho, and Wyoming. Whites disdain-fully called them "Diggers" because they subsisted mainly on roots dug from barren soil.

other parties arrived, when we would move on with them, and thus be better prepared to stand the Indians off if they attacked us.

Two days after the stampede Washakie[26] and his band of Snake Indians[27] camped near us, and when we told him, or rather when his old friend Robinson told him, what had happened, he started off with two or three hundred warriors after the Bannocks. At the end of four days he came back with a drove of horses, ours among them, and told us to help ourselves. Of course there had to be a powwow and smoke over his success, and during the ceremony he passed whisky around for all hands to drink with him. When he came to me, after looking at my small frame, he took the powder measure from his belt, filled it, and gravely handed it to me with the remark "Little Breeches, drink that." I was known on the plains as "Little Breeches."

During the evening of this powwow many of the Indians were howling drunk around the camp, and, I am sorry to say, most of the white men were in the same condition. I was rolled up asleep under our wagon, when I was seized and thrown on to an Indian pony by a son of the chief Washakie. I promptly slipped off on the other side as soon as I could free myself from the blanket, and ran for the storehouse, where I placed myself under the protection of Robinson. The young Indian came after me and explained that he wanted me to go

26. Washakie was a Shoshoni chief of mixed Shoshoni and Umatilles blood, born about 1804. Noted for his friendship with whites and as a warrior against tribal enemies, he became the chief of the eastern band of Shoshoni of Wyoming, known as Washakies Band. A devout Episcopalian and friend of missionaries, he greatly aided emigrating whites in the 1850s. He died on 20 February 1900 and was buried with full military honors at Fort Washakie, Wyoming, where a monument was erected over his grave.
27. A name applied to different bands of Shoshoni Indians, most persistently to those of eastern Oregon.

to his camp with him, and that he meant me no harm. As he was quite drunk at the time, we concluded not to discuss the matter until the next day. The following morning Washakie himself came, and after a long talk Robinson said that I had better go, as the chief had promised to bring me back safely at the end of ten days; that if I did not go willingly he would take me anyhow, and in that case there was no telling when I might get back. It was agreed that if the party had to go on before my return, my belongings should be left at the ferry for me, and that I should finish my journey with some other party. The Indians started up the Green River that afternoon, and had it not been for my fear of treachery I should have enjoyed my ten days among them very much. I learned afterward that Washakie had always been a staunch friend of the white men, and served them well on many occasions. He was very tall—over six feet—and the finest-looking Indian I ever saw. He was most kind and generous to me always, and brought me back at the time he had promised.

While I was with them the Indians hunted nearly all the time, and killed large quantities of game of various kinds. The tribe consisted of about a thousand people, and when we camped, their ponies and dogs seemed to cover the country for miles around. The ponies were so well trained that a warrior could walk a few steps from his wigwam and whistle or call his pony from the drove feeding on the prairie some distance away. I belonged to the chief's mess, so to speak, and had to sleep in his tepee, which was the most disagreeable part of my experience; the sleepers were too numerous and the air too foul for comfort. During the day we marched or hunted, and as soon as we were camped I was expected to wrestle with some of the Indian lads of my own age, which always seemed to amuse the chief. I could throw the boys, as a rule, but as their hides were well greased I never could hold them. Washakie taught me to shoot with bow and arrow, and to use the lasso, and as soon as we started put his squaws to work making buckskin clothing for me. These garments fitted me well enough, and were things of beauty, with their fringe and beads.

One incident of this visit I recall vividly. We were camped near the river, where the willows grew plentifully, and, for want of something better to do, I cut one of these and made a whistle. When I walked in among the warriors and gave a sharp blast on my whistle there was a scattering and seizing of arms that caused me some uneasiness. Not one of the tribe had ever seen such a thing, and during the next two days I was kept busy whittling out whistles. It was a curious sight to see grown men, and women, too, for that matter, walking about, solemnly tooting on a willow whistle.

At the time promised I was back at the ferry, and found my party waiting—not so much for me, because I found afterward that they all believed that I was gone for good, but to accumulate force enough to face the Bannocks, who were in ugly mood over the loss of their horses. Before we reached the ferry Washakie had a long talk with me, in which he pointed out the advantages that would come to me if I would let him adopt me—the ponies I would own, and that I might some day even have one of his daughters for my wife; but Indian life had less charm for me the more I saw of it. I thanked him as best I could, and was very glad when we had put the river and many miles of prairie between us and my Snake friends. The presents he gave me—bows and arrows, pipes, and buckskin clothing—I carried to Salt Lake City, and some of them eventually back to Washington.

CHAPTER 3

In the Mormon Country

AFTER crossing Green River our course lay along Ham's Fork[1] in the direction of South Pass,[2] the highest point of the Rocky Mountains we had to cross. We passed the wreck of the supply trains of our army burned by the Mormons[3] in 1857. The wagons had been drawn up in a circle

1. Ham's Fork, a village also known as North Kemmerer, was located in Lincoln County, Wyoming. The name dates from 1824, probably given by one of the trappers in the area. One of the oldest settlements in the region, it was both a Pony Express and a home-stage station on the overland route. A large garden supplied fresh vegetables for the summer.
2. A 7,526-foot open strip of high country at the southern tip of the Wind River range. This break in the continental divide was long used by Indians and later became the most prominent emigrant passage. Gold was discovered in the long, treeless 25-mile pass in 1842, but the "boom" period came long after Evans and his party noted this area. Strip mining for low-grade iron ore has been more recently conducted by U.S. Steel in the area.
3. The common pseudonym for the Church of Jesus Christ of Latter-day Saints, organized by Joseph Smith and five others at Fayette, New York. Persecuted for their beliefs, this movement emigrated west to Illinois and Missouri, then to the Salt Lake valley in 1847. In 1857–58, Brigham Young and his group refused to obey Federal laws, which led to a U.S.

A SAILOR'S LOG

and there burned—the circle still showing, and dotted here
and there with tires and such ironwork as the Indians had
not cared to carry away. At one place we struck alkali dust,
and as soon as our water gave out we found ourselves and our
animals in pitiable condition. Our lips and eyes grew sore,
and our tongues swelled until we could scarcely talk. After
we had passed the dangerous place, we came upon an emigrant who had a barrel of whisky in the tail of his wagon.
There was no spigot in it, and he refused to put one in, but
after a long, wordy contest he agreed that he would bore a
gimlet hole in the barrel, each man should select a straw,
and for two bits he could suck all the whisky he wanted
without drawing breath. They selected straws very carefully,
and I remember how each man held on until he was blue in
the face before admitting that his drink was done.

On entering South Pass we camped at Pacific Spring[4] and
made ourselves comfortable, as there was no longer fear of
trouble with the Indians, and our animals needed rest and
grass. The spring covered a space of forty by thirty feet, and
the water bubbled up cold and clear as crystal and ran toward
the Pacific—hence its name. A few doves or wild pigeons
were feeding about the camp. The guide bet me that I could
not kill one with my rifle, and this led to my killing my first
elk. I was anxious to win the bet, and was following the bird
as he flew about on the trees to make sure of a fair shot. In
this way I wandered off from the trail into the thick cover on
the side of the pass, and was about to fire at the pigeon,
when I heard a breaking of twigs near me, but above me, on
the mountain. My first idea was Indians, and, standing perfectly still in my tracks, I took a quiet look. Within thirty
yards of me was a magnificent animal looking straight at me,

military expedition being sent into the territory to restore order and support Federal courts and justice.
4. A favorite campsite for emigrants "just over the hump." The spring's
waters originate less than four miles from the continental divide and eventually flow to the Pacific Ocean.

his head and antlers only showing through the thick cover. I raised the gun to my shoulder very quietly, and, taking good aim at a spot between his eyes, fired. He made a great bound down the side of the mountain in my direction, and at the same moment I started for camp as fast as my legs could carry me, and did not stop until I got there. Bromley asked me if I had killed the bird, to which I replied that I had not, but I believed I had killed the father of all deer. Up to that time I had never seen an elk. When we reached the spot we found a beautiful specimen, with grand antlers, with a bullet fairly through his brain. I had killed him stone dead, and he had slid almost to where I stood when I fired. The bet was called off, and removing the head, we skinned the game, and the entire party had all the meat they wanted for several days.

Afterward we saw immense herds of elk, many thousands in a herd, and we had no trouble in killing them whenever we chose. We also saw and killed a number of mountain sheep, a very curious animal with enormously large horns. The guide told marvellous stories of their jumping down great distances, landing on their horns, which might, for all I know, have been true; but I never saw one of them do it. They were wary and hard to get at, as compared with other kinds of game, and I never saw much of them—only for a moment before I fired, and then the sheep was either dead or off out of sight like a flash.

After leaving South Pass we fell in with a Mormon train, consisting mostly of women from Wales, bound for Salt Lake City. These people, who seemed a decent lot, had few large wagons, but appeared to depend for transportation on a species of handcart, which contained their belongings and were pushed along by the women. A few wagons carried the provisions, and these were looked after by the dozen or so men of the party. All the work was done by the women, which was a foretaste of what their lot was to be after arriving at their destination.

In the forenoon of a beautiful day we had our first view of

Salt Lake City as we slowly wound our way down Echo Cañon.[5] The mountains rose to a great height on either side, and were still surmounted by the low stone breastworks thrown up by the Mormons to oppose the entry of United States troops[6] two years before. Through the cañon ran a small but swift stream, and upon this the beavers were industriously building their dams, some of which were really works of art. These curious beasts were to be seen in hundreds—some cutting the logs for the dams, and others using their curious flat tails as trowels to cement the face of the dam with mud. Many of the dams had been cut in order to make the road available, but, when left to themselves, the beavers soon had them repaired. The beavers have disappeared, as have the buffalo and other large game of the West, but in their case the excuse can be made that the fur was used to some good purpose; in the case of the big game no such excuse can be offered: it was in a great measure simply senseless, brutal killing for the sake of killing.

My first impressions of the city and Salt Lake Valley, with Great Salt Lake lying blue in the distance, were very pleasing, and a closer inspection did not change them. The city was beautifully laid out, and the houses were generally of a character to indicate comfort, and often wealth and refinement. The water from a rushing mountain stream had been introduced, and, besides answering for household purposes, it ran through the gutters on both sides of the principal

5. Picturesque Echo Canyon, located west of Emory, Utah, contains the famous landmarks "Jack in the Pulpit," "Steamboat Rock," "Gibraltar," "The Sphinx," and "The Giant's Teapot." Mormons erected fortifications here, expecting battles with U.S. troops that never occurred. Later, the Union Pacific Railroad passed through here. Some cliffs rise 1,000 feet.
6. In 1857–58, President James Buchanan sent Federal troops under Colonel Albert Sidney Johnston to subdue the Mormon people in Salt Lake valley. Mormon guerrilla tactics and raids on Federal supplies prohibited actual punitive action before an armistice was effected between the Federal government and Brigham Young on 16 June 1858. Johnston and his expedition marched into Salt Lake City without bloodshed.

streets, thus insuring cleanliness and good sewerage. Many of the houses had gardens about them filled with vegetables, and the most delicious small fruits. The residences of Brigham Young[7]—he had two—were beautifully constructed and surrounded by elaborate flower gardens, which were kept in the most perfect order.

I made my home while in the city with the family of Mr. Hooper,[8] who was a Mormon, though not a polygamist. They, as well as the people generally whom I met, were kindly and courteous, and did all in their power to make my stay among them agreeable. Mrs. Hooper was worried for fear that I might be converted to Mormonism without the knowledge or consent of my parents, but I assured her that I felt myself strong enough to stand any amount of temptation in that line, and that I really was not in the least danger.

I had command of plenty of horses, and amused myself by making excursions to Camp Floyd,[9] or Salt Lake, or other attractive places. Frequently I went to the country for a day's shooting, and as game of all kinds was plentiful I made very good bags. One day, when I had wandered rather too far into the thick woods on the side of the mountain, I had an excit-

7. Born in 1801, the Mormon leader and colonizer converted to Mormonism in 1832 and became head of the church upon the death of its founder, Joseph Smith. Young led the sect's migration to the valley of the Great Salt Lake and directed settlement of Deseret, which Congress recognized as the Utah territory in 1850. Young became territorial governor, although he was removed during the dispute with the government in 1857–58. He remained the effective leader of the church and shaped administrative machinery that enabled the survival and development of the Mormon faith. He adopted polygamy and fathered fifty-six children before his death in 1877. Young's residences included Lion House and Beehive House—both on South Temple Street—which are still maintained as museums.

8. Most likely the family of William Henry Hooper.

9. Camp Floyd was named for Secretary of War John B. Floyd. It was established by the U.S. Army on 24 August 1858 in Cedar Valley (west of Utah Lake) and was renamed Fort Crittenden in 1861.

ing experience. I had dismounted from my horse and was advancing slowly and quietly through the thick cover, which was so dense that the sunlight was almost shut out, when I saw some distance ahead of me a curious black object. After watching it for some time without being able to make out what it was I gave it one load of No. 4 shot to see what would happen. I was thoroughly surprised at the result. It proved to be a Digger Indian,[10] with a large black felt hat on his head, digging roots. As he straightened himself up he seemed to me ten feet tall, and I lost no time in mounting my pony; neither did he in mounting his. There was no time to explain matters, and I bolted down the mountain road with the Digger in hot chase. He occasionally sent an arrow over me, and generally behaved in a way to hasten me into town in the shortest possible time. As I reached the front gate of Mr. Hooper's house the Indian pulled up about three hundred yards away and sat on his pony, waiting apparently to see what would happen next. He only waited a few seconds when I appeared with my Colt's rifle, and then we had a spirited race for the mountains, only in this case I was the pursuer, and I surely put him to his best speed to escape. I was more careful after that how I shot at things until I could make out what they were.

As a rule, the city was orderly and peaceful. At times the Indians would come in in considerable numbers, and, having filled up with whisky, would proceed to make themselves disagreeable by shooting arrows at people, and misbehaving in other ways. When they got too bad, word would be sent

10. The English translation of Naunuents, the name of a small tribe near St. George, in southwestern Utah. It was the only Paiute tribe to practice agriculture, hence the original significance of the name "digger." In time, however, whites derisively applied the name to every tribe known to use roots extensively for food. Digger Indians included many tribes of California, Oregon, Idaho, Utah, Nevada, and Arizona, who spoke widely different languages and embraced perhaps a dozen distinct linguistic stocks.

out to Camp Floyd, and the soldiers would come in and run them out of town—generally killing a few. On one of these occasions I was sitting on the front porch reading a newspaper, when suddenly an arrow drove into the weather-boarding very close to me, and before I could move, a second one came and caught me in the shin bone. My double-barrelled shotgun was in the hall near by, and as I came out with it I discovered a half-drunken Digger standing in the middle of the street, laughing at the joke he had perpetrated on me. I don't think he enjoyed the rest of the afternoon much, as the men in the drug store at the corner had him laid on his back while they picked shot out of him until after dark. The next time I saw my friend he looked as if he had had the smallpox. I presented him with five pounds of brown sugar, and watched with interest while he sat on the pavement and ate the whole of it.

As I was to represent Utah in the navy, I felt it my duty to call on Mr. Young, and at the same time I hesitated to do so, because a pony-express horse, which I had borrowed for a ride on the Fourth of July, had run away with me, and before I could stop him had seriously damaged some beautiful flower beds in Mr. Young's yard. However, I did call, and found the Mormon leader a rugged, hard-looking man, but withal kindly in his manner and good enough to wish me success in the profession I had selected. Without entering into the question of how far he was right in what he had done and was then doing—questions now forever settled by the laws of the land—we must admit that Mr. Young was a man of wonderful ability and a natural leader of men. Otherwise he could never have led his people through the tremendous difficulties they encountered, and then made of the desert a flowering garden.

When I had been sufficiently long in Utah to claim residence I began preparations for my return journey. The call of the sea was strong upon me, and I could not resist it even had I wished to do so, which I certainly did not. The sea and the ships were constantly in my mind, and I was anxious to begin. I secured a seat on the overland coach and left for the East about the middle of July, 1860.

We had a pleasant trip, all things considered. Riding on top of a coach is well enough in the daytime, but not so pleasant at night. I was small for my age, and soon found a way of stowing myself so that I could sleep with a fair amount of comfort. But when it rained, which it often did at night, I was most uncomfortable. The choice was between getting wet or being smothered under blankets—and I generally got wet. The coach stations were reasonably close to each other, and we made good speed all the way. As soon as we arrived at one of these stations all hands went for food— generally very poor—and when that was finished, six wild, kicking, bucking mules were hitched up, and away we went at a full run. The drivers were experts in their line, and the mules usually ran four or five miles before they were pulled down to their regular paces. After that, woe to the unfortunate mule that tried to shirk his fair share of the work!

The party was well armed and thoroughly able to stand off any small band of Indians; but the red men as a rule seemed to fancy the emigrant trains rather than the coaches, and we escaped without serious molestation. During the time we were on the South Platte we had one or two very severe hailstorms, which for a time threatened to destroy the whole outfit. When they struck us, usually accompanied by a hard gale of wind, the mules backed up under the lee of the coach, and no amount of beating would induce them to move until the storm had passed; then they would go on as cheerfully as before, the driver launching at them such a volley of oaths and abuse as could come only from the driver of an overland coach. No other human being could match him. The passengers during these storms found shelter as they could, either in or under the coach, or among the mules. At times the hail covered the prairies as far as one could see to a depth of two or three inches. Some of the hailstones were large enough to disable a man if they struck him on the head.

While we were resting at Mayersville, Kansas, [11] we experienced a wind storm which lingers in my mind, although I have since seen storms of about all kinds and sizes. It came up very suddenly, and we at first took refuge in a long, narrow frame building used as a storehouse. The wind struck this house end on and soon lifted one end a foot or so from the ground. We then retreated behind a stone wall, but the stones began to fly from the top, and we concluded to follow the example of some of the natives and go out on the open prairie, lie down flat on our faces, head to wind, and hold on to the grass as best we could. In this position each one soon had a considerable sand shoal about him. There were several emigrant trains and a band of Indians camped on the prairie, and these were soon off before the wind as fast as they could go. The "prairie schooners," as the wagons were called, would run some distance before the wind, and then, as they got canted one way or the other, would capsize and spill out women and children and whatever else happened to be in them. The last we saw of the Indians, as they disappeared in the clouds of sand and gravel, the men were riding their ponies, shouting and yelling, and the squaws doing what they could to save their belongings. A few days after this we crossed the Missouri River, I found myself again in civilization, and I was soon on a train bound for Washington, where I arrived late in August.

On September 15th I went to Annapolis, passed my exam-

11. Evans may have been referring to Mairestown (also Mairsville) in Shawnee County, about fourteen-and-one-half miles southeast of present-day Tecumseh, or ten miles east/southeast of modern Topeka. With possibly fifty residents—dominated by the Maires family—the town at best had a hotel and a few stores. It never played a dominant role in the area due to its proximity to Tecumseh and Topeka and its situation on a small territorial road.

ination, and, after a few days' leave, reported September 20th on board the frigate Constitution[12] as an acting midshipman.

I have so far picked the oakum,[13] now let me spin my yarn of forty years of naval life.

12. Arguably America's most famous fighting ship, the obsolete wooden sailing frigate served as a receiving ship at the Naval Academy in Annapolis, Maryland, at the time of the Civil War. Built by the Treasury and War departments, she was launched at Boston, Massachusetts, on 21 October 1797. The *Constitution* cost $302,718.84 to construct; she displaced 1,607 tons and mounted a battery as of 14 September 1861 of sixteen guns. She can be toured at historic Charlestown Navy Yard in Boston.
13. Loose hemp or jute fiber.

CHAPTER 4

A Cadet at Annapolis

I passed my entrance examination to the Naval Academy [1] September 15, 1860, and reported, as an acting midshipman, as I have before stated, on board the frigate Constitution—"Old Ironsides"—on the 20th of the same month. The examination, fortunately for many of us, was a very simple one; nothing like the elaborate and trying affair of to-day, otherwise many of us would not have followed the navy as a profession. The candidate had to be sound physically, and have a fair foundation on which to build the education required of a sea officer, who was not in that day expected to be an engineer, a chemist, a scientist, an electrician, a lawyer, an artist, etc., as is the case to-day—only a seaman and a gunner, with the necessary knowledge of things that per-

---

1. Established in 1845, the nation's training school for young officers was moved from Annapolis, Maryland, to Newport, Rhode Island, in early May 1861, but was returned in the summer of 1865. A disruptive wartime period witnessed few curricular changes to meet the challenges of the new technical developments that were revolutionizing naval warfare. Senior admirals felt they made midshipmen too scientific at the expense of practical training.

tained to the sea. The superintendent, Captain George S. Blake,[2] was assisted by half a dozen officers, selected for their fitness, and as many civil professors. Among the officers were two brothers, C.R.P.[3] and George Rodgers,[4] lieutenants,

2. Fifth Superintendent of the Academy (15 September 1857 to 9 September 1865), this mild-mannered but strict disciplinarian—he forbade cardplaying or physical sport among the students, for example—held the longest tenure of any superintendent before the end of World War II. Born in 1803 at Worcester, Massachusetts, he was appointed midshipman in 1818, engaged in anti-pirate duty in the West Indies, commanded the brig *Perry* in the 1840s, and was a fleet captain in the Mediterranean, 1849–52. Blake was assigned to special duty in connection with building the Stevens Battery at Hoboken, New Jersey, in 1855. His strenuous measures in 1861 saved the Naval Academy from capture by hostile elements by moving it to Newport, Rhode Island, for the duration of the Civil War. Later, he served as a lighthouse inspector before his death on 24 June 1871.

3. Christopher Raymond Perry Rodgers was the sixth Commandant of Midshipmen, 1860–61. Born in Brooklyn, New York, on 14 November 1819, he was the son of George Washington and Anna Maria (Perry) Rodgers, and the nephew of Commodore Oliver Hazard Perry. Appointed midshipman from Connecticut on 5 October 1833, he served against the Seminoles in Florida and in the Mexican War. He commanded the steam frigate *Wabash* and was fleet captain to Rear Admiral S. F. Dupont in blockade duty along the North Carolina coast. Rodgers participated in the Battle of Port Royal, November 1861; commanded naval force ashore at Fort Pulaski, Georgia, 27 January 1862; commanded the USS *New Ironsides* in her attack on Charleston, 7 April 1863; and commanded the steam sloop *Iroquois* on special service, 1863–65. Promoted to captain in 1866, he was Commandant, Norfolk Navy Yard, 1865–67; commanded the steam frigate *Franklin* with the Mediterranean Squadron, 1868–70; promoted to commodore, August 1870; assigned to special service in Europe, 1871; Chief, Bureau of Yard and Docks, 1871–74; and promoted to Rear Admiral, June 1874. During his administration as the eighth Superintendent of the Naval Academy, 1874–78, five top-ranking midshipmen were allowed to wear a star on their collar. Rodgers was Commander, Pacific Station, 1878–80. He retired after forty-eight years of service on 14 November 1881, and died on 8 January 1892.

4. George Washington Rodgers was the seventh Commandant of Midshipmen, 1861–62. Born in Brooklyn, New York, on 30 December 1822, he was the brother of C.R.P. Rodgers. Appointed midshipman on

both of whom made their mark on the service, and wrote their names high up on the history of the navy which they loved so well and did so much to honour. We have never had two officers whose standard of honour and duty was higher or whose conduct reflected greater credit on the country than that of those two. C.R.P. Rodgers was commandant of midshipmen and George Rodgers was captain of the Constitution, and to them I owe everything in my professional life.

We had one hundred and twenty-seven men in the class when we settled down to work, an average lot, from all parts of the country, and representing the various classes of American life—North, South, East, and West. I was the only one from Utah,[5] and I believe the first one ever appointed from that Territory either in the navy or the army. Our life on board ship was pleasant and novel, and our education on the lines that would fit us for the duties we would in the future have to perform. English studies occupied a considerable part of our time, but practical seamanship and gunnery were considered the important things, and they were hammered into us so hard by our honoured captain that we had to learn them in spite of ourselves. Many showed wonderful cleverness, and

---

30 April 1836; served in the Mexican War, 1846–48; and coastal survey, 1849–50. He organized the defense of the Naval Academy and of the frigate *Constitution* prior to their relocation, and commanded her and midshipmen during the trip to Newport. Characteristically, he had the academy reorganized and in full operation within three days of arrival in Rhode Island. Promoted to commander in January 1862, he was appointed Rear Admiral John Dahlgren's chief of staff in July 1863; distinguished for bravery in silencing Fort Sumter and batteries on Morris Island; killed in attack on Fort Wagner, Charleston Harbor, on 17 August 1863.

5. Evans was mistaken about being the first Utah cadet at the Naval Academy. Fifteen-year-old Edward S. Ruggles was appointed on 21 September 1858. The first Utah appointee to West Point was Missouri-born Samuel McKee, 19, who was a cadet from 1 July 1854 to 1 July 1858. He served in the Mounted Rifles, 1st Dragoons, 1st Cavalry, and was mortally wounded at Cold Harbor on 3 June 1864.

after a few months the class standing in seamanship placed the men about as they have since stood in the service.

The Constitution was moored at the end of a long, narrow wharf, which was the only means of approach unless by boat, so that the class was completely isolated from the older classes. We never came in contact with them except when on shore for drill, or on Saturday, when we passed their quarters on our way to the town on liberty. All our recitations and most of our drills took place on board ship. Under such conditions the disgraceful hazing, which later on gave the Naval Academy such a bad name, was impossible, even had the temper of the midshipmen been such as to tolerate it. At the time of which I am writing hazing was absolutely unknown, and I am sure that any attempt to practise it would have led to a duel behind old Fort Severn.[6] It was not until we reached Newport,[7] and the senior classes had been ordered into service, that this brutal, and I must say cowardly, practice took root and grew until it was a disgrace to all those engaged in it. By some means the classes entering after 1862 got the idea from West Point, and in their zeal to emulate really went far beyond the practices of that excellent institution, where hazing of a certain kind was a tradition, and considered necessary to the discipline of the cadets among themselves. With us the proper class distinctions and respect were traditions which did not require hazing to enforce them. I remember very well, one Saturday afternoon, two of us, both

6. A cylindrical work, enclosed by a fourteen-foot-high stone wall, Fort Severn was constructed on Windmill Point on the south side of the Severn River at Annapolis in 1808. It was transferred from War to Navy Department control upon the founding of the Naval Academy in 1845.
7. In late April 1861 the Navy Department determined to move the Naval Academy from Annapolis, Maryland, in the hostile border-state climate near the nation's capital, to a more secure location in the north. Newport, Rhode Island, was the chosen site, and the USS *Constitution,* which had served as a training ship at Annapolis, and the hotel Atlantic House were utilized as dormitories and classrooms at Newport for the duration of the war.

very small, were passing the quarters of the first class on our way to town on liberty, when two seniors thought it would be good fun to put us down on the grass and sit on us. They promptly carried out their plan, and sat on us five minutes or so and then let us go. We returned to the ship mad all over, and in a few minutes we swarmed back with most of our class, and there was a beautiful fight which resulted in many black eyes and the destruction of much furniture in the first-class quarters. This was about the nearest approach to hazing we ever had.

The discipline was strict on board ship from the start, and we were expected to observe the regulations as soon as they had been made clear to us. I had formed a warm friendship for a young fellow from Mississippi named Baldwin,[8] and he somehow became involved in a quarrel with a man twice his size; the quarrel soon led to a fight, and the large man attempted to strike Baldwin with a camp stool, when I grabbed him from behind, preventing the blow, and thus myself became part of the row. The next morning I was sent for on the quarter-deck, and, after having the Articles of War read to me and receiving a long lecture on the enormity of my offence, was locked up in a dark room in the wardroom. Some one had reported that Baldwin had a knife in his hand during the fight, and that I called out to him to use it and that I would help him. After being locked up I made up my mind that my time had come, in view of the many offences mentioned in the Articles of War for which the punishment was "death or such other punishment as a court martial may inflict." I wrote a hurried note to my uncle in Washington to come at once if he wished to see me alive, as I was sure that I was soon to be hanged at the yardarm. He answered

8. James Gardner Baldwin was admitted to the Naval Academy from Columbus, Mississippi, on 29 September 1860. Subsequently, Baldwin apparently went south and became a midshipman in the Confederate States Navy.

that discipline was good for me, and that he would wait a few days, or until sentence was pronounced. After three days' confinement I was sent for by the commanding officer, and told him exactly how I became involved in the fight, when I was at once sent to duty, and some one else took my dark room.

On board ship we had our hammocks to sleep in instead of bunks, and our messing was regulated just as it would have been on a cruising vessel. In fact, we lived under service conditions; and while it is now the fashion to decry such training in favour of barracks on shore, I have yet to be convinced that for the conditions then existing it was not the best. Many officers of that school have achieved great success both afloat and ashore, and have certainly met all the requirements of the service as fully as those of the new school can ever meet the requirements that will face them. Our first impressions of the service were received on board ship, and the discomforts of ship life were met and overcome in a way that made such discomforts and even much greater ones seem very trivial afterward. We grew into ship life gradually and naturally, and our knowledge of the ship and all her parts was complete; such knowledge can be acquired in no other way, and while many able officers hold that this is not a matter of importance on this point, I have also still to be convinced of the soundness of their reasoning.

During the winter of 1860-'61 the anxious faces of our officers foretold the storm of war that broke so suddenly in April of the latter year. It was a time of great suspense for all hands; naturally the greatest strain came on those in authority, but the midshipmen had their loads to bear as well. Many of us came from the South, and as the States one after another either seceded or threatened to do so, we had to make up our minds what we were going to do. Conferences were frequent and serious, but never in one of them was there a disloyal word uttered. Every man followed the example set by the Southern men among the officers.[9] So long as we were inside the academy limits, or until our resignations were accepted, we were officers of the navy and would behave as such. Lieutenant Hunter Davidson,[10] afterward the torpedo expert of the Confederacy, was probably more responsible for this position than any other man, though both C.R.P. and George Rodgers were constantly giving us good advice.

During the month of April, 1861, our studies were practically suspended, and preparations were made to defend the academy and the ship Constitution in case of attack. Drills were constant, and every precaution taken to give the enemy a warm reception in case he came. A Confederate cavalry company was organized on the north bank of the Severn River,[11] and for several days they drilled in plain sight of the ship; but when a few boats were sent after them they disappeared, and the next soldiers we saw wore blue uniforms. We had been told that the Confederates in Baltimore had organized an expedition and were coming down in steamers to capture us. A bright lookout was kept for them, and one

9. Fifty-five midshipmen and 267 acting midshipmen (of whom only eight did not attend the Naval Academy) left between 1 December 1860 and 21 December 1861 to join the Confederacy. For further data, see William S. Dudley, *Going South: U.S. Navy Officer Resignations and Dismissals on the Eve of the Civil War* (Washington: Naval Historical Center, 1981).

10. Born in the District of Columbia, Davidson was appointed midshipman from Fairfax County, Virginia. He invented a boat-lowering device for the service while an instructor at the Naval Academy in 1859. Upon Virginia's secession, Davidson resigned from the service, but Secretary of the Navy Gideon Welles subsequently ordered him dismissed from the Navy. He became an expert on torpedo, or mine, warfare in the Confederate Navy Department, rising to the rank of commander. He joined the Argentine Navy as a torpedo expert after the war, later settling in Paraguay.

11. This may have been a local band of secessionists or southern-sympathizing Maryland militia, since the state never joined the Confederacy and many Marylanders simply joined Virginia units.

dark night, about two o'clock in the morning, the lookout reported a large steamer coming in from the bay. General quarters were sounded, and in a few minutes we were ready; and there we stood waiting for the word to fire. The cabin bulkheads had all been taken down, and four thirty-two pounders run out the cabin stern ports and loaded with grape and canister.

The steamer slowly came on until she could be plainly seen with the naked eye moving up directly astern of us, as if to avoid our broadside and carry us by boarding. Captain Rodgers's clear voice rang out: "Ship ahoy! What ship is that?" The gun captains had the guns trained on the mass of men we could now see crowded about the decks and not more than three hundred yards away. Twice more the clear voice rang out: "Ship ahoy! keep off, or I will sink you!" and then a voice we all recognised answered: "For God's sake, don't fire! We are friends!" It was the voice of our chaplain, who had been North on a short leave, and on his return found Colonel B.F. Butler[12] and the Eighth Massachusetts Regiment[13] at Havre de Grace, Maryland,[14] blocked in their effort to reach Washington.

12. Major General Benjamin F. Butler was the Massachusetts political general who was instrumental in securing free movement through the inflamed border state of Maryland in order for military men and materiel to reach Washington. His subsequent Civil War career was controversial and included the occupation of New Orleans, amphibious expeditions to the North Carolina coast, and command of the Army of the James. He returned to politics following the war and was the Greenback Party candidate for President in 1884.

13. One of the first four northern regiments to respond to the call after the opening of hostilities, this gray-clad militia outfit gathered in Boston on 16 April 1861 under Colonel Benjamin F. Butler. It aided in relieving the beleaguered capital, and was subsequently stationed at Relay House near Baltimore from May to July. The unit mustered out in Boston on 1 August 1861.

14. Incorporated in 1785 on a site settled in 1658 and developed as a river-crossing stop on the main north-south Post Road. Havre de Grace

Colonel Butler had seized the ferry steamer Maryland,[15] and, embarking his regiment on board of her, sailed for Annapolis, fortunately bringing with him our chaplain—I say fortunately, because he seemed the only one on board who knew enough to answer the hail from the Constitution, and in a few seconds more we should have opened fire, and no one can doubt what the result would have been. The splendid record of this fine regiment would never have been written; it would have ended there and then, and what one may fairly call the variegated career of General Benjamin F. Butler would have been very short and inglorious.

As soon as the character of the strange craft was satisfactorily established, she was directed to haul up alongside of us, which she did, and remained there until daylight, when the midshipmen were landed under arms, formed with those on shore and marched to the wall in the vicinity of the gate leading to the town of Annapolis, and there deployed in line of battle to cover the landing of the Eighth Massachusetts. We stood in this position until the last soldier was ashore and the regiment had formed line in rear of the midshipmen's quarters and stacked their arms, when sentries from our battalion were posted and the rest of us returned to our quarters. Not a shot had been fired by either side, though the excitement was intense, and there was a readiness on both sides to fight. Both parties hesitated to fire the first shot, and the Confederates contented themselves with pitching stones over the wall, which we caught and tossed back. The newspapers gave graphic accounts of how Butler and his men had recaptured the Constitution and the Naval Academy! They never fired a shot nor saw a rebel to shoot at. The magazines of the Constitution were mined, and she and her crew would have

later became a railroad crossing near the confluence of the Susquehanna River and Chesapeake Bay.
15. A railroad ferryboat of the Philadelphia, Wilmington, and Baltimore Railroad that crossed the Susquehanna River between Perryville and Havre de Grace.

been blown to atoms before surrendering if the rebels had attacked her.

Everything was now made ready as soon as possible, and the ship hauled out into the bay and prepared to transport us to some Northern port. The midshipmen on shore gave up their quarters to the officers of the Seventh New York Infantry[16] and the First Rhode Island Artillery[17] under Colonel Burnside,[18] these regiments having arrived immediately after the Eighth Massachusetts. Our routine was entirely broken up, and our time given to guard and picket duty, until all preparations had been made for our trip North, when orders were given to assemble ready for embarkation. Then followed a scene which those who participated in it can never forget or recall without a tendency to moist eyes. The good fellows from the South who had determined to go with their States

16. The crack New York City militia unit that responded to Lincoln's call for volunteers on 19 April 1861, the Seventh Regiment performed three months' service defending Washington until June 1861, when it returned to New York City. Mustered again for three months' service in May 1862, the regiment was sent to occupy Baltimore against rioting. The unit performed duty again in Baltimore in 1863 before being returned to New York City to suppress draft riots on 16–21 July 1863.

17. Evans errs in that Burnside commanded the 1st Regiment of Volunteer Infantry, not the artillery. This three-month unit performed ably in relieving the besieged capital and participated in the disastrous First Bull Run campaign of July 1861. It returned to Rhode Island and mustered out on 2 August 1861.

18. Ambrose E. Burnside (1824–81), a West Point graduate and Major General of the Rhode Island militia, organized the 1st Rhode Island Volunteer Infantry for a three-month deployment to help relieve the beleaguered capital in April 1861. Subsequently, Burnside advanced through successive brigade, division, and corps command to Commander, Army of the Potomac. He was responsible for the ill-fated Fredericksburg campaign in 1862. An able subordinate but mediocre in independent command, he later took charge of the Department of the Ohio, successfully defended Knoxville, Tennessee, against Confederate attack in November 1863, and returned to lead his old IX Army Corps in the Army of the Potomac before resigning in April 1865. He served as Governor of Rhode Island from 1866 to 1868, and as U.S. Senator from that state, 1874–81.

said good-bye to their classmates, and as the rest of us formed ranks to embark, Captain C.R.P. Rodgers stepped out to say a few words to us before leaving the dear old Alma Mater. After a strong effort he managed to say, "My boys, stand by the old flag!" and then broke down. We were all in tears, and only braced up when we heard the men of the Seventh New York cheering us, which we returned in a feeble sort of way—scrambled into the boats, and two hours later were once more on board "Old Ironsides." That was the last we saw of the Naval Academy at Annapolis until after the civil war had done its work. The army took possession, repaired the railroad and locomotives, and after a month or so of hard work reopened communication with Washington.

The Constitution was towed to New York, from there to Newport, Rhode Island, where she was anchored in Brinton's Cove, off Fort Adams,[19] and all the senior classes were ordered into active service. My class, now about seventy strong, was the only one left, and we were anxious, of course, to join the others; but we had not yet sufficiently advanced to make us of much value. Once more we settled down to routine and hard work. Fort Adams was unoccupied, so we were transferred there, where we could have roomy quarters and convenient recitation rooms, and at the same time man the guns in case of need. It was all a lark to most of us, and the time given to study did not amount to much. The officers soon found that, if we were to do any serious work, proper quarters would have to be provided; and as the idea of a return to Annapolis was abandoned, the Atlantic Hotel, in the heart of Newport, was secured on long lease, duly fitted for our accommodation, and there we were marched, bag and baggage.

19. One of the largest of the pre-Civil War seacoast fortifications, Fort Adams was constructed in 1799, being named for the second President of the United States. It was rebuilt in 1824–51 to protect the entrance to Narragansett Bay.

In the meantime, steps were taken to quarter the new class, a very large one, which had been appointed. The Constitution and the Santee,[20] which had been sent North for this purpose, had been moored at suitable docks built on the inside of Goat Island[21] in the inner harbour, and the sloops of war John Adams[22] and Marion[23] were anchored near them, to be used for practical seamanship and gunnery drills afloat. This made the most complete outfit in ships the Naval Academy had ever seen and the most useful.

That master of his trade, Stephen B. Luce,[24] had charge of drills afloat, and scarcely a day passed that we were not under

20. This sailing frigate built at Portsmouth Navy Yard cost $229,022.43 and was launched on 16 February 1855. Displacing 1,726 tons, her armament varied from 25 to 50 guns during the war.

21. A small island in Narragansett Bay, near Newport, Rhode Island, Goat Island was the site of a postwar torpedo station.

22. Originally built as a corvette in 1799, the USS *John Adams* was rebuilt in 1830 at Norfolk Navy Yard at a cost of $119,308. She displaced 700 tons, was armed with 8 to 10 guns, and had a top speed of 9 knots. The sailing sloop sold at public auction in Boston on 5 October 1867 for $10,000.

23. A 566-ton sailing sloop of war, with a top speed of 11.5 knots, the USS *Marion* was built at the Boston Navy Yard in 1838 for $212,842.51. She was rebuilt as a screw steamer at Portsmouth Navy Yard, 1871–76. Her sixteen guns, mounted in 1853, progressively declined to ten as of 1887. She made her first cruise in 1839 and sank in Rio de Janeiro. She was raised, cruised on various stations, and was used as a practice ship for midshipmen until 1870. The *Marion* was ultimately turned over to the San Diego naval militia in 1897.

24. Born in 1827, Luce was appointed midshipman in 1841 and saw service in the Civil War. He authored a text on seamanship while on the faculty of the Naval Academy and was Commandant of Midshipmen there from 1865 to 1868. Identified throughout his naval career with training and education, Luce helped found the U.S. Naval Institute. A scholar and writer in uniform, Luce has been termed the "father" of the senior service school—the Naval War College at Newport, Rhode Island—over which he presided as its first president in 1884. Retired as rear admiral in 1884, Luce nevertheless returned to the war college for special duty from 1901 to 1910.

his watchful eyes at some sort of practical seamanship. Every Saturday we went outside in one or other or both of the ships, and then the work was most thorough and complete, each midshipman in turn taking charge of the deck for different evolutions. On our way in, in the afternoon, we could generally tell when our work had been satisfactory; if it had not been, the ship was sure to fetch up hard and fast before we reached our anchorage, anchors carried out, and the vessel hove off, properly berthed and everything made snug and shipshape, before we could leave her. For all this work we had only midshipmen—no man to help us. Everything must be done with our own hands, and thus we learned, and learned thoroughly, what a man had to do in every position on board a sailing ship, from passing a close reef to sweeping down the quarter-deck. We learned how to do it ourselves, and how to make others do it under our instruction, and many of us still cling to the notion that there could not have been better training. If the weather happened to be such that we could not get under way, we sent down yards, masts, and rigging, and proceeded to refit everything. Before the year was out there were very few in the class who could not, with their own hands, do any job of work required of a petty officer or seaman.

The quartering of the senior class on shore and all the others on board ship had a very bad effect, and it was years before the academy recovered its normal condition. All the traditions of the school, the discipline among the classes themselves—which was, and always must be, dependent on traditions and customs—were lost sight of, and, as I have before said, hazing took root on board the Constitution and Santee. It took twenty years to break up this unnaval practice, and even now it occasionally shows its ugly head, generally with the result that some promising youngster has to be dismissed and thus lost to the service.

CHAPTER 5

The Early Days of the War

As soon as war was an assured thing, my family demanded that I should resign, come South and fight for my State; but it did not seem to me that this course was imperative. My next younger brother[1] enlisted at the age of fourteen in the Washington Artillery,[2] and went to the front under

1. Samuel T. Evans (1847–90) followed in his father's profession and became a renowned physician in Union City, Tennessee. He joined Pelham's Battery of J.E.B. Stuart's Horse Artillery, Army of Northern Virginia, rising to the rank of lieutenant and suffering a horrible wound at Fredericksburg that incapacitated him and ultimately contributed to his death. Evans served as a "special courier" between General Robert E. Lee and Confederate President Jefferson Davis, and apparently, he was the courier who conveyed Lee's Petersburg evacuation dispatch to Davis in Richmond just before Appomattox in 1865. Ironically arrayed in the Civil War on the opposite side from his brother Robley, Samuel Evans became an assistant surgeon in the U.S. Navy in the 1870s.
2. It is unclear as to the particular Washington Artillery unit Evans cites. The famous Washington Artillery of New Orleans was one; another came from Tidewater Virginia. It is apparent from obituaries that Samuel T. Evans did fight with the famous horse artillery of Captain John Pelham of J.E.B. Stuart's cavalry corps.

Pelham;[3] so that there was one member of the family on each side, which was a fair division if he saw his duty in that way. I was much assisted in these dark and trying days by the advice of Captain Rodgers, who pointed out to me very clearly what my duty was. I concluded to stick by "The Old Flag," and let my family ties look after themselves, and so informed my mother, who was much grieved and shamed by my determination. She finally wrote my resignation, sent it to the Navy Department, where it was accepted, and without previous warning I found myself out of the service, despite my determination to stay in.

What to do under such conditions was a serious question to me, and I was again assisted to the right course by Captain Rodgers, who telegraphed to Washington, explaining matters. I was out only about twenty-four hours, but they were very unhappy ones for me, and I was relieved when my reappointment came by wire. My mother, thinking she had finally disposed of the matter, went to Richmond to nurse my brother, who had been badly wounded, and there waited for me to join her. She was naturally much disappointed at the result of her efforts, and wrote me a very severe letter, which she sent through the lines by a blockade runner, who mailed it. When it came to me it showed no signs of having been opened, but I found that it had, and many parts of it underlined with blue pencil. Many of my letters during the war mailed in the same way had been similarly treated, showing that in my case at least the post-office had their eyes on me.

My brother fought gallantly, was twice wounded, and served to the end of the war. As soon as he could make his way North he came, and never showed any bitterness over

3. John Pelham was an Alabama-born West Point cadet. He joined the Confederacy, rising to the rank of major and commanding a battalion of horse artillery. He established a reputation for dash and speed in battle, operating frequently with the famed cavalry of J.E.B. Stuart. Mortally wounded at the Battle of Kelly's Ford, Virginia, on 17 March 1863, Pelham became a postwar hero of the Lost Cause.

my course. The other members of my family did not behave in quite the same way, but after some years my mother changed her views, and fully forgave me before she died.

In June, 1862, we started on our first real practice cruise, using for the purpose the sloop of war John Adams. We were crowded into her like sardines in a box, and had no end of hard work, with whatever we could find to eat, and all in all about as little comfort as a set of youngsters ever experienced; but we made great headway in learning our business as seamen. The ship was uncomfortable, as all her class were, but at the same time seaworthy and safe. She would run well when off the wind, but with everything braced sharp up when there was any sea on she would butt three times at a sea and then go round it. Before the wind she rolled so that all hands had trouble in sleeping at night; but with all her defects she carried us safely as far south as Port Royal, South Carolina,[4] and brought us safely back to Newport.

On our way South we stopped a few days at Hampton Roads[5] and Yorktown,[6] where we had a chance to see the effects of the war. At Yorktown, particularly, we were much interested. The rebel General Magruder[7] had just evacuated

4. Port Royal was the major coaling, refitting, and supply station for the Union naval South Atlantic Blockading Squadron. Located between Charleston, South Carolina, and Savannah, Georgia, it was captured on 7 November 1861 by Flag Officer Samuel F. Du Pont's expedition of seventy-five warships and 12,000 troops.
5. The channel—about eight miles long—formed by the James, Nansemond, and Elizabeth rivers as they come together and flow into the Chesapeake Bay. It was the site of major strategic operations by Union forces against Richmond, especially the battles of the *Merrimac (Virginia)* with Union naval forces in March 1862.
6. A colonial town and site of the 1781 surrender of George Cornwallis to George Washington, Yorktown was the scene of the Union siege from 5 April to 3 May 1862, when John B. Magruder's Confederates blocked George B. McClellan's access to Williamsburg and Richmond.
7. Virginian John Bankhead Magruder (1807–85) was a graduate of West Point, professional artillerist, and a commander at the first land

the place, and was retreating up the peninsula, closely followed by the army under General George B. McClellan.[8] The wells had all been poisoned, and the roads in many places mined and torpedoes planted, so that we had to be very careful where we went and what we did. However, midshipmen are notoriously hard to kill, and with the assistance of the cavalry escort which was kindly furnished us, we managed to escape without damage except by falls from the cavalry horses, which all hands seemed determined to ride. Horseback riding was not a novelty to me, and I contented myself with going as quietly as I could in a wagon.

At Port Royal we saw Admiral Dupont's[9] splendid fleet, comprising many of the finest ships in the navy, fresh from their encounter with and complete victory over the rebel forts. Among them all, the Wabash seemed to me the most perfect; she flew the admiral's flag, and on board of her I had

---

battle of the war, Big Bethel, Virginia. His theatrical defense of the peninsula in the spring of 1862 successfully delayed George McClellan's march on Richmond. A vain individual, nicknamed "Prince John" for his elaborate lifestyle, he was even more successful in the trans-Mississippi West.

8. Born in Philadelphia in 1826, McClellan graduated from West Point in 1846. A brilliant organizer as the Union's General-in-Chief in early 1862, he commanded the Army of the Potomac on the peninsula and at Antietam. Falling from favor due to his inability to prosecute the war with alacrity, he was the unsuccessful Democratic nominee for President in the 1864 election. McClellan died in 1885.

9. Samuel Francis Du Pont was born on 27 September 1803, became a midshipman on 19 December 1815, and a lieutenant on 26 April 1826. He was promoted to commander on 28 October 1842, captain on 14 September 1855, and rear admiral on 6 July 1862. Scion of the famous Delaware industrialist family, Du Pont was head of the board that organized the blockade against the Confederacy and planned amphibious operations on the southern coast. He commanded the South Atlantic Blockading Squadron from 1861 to 1863, achieving the capture of Port Royal, Beaufort, and other Confederate positions. But he failed to take Charleston in April 1863, which led to his imagined censure by Washington officials. Du Pont died on 23 June 1865.

the pleasure of again meeting Captain C.R.P. Rodgers, who was fleet captain to Admiral Dupont.

I shall always remember an incident of my visit to this ship. As we went over the side, a large black bear stood on his hind legs at the gangway, among the side boys, hat in hand, and saluting each officer as he went on board. I saw him as I came up the side, and not proposing to give him a chance at me, jumped for the main chains and went over that way, much to the amusement of the officers. A short time after this his bearship came to grief, and had to be sent on shore. He was very fond of alcohol, and, having filled up and become ugly, turned into the bunk of one of the lieutenants, who, finding his bed occupied, turned in somewhere else until his time came for duty. The quartermaster being sent down during the night to call the lieutenant, and getting no answer, undertook to awake him by shaking him, which so enraged the bear, in his half-drunken condition, that he bit the quartermaster so badly that he lost one of his legs.

During this cruise the midshipmen were stationed as a crew for the vessel, and did all the work of the different ratings. When off Hatteras[10] on our way North our efficiency was thoroughly tested. At about ten o'clock the ship was struck by a sudden heavy squall, accompanied by rain and hail. All hands were called to reef topsails, the watch on deck having successfully handled the light sails. We were close enough to Diamond Shoal[11] to make haste a matter of importance, and the officers hustled us up without much ceremony.

10. Cape Hatteras is the easternmost point in North Carolina on the tip of Hatteras Island. It is noted for its storms and as the site of the sinking of the USS *Monitor* in December 1862.
11. A series of three shoals that extend southeast from Cape Hatteras into the Atlantic Ocean off southeastern Dare County, North Carolina. The shoal is also known as the "Graveyard of the Atlantic" because of the constant, dangerous turbulence caused when warm Gulf Stream waters collide with cold Arctic waters from farther north.

The topsails were quickly reefed, and I had just secured the lee earing on the main topsail yard when I heard the order, "Hoist away the topsails!" I was straddling the yard at the time, and just about to swing to the foot rope and lay down from aloft; but I changed my mind very suddenly, and instead hugged that topsail yard until I am sure you could have found the marks of my arms on the paint. It was as black as a pocket, raining in torrents, and as the yards were braced up the topsails filled and the ship made a butt at a heavy sea. I thought my time had come. I reached the deck, however, in safety, only to be properly dressed down by the officer of the deck for being slow in laying down from aloft! We were back at Newport again in September, better for our work, and ready to enjoy the short leave that was then given us.

My family had all gone South, and it was a question what I should do with myself; but as my uncle's house in Washington was in charge of a housekeeper, I concluded to spend my time there, which I did very pleasantly. The good woman who had charge of the house called me one night to inform me that there was a burglar in the cellar, and would I put him out? I was not anxious for the job, but my position as an officer forbade my declining; so with a small revolver in one hand and a lighted candle in the other I sought the burglar in the coal cellar. I had hardly entered the passageway leading past the door of the room in which he was located when a large chunk of coal whizzed past my head, and very close to it. I dropped the candle, which fortunately went out, putting us on more even terms, and after ten minutes I turned my man over to the police with a bullet through his thigh. I learned that night not to hunt burglars with a lighted candle; experience sometimes teaches things in a very forcible way.

During this leave I had a curious meeting with my rebel brother, whose command was operating on the Virginia side of the Potomac, a few miles away. I went one evening to an oyster house with a friend to eat some raw oysters. The place was one that all of us had known and frequented for years. As I entered the door I observed a tall, handsome young fellow who was finishing what he had ordered, and at the same moment I saw him give me a quick glance of recognition. He drank up his glass of beer, and then walked briskly out of the place, while I called for oysters on the half shell, and ate them very slowly. My brother knew what I would do, and he did not hesitate the least bit in his movements; but I had some very serious thinking to do while the man opened oysters for me, and I must admit that I ate more oysters than I wanted.

I could have gone to the exact spot where my brother's skiff was hauled out, but I was giving him all the time I could to get there ahead of the provost guard. Finally, my friend asked me if I were going to eat all night, when I paid my shot and we went out together. I asked if he had recognized my man; he replied that he had not, and then asked me in turn what I was going to do about it. Before I had time to reply, a squad of the provost guard came by, and to the officer in charge I reported that there was a rebel officer in the city—that I had seen and recognised him, and knew him as such. At first he seemed disposed to arrest me, but at last concluded to go after the real offender. After the war, my brother told me that he just managed to escape, and that he had concealed his boat at the spot where I imagined it was. As a result of this incident I was twice arrested and taken before the provost marshal on suspicion of holding intercourse with rebels. The last time I told the officer confidentially who the man was I had reported, and after that I was not annoyed.

Part of my leave I spent in a trip to the Army of the Potomac, to get an idea of how they conducted their business. I had a pass, and was described as an aid to the wounded. The horse I rode was hired form a livery stable,

and came near never reaching its owner again. I soon saw
enough to convince me that the army would not suit me;
that it was not to be compared to the navy for comfort or for
getting results. The army seemed to be continually fighting
and killing people, without arriving at any satisfactory conclusion as to who was whipped, both sides frequently claim-
ing the same fight. There was much straggling in the rear of
the army, and several times on my way back to Washington
I was asked for my horse, and was once shot at because I
declined to comply with the request. When I finally recrossed
the Long Bridge[12] into Washington I made up my mind that
I had learned all I wanted to know about the army.

October, 1862, found us all back at Newport, and once
more settled down to hard work and study. The demand for
officers was so great that the class was divided into two sections, and the instructions arranged so that the first section
could be graduated in the following June. It was not my
good fortune to be one of this first section; but I lost nothing
by this, as we shall see later on.

There was in this section, however, one of whom we were
all very fond—the young Frenchman, Pierre d'Orléans,[13]
Duc de Penthièvre, who preferred to acquire his professional
education under American auspices. He was a fine, manly

12. This was the principal bridge that spanned the Potomac from Virginia into Washington at the time of the Civil War. Originally a single
span for foot and horse traffic, a second, separate span of bridge was added
adjacent to the first in 1863 to carry military rail traffic to Alexandria.
Modern railroad and highway bridges now perpetuate the memory of this
major artery into Civil War Washington from the south.
13. Son of Admiral Prince de Joinville and grandson of King Louis Phil-
ippe, who occupied the throne of France, 1830–48. *Persona non grata* in
his homeland under the Second Empire, he was admitted to the academy
in 1860 on condition that his family would defray the expense of his
education. Popular with his classmates, who called him Pete, he relished
the democracy of the American midshipmen. Pierre d'Orléans resigned
from the U.S. Navy on 30 May 1864.

young fellow, known in the class as "Pete," and you might expect to find him mixed up in all the class scrapes and troubles. I remember him particularly as a cunning hand with the small sword, and a generous giver of very good French chocolate, an article which he consumed and gave away in enormous quantities.

During the winter of this year I again made acquaintance with the dark room on board the Constitution. Two of us were walking about during the evening in the park opposite our quarters, when I saw a watchman sneaking through the trees to catch some fellows who were violating regulations. The chance was very tempting, and without waiting to count the cost I landed a good-sized stone fairly behind the watchman's ear, sending him to the hospital for repairs. Unfortunately for me, there was a citizen near by who gave the commandant so good a description of me that I was sent for the next morning, and promptly sent on board ship and locked up. This was bad enough in all reason, but I soon made it much worse. The officer of the day, wishing to show proper respect for a senior, smuggled me a novel and a candle, and, having arranged my blanket so as to shut out curious eyes, I read my novel in peace until the sentry, a sailor with a cutlass, pried the blanket to one side. I blew the candle out at once, and then arranged the spring in the candlestick so that I could shoot the candle out when ready. Then I lighted it again, and taking a position favourable for my purpose, I waited for the sailor; and, as he again cautiously pried the blanket aside, I fired the candle through the opening. Unfortunately, it struck Jackey[14] in the eye, and thinking that his head was shot off he bolted from his station.

In a short while the commanding officer was on the scene, and then an end was put to my sport. I was marched out, the room searched, the door boarded up solid, and the key again turned on me. This time there was not the least sem-

14. "Jackey," or Jack-Tar, was a euphemism for sailor.

blance of fun about it. For two weeks I was kept locked up and then released; but for several days I could not do anything, as the light hurt my eyes dreadfully. It seemed to require a very practical demonstration to convince me that I had to do what I was told. This last experience went a long way in that direction.

CHAPTER 6

First Active Service

THE first section of the class was graduated in June, 1863, and at once ordered into service. The second section was distributed among the three practice ships, which were to take the junior classes out for the summer. I was one of five who were detailed as watch officers for the sloop of war Marion, as the Navy Department was unable to spare a sufficient number of watch officers for all the ships. We had a captain, of course, an executive officer, and a navigator, and five first-class men in the wardroom. Our crew consisted entirely of midshipmen, who did all the work usually done by sailors, including scrubbing the decks and cleaning the ship. We were to cruise along the coast, making Newport our headquarters, while the other ships went abroad.

The first night out we were beating clear of Block Island.[1] I had the deck, when, at 2 A. M., with a good stiff breeze, the captain ordered me to tack ship and shorten sail in stays. The helm was put down and I was getting on famously,

1. An island off southern Rhode Island that extends to Long Island Sound.

when the quartermaster stepped out from the wheel and reported, "Wheel ropes carried away, sir!" In turn, I reported to the captain, "Wheel ropes are carried away, sir!" His reply was, "Well, wheel ropes carried away, what do you do?" and as far as I could see he paid no further attention to me until the ship was close hauled on the other tack, with the light sails furled. Then, in a quiet, kindly way, he pointed out to me where I had been wrong, at the same time commending my general work. And so it was during the entire cruise: every man of us had to rely on himself; but at the same time a careful, conscientious officer was watching us and correcting us when we went wrong. Many officers in the service to-day remember gratefully the summer cruise of the Marion, Captain E.O. Mathews[2] commanding.

In the course of the month of July the rebel cruiser Florida[3] appeared off the coast, and the merchants of the exposed cities cried out for protection. The Marion was sent out, among other ships, to look for the privateer—an old-fashioned sailing sloop after a modern steam sloop of war! At the same time several vessels were chartered in New York, guns and men tumbled on board, and sent out to cruise off the coast. In one of these I served.

Captain J.W.A. Nicholson[4] was ordered to command a

2. Edmund O. Matthews became an acting midshipman on 2 October 1851 and was promoted to captain on 14 September 1881. Made a commodore on 21 July 1894, he achieved the rank of rear admiral three years later, and retired on 24 October 1898.
3. CSS *Florida* was the first Confederate cruiser contracted abroad. Secretly built in England under the name *Oreto,* she was a twin-bladed screw steamer of about 700 tons, with four to nine guns, a top speed of 9.5 knots, and a 146-man complement. Under the command of Captain John N. Maffitt, this ship scourged the seas of Union commerce until captured—under questionable circumstances—at Bahia, Brazil. The *Florida* was subsequently destroyed in a collision with a Union ship in the Chesapeake Bay in 1864.
4. James W.A. Nicholson began his naval career as a midshipman on 10 February 1838. He attained the rank of captain on 25 July 1866, commo-

new steamer, the Governor Buckingham,[5] built by Mallory.[6] He had only one officer, a volunteer acting ensign, so he applied to Captain Mathews, who told him that I could be spared, and could perform the duty of watch officer. The following day I received a telegram from the Department appointing me an acting lieutenant, and ordering me to report to Captain Nicholson for duty, which I did at once. The captain seemed somewhat surprised at my youthful appearance, but nevertheless directed me to find a crew for the Buckingham, get the guns on board, coal, and prepare for sea, and report to him when everything was ready. He was serving as one of the officers of the yard at the time. On board the receiving ship I was abused by the executive officer because I did not have the proper papers from the commandant, and cursed all over the quarter-deck and into the cabin by the captain, who was a fine old seaman, but dreadfully profane. He finally gave me thirty men, and surely not the best I ever saw!

On board the Buckingham I found a very curious state of things. The contract read that the merchant captain, his officers and crew, were to work the ship during the daytime under the orders of the naval captain, and to feed the officers but not the crew. At sundown the navy men were to take charge of the ship and do all the night work. The engines were to be run by the owners under orders of the naval captain, the navy to furnish the coal. For all this the Government was to pay one thousand dollars per day.

As soon as I had my crew on board I hauled the ship into the ordnance dock, took on three small guns and the neces-

---

dore on 8 November 1873, and rear admiral on 1 October 1881. Having retired on 10 March 1883, he died on 28 October 1887.

5. A wooden screw steamer of 886 tons, four to six guns, and a top speed of 8 knots, the USS *Governor Buckingham* was constructed at Mystic, Connecticut, and purchased on 29 July 1863 for $110,000. She was sold two years later at New York Navy Yard for $38,000.

6. Charles Mallory was a shipbuilder in Mystic, Connecticut.

sary ammunition, and at once anchored off the yard and began coaling. We had only taken in a few bags, when one of the men, a little the worse for liquor, concluded that I was neither old enough nor large enough to make him work; on the contrary, he would show me a thing or two. I landed on top of him from the deck above with a heavy brass trumpet, and he was convinced of his mistake in less than half a minute. I tied him up securely, bandaged his head, and locked him up in a coal bunker. Early the next day I reported the ship ready, and that afternoon we sailed in search of the Florida. Several chartered vessels went on the same mission about the same time, and one of them, the Ericsson,[7] was fortunate enough to sight the privateer about fifty miles northeast of Sandy Hook.[8] She was also fortunate enough to get away from her when the Florida gave chase! She steamed much faster on the trip in than she did going out. I had expected to be punished for my encounter with the man, but Captain Nicholson considered the peculiar circumstances under which I was working, and dismissed the matter with a caution—not to me, but to the man, who afterward proved himself a very good sort of a chap.

We ran as far north as Cape Sable[9] with the Buckingham, and then cruised slowly back, reaching New York safely after an absence of three weeks, without seeing the Florida, which was no doubt fortunate for us, as we were not fast enough to get away from her, and certainly not strong enough to fight her. But we satisfied the merchants of New York, and that was what it was all about. I had done the duty of executive officer, navigator, and watch officer, besides drilling the men for two hours every day. Captain Nicholson was good enough

7. A chartered steamer not accorded the government rank of "USS."
8. A peninsula of eastern New Jersey at the entrance to Lower New York Bay.
9. It is unclear whether Evans refers here to a promontory of extreme southern Nova Scotia or an island off Nova Scotia, east/northeast of Halifax.

to commend me for my service. Our acting ensign had been
found asleep on watch shortly after we sailed, and was not
again put on duty, the captain and I standing all the night
watches. One part of the contract I remember was faithfully
carried out: I mean the feeding of the officers. I never have
lived so well at sea since. Every night during the mid watch
a beautiful lunch was served to the officer of the deck, including a bottle of wine if he wanted it.

After the return of the Buckingham I was sent back to the
Marion, and was then given command of the yacht
America,[10] two guns, and a crew of twenty-four midshipmen. In company with the Marion we again sailed in search
of the Florida, but failed to come up with her. I enjoyed
every day and hour of my first command, and never missed a
chance to race with anything, from a steamer down to a pilot
boat. For some time I was cruising by myself off Cape Cod[11]
and toward the Banks,[12] and while so employed overhauled
an English steamer, the skipper of which was not disposed to
pay much attention to me. Two shells across his bow seemed
to have no effect, but the third, which landed in his main
hatch, brought him to very quickly. On my way back to
Newport I sighted a schooner off Nantucket Shoals,[13] and
stood toward her. She made every effort to escape, but the

10. The USS *America* was a sailing yacht of 100 tons and three guns that
was discovered in Dunn's Lake, St. John's River, Florida, and purchased
by the Navy Department on 19 May 1863. Originally brought to
America from Great Britain, she ostensibly was to take Confederate commissioners to that country. General B.F. Butler bought the *America* for
$5,000 on 20 June 1873 in Annapolis, Maryland, where she was school
ship at the Naval Academy.
11. The famous hook, or spit, of land south of Boston, Massachusetts.
12. Shoals of the western Atlantic that lie off southeastern Newfound-
land, Canada, comprising about 36,000 square miles.
13. The shoals off Nantucket Island, south of Cape Cod, Massachusetts,
which are separated by Nantucket Sound, an arm of the Atlantic.

wind was very light, and we slowly fanned up on her quarter. I saw that she was a whaler homeward bound, and the men of the crew were amusing themselves catching mackerel. I had not, up to this time, shown my colours. When I hoisted the flag I hailed, "Schooner ahoy!" "Hello!" came back. "Have you seen anything of any pirates offshore?" "No; bein't you a pirate?" The captain had mistaken the character of my ship, and when he discovered his error promptly swung out a boat and sent me a mess of the finest mackerel I ever saw.

We returned to Newport late in September, and were rejoiced to find that the Navy Department had decided to send us into service immediately. Our educations were not complete, but we knew enough to look out for a ship and stop bullets, which were the important things. We were commissioned as acting ensigns from October 1, 1863.

After ten days' leave I reported on board the United States steamer Powhatan[14] at Philadelphia, where she was refitting for service in the West Indies. I was at once given a watch and division of guns, and two classmates and I composed the watch officers of the ship. Captain William Ronckendorf[15] was the commanding officer, and it has been truly said of him that he could make himself disagreeable in more different ways than any man who ever wore naval uniform. I agree perfectly with the man who said it.

After ten days' hard work we put to sea with a fairly good crew and a large complement of officers, all anxious for active

14. A wooden side-wheel steamer and first-class sloop, the USS *Powhatan* displaced 2,415 tons, had a top speed of 18 knots, and was armed between 1861 and 1865 with anywhere from three to twenty-four guns of varying calibers. She was commissioned on 25 August 1860 and sold in 1886.
15. William Ronckendorf became a midshipman on 17 February 1832, was promoted to captain on 27 September 1866, and to commodore on 12 February 1874. Placed on the retired list on 9 November 1874, he died on 27 November 1891.

The Powhatan

service. Although we had many officers, we were kept in three watches, because the captain would not trust volunteer officers to take the deck. We had seven of these gentlemen, excellent men, who had commanded ships, many of them, before I was born; but they knew nothing of man-of-war routine, and this we had to teach them. Drills were constant— forenoon, afternoon, and generally once during the night. In addition I was made midshipman of the foretop, and spent a good portion of my time aloft instructing the green men of the crew in bending and unbending sails, and the thousand and one things a topman has to know. Every time the men were sent aloft, up I went, day or night, rain or shine. By the time we reached Cape Haytien,[16] which was headquarters of the Flying Squadron, to which we belonged, I had about concluded that I at least had work enough to keep me from rusting out.

Upon our arrival at Cape Haytien the captain reported us for duty as flagship of the squadron, and the next day we flew the flag of Rear-Admiral James Lardner,[17] one of the finest specimens of the old navy. He was the very opposite of our captain—a splendid seaman, a courteous, kindly gentleman, brave to the point of recklessness, an honour to the service, and a man under whom all were glad to serve. Tall and commanding in figure, with close-cropped, snow-white hair and mustache, he looked what he really was, the ideal commander. As soon as he came on board many of the petty annoyances from which we had suffered ceased, and we became contented and happy. It is difficult to convince any one to-day of how completely the captain ruled things in the time of which I am writing. There was no law off soundings beyond the captain's will, unless you had an admiral on board,

16. A city of northern Haiti on the Atlantic coast.
17. James K. Lardner began his naval career as a midshipman on 10 May 1820. He attained the rank of captain on 19 May 1861, commodore on 16 July 1862, and rear admiral (while on the Retired List) on 25 July 1866. He died on 12 April 1881.

when his will became the law. Officers could be, and to my knowledge were, kept on board for months without ever being allowed on shore, because the captain thought it was better for them!

Admiral Lardner had some peculiarities which were striking; anything that savoured of insubordination or disrespect brought the severest punishment, generally a tongue-lashing the recipient remembered all his life. To a naturally fluent tongue the admiral added a vocabulary of oaths so fine that it was musical, and when aroused he did not hesitate to speak his mind in the language all seamen understand. At the same time his black eyes shone like fireflies, and his white mustache bristled, each hair standing on end. He certainly was a darling, and much beloved by all of us.

When the Rhode Island[18] was his flagship, Captain Trenchard,[19] who commanded, had a very accomplished steward, a coloured man, who had become so expert in catching flies off the captain's bald head that he was never annoyed by them. Admiral Lardner had for his steward a fine, large, heavy-handed Irishman, who watched the coloured man with great envy while his master, undisturbed, enjoyed his meals. Pat's master thrashed at the flies, and swore roundly as they lighted on his close-cropped hair. The coloured man went on catching flies with a quick, dexterous movement of his right hand until Pat could stand it no longer. Drawing back, he made a vicious swing at a fly, but, instead of catching it, he caught the admiral an awful blow on the back of his head.

18. A wooden side-wheel steamer of 1,517 tons, and a top speed of 16 knots, the USS *Rhode Island* was armed between 1861 and 1865 with four to twelve guns. She was purchased on 8 July 1861 from Spofford, Tileston & Co. for $185,000, and sold at public auction on 1 October 1867 for $70,000.

19. Stephen D. Trenchard became a midshipman on 23 October 1834, was promoted to captain on 25 July 1866, to commodore on 7 May 1871, and rear admiral on 10 August 1875. He retired on 10 July 1880, and died on 15 November 1883.

The admiral, thinking there was a mutiny, grabbed the carving knife, and made after Patrick, who retreated to the spar deck, and there was a hurdle race fore and aft—the officer of the deck and the orderly trying to catch the admiral, who was doing his best to put the carving knife in the back of Pat, who finally escaped, but never bothered any more about flies on the admiral's head.

One of the crew of the admiral's barge, a man the admiral was very fond of, died, and, as a mark of great respect, he went to the grave to see the poor fellow buried. The grave diggers had, for some reason, dug a very shallow grave, which so incensed the admiral that he spoke to them very severely, and not receiving a satisfactory reply, seized a stick and made after them. They ran, but he was too quick for them; he caught them and forced them to return, and while we stood around waiting, made them dig a proper grave in which poor Jack was decently buried.

The duty of the Flying Squadron was to look after the rebel privateers in the West Indies, and see that they did not interfere with the Pacific mail steamers on their regular trips. In order to do this most effectually, some vessel, often the flagship, met the steamer at Mariguana Island,[20] and convoyed her clear of Navassa,[21] where she was left to depend on her heels for safety. The convoying vessel got her mail first, and generally a file of late papers from home, so the duty was considered choice, and all hands were anxious for the job. As soon as the mail steamer was out of sight a cruise around the south side of Cuba was in order, generally including Havana[22] and Key West, and then back to Cape Haytien.

The vessels of the squadron were kept constantly cruising

20. An island in the Bahamas that lies between the Acklins on the northwest; the Caicos and Turks to the southeast; and Cuba to the northeast.
21. An island located off the west coast of Haiti between Haiti and Jamaica.
22. The capital of Cuba, Havana is situated in the northeastern part of the island, on the Gulf of Mexico.

through the Windward Islands[23] and as far south as the Spanish Main,[24] and though we used our best exertions we never came up with a privateer, because none of them visited that part of the world. For several months we cruised constantly, disguised as a Frenchman, and showing French colours to passing vessels, with the idea that we might thus decoy the Alabama[25] within range of guns. During a part of this time we had yellow fever on board, and to get rid of it we steamed out into the trade winds, stopped the engines, put the ship under sail, and slowly cruised around with the wind abeam, until the fever disappeared. The admiral was very fond of sailing, and there was no end to sail and spar drills. He would reef the buckets of our paddle wheels, set studding sails on both sides, and run off to leeward, apparently for the fun of beating back again.

Once we thought we had the Alabama sure. We were anchored at Cape Haytien, when a messenger arrived from the consul at St. Nicholas Mole[26] with word that the Alabama was anchored in that harbour. In a few minutes we were under way, heading to the westward, all sails set, and using pork in our furnaces to get all the speed we could out of the old ship. She really made fourteen knots all the way.

23. Located in the southeastern West Indies, the Windward Islands comprise the southern group of the Lesser Antilles from Martinique south to Grenada.
24. Principally identified as the mainland of Spanish Colonial America, especially along the south coast of South America. The name also applies to the Caribbean Sea and adjacent waters, especially at the time when they were infested with pirates.
25. Arguably the most famous of the Confederate raiders, the CSS *Alabama* was constructed by Laird shipyards in Liverpool, England. A screw sloop of 1,050 tons, she mounted a battery of eight cannon, and had a top speed of 13 knots and a complement of 145 men. Her twenty-one-month career saw her cruise nearly 75,000 miles, and take sixty-four prizes worth $6.5 million. The *Alabama* was sunk off Cherbourg, France, by the USS *Kearsarge* on 19 June 1864.
26. The breakwater and harbor at Port-au-Prince, the capital of Haiti.

On the way down the ship was cleared for action, and every preparation made to fight and fight hard. The admiral did not intend that the Alabama should get away from him, as she had from several others who had sighted her. As we approached the harbour preparations were made for anchoring; men were stationed by both anchors to let go when ordered, but the anchors were lashed so securely that nothing short of an axe could have got them clear. It was the intention, if we found the Alabama in port, to approach her at full speed, and when very close to back the engines and order both anchors let go, which failing, she would, of course, be sunk in the collision that would follow. We stood at our stations peering into the dark as we tore around the harbour at twelve knots, much to the surprise of the people on shore, but there was no Alabama.

The next day we found that an English sloop of war had caused all the trouble. Fortunately for her, she had gone out in the afternoon for target practice, and remained outside overnight. If she had been anchored inside, nothing could have saved her, as the admiral had made up his mind what he was going to do, and would not have waited to ask any questions. We agreed among ourselves that the captain of that ship ought to buy a lottery ticket!

Our men were kept on board so long, and we were so steadily under steam, that they became very irritable and ugly. Fights were of daily occurrence, and some of them serious. If a deck hand interfered in any way with a man from the engine room, there was a fight on the spot; and even the firemen fought among themselves on the slightest provocation. The heat seemed to make them particularly ugly. Several men lost their lives in this way, and the admiral finally went to St. Thomas[27] to give shore liberty to the crew.

When we arrived we found the English Flying Squadron[28]

---

27. One of the Virgin Islands in the West Indies.
28. Evans possibly refers here to the British West Indian Squadron.

in port, but while the feeling against them was very bitter, we did not consider it a good reason why our men should be kept on board; so the starboard watch, consisting of one hundred and fifty men, were sent on shore for twenty-four hours. It was only a few hours before word came off that there was trouble ashore, and later a letter from the English admiral, saying that our men were rioting with the English sailors, some of whom had been killed. Admiral Lardner directed the captain to send the other watch on shore. And then there was a fine time, sure enough! The Danish garrison was turned out and attempted to arrest some of the leaders; but they were soon driven back into their forts, and the English and our men went at it again. The native negroes all sided with the English, and our people had them to contend with as well. Just before sundown the general recall was hoisted as a signal for all hands to repair on board, and such boats as we could man were sent in charge of officers to bring the men off. I was sent in the admiral's barge, the crew of which were picked men, and I anticipated no trouble with them; but on nearing the landing, where two or three hundred men were fighting with such weapons as they could find, I heard the stretchers begin to rattle in the bottom of the boat, the oars were tossed, and before I knew what had happened every man of the crew was out of the boat and into the fight, stretcher in hand. I followed, also armed with a stretcher, a very handy piece of white ash, and soon had my boat nearly loaded with men. But, unfortunately, I saw one of our men with three or four natives after him, and went at once to his assistance. As I grabbed him by the arm one of the negroes struck at my head with a broken oar, but only hit me across the shoulders, which probably saved my life. I was knocked down, of course, but quickly regained my feet with a fine round stone in my hand, which I planted squarely in the negro's mouth, and he gave no further trouble. By midnight we had our people on board, and found that three had been killed and many more or less seriously wounded, while the English were in about the same fix. Some of the rum mills on the water front were badly wrecked. After this experience our men had no more shore liberty until we got back to the United States.

Many years afterward I visited St. Thomas, and at the best hotel I saw a coloured porter without any front teeth, who told me, when I asked him what had become of them, "A little Yankee midshipman hit me in the mouth with a rock!" He was my friend with the broken oar.

During the time we were lying at headquarters the watch officers had a peculiar duty to perform in addition to their regular work. The officer who had the first watch at night was obligated to be ready for duty at four the next morning. As soon as the men had had their coffee, he left the ship with two boats and the fishing seine, and was expected back by eight o'clock, with fish enough for the whole crew. The fishing ground was five or six miles away, and to get to it we had to find our way through a tangle of shoals and coral heads, but once on the ground we could fill both boats with tarpon or other splendid fish at one haul of the seine. Usually we reached the ship just in time for breakfast, and then went on duty for four hours, which made a pretty long forenoon of it. However, we were young and strong, and could stand almost anything.

One morning while exercising at sail drill, we had a sad accident, which was long remembered by the whole crew. We had two brothers on board, one a seaman about twenty-three years old, and the other a landsman about eighteen; both excellent men, very active and promising. The younger one missed his footing in the foretopmast rigging, and fell to the deck and died in a few hours. We were quarantined at the time, and could not bury his body on shore; neither could we buy screws for his coffin when we found that there were none on board. The coffin had to be nailed up, which was anything but a pleasant performance, as the carpenter, a little nervous, I suppose, hit the coffin lid much oftener than he did the heads of the nails. I never understood why the captain insisted on burying the body in a coffin, but he probably had a reason of his own which he did not confide to us.

Just before sundown two boats were called away and dropped to the gangway—one for the body, and the other to tow it out to sea, where it was to be buried. All hands were called to bury the dead, and I was ordered to take charge of the boats when everything was ready. The coffin was placed on the quarter-deck, the officers and men paraded, and the captain had pronounced a few words of the burial service, when a loud, prolonged squeak was heard, and the lid of the coffin slowly raised several inches. It was the most terrifying sound I ever heard in my life, and the effect was startling; most of the men bolted forward, and the officers were very pale. I was standing near the head of the coffin, and my legs were only prevented from carrying me away by the fact that my hands were firmly gripping the spokes of the wheel. The trouble was soon manifest: the gases formed in the body had caused it to swell and lift the lid of the coffin, and the nails in drawing out made the awful noise that had so startled over three hundred men.

There was some delay in getting things ready again, and when I finally left the ship with a crew of petty officers, towing the boat with the body in it, the moon had risen. Out over the bar we went, pitching into rather a rough sea until I thought we had reached the right spot, when the boat was hauled up alongside and the body consigned to the deep. Then we started back for the ship. We had gone only a few hundred yards when the men fell into a perfect panic; some of them even dropped their oars overboard, and all hands stopped pulling, their faces white and terror-stricken. The stroke oar, a splendid specimen of manhood, fairly shook as he said to me, "He's coming, sir!" I turned, and looking out to sea, was not surprised at the condition of the men, for I was horrified myself at what I saw. The coffin was standing upright in the water, and as it rose on the seas it seemed, in the moonlight, to be making great jumps after us. It certainly was a most nerve-shattering sight, especially after the unpleasant scene on board ship. There was only one thing to do, and after quite a struggle with the men we pulled back, knocked the head of the coffin in and allowed it to sink. It was the most uncanny job I ever did in my life, I think, and I was glad when we were back on board and the boats hoisted up. No real danger could have frightened any one of the crew; they were a splendid, manly lot, and showed great spirit when in action; but just a touch of the supernatural, the least bit, and they were ready to hide their heads in the bottom of the boat.

Havana was, for some reasons, the most pleasant port to visit on the station; we got fine cheap cigars, and sometimes good meat there, but we hated it more than any place we had to go to, because the people were so bitter against us. The Southerners who lived there were not so bad, but the Spaniards were almost unbearable. On several occasions we found blockade runners anchored in the harbour, and their crews would pelt our boats with lumps of coal as we passed back and forth, all of which we could avoid by pulling a bit farther away; but the abuse on shore we could not avoid, as we were obliged always to land in uniform. Under such conditions collisions were frequent, and as a rule we were content with the way we came out of them. In the matter of coal we were held strictly to the law, while the blockade runners were allowed great latitude, and in consequence were very successful.

In 1864 Jeffrard[29] was ruler of Hayti, and his iron hand was felt by all classes. He was thoroughly hated but at the same time feared by the people generally. Revolutions, shoot-

29. Nicholas Fabre Geffrard was a Haitian general and President of the Haitian republic from 23 December 1858 to 13 March 1867. In 1864 he signed a treaty of amity, commerce, navigation, and criminal extradition with the United States. Geffrard also attempted to induce ex-slaves to emigrate from America, and his presidency witnessed efforts at internal reform and stimulation of culture and education.

ings, and hangings were the order of the day; the people seemed happy, and appeared to enjoy all these diversions. The ordinary routine was somewhat varied during one of our stays in Cape Haytien by the discovery of a gang of cannibals, who occupied a strong position in the mountains near the Old Castle.[30] Jeffrard went after them, captured the whole lot, brought them to Cape Haytien, where they were confined for a few days, and then shot. It was reported and believed at the time that several barrels of human flesh had been captured with the prisoners, and that some of it was produced in evidence before they were shot. The favourite morsel was said to be the palm of the hand. If one could judge from appearances, we were sure Jeffrard made no mistake in shooting this lot, for they certainly were the worst-looking cutthroats we had ever seen.

During the month of October, 1864, a rumour came that we would soon be ordered to the United States for more active duty than we had been having in the West Indies. The next mail brought the order, and all hands, from the admiral down, were as happy as boys out of school. Our preparations for departure were quickly made, and we said good-bye to the West Indies, yellow fever, rebel sympathizers, heat, filth, and hard service—the whole outfit—without a single pang. The old ship seemed to know that she was homeward bound, and did her best. Early in November we anchored in Hampton Roads, and as soon as possible all hands, as they could be spared from duty, sought the dissipations of the city of Norfolk, which at that time was not the best place in the world for those wearing United States uniform. However, we did manage to enjoy a good square meal and the conversation of people of our own race. Only those who have served away

30. This may have been the ruins of Henri Christopher's "Sans Souci" or "The Citadel Laferrier," upon which Haitians labored from 1804 to 1817 atop Mount Bonnet à l'Évêque.

from home can appreciate what all this means, and how we enjoyed it.

Soon after our arrival, Admiral Lardner was detached, and left the ship with the respect and affection of every officer and man aboard. A few days later Captain Ronckendorf was sent to other duty, and Commodore Schenck[31] took his place. In our new commander we had one of the ablest men of the navy, and one who soon endeared himself to all on board. He found a splendidly drilled crew and a ship thoroughly organized in every department and detail, and he showed his appreciation of it all. Our men were all long-service men, and there was not the demoralization that always comes with a draft of new men to be whipped into shape with a lot of old ones. I am sure we did not require a dozen men to complete our complement.

We lost one man in a curious way. We had among the crew a "bounty jumper"—so called because he had drawn a bounty on enlistment and then deserted. In fact, he had repeated this trick a good many times before he finally fitted into his place on board the Powhatan. He was a plausible sort of a chap, and had made himself a favourite with the men on board to such an extent that the petty officers had made him caterer of their mess, and had given him quite a large sum of money with which to buy stores. When we anchored, well up toward the middle ground, a number of bumboats came off to trade with us, and when they left it was soon discovered that the "bounty jumper" had gone with them, taking all the mess money. A boat was soon ready to follow them, manned by a crew of petty officers, as they would be sure to pull harder than any others in the ship. I

31. James Findlay Schenck, having become a midshipman on 1 July 1825, attained the following ranks in his naval career: commander, 14 September 1855; commodore, 2 January 1863, and rear admiral, 21 September 1868. Having retired on 11 June 1869, he died on 21 December 1882.

was sent in charge of the boat, and soon picked out the canoe containing the deserter by the frantic efforts she was making to escape, which she finally did, owing to the long start she had. All the canoes, half a dozen or more, landed at the same place five minutes ahead of me, and in the semi-darkness I could not see where the men disappeared. I at once notified the guards about the fort of what had happened, and asked the officer of the day to order the man's arrest, which he did. Then I went back to my boat, and found that the crew had been looking about, but found nothing of importance. Just as I was about to shove off, a tall, powerful boatswain's mate said: "Let me look under this wharf, sir; it is low tide; he may be there." Off he went, and was gone five or ten minutes. I could hear him occasionally splashing around, but not making noise enough to indicate any trouble. Finally, he came back, reported, "He's gone, sir!" and I returned to the ship at once. The next morning the body of the man we had been looking for was found under the wharf with his throat cut from ear to ear, and no money on his person. His was one of the vacancies we had to fill from Norfolk.

CHAPTER 7

The First Fort Fisher Campaign

A DMIRAL PORTER[1] assumed command in November, and at once began assembling a powerful fleet. Every preparation was made for active service. Boilers and machinery were overhauled, magazines, shell rooms, and storerooms replenished, and constant target practice was had with all guns. By the end of November the largest fleet ever seen

1. Born in 1813, David Dixon Porter began his naval career as a midshipman on 2 February 1829. He was the scion of a naval family that included father David, distinguished naval officer and diplomat; brother William D., commodore on western rivers; adopted brother David G. Farragut; and cousin General Fitz-John Porter. An energetic naval veteran of the Mexican War, Porter's service in the Civil War included the relief of Florida's Fort Pickens in the spring of 1861; command of a mortar flotilla during the assault on New Orleans via forts Jackson and St. Philip; command of the Mississippi Squadron involved in the capture of Vicksburg; the abortive Red River expedition; command of the North Atlantic Blockading Squadron; and the capture of Fort Fisher. Porter was the Navy's senior admiral after the war, although he was identified increasingly with the old style of naval command and management rather than progressive new navalism. Promoted to the rank of full admiral on 15 August 1870, he died on 13 February 1891.

under the American flag was assembled in Hampton Roads, all classes, from the largest monitor to the small gunboat, being represented. Our destination was a secret, carefully guarded; but we surmised from what was taking place that some important move was contemplated, and in this we were not mistaken. It was evident from the daily target practice that the admiral meant we should hit something when the time for action came, and the landing of the men on the beach for drill was an indication of possible shore service.

The Ticonderoga,[2] anchored near us, was firing at target one morning, and making such good practice that we were all watching her with great interest, when one of her pivot guns, a large-calibre Parrott,[3] was fired. There was a terrific report, as if the shell had burst at the muzzle of the gun, a great cloud of smoke, and then something struck close to her, making a great splash in the water. At the same time, or shortly afterward, the shot she had fired fell near the target. About two feet of the muzzle of the gun had blown off, straight up in the air, and come down within twenty feet of the ship. It was the most curious of the many accidents we had then and afterward with the Parrott rifles. This particular gun, though two feet shorter than it was intended to be, was continued in service, and did good work.

Early in December the troopships arrived—thirteen thousand men under General B.F. Butler—and still our destination was a secret.

2. Built at the New York Navy Yard for $330,746.50, the *Ticonderoga* was launched on 16 October 1862, and commissioned on 12 May 1863. She was a wooden screw-sloop that displaced 1,533 tons, had a top speed of 10.5 knots, and mounted thirteen to fourteen guns. She was sold in August 1887 for $15,900.
3. A Parrott gun was an iron, rifled artillery piece distinguished by its single reinforcing band on the breech. It was developed by Robert Parker Parrott, veteran artillerist and superintendent of West Point Foundry in Cold Spring, New York. One of the most widely used rifles of the Civil War, the Parrott gun fired shells ranging from 10 to 250 pounds, and

About this time I received a letter by flag of truce from my brother, who was serving as a captain of scouts on General Lee's staff, in which he said, "We will give you a warm reception at Fort Fisher[4] when you get there!"—showing that our intended move was not so much of a secret to the rebels as it was to us. The information must have been sent from Washington, as no one in the fleet, outside the admiral's immediate official family, knew anything about it. When I showed the letter to Commodore Schenck, which I was required to do by the regulations, he seemed much surprised, and sent me with it at once to Admiral Porter, who was very indignant when he had read it. For myself, I thought my brother had only made a good guess; there were only a few important places on the Southern coast remaining in the hands of the rebels, and, as our preparations surely indicated an important move, he guessed, and guessed correctly, that we were after the most important of the lot.

Toward the middle of December all our preparations had been completed, and we put to sea under sealed orders. It was a grand sight as we passed Cape Henry;[5] all the water as far as one could see was covered with ships, and among them the flower of the navy. Commodore James Findlay Schenck

---

proved to be one of the most capable, if not always accurate, pieces of rifled artillery.

4. An enormous Confederate L-shaped earthwork that formed the key to the Cape Fear defenses guarding the river approach to Wilmington, North Carolina. A fall 1864 expedition of 6,500 troops in sixty naval vessels, led by Rear Admiral David D. Porter, failed because of poor relations between General Benjamin Butler and Porter, inept handling of landing and assault operations, and the stalwart Confederate defense of the area. Butler retired with his land force to Fort Monroe and informed his superiors that he had used discretion in withdrawal although still under orders to continue the siege of the fort. He was relieved of command by General Ulysses S. Grant and sent home to Massachusetts, ridding the Lincoln administration of this politico-military thorn.

5. The cape in southeastern Virginia, east of Norfolk, at the entrance to the Chesapeake Bay.

commanded the third division of the fleet, and flew his flag
on the Powhatan. The fleet was formed in three columns, the
transports and storeships in the centre.

After passing Cape Henry we experienced beautiful
weather, and got around Hatteras in almost a dead calm,
much to the delight of the troops, who were dreadfully
crowded on the troopships. On December 22d the fleet, having parted company with the transports, anchored in column
thirteen miles off the mouth of Cape Fear River,[6] and then,
of course, we knew what we had in hand. That afternoon it
came on to blow hard from southeast, and when the sun went
down the sight was a grand and threatening one. The seven
monitors at the head of the column held on well at their
anchors, but would disappear entirely from sight as the heavy
seas swept over them. The ships soon began to drag, and all
hands were kept on deck during the entire night, ready to
do what was possible in case of collision. When daylight
came the monitors were still in place, but the rest of the fleet
was scattered over a space of sixteen miles, and nowhere
could we make out a single transport. At sundown of the
23d the fleet was again anchored in good condition, none the
worse for the shaking up it had had; but still we wondered
what had become of the transports, as none of them showed
up. It turned out later that they were safely anchored well
inshore of us, waiting for the stragglers, who had been blown
out of place in the gale, to come up.

Before leaving Fortress Monroe,[7] General Butler had pro-

6. The river was strategically important to the Confederacy because it
enabled blockade runners to reach Wilmington, North Carolina, with
their precious cargoes. Wilmington was the South's most active port in
this regard, and closure of the river became a major objective of the
Federal naval blockade.
7. Originally the site of Colonial, Revolutionary, and later permanent
fortification at Point Comfort, where the James River enters the Chesapeake Bay. Called fortress prior to 1832, its construction began in 1819,
and it was named for the seventh President.

posed a "powder boat," by the explosion of which he hoped to seriously injure the forts on Federal Point,[8] including Fort Fisher. Indeed, he was confident that he would dismount most of the guns and level the works. An old steamer, the Georgiana,[9] had been loaded with several hundred tons of powder, and turned over to the navy to explode at the proper spot. A crew of volunteers, commanded by Captain A.C. Rhind,[10] had her in charge, and on the evening of December 24th took her in for the final act in her career. No man in the navy believed for a moment that she would do much harm, but none of us anticipated how little injury would come from the explosion.

At eleven o'clock that night Admiral Porter steamed about the fleet in his flagship, the side-wheeled steamer Malvern,[11] and made signal: "Powder boat will blow up at 1.30 A. M. Be prepared to get under way, and stand in to engage the fort!" After that there was no sleep for any one; we stood and watched and waited as the hours slowly dragged by. Half past one came, and no explosion, and we were fearful of some mishap; but just as the bells struck two o'clock it came. At first a gentle vibration, then the masts and spars shook as if they would come down about our ears; and then came the

8. The promontory on the Cape Fear River at the Atlantic Ocean, south of Wilmington, North Carolina, upon which Confederates crowned numerous batteries.

9. It is unclear which one of the U.S. steamers mentioned in the *Official Naval Records* is the ship mentioned by Evans.

10. Alexander C. Rhind became a midshipman in September 1838. He attained the rank of captain on 2 March 1879, commodore on 30 September 1876, and rear admiral on 30 October 1883. Retiring on 31 October 1883, he died on 8 November 1897.

11. An iron steamer, the gunboat USS *Malvern* displaced 627 tons, was armed with eight to twelve guns, and had a complement of 625 men. Purchased from Boston prize court for $137,000, she was commissioned on 9 February 1864 and became Admiral D.D. Porter's flagship at Fort Fisher on 15 January 1865. She was sold at public auction on 25 October 1865 for $113,500.

low rumble like distant thunder, while the sky to the westward was lighted up for a few seconds, and then great masses of powder smoke hung over the land like thunder clouds. The powder boat had blown up surely, and as the fleet rapidly formed for battle there was great curiosity everywhere to see what the effect had been.

At daylight we were heading in for the fort, and almost in range, when we saw General Butler's flagship coming in at full speed, heading straight at Fort Fisher, which looked to us very grim and strong, and totally uninjured. Everything was very quiet until the general got fairly within range, when there was a flash from the fort and a prolonged roar, and all the guns on that face of the work opened on his ship. If he had had any notion that he could land unopposed he was quickly undeceived, and the way that ship turned and got offshore spoke well for the energy of her fireroom force! The last we saw of her she was running east as fast as her engines could carry her. The powder boat had proved a failure, and the general was grievously disappointed. A rebel newspaper reported that a Yankee gunboat had blown up on the beach and all hands lost.

The fleet stood on in column, the monitors[12] leading until in position, when the leader anchored; and then the rest anchored in succession as they reached their places. It was a beautiful evolution and beautifully performed. As soon as the monitors came in range, all the guns that would bear opened furiously; and as the range was only seven hundred yards, the hits were frequent. The rebels seemed to conclude very quickly that they could do nothing with the ironclads, so they held their fire for the wooden ships. Then the Minne-

12. Monitors were a class of iron naval vessel descended from the USS *Monitor* designed by Swedish inventor John Ericsson. These ships were conspicuous for their armored flush-deck arrangement with a revolving turret that contained a variety of heavy cannon.

sota[13] took her place, and as her anchor went down her batteries opened, first a broadside from the spar deck, and then her gun-deck broadside roared its Christmas greeting. At the same moment all the rebel guns replied, and the ship was completely enveloped in the smoke from her own guns and the bursting rebel shells. For a moment it looked as if she must be disabled, but then her guns began to speak out with a welcome sound, and we knew she was all right. The Wabash[14] and the Colorado[15] followed the Minnesota, and quickly dropped into their places, opening as they did so with their tremendous batteries. In rapid succession each vessel of the fleet passed them on the off side, firing through the intervals between them, and thus the battle line was formed. At times the shower of shells coming over the vessels engaged gave us a foretaste of what was in store for us, but the losses were wonderfully few.

13. The frigate USS *Minnesota* was a wooden screw-steamer that displaced 3,307 tons and mounted forty guns. Built at the Washington Navy Yard for $691,408.14, she was launched on 1 December 1855. Best known for her fight with the CSS *Merrimack (Virginia)* while grounded after her sister ship the *Cumberland* sank on 8–9 March 1862, she served as a training ship from 1875 to 1895, and was loaned to the Massachusetts Naval Militia from 1896 to 1900. The *Minnesota* was sold for $25,738.38 in 1901.

14. Built at the Philadelphia Navy Yard, the frigate USS *Wabash* was a wooden screw-steamer that displaced 3,274 tons and mounted forty-six guns of various calibers and configurations. She was launched on 25 October 1855, having cost $854,429.74. She was decommissioned on 14 February 1865 at the Boston Navy Yard.

15. A wooden, screw-propelled steam and sail frigate, the USS *Colorado* was built by the government at a cost of $814,012.88. Launched on 19 June 1856 and commissioned on 3 June 1861 at Boston Navy Yard, she displaced 3,425 tons, mounted forty-four guns, and had a top speed of 9 knots. Notably, the *Colorado* underwent fourteen changes in her battery during her Civil War service—that is, from 2 May 1861 to 1 October 1865. A sister ship in class to the *Merrimack* and *Minnesota* of Hampton Roads fame, the *Colorado* was sold on 14 February 1885 for $26,700.

Just as the Powhatan dropped her anchors an incident occurred which caused much bitter comment afterward. The
Brooklyn,[16] the next ship to us in line, was commanded by
Captain James Alden,[17] whose conduct at the battle of Mobile Bay[18] had not met the approval of Admiral Farragut.[19]
In taking his position in line he held his fire until his anchor
was down, when he fired a broadside very smartly, which
brought from the admiral the signal, "Well done, Brooklyn!"
the only signal of commendation made during the fight. The
general feeling was that it was a theatrical performance, and
that the signal did injustice to many veteran officers who had
handled their ships with consummate skill. However, the
signal undoubtedly went far toward removing the stigma of
Mobile Bay, and the friends of Captain Alden rejoiced over
it.

We had been up, many of us, all night, and our only
breakfast had been coffee and hard-tack. As we approached
our position Commodore Schenck sent me aloft with a pair

16. This wooden screw-steamer mounting twenty-four guns served with
the West Gulf, the North Atlantic, and the Brazilian squadrons. Built
by contract for $417,921, the USS *Brooklyn* was commissioned on 19
December 1861, and sold on 25 March 1891 at the Norfolk Navy Yard
for $13,128.
17. James Alden was warranted a midshipman on 1 April 1828. He was
made captain on 2 January 1863, commodore on 25 July 1866, and rear
admiral on 19 June 1871. Having retired on 31 March 1872, Alden died
on 6 February 1877.
18. The battle took place on 5 August 1864 when Rear Admiral David
G. Farragut's fourteen wooden ships and four monitors successfully defeated a Confederate defense at Fort Morgan, as well as three Confederate
gunboats and the ironclad CSS *Tennessee*. Farragut is reputed to have uttered his famous "Damn the Torpedoes, Full Speed Ahead!" after the
monitor *Tecumseh* was lost to a mine (torpedo) in Mobile Bay.
19. David Glasgow Farragut (1801–70) was a crusty sea dog who served
in the War of 1812 and commanded the West Gulf Blockading Squadron, which captured New Orleans in April 1862. Ill health prevented his
participation at Fort Fisher. Made a full admiral after the Civil War,
Farragut commanded the European Squadron from 1867 to 1868.

of glasses to locate, if possible, some guns that were annoying him. It was a raw, cold morning, and I had on a short double-breasted coat, in the pockets of which I had stowed several pieces of hard-tack. When I had taken my place in the mizzen rigging, just below the top, I put the corner of a hard-tack in my mouth, and was holding it between my teeth while I took a look through the glasses for the guns. I caught them at once, and saw gunners train one of them around until I could only see the muzzle of it, which interested me, because I knew it was pointed directly at us. There was a puff of smoke, something like a lamp-post crossed the field of the glass, and a moment after the rigging was cut four feet below me, and I swung into the mast. I at once thought of my hard-tack, but it was gone, and I never found even a crumb of it. I am sure that I swallowed it whole. When I had reported what I had made out of the battery I was directed to lay down from aloft to my station, which was in charge of the after division of guns; but I hesitated to do so, because my knees were shaking, and I was afraid the men would see it. However, I had to come down, and as soon as I reached the deck I stood up and looked at my legs, and was greatly relieved to find that they did not show the nervous tremor that worried me so. I soon forgot all about it as I became interested and warmed up to my work.

We had only eighteen inches of water under us when we finally anchored and began firing rapidly in obedience to signal from the admiral. There was a wreck of a blockade runner between us and the battery at which we were to fire, and it was soon evident that this had been used as a target and the range was well known. One or two shots were fired in line with it, each one coming closer to us, and then they struck us with a ten-inch shot. Four more followed, each one striking nearly in the same place, on the bends forward of the starboard wheel, and going through on to the berth deck. Then for some reason the shot and shell began going over us, striking the water thirty or forty feet away. Probably the

gunners on shore could not see the splash of these shots, and
thought they were striking us. If they had not changed their
range when they did they would have sunk us in an hour. As
it was, we hauled out at sundown pretty well hammered, and
leaking so that we had to shift all our guns to port in order
to stop the shot holes.

We had damaged the fort to the extent of dismounting
some of the guns and burning the barracks and officers' quarters. When the whole line was fairly engaged the sight was
magnificent, and never to be forgotten by those who saw it.
No fort had ever before been subjected to such a fire, and the
garrison could only make a feeble response; most of them
were driven into the bombproofs, where they remained until
we hauled off for the night. The heaviest losses on our side
had been caused by the bursting of the one-hundred-pound
Parrott rifles; thirty-five or forty men had been killed or
wounded in this way.

The transports in the meantime were got together, and
while a slow, steady fire was kept up on the forts by the
monitors and a portion of the fleet, the rest of us devoted
our energies to getting the troops on shore. The weather was
favourable for the purpose, and in one day and night we
landed General Butler and his thirteen thousand soldiers with
their ammunition and stores. Then for two days more we
hammered away at the fort, expecting every hour to see them
carried away by the army; but we were not to have that pleasure. Some officers and men did get very near the fort, but,
without making the effort, the general decided that the
works had not been seriously damaged as defensive works,
and were too strong to be carried by assault. He therefore
asked that we reembark his men, which we did, and he sailed
for the North. So ended the first attack on Fort Fisher, which
had promised so much to the national cause.

CHAPTER 8

The Assault on Fort Fisher

ADMIRAL PORTER was not willing to give up so easily, and on his representations, concurred in by General Grant,[1] the second expedition was organized. The fleet was ordered to Beaufort, North Carolina,[2] and such vessels as could do so entered the harbour; the rest anchored outside, and all hands worked day and night coaling and filling up with ammunition and stores. Any one who has served on that

---

1. Union General Ulysses S. Grant (1822–85) was the victor of campaigns in the west from forts Henry and Donelson, and from Vicksburg to Chattanooga. Subsequently promoted to General-in-Chief of all the Union armies, he devoted his personal attention to the destruction of the Confederacy's principal military force in the east under General Robert E. Lee. Grant was a mediocre President of the United States from 1869 to 1872 whose greatest monument was his *Personal Memoirs,* published in 1885.
2. A coastal town and seat of Carteret County, Beaufort was laid out in 1715, north of Wilmington near Morehead City. The town was captured by Federal forces during General Ambrose Burnside's expedition to North Carolina in April 1862. Its sheltered anchorage behind the Cape Lookout promontory afforded the U.S. Navy a superb fueling station and base for operations along the coast.

coast in the winter months will know the difficulties with which we had to contend; to those who have not, no adequate idea can be given. Gales of wind were of almost constant occurrence, and, as we were in the open sea, the vessels rolled so that frequently we had to use life lines on our decks to prevent the men from being washed overboard. On many occasions vessels had to slip their cables and go to sea to ride out the storms.

Notwithstanding all this, in two weeks we were ready to try it again, and this time success seemed to be in the air. That gallant soldier, General Alfred Terry,[3] was in command of the army contingent; his men were enthusiastic and anxious for the fight, and he and Admiral Porter were working in harmony—a fact of itself promising the very best results. It was agreed between the commanders that a naval brigade should be landed to assist the army in the assault, by attacking the sea face of the fort, while the army went in on the northwest angle. Volunteers were called for from the navy for this service, and it was gratifying to see the officers and men come forward, almost in a body, for a job they knew would be a desperate one. So many volunteered that finally a detail had to be made from each ship, and there were many sorely disappointed ones when the names were published.

It was my good fortune to be officer of the deck when the order came on board directing the movement, and so I had my name put first on the list of those who volunteered. At

3. Born in 1827, this Union general was one of the relatively few non-West Point graduates to reach senior rank during the Civil War. He served primarily along the south Atlantic coast, participating in the Port Royal and Fort Pulaski captures. He succeeded General Benjamin Butler in leading the expedition that finally captured Fort Fisher, for which he received the official thanks of Congress. Later, Terry commanded a corps under Sherman. In 1876, he was Colonel George Custer's departmental commander at the time of Little Bighorn.

this time there were four classmates on board—Harris,[4] Kellogg,[5] Morris,[6] and Evans. All volunteered, and as only two could go, we agreed that Harris and Kellogg, being in the first section of the class, should have one chance between them, and Morris and I being in the second section, should have the other chance. Harris won his chance on the toss of a penny; but I, being a Virginian and having no particular family ties, insisted that I should go rather than Morris, who came from New York and would be sadly missed if he were killed. To all of this Morris naturally objected, and we seemed a long way from any conclusion, when he suggested that we leave the selection to Lieutenant-Commander George Bache,[7] who was to command the men from the Powhatan, which was done, and Bache selected me.

January 13th found us again in front of Fort Fisher,[8] and this time we came to stay. The fleet opened on the fort, and

4. Ira Harris became an ensign on 28 May 1863 and graduated from the Naval Academy in 1864. He rose to the rank of lieutenant commander on 12 March 1868. Having fought in the Spanish-American War in 1898, he was honorably discharged on 17 January 1899.
5. Augustus Greenleaf Kellogg, a native of Ohio, was appointed to the Naval Academy from Illinois. Graduating an ensign on 28 May 1863, he rose to the rank of commander by 11 July 1880. His name was placed on the retired list on 15 December 1891.
6. A native of New York, Francis Morris graduated from the Naval Academy in 1864. He attained the rank of commander on 15 April 1882, a year before his death in Newport, Rhode Island.
7. George M. Bache was warranted an acting midshipman on 19 November 1857, and became a lieutenant during the second year of the Civil War. Rising to the rank of lieutenant commander on 25 July 1866, he retired on 5 April 1875 in the rank of commander. Bache died on 11 February 1896.
8. This second expedition—24 December 1864–15 January 1865—was led by Rear Admiral David D. Porter, with forty-four ships and 8,000 troops under Brigadier General Alfred D. Terry. The operation reflected solid joint cooperation between the Union Army and Navy. With the fort's capture at mid-month, the Confederacy's only East Coast port still open to the outside world had fallen.

kept up a constant and accurate fire. We soon found a great difference in the garrison from the one we had fought in the first attack. They stood up and fought their guns most gallantly, and would not be driven into the bombproofs. A division of gunboats was sent close in to cover the landing of the troops, which was done by the boats of the fleet in a sea heavy enough to make care necessary. I was in charge of the commodore's barge, a very handsome, large, able boat, fit to carry thirty-five or forty men. We made the first landing with over two hundred boats, and the sight was a notable one as we pulled in, an occasional shell splashing among us, and the bullets spluttering on the surface of the water.

As soon as the order was given to land we went for the beach at full speed, and, after passing the first breakers, turned our boats and backed them in until our passengers could land almost with dry feet but to get them out of the boats at the right moment was almost impossible. They would wait too long, and as a result most of them were rolled up on the beach by the surf, soaking wet. But once on shore it was glorious to see how they knew their business and the way they did it. As soon as they got their feet they spread out into a skirmish line, and the rifles began to crack. When I came in with the second load those on shore had captured some cattle, and were skinning them, and did not seem the least bit worried by the fire of the skirmishers, only three or four hundred yards away. Before dark we had all the men landed, and enough ammunition and stores to make them safe and comfortable in case it should come on to blow. During the night we completed the landing of stores and supplies and some thirty-pound Parrott guns, which were immediately put in position facing General Bragg,[9] who was coming

9. Braxton Bragg (1817–76) had been a controversial commander of the Confederate Army of Tennessee. At the time of the Fort Fisher expeditions, he was departmental commander of North Carolina, headquartered at Sand Hill, three miles north of the beleaguered post near Wilmington. Bragg also served as senior adviser to President Jefferson Davis. Criticism

from the direction of Wilmington to re-enforce the garrison
of Fort Fisher. The bombardment was kept up during the
14th, while the army got into position for the assault, which
had been fixed for the afternoon of the 15th.

The premonitions that men have before going into battle
are very curious and interesting, particularly when they come
true. We had on board the Powhatan a fine young seaman
named Flannigan, who came from Philadelphia. On the
night of the 14th of January he came to my room with a
small box in his hand, and said to me, "Mr. Evans, will you
be kind enough to take charge of this box for me—it has
some little trinkets in it—and give it to my sister in Philadelphia?" I asked him why he did not deliver it himself, to
which he replied, "I am going ashore with you to-morrow,
and will be killed." I told him how many bullets it required
to kill a man in action, and in other ways tried to shake his
conviction, but it was no use—he stuck to it. He showed no
nervousness over it, but seemed to regard it as a matter of
course. I took the box and, after making a proper memoran-
dum, put it away among my things. On the afternoon of the
next day, when we were charging the fort and just as we
came under fire, at about eight hundred yards, I saw Flannigan reel out to one side and drop, the first man hit, with a
bullet through his heart. I stepped quickly to his side and
asked if he were badly hurt; the only reply was a smile as he
looked up into my face and rolled over dead. The box was
delivered as he requested, and I afterward assisted in getting
a pension for his sister.

January 15th proved a beautiful day for our work, clear
and warm enough, with a smooth beach for our landing. At
early daylight the whole fleet opened on the fort, and poured
shells in on it at a fearful rate. After a hasty dinner at noon
the signal was made at one o'clock, "Land naval brigade." In

---

for his handling of the Fort Fisher defense focused on his ineffective application of the reserves against the Federal rear during the three-day siege.

a few minutes we were off, cheered by our shipmates, and pulling for the shore, where we landed unopposed and without serious accident, about one mile and a half from the northeast angle of Fort Fisher. On the way ashore some evilly disposed person fired a shot at us, which struck the stroke oar of my boat, cut it in two, and sent the handle spinning across my stomach with such force that I thought I was broken in two. On landing we were quickly formed in three divisions, with the marine battalion in the lead.

During the forenoon a force of firemen had landed under Lieutenant Preston [10] to dig rifle pits, well to the front, and these were to be occupied by the marines, who were to keep down the rebel fire until the sailors, armed with cutlass and revolver, reached the parapet. When the divisions were formed, we advanced until we reached a point about twelve hundred yards from the fort, where we halted and waited the signal to charge, which was to be the blowing of the steam whistle on the flagship, repeated by other vessels of the fleet. All the guns that we could see had been dismounted or disabled in the bombardment, but after we landed there was one large rifle that opened on us and did some damage. The shells generally struck short of us, and would then ricochet down the level beach, jumping along for all the world like rabbits. To avoid this shell fire the divisions had been marched by the flank to take advantage of what shelter the slope of the beach offered. It thus happened that the three divisions forged up abreast of each other, and we charged in this formation—three columns abreast, the marines leading. While we were waiting for the army to report ready, our men had a good rest, and seemed to be in excellent spirits. The rebels were firing at us slowly, but doing no damage to speak of. Curious little puffs of sand showed where the Enfield rifle

---

10. Samuel W. Preston became an acting midshipman on 4 October 1858. Having attained the rank of lieutenant on 1 August 1862, he was killed in the attack on Fort Fisher on 15 January 1865.

balls were striking, but they only hit a man now and then by accident.

At three o'clock the order to charge was given,[11] and we started for our long run of twelve hundred yards over the loose sand. The fleet kept up a hot fire until we approached within about six hundred yards of the fort, and then ceased firing. The rebels seemed to understand our signals, and almost before the last gun was fired manned the parapet and opened on us with twenty-six hundred muskets. The army had not yet assaulted, so the whole garrison concentrated its fire on us. Under the shower of bullets the marines broke before reaching the rifle pits that had been dug for them, and did not appear again as an organization in the assault. Most of the men and many of the officers mixed in with the column of sailors, and went on with them. About five hundred yards from the fort the head of the column suddenly stopped, and, as if by magic, the whole mass of men went down like a row of falling bricks; in a second every man was flat on his stomach. The officers called on the men, and they responded instantly, starting forward as fast as they could go. At about three hundred yards they again went down, this time under the effect of canister added to the rifle fire. Again we rallied them, and once more started to the front under a perfect hail of lead, with men dropping rapidly in every direction. We were now so close that we could hear the voices of the rebels,

11. After establishing a beachhead in the late afternoon of 13 January 1865, General Alfred Terry's three white and one black divisions constructed their own line of entrenchments across the neck of the peninsula upon which the fort was situated, thus severing land communication for the besieged Confederates. Admiral David Porter's naval armada subjected the Confederate positions to a grueling bombardment, and early on the morning of 15 January, the Federal land offensive began with an assault by 1,600 sailors and 400 Marines from Porter's fleet. The naval force took heavy casualties but diverted the garrison sufficiently so that three brigades of Terry's soldiers could penetrate the fort in bitter close-in fighting. The outcome hung in the balance until evening, when a reserve brigade was committed and overwhelmed the defenders.

and what they said need not be written here. The officers were pulling their caps down over their eyes, for it was almost impossible to look at the deadly flashing blue line of parapet, and we all felt that in a few minutes more we should get our cutlasses to work and make up for the fearful loss we had suffered.

At this moment I saw Colonel Lamb,[12] the Confederate commander, gallantly standing out on the parapet and calling on his men to get up and shoot the Yankees. I considered him within range of revolver, so took a deliberate shot at him. As I fired, a bullet ripped through the front of my coat across my breast, turning me completely around. I felt a burning sensation, like a hot iron, over my heart, and saw something red coming out of the hole in my coat which I took for blood. I knew, of course, that if a bullet had gone through this portion of my body I was done for; but that was no place to stop, so I went on at the head of my company. As we approached the remains of the stockade I was aware that one particular sharpshooter was shooting at me, and when we were a hundred yards away he hit me in the left leg, about three inches below the knee. The force of the blow was so great that I landed on my face in the sand. I got a silk handkerchief out of my pocket, and with the kind assistance of my classmate, Hoban Sands,[13] soon stopped the blood, and again went to the front as fast as I could.

12. William Lamb, the stalwart North Carolinian commanding the Fort Fisher complex, ably defended his position against both Federal expeditions. He was severely wounded and captured at the time of the post's surrender on 15 January 1865. A Norfok, Virginia, publisher prior to his enlistment at age 25, on 18 April 1861, Lamb was appointed captain of Company C, 6th Virginia Infantry, and subsequently colonel of the 36th North Carolina Troops (2d North Carolina Artillery) in September 1862. He was confined at Fort Monroe after the fall of Fort Fisher until transferred to his home on 1 May 1865.
13. James Hoban Sands was born in the District of Columbia, and was appointed to the U.S. Naval Academy from Maryland in 1859. He ultimately attained the rank of rear admiral, and served as Superintendent of

About this time the men were stumbling over wires which they cut with their knives—they proved to be wires to the torpedoes over which we had charged, but they failed to explode. My left leg seemed asleep, but I was able to use it. The stockade, or what remained of it, was very near, and I determined to lead my company by the flank through a break in it, and then charge over the angle of the fort, which now looked very difficult to climb. I managed to get through the stockade with seven others, when my sharpshooter friend sent a bullet through my right knee, and I realized that my chance of going was settled. I tried to stand up, but it was no use; my legs would not hold me, and besides this I was bleeding dreadfully, and I knew that was a matter which had to be looked to. I heard some one say, "They are retreating!" and looking back I saw our men breaking from the rear of the columns and retreating. All the officers, in their anxiety to be the first into the fort, had advanced to the heads of the columns, leaving no one to steady the men in behind; and it was in this way we were defeated, by the men breaking from the rear. Two minutes more and we should have been on the parapet, and then—nobody can even guess what would have happened, but surely a dreadful loss of life. As the men retreated down the beach they were gathered up and put into the trenches to oppose Bragg, and there served until after the fort was captured. Of the eight of us who went inside the stockade all were shot down; one, the colour bearer of my company, was halfway up the parapet when he received his death wound.

When I received the wound in my right knee I began at once to try to stop the flow of blood. I used for the purpose one of the half dozen silk handkerchiefs with which I had provided myself, but I was so tired and weak from loss of blood that I was some time doing the trick. In the meantime

the Naval Academy from 1905 until his retirement in 1907. Sands died on 27 October 1911.

my sharpshooter friend, about thirty-five yards away, continued to shoot at me, at the same time addressing me in very
forcible but uncomplimentary language. At the fifth shot, I
think it was, he hit me again, taking off the end of one of
my toes, tearing off the sole of my shoe, and wrenching my
ankle dreadfully. I thought the bullet had gone through my
ankle, the pain was so intense. For some reason, I don't know
why, this shot made me unreasonably angry, and, rolling
over in the sand so as to face my antagonist, I addressed a
few brief remarks to him; and then, just as some one handed
him a freshly loaded musket, I fired, aiming at his breast. I
knew all the time that I should kill him if I shot at him, but
had not intended to do so until he shot me in the toe. My
bullet went a little high, striking the poor chap in the throat
and passing out at the back of his neck. He staggered
around, after dropping his gun, and finally pitched over the
parapet and rolled down near me, where he lay dead. I could
see his feet as they projected over a pile of sand, and from
their position knew that he had fought his last fight. Near
me was lying the cockswain of my boat, Campbell by name,
who had a canister ball [14] through his lungs, and was evidently bleeding to death. When he saw the result of my shot
he said, "Mr. Evans, let me crawl over and give that— —
another shot." He was dead almost before I could tell him
that the poor fellow did not require any further attention
from us.

One of the marines from the Powhatan, a splendid fellow
named Wasmouth, [15] came through the stockade, quickly

14. Canisters were constructed of a cylindrical case that held four tiers of
48-iron balls packed in sawdust. They broke apart upon firing to produce
a scattershot effect, which was especially effective at a range of 300 to
600 yards. Charging troops were usually badly broken up or annihilated
by this lethal projectile.
15. Henry Wasmuth was a private in the Marine detachment under 1st
Lieutenant F.H. Corrie on board the Powhatan, having enlisted in the

gathered me up under one arm, and before the sharpshooters could hit him laid me down in a place of comparative safety; but a moment afterward the fleet opened fire again, and the shells from the New Ironsides[16] and the monitors began falling dangerously near us. Occasionally one would strike short and, exploding, send great chunks of mud and pieces of log flying in all directions. Wasmouth again picked me up, and, after carrying me about fifty yards, dropped me into a pit made by a large shell. Here I was entirely protected from the rebel fire, and several times called to him to take cover, but he said each time, "The bullet has not been made that will kill me." I was very drowsy and almost asleep when I heard the peculiar thug of a pullet, and looking up, found poor Wasmouth with his hand to his neck, turning round and round, and the blood spurting out in a steady stream. The bullet had gone through his neck, cutting the jugular, and in a few minutes he dropped in the edge of the surf and bled to death. He certainly was an honour to his uniform.

Just as our men began to break, the army made their charge, and were able to make a lodgment on the northwest portion of the works before the rebels, who had taken us for the main assaulting column, saw them. When they discovered them, however, they went at them with a savage yell, and for seven hours fought them desperately, the same bomb-proof in several cases being captured and recaptured five or six times. A number of sharpshooters remained on the sea

---

corps on 11 June 1861. He died of wounds at the naval hospital in Portsmouth, Virginia, on 16 January 1865.

16. Rated by the Navy as an ironclad screw steamer of 3,486 tons (by maritime historians as a 4,120-ton "broadside ironclad"), the USS *New Ironsides* mounted twenty guns, and had a top speed of 7 knots and a 449-man complement. The ship was built by Merrick & Sons of Philadelphia, Pennsylvania, for $865,514.66. The *New Ironsides* was commissioned on 21 August 1862, decommissioned on 6 April 1865, and burned on 16 December 1866 at the League Island Navy Yard.

face and northeast angle, and shot at every moving thing. No doubt this was owing to the fact that quite a number of marines were scattered about the beach wherever they could find cover, keeping up a steady fire.

After Wasmouth was killed I soon fell asleep, and when I awoke it was some time before I could recall my surroundings. The tide had come in, and the hole in which I was lying was nearly full of water, which had about covered me and was trickling into my ears. I could see a monitor firing, and apparently very near, and the thought came to me that I could swim off to her if I only had a bit of plank or driftwood, but this I could not get. It was plain enough that I should soon be drowned like a rat in a hole unless I managed to get out somehow. Dead and wounded men were lying about in ghastly piles, but no one to lend me a helping hand. By this time I could not use my legs in any way, and when I dug my hands into the sides of my prison and tried to pull myself out the sand gave way and left me still lying in the water. Finally, I made a strong effort, and rolled myself sideways out of the hole. When I got out I saw a marine a short distance away, nicely covered by a pile of sand, and firing very deliberately at the fort. I called to him to pull me in behind his pile of sand, but he declined, on the ground that the rebel fire was too sharp for him to expose himself. I persuaded him with my revolver to change his mind, and in two seconds he had me in a place of safety—that is to say, safe by a small margin, for when he fired, the rebel bullets would snip the sand within a few inches of our heads. If the marine had known that my revolver was soaking wet, and could not possibly be fired, I suppose I should have been buried the next morning, as many other poor fellows were. As soon as I could reach some cartridges from a dead sailor lying near me I loaded my revolver, thinking it might be useful before the job was finished.

When I was jerked in behind this pile of sand, I landed across the body of the only coward I ever saw in the naval

I persuaded him with my revolver to change his mind

service. At first I was not conscious that there was a man under me, so completely had he worked himself into the sand; he was actually below the surface of the ground. The monitors were firing over us, and as a shell came roaring by he pulled his knees up to his chin, which hurt me, as it jostled my broken legs. I said, "Hello! are you wounded?" "No, sir," he replied; "I am afraid to move." "All right, then," I said; "keep quiet, and don't hurt my legs again!" The next shell that came over he did the same thing, and the next, notwithstanding my repeated cautions. So I tapped him between the eyes with the butt of my revolver, and he was quiet after that. The poor creature was so scared that he would lie still and cry as the shells flew over us. As I said before, he was the only coward I ever saw in the naval service.

From my new position I could see the army slowly fighting its way from one gun to another, and it was a magnificent sight. They knew their business thoroughly, these gallant fellows from the Army of the Potomac, and in the end, at ten o'clock that night, won a victory that will live as long as heroic deeds are recorded. I can recall to this day the splendid courage of General Curtis,[17] leading his brigade; he seemed to stand head and shoulders above those around him; and while I looked at him he went down, but was soon on his feet, only to go down a second time, shot in the eye. As darkness approached and the cold began to be felt, our men seemed to fight with more desperate determination, and the advance was more rapid. The Confederates were doing, and

17. Newton Martin Curtis (1835–1910) was commander of the 142d New York, which enjoyed long service in the eastern theater. He participated in the Butler-Porter ill-fated first expedition against Fort Fisher, and commanded a brigade in General Alfred Terry's land force during the second expedition. He was awarded the Congressional Medal of Honor as the first Federal soldier inside the fort. Curtis ultimately rose to the rank of Brevet Major General and became a prominent New York State politician after the war.

had done, all that human courage could do, but they were wearing out, and the arrival of fresh brigades on our side discouraged them.

The scene on the beach at this time was a pitiful one— dead and wounded officers and men as far as one could see. As a rule, they lay quiet on the sand and took their punishment like the brave lads they were, but occasionally the thirst brought on by loss of blood was more than they could bear, and a sound-wave would drift along, "Water, water, water!" and then all would be quiet again. It was one of the worst of the awful features of war. Just as the sun went down, and it did seem to go very slowly that afternoon, I saw an officer coming up the beach dressed in an overcoat and wearing side arms. As he approached me I recognised Dr. Longstreet, and begged him to lie down, as the bullets were singing around his head. He took a canteen off a dead marine and gave me a swallow of sand and water, and did the same for another wounded man. Then, turning his face toward me, he said, "We will have you all off the beach to-night," and was moving on to the front, when a bullet struck him in the forehead. He sprang several feet in the air, fell at full length on his back, and lay quite still and dead. His resignation had been accepted a week before, and as soon as this fight was done he was going home to Norfolk to be married.

After the death of Dr. Longstreet I saw another man coming toward me; but he was taking advantage of all the cover he could get, and arrived without accident. He was a fireman from the gunboat Chicopee, [18] and said he had come after me, but had only a coal-shovel with which to aid me. He said if I could sit in the coal-shovel he could drag me off! The twi-

18. A wooden, double-ended, side-wheel steamer of 650 new tons, the USS *Chicopee* mounted ten to thirteen guns of various calibers and had a 135–73 man complement and a top speed of 11 knots. Acquired by contract at Boston, Massachusetts, from P. Curtis for $157,000, she was launched in that city on 4 March 1863, and eventually sold in Washington, D.C., in 1867 for $4,000.

light was deepening, and it seemed improbable that a sharpshooter could hit either of us, so I managed to get seated on
the shovel, and the fireman, with both hands behind him on
the handle, started to pull me off, but had only gone a few
steps when a bullet struck him, passing through both arms
below the elbows. That ended my trip on a coal-shovel, and
I spent the time until dark making my friend as comfortable
as possible. Then I heard some one calling my name, and in
a few minutes two men came who said Captain Cushing [19]
had sent them to find me and bring me off. They had only
their hands, but they used them most willingly and tenderly.
One would put me on his back and carry me, while the other
held me on. When the first one was tired, the two would
change places; and thus I was carried, shot through both
legs, a distance of a mile and a half.

The outfit for the care and comfort of the wounded consisted of a large fire made of cracker boxes and driftwood, a
fair supply of very bad whisky, and a number of able and
intelligent medical officers. To the vicinity of this blazing
fire I, among a large number of wounded men, was carried,
and stretched out on a piece of plank with my head on a
cracker box, where I enjoyed the warmth, which was very
grateful in the chill of the January evening. My clothing was
saturated with blood and salt water, and thoroughly filled
with sand. My wounds were in the same condition. A rebel

19. Born in 1841, William Barker Cushing began his naval career as
acting midshipman on 25 September 1857. A failed midshipman at the
U.S. Naval Academy, he joined the Union Navy, rising from acting master's mate to captain at war's end. He is famous for destroying the ram
CSS *Albemarle* on 24 October 1864 in the Roanoke River with a torpedo-
tipped spar. At Fort Fisher Cushing marked the channel, working in a
small skiff for six hours under heavy fire, and he led sailors and Marines
from Admiral David Porter's squadron on the land assault. He spent the
last months of the war on hazardous mine-removal duty. While commanding the USS *Wyoming* in 1873, he intervened with Spanish authorities in Cuba to prevent the execution of American sailors detained there.
He died the following year.

gunboat in the bayou back of the fort was using our fire as a target, and finally succeeded in landing a shell fairly in the middle of it, much to our discomfort. When the shell exploded several men were killed, and the fire blown about over the rest of us. The doctor finally got to me, and after cutting off my trousers and drawers well up on my thighs, split them down the sides and threw them into the fire. Then he ran a probe, first through one hole, then the other, said I was badly wounded, gave me a stiff glass of grog, and passed on to the next man, leaving me practically naked. A brother officer, seeing my condition, took the cape off his overcoat and wrapped it about my legs, and this, with the assistance of the grog, soon made me very comfortable.

About half past nine that night Captain Breese,[20] who commanded the brigade, succeeded in getting a lifeboat in through the heavy surf breaking on the beach, and at once wounded officers were tumbled into her, while the crew stood in the water holding her head on to the seas. My turn came at last, and two friends landed me in the boat with my legs hanging over the stern; then the crew jumped in, the cockswain sat down calmly on my knees, gave the men the word, and out we went through the surf in beautiful style. The boat was from the gunboat Nereus,[21] Captain Howell[22] com-

20. K. Randolph Breeze was warranted a midshipman on 6 November 1846. He subsequently became commander on 25 July 1866, and captain on 9 August 1874. Breeze died on 13 September 1881. He is listed as Admiral David Porter's Fleet Captain at Fort Fisher.
21. A wooden screw-steamer of 1,244 tons that mounted eleven or twelve guns and had a top speed of 11 knots, the USS *Nereus* was purchased on 5 October 1863 in New York from William P. Williams for $160,000. Commissioned on 19 April 1864 and decommissioned on 15 May 1865, she was sold at public auction on 12 July 1865 for $73,000.
22. John G. Howell, warranted a midshipman on 9 June 1836, was promoted to captain on 25 July 1866. He became commodore on 29 January 1872, and was assigned Chief, Bureau of Yards and Docks, on 22 September 1874. Attaining the rank of rear admiral on 25 April 1877, he retired on 24 November 1881 and died on 12 September 1892.

manding, and to her we were taken. We found her rolling in the trough of the sea, but the officer of the deck had all preparations made, and we were quickly hoisted up to the davits, and willing hands soon transferred us to the deck. Just as they were putting me on a cot, before taking me below, I saw a signal torch on the parapet of the fort calling the flagship, and a moment later I read this signal: "The fort if OUR—" and then everything broke loose! Nobody waited for the completion of the signal; all hands knew what that last letter would be. There was a great burst of rockets and blue lights, and the men manning the rigging cheered as the guns roared with saluting charges. Long after I was comfortably swung in the wardroom I could hear the fleet rejoicing over the downfall of the great rebel stronghold.

The officers of the Nereus, from the captain down, spent the night doing all in their power to make us comfortable. We had a good supply of whisky and a pitcher of morphine and water, and they gave us plenty of both. Shortly after daylight signal was made to transfer all wounded men on board to the Santiago de Cuba,[23] and for vessels having dead on board to hoist colours at half-mast. I shall never forget the sight that greeted me when I was carried on deck to be put in the boat. The fleet lay just in the position in which it had fought the day before, and it seemed to me that every ship had her flag at half-mast lazily flapping in the drizzling rain. The weather was cold and raw, and all our wounds were stiff and sore, and every movement of those helping us caused indescribable suffering. In the excitement of the charge, getting wounded was fun, but we had a different problem to solve, and it required real nerve to face it.

23. This wooden, side-wheel steamer of 1,850 new tons, a top speed of 14 knots, and ten to thirteen guns was purchased on 6 September 1861 for $250,000. Commissioned on 5 November 1861 at New York Navy Yard and decommissioned on 17 June 1865 at Philadelphia Navy Yard, the USS *Santiago de Cuba* was sold at public auction on 21 September 1865 for $108,000.

CHAPTER 9

Experiences of a Convalescent

THE Santiago de Cuba was soon loaded to her utmost capacity, and early in the forenoon we started for Norfolk, Virginia. My friends Kellogg and Morris had kindly packed all my traps for me, and sent them on board so that I had a change of linen. The officers of the ship devoted themselves entirely to our comfort. Lieutenant-Commander Farquhar,[1] the executive officer, put four of us in his room and made us feel that everything he had belonged to us. If we had been his own brothers he could not have treated us with greater kindness. Before we passed Hatteras the fresh water ran low, and we had to drink warm water from the distillers, but we regarded that as a small matter so long as we could have a drop of whisky with it.

The chaplain was a good soul, and was unremitting in his attentions to those who needed them. Once, when he came to see us, he said to one who was pretty badly used up, "My

1. On 27 September 1854, Norman H. Farquhar became an acting midshipman. He was promoted to captain on 4 March 1886, commodore on 21 July 1897, and rear admiral on 25 December 1898.

friend, you should be very thankful that it is no worse!" To
which the officer replied, "I am, but I would be a d——d sight
more thankful if it had not been so bad!" This did not evoke
a reply from the man of God, who seemed to consider it
quite a new view of the situation; but to the rest of us it
sounded like good common sense.

After a very comfortable trip, all things considered, we
arrived at Norfolk at daylight in the morning, and hauled
alongside the wharf at the Naval Hospital.[2] We were landed
without delay, and I found myself on a comfortable bed in a
large, clean-looking ward. I slipped my revolver under the
pillow, and pulling the blankets up about my chin, went to
sleep and did not awake until ten o'clock that night. The
surgeon in charge and his principal assistant were standing
by the bedside, and after a careful examination of my wounds
they retired to the end of the room for consultation, when I
distinctly heard the senior one say, "Take both legs off in the
morning." I did not get much sleep that night, but I did do
some very serious thinking.

The following morning the assistant, who was a personal
friend of mine, came in, and after a few words of greeting
began to tell me how seriously I was wounded, and how
dangerous wounds about the knee were. I saw at once that
he hated to tell me what he was going to do to me, so to
relieve the situation I told him that I had overheard the conversation the night before; that I had thought very seriously
of the matter, and that I preferred to die with my legs on;

2. Naval facilities located at Norfolk, Virginia, and adjacent Gosport and
Portsmouth date to Colonial times, with Revolutionary-period shipbuilding facilities eventually evolving into the present-day Norfolk Navy Yard.
The Portsmouth Naval Hospital was constructed in 1827. The Gosport
yard was destroyed at the outset of the Civil War by Federal authorities.
Capture of the Norfolk base by Confederates—and its recapture by Union
forces—prevented large-scale refurbishment during the war, but construction for the new steel navy of the late nineteenth century stimulated the
locale's rebirth as a major naval base.

that I was only eighteen years old, and the thought of living my life without my legs was more than I cared to face; that as the legs belonged to me, I thought I had a right to say what was to become of them; and that I asked the doctors to do what they could for me with my legs on, and if I died it was no matter. He heard me very quietly, and I thought with sympathy, but when I had finished he said, "You know, Evans, orders have to be obeyed!" Thinking that he had misunderstood me, I went over matters again, and wound up by asking that they put me out on the lawn on a cot rather than cut me to pieces; that I would find some one to take me to a hospital farther North. Again came the reply about obeying orders. Reaching over, I pulled the gun from under my pillow; I told him that there were six loads in it, and that if he or any one else entered my door with anything that looked like a case of instruments I meant to begin shooting, and that he might rest perfectly sure that I would kill six before they cut my legs off. This brought matters to a crisis at once, and in a few minutes the surgeon in charge came in very angry and full of threats. But the result was that they left my legs on, and paid very little attention to me in any way for two weeks, when they found I had fever and must be looked after.

To the wife of the doctor who was going to operate and his little daughter I owe my life. Had it not been for their kindness and care I should undoubtedly have died. It would be difficult to make any one believe to-day the conditions that existed in the Norfolk Hospital at the time of which I write. No doubt the medical officers did the best they could with the tools they had to work with, but the tools were awfully bad. Hospital diet was unknown, and we lived on regular rations—at least I did, until bacon and cabbage knocked me out, strong as I was, and it was then that the doctor's wife and daughter saved me. Such a thing as a trained nurse was absolutely unknown, and there were none of the modern conveniences for handling men in my perfectly

helpless condition. No language of man can convey any idea
of the quantity and variety of vermin in that hospital. I have
lived my whole life in hopes that it would burn down and
that I might be there to see the slaughter!

When it was discovered that I had fever I was placed in a
room with two other officers—Paymaster Schenck,[3] who had
been wounded in the first fight at Fort Fisher, and a volunteer lieutenant named Vassallo,[4] who had been literally pep-
pered in the same fight by the bursting of a Parrott gun
which he was firing. Schenck, who was the jolliest, best soul
in the world, kept us amused with his stories, and read to us
or wrote letters for us when we were unable to do so for
ourselves. Erysipelas soon developed in my right leg from the
attendant using a dirty sponge, and then came an abscess in
the right knee. In the meantime bedsores added to my mis-
ery, and all the bones on my right side, hip, knee, and ankle
came through the skin. In fact, I was a skeleton, and nothing
more. For nurse in this room we had a fine chap named Milligan, an enlisted man, who had been wounded and was conva-
lescent, six feet tall and as strong as an ox, and scrupulously
honest, but he knew nothing about nursing. Milligan had a
pass book, and every third day he would go to Norfolk and
buy things for us, generally sugar and coffee and whisky. At
five o'clock in the morning he would turn out and make a
pot of strong coffee, and each patient would have a cup of it
with enough whisky put in to make it bite. Then we would
smoke a cigar or two and be ready for what breakfast we
could get. Looking back at it now, the wonder is that any of
us got well.

3. Caspar Schenck rose from acting assistant paymaster on 6 July 1861
to assistant paymaster on 14 September of that year, and to paymaster on
5 February 1862. He eventually became pay director on 6 December
1880, and was placed on the retired list on 26 September 1897.
4. L. Gustav Vassallo was warranted an acting master on 11 June 1862,
and an acting volunteer lieutenant on 7 November 1864. He resigned on
1 November 1868.

After Fort Fisher

After a time Schenck recovered from his compound fracture and went home, and later on Vassallo also. Then I was left alone to watch the trees grow outside my window. As spring advanced into summer one branch spread out and almost covered it. I amused myself by sketching this branch each day when I was strong enough to do it. Often I was too weak to lift my hand, much less use a pencil. Several times the doctors gave me up, and though they never told me so, I knew when they thought I was going to die by the appearance of the chaplain, who never hesitated to tell me that I was dying, and also just where I was going to bring up after I was dead. Fortunately, I did not believe him in either of his statements. One of them was clearly wrong, and the other has yet to be decided.

The Powhatan came to Norfolk early in February, and I then heard for the first time an accurate account of our losses in the Fort Fisher fight.[5] All the officers from our ship had been wounded, and out of the sixty-two men in my company fifty-four had been either killed or wounded. The naval brigade as a whole had been fearfully punished, but we did what was expected of us—drew the garrison away from the point selected by General Terry for his assault, thereby aiding the army to get in.

Early in June my wounds had healed, and I made up my mind to get away from the hospital if I could. I told Milligan, who was a carpenter by trade, to go to the carpenter shop and make me a stretcher narrow enough to go in the aisle of a car, and to use a hammock to cover it. When he

5. The Union suffered the following casualties at Fort Fisher: 184 killed, 749 wounded, and 22 missing, with naval casualties of 686 and an additional 25 Federals killed, 66 wounded, and 13 missing—mostly from the 169th New York—in a mishap involving the fort's magazine the day after the surrender. Confederates suffered the loss of 1,200 North Carolinians and 600 additional men either killed, wounded, or captured with Colonel William Lamb (severely wounded) and local Confederate sector commander Major General W.H.C. Whiting (mortally wounded).

had done it he managed to get me on the stretcher and cover me with a sheet. Then I sent for the surgeon in charge, who was so surprised that he fell in with my plan and allowed me to go, or rather to be taken, to the Bay Line[6] steamer for Baltimore. In fact, he sent Milligan with me to take care of me until I reached my home, which was then in Philadelphia. I have sometimes thought the dear old doctor was very glad to get rid of me. I was taken across the harbour in a small boat, and nearly drowned in a squall that struck us on the way; but we managed to make the steamer finally, and here my troubles began again. The stretcher would not fit in anywhere! Finally, the captain stowed me in the ladies' cabin, where some beautiful rebel girls gave me the benefit of their tongues. I was as patient under this as I could be, and when we got into Chesapeake Bay that night, and they were all very seasick, I had my innings.

On board the steamer I found a company of the Twelfth Infantry,[7] who took charge of me and showed me every kindness and attention. At Baltimore they carried me to the train, but the sergeant in charge of the squad concluded that I could go more comfortably by boat through the canal, so took me there and saw me snugly berthed before he left me. At Philadelphia my uncle, who had returned from the South, met me with a fireman's ambulance, and I was soon comfortably housed and cared for by loving hands. In taking me into the house, on account of a sharp turn in the stairs, the

6. A steamship company that plied the Chesapeake Bay between Hampton Roads, Virginia, and Baltimore, Maryland.
7. A regular unit was organized on 4 May 1861 at Fort Hamilton, New York Harbor, by direction of the President. It became part of George W. Sykes's regular contingent and campaigned with the Army of the Potomac from the Peninsula Campaign in the spring of 1862 to the siege of Petersburg. The 12th U.S. Infantry departed for New York in November 1864. It is difficult to ascertain which company may have assisted Evans, for the 1st Battalion was on duty at prisoner of war and draft rendezvous camps in Elmira, New York, and the 2d Battalion was at Fort Hamilton until July 1865.

stretcher had to be shoved out of a second story window, which alarmed Milligan very much, but did not worry me, as I knew nothing about it.

My convalescence was slow and very tedious. My right leg had been allowed to contract to such an extent that I could not get my foot to the ground, and the tendons of my left leg had healed into the wound in that leg and seemed very much too short. When I stood on my left foot my heel would not come to the ground, and when I tried to force it down the pain in the calf of my leg was very severe. However, I stuck to it, and after a few months the left leg worked fairly well. Then I went to duty at the Philadelphia Navy Yard,[8] where I remained only a short time, when I was ordered to ordnance duty at the Washington yard.[9]

8. One of the nation's oldest naval facilities, the yard was established in 1801 in the Southwark section of the city. It was located there during Evans's duty, but was moved three miles south to League Island at the confluence of the Schuykill and Delaware rivers in 1876, where it remains today. During the Civil War the yard served as both a recruiting station and repair facility, and its laborers constructed nine ships, including the ironclad *Tonawanda* (later *Amphitrite*), despite inadequate and obsolete shipbuilding facilities. Political machinations in the city and state succeeded eventually in relocating the yard so as to open Southwark to urban development. The new yard evolved into a major construction and repair facility in the late-nineteenth and twentieth centuries.
9. One of the first naval installations erected after the U.S. Navy was established. Located about one mile southeast of the Capitol, it has served the country in one capacity or another continuously since its founding. Many of the early warships of the Navy were constructed or repaired here, although through the nineteenth century it became prominently associated with naval ordnance development and fabrication. At the end of the Civil War, the yard was the scene of two massive auctions of war-surplus vessels. The yard's proximity to Congress probably shielded it from many postwar assaults of political patronage that facilities elsewhere in the country faced.

CHAPTER 10

Sea Service in the Orient

THE desire to get back to sea duty was very strong, but my condition absolutely forbade it. I could not use my right leg, and was compelled to walk with crutches. The idea came to me that my right knee could be broken again, and my leg set at such an angle that I could walk on it. I returned to Philadelphia and consulted Dr. Samuel Gross,[1] who made me very happy by saying that he would undertake the job. I was soon under chloroform, and the operation successfully done. An instrument was put on my leg by which it was hoped that the motion of my knee might be restored, and I was cautioned to work it every day for that purpose. It caused me great pain, and after torturing myself with it for

---

1. It is unclear which of a father-son team of Philadelphia physicians Evans consulted in 1865. The elder Samuel David Gross was a prominent surgeon who authored *A Manual of Military Surgery* in 1861 and long held the chair of surgery of Jefferson Medical College. His son, Samuel Weissell Gross, served as a surgeon at the Philadelphia Hospital during the Civil War and authored numerous treatises on medicine, and succeeded his father at Jefferson, being one of the first men in Philadelphia who employed antiseptic surgery.

a year and a half, without any apparent benefit, I buried it in the Indian Ocean.

The question of my promotion now came up, and the Medical Board promptly had me placed on the retired list, on the ground that I could not perform all my duties at sea. There was nothing for it but to go to Congress for relief, which I did. Being the only officer in the navy retired for wounds received in battle, I was put back on the active list, and shortly afterward advanced some thirty numbers, in company with three other classmates. This advancement was the result of being selected by a Board of Admirals, no one of whom I knew; nor did I know a single member of Congress, Senator or Representative, at the time, yet my promotion caused me no end of trouble. I have always supposed that it was made purely on my record, as I knew nothing about it until I was sent for at the Navy Department and there told of it. The following extract from the report of Lieutenant-Commander James Parker,[2] who was the senior officer on shore in the attack on Fort Fisher, was a matter of pride to me as a young officer, and is of interest in this connection:

> "Acting Ensign (Regular) R.D. Evans was wounded in the leg just after reaching the end of the palisade; he bound up the wound with his handkerchief, and then pressed on until he fell with a second wound in the knee joint.
>
> "From all I can learn, his bravery and determination to enter the fort were equalled by few and excelled by none.
>
> "He now lies in a critical state at the Naval Hospital, Norfolk."

After I had been confirmed as a lieutenant, the question of sea service once more came to the front, and I determined to settle it once for all by going to sea and making the effort to

2. James Parker, who became a midshipman on 14 November 1846, was an acting lieutenant as of 8 May 1861, and was promoted to lieutenant commander on 16 July 1862. He resigned from the Navy on 31 May 1866.

do all the duties required of me. Captain Daniel Ammen[3] was going out to China in command of Admiral Rowan's[4] flagship, the Piscataqua,[5] and to him I applied. He very kindly asked for my detail to his ship, and my orders were made out immediately.

The Piscataqua was fitting out at Portsmouth, New Hampshire,[6] and I reported on board of her in October, 1867. After several weeks' delay, we sailed from Portsmouth for New York, where the ship was docked and some necessary work done to complete her. She was a new ship, and this was to be her maiden voyage. Toward the end of November we were finally ready for sea, and anchored off the Battery, New York,[7] to await our orders. A violent northeast gale came on, with a heavy snowstorm, and in the midst of it the apothe-

3. Daniel Ammen was warranted a midshipman on 7 July 1836. He was promoted to captain on 25 July 1866, commodore on 1 April 1872 and rear admiral on 11 December 1877. Retiring on 4 June 1878, he died on 11 July 1898.

4. Stephen C. Rowan, beginning his naval career as a midshipman on 1 February 1826, was promoted to commodore on 16 July 1862, rear admiral on 25 July 1866, and vice admiral on 15 August 1870. Placed on the retired list on 26 February 1889, he died on 31 March 1890.

5. A screw sloop of 2,354 tons, twenty guns, a top speed of 13 knots, and a 325-man complement, the USS *Piscataqua* was built at the Portsmouth Navy Yard for $1,071,175.11. Launched in 1863, her name changed to *Delaware* on 15 May 1869. The sloop was decommissioned in 1870, sunk at the New York Navy Yard in 1876, and sold in February 1877 for $5,175.

6. With its fine harbor at the mouth of the Piscataqua River, the Portsmouth Navy Yard was the site of Colonial shipbuilding activity for the British Royal Navy. A number of early U.S. Navy vessels were constructed at the yard, and during the Civil War some 2,000 workers constructed two ironclads, seventeen steamers, and two tugboats at the facility. The rebirth of the Navy during the late-nineteenth century saw improvements and construction of a Marine hospital, a prisoner of war camp for survivors of the Battle of Santiago, and new facilities to accommodate the technologically advanced warships of the fleet.

7. Once a Colonial battery site at the southwestern tip of Manhattan Island (New York City).

cary thought it a good time to kill himself, which he did by taking poison. Then the ship walked away with her anchors during the night, and in the morning we had two large schooners under our bows with their chains and our own beautifully twisted together—so effectually, indeed, that it took us all day to clear them. The decks were covered with snow to an average depth of two feet, and this was frozen as hard as a nail, so that there was not much comfort on board. However, there is an end to all things, and at last, having buried the apothecary, who had caused so much trouble, we put to sea.

In the wardroom we had a splendid mess of twenty-three members, and in the steerage we carried nineteen midshipmen, just graduated from Annapolis, many of them being older than the watch officers. Admiral Rowan and Captain Ammen were well known in the professional world as officers of great ability and reputation, without superiors in any service.

As we passed out by Sandy Hook,[8] the caterer of the midshipmen's mess appealed to the officer of the deck to detail some men to find their mess stores, which he did, and two barrels of potatoes were dug out of the snow, all frozen hard; and these were the only food that the youngsters had provided to last them to Rio. Captain Ammen gave them a barrel of peanuts, which, with ship's rations, was all they had to rely on. Both the admiral and the captain were officers of the old school, and believed in old-time methods.

The midshipmen were stationed in three watches and were sent aloft whenever the men went up, and were expected to call the officers of the relief watches and light their candles. The war had broken up many of these old customs, and this was the first effort to renew them. Of course the youngsters kicked hard, but the routine was carried out to the end of the cruise, much to the benefit of all concerned. Quite a

8. A peninsula of eastern New Jersey at the entrance to New York Bay.

number of the nineteen are still living, all distinguished as excellent officers, and if you should ask any one of them he would tell you that this first cruise was the making of him. The captain carried a case of beautiful duelling pistols which he thought his young officers might want to use.

The Piscataqua was one of those long, narrow productions so much in fashion about the time our civil war closed. She had many bad qualities, but no good ones. She did, however, serve as an object lesson to show the naval constructors what bad work they were doing, and helped them to something better. She could carry sail well off the wind, and made good speed when pressed, but on the wind she could do nothing. As a steamer she was a notable failure. When forced, she could do twelve knots in smooth water, but while doing it she would fairly shake the teeth out of your head. If it had not been for the strong diagonal bracing of the hull the stern would have dropped off before we reached our destination. Fortunately for the comfort of all hands, we sailed most of the time, and thus avoided the excessive vibrations caused by the screw, which at times really prevented any one in the after part of the ship from sleeping.

We stood well out to the eastward, and carried good winds down to the line, where Father Neptune had a hard job, as we were all green hands to him, except a few of the older men. After the usual visit—dirty soapsuds for shaving and much salt water for ducking—he gave us certificates, and we steamed for a few days before we caught the welcome trades. Once we got them, however, we held them almost to our anchorage in Rio Harbour,[9] where we arrived January 15, 1868, thirty-one days out from New York.

Rio was, comparatively speaking, free from fever at the time of our visit, and we enjoyed it to the utmost. The opera, in which Aimée was the star, was very good; the restaurants gave us fine food after our sea grub, and the suburbs

9. The famous city of southeastern Brazil on Guanabara Bay.

were charming. When we had been in port a few days a Russian practice ship came in filled with midshipmen. They and our youngsters fraternized on shore, and that evening owned the largest theatre in the city. A party of fifteen or twenty midshipmen in Russian uniform took charge of the stage and ran the performance to suit themselves, which did not please the audience; and the result was that all the morning papers had hard words for the Russian ship and her crew. During the forenoon of the following day all our midshipmen were sent for by the admiral and quarantined to the ship. He was the only one who had detected our gang in the Russian uniforms.

Leaving Rio January 29th, we ran down to the "roaring forties" and squared away for the Cape of Good Hope.[10] During this trip we had a good chance to see what the ship would do running in a hard gale, for we had nothing but gales all the way over. We found that she ran fairly well, but was most uncomfortable, rolling from thirty-seven to forty-five degrees, and keeping it up for days without a let up. We fairly rolled our way to the Cape, arriving at Simon's Town[11] February 19th. We had tried the "brave west winds," and were ready to admit that they were all that had been claimed for them, and as much more as anybody wanted to say; and the seas that came with and were made by them were worth a trip around the world to see. Coming as they did all the way around Cape Horn and across the South Atlantic, they acquired a force and grandeur never seen in any other part of the world. At times our big ship would settle down between two great mountains of water, and one involuntarily held his breath for a moment until she climbed the side in front of her; and then, as she settled down again, the great white-crested following sea raced after her, looking as if it must board her and sweep everything before it.

10. A promontory on the southwestern coast of South Africa.
11. A town south of Cape Town, South Africa, on False Bay.

Each day at noon we threw overboard a bottle tightly corked, and containing the latitude and longitude, with the request that the finder send the slip of paper to the Navy Department at Washington, giving the location where the bottle was found. This was done in order to help, if possible, in determining the force and direction of ocean currents. In the afternoon we usually amused ourselves fishing for albatross. We used a blunt-pointed hook, which generally caught under the projecting bill, and by keeping a steady strain on the line the beautiful bird was landed on deck unhurt. Some of those we caught measured ten feet from tip to tip. After robbing them of a few feathers, and placing about their necks a brass shield with the date and name of the ship, we threw them overboard to rejoin their companions.

The anchorage in Simon's Bay [12] was at times very uncomfortable, owing to the heavy sea that set in when the winds blew home, which they frequently did. It was selected in preference to Cape Town [13] because at that season of the year the prevailing winds were supposed to be more favourable for boating, but we all agreed that it was rough enough where we were. Frequently all hands in a boat would land or reach the ship thoroughly soaked with salt water.

The trip around to Cape Town was a very delightful one, and I made it several times. Part of the way we drove on a beautiful firm beach, and then took the road over some picturesque mountains, where the scenery was very characteristic of South Africa. We usually rested and had breakfast at the Halfway House, [14] and then jogged along slowly through the

12. A site on the western side of False Bay on which the naval base of Simonstown is now located. Offering a sheltered winter anchorage, it became popular with the Dutch East India Company vessels after 1742 and was named for Governor Simon van der Stel.
13. The legislative capital of South Africa, located on the Atlantic Ocean in the extreme southwestern part of the country.
14. The famous and popular Rathfelder's Inn at Diep River, halfway between Cape Town and Simonstown, South Africa. A veritable institu-

grape district, stopping now and then to enjoy the delicious fruit, or maybe a glass or bottle of the excellent wine made hereabouts. On arriving at Cape Town, we always went to the Royal Hotel,[15] where we were well treated, and found the food most enjoyable after our sea fare of hard-tack and "salt horse." Once I joined a party for a trip to Table Mountain, from which we had a magnificent view of all the surrounding country and the coast for many miles. For once in my life I drank Bass ale when it was perfect—all the surroundings conspired to make it so. I was dead tired when lunch time came, and the ale was brought on, not too cold, with cold roast beef and cheese. I have often said that it was worth the price of this trip to know how good ale could be when it was at its best. We left Simon's Town, after a stay of ten days, with sincere regret, and started for our long and tedious run across the Indian Ocean.

We could not carry coal enough to steam the whole distance, and therefore relied on our canvas,[16] which made the trip pleasanter and more interesting than it would otherwise have been. Officers and men soon shook down into their places, and the healthy rivalry that does so much to make our service what it is showed itself. Each watch was ready to

tion to Cape Town residents, officers of the British Army and Royal Navy, invalids from India, and travellers alike. Among its guests were Prince Albert, Lady Duff Grodon, and Evans. Apparently, the Halfway House formed the background of much of the social life of the cape peninsula in the first decades of Queen Victoria's reign.

15. A popular Cape Town hotel that was constructed in 1861 as the Hotel de Europe. Its name changed in 1867 to The Royal Hotel. Located on Plein Street, it was particularly noted for its inexpensive drinks, including American beverages. It was demolished in 1936.

16. Many U.S. Navy ships of the early steam period carried sails for auxiliary power. In the budget-constrained Reconstruction period, the Navy Department customarily ordered ships to rely primarily on sail power to conserve fuel on foreign station. Old Navy commanders may also have preferred the well-known sail power to the relatively unknown steam power, which was subject to breakdown.

wager anything that it could make sail or reduce it to a squall in half the time the other could, and the gun divisions had the same feeling. We were drilled constantly, as the admiral would not tolerate any but the very best work, particularly with the guns. He had a fashion of coming out of his cabin in the middle of the night and, without previous warning to any one, ordering the alarm for general quarters sounded. On such occasions he would order a shot or shell fired from each gun in the battery, carefully taking the time himself, and the last one to fire usually heard some very plain words from him.

One night I was the officer of the deck when he had an exercise of this kind, and one of my guns fired the first shot. It was fired just as I reached the gun and before things were ready, and caused considerable trouble by parting side tackles and other gear. Several minutes elapsed before another gun was fired, and the officers of the other divisions claimed that my gun captain had obtained his cartridge by unfair means, while I myself was satisfied that the gun had really been fired before the magazine was opened; but of course I said nothing about it, and stood up for my man, praising his promptness. After a few days he told me all about it: he had the cartridge in his hammock, where he had carried it since the last exercise, determined to be among the first. The powder boy swore that he got the cartridge from the powder division and carried it to the gun and handed it to the loader. He even remembered particulars: how the man in the powder division had said to him, "You are pretty d—d quick this time!" How could you doubt such evidence? Of course, it was all right, and the gun had been properly loaded and fired.

After a very pleasant run across the Indian Ocean we passed Java Head [17] and hurried on to Singapore, [18] where the

17. A promontory of southwestern Java Island through which Sunda Strait passes. It connects the Indian Ocean and the Java Sea.
18. Singapore was the capital of British Malaya (now Malaysia) on Singapore Strait.

Hartford[19] was waiting for us to relieve her; and it was here
that we had the first news of Admiral Bell's[20] death. He had
been drowned at Osaka,[21] in Japan, while attempting to
cross the bar in his barge. The sea was breaking very heavily,
and, before leaving the ship, the danger was pointed out to
him; but the ministers were in peril on shore, and he decided
to take the chance, and so lost his life. The boats of the ship
were prepared as soon as he shoved off, so confident were the
officers that he would come to grief, and the moment his
barge was capsized they were hurried to the rescue, and succeeded in saving most of the crew.

Singapore proved a charming place to me. The people were
most hospitably disposed, and the mode of living well suited
to the climate. For the first time in my life I tasted real
curry. Of course I had eaten the rice paste, served in the
United States with its offensive hot yellow gravy, but here in
Singapore we had the real thing—fresh curry powder each
day, rice that was like a pile of snow flakes, Bombay duck, a
flat, dried fish baked crisp, and Borneo red fish. When prepared like this, one has the finest breakfast dish in the world,
and one that can be had only in the tropics, because only
there can the fresh curry powder be obtained, and without
that you can't have real curry. We also had for the first time
the mangosteen, which some one has described as strawber-

19. This well-known fighting ship of the Union Navy had been Admiral
David Farragut's flagship at Mobile Bay. A wooden screw steamer of
2,900 tons, with a battery of twenty guns and a top speed of 13.5 knots,
the USS *Hartford* was acquired by the government at a cost of
$502,650,16. Launched on 22 November 1858 at the Boston Navy
Yard, she was still in service as late as 1921 at Charleston, South Carolina. The *Hartford* sank at her berth in 1956.
20. Henry H. Bell, warranted a midshipman on 4 August 1823, rose to
the rank of commander on 12 August 1854, commodore on 16 July
1862, and rear admiral on 25 July 1866. Placed on the retired list on 12
April 1867, he drowned on 11 January 1868.
21. A city in southern Honshu Island in Osaka Bay, an inlet of the
Pacific Ocean.

ries and peaches and cream mixed; but the description only gives a faint idea of the excellence of the fruit. Of course, all other tropical fruits were in abundance, and the people of Singapore knew how to serve them. All our spare time was given to enjoying the hospitality which the people were most lavish in extending to us, and we went on our way to Hong-Kong with much regret and many hopes that we might soon be back.

We had been sent to the East with orders to punish the natives of Formosa for their ill treatment of some ship-wrecked Americans, and we were all ready for the job—organized, armed, and equipped; but before we arrived the affair had been settled by Admiral Bell, so we were saved the trouble. A large force had been landed, and a fight resulted, in which Lieutenant-Commander Mackenzie[22] had lost his life, he being the only man killed.

When we arrived at Hong-Kong[23] piracy prevailed to such an extent that the admiral sent Cushing in the Maumee[24] to look after the pirates and break them up. As this was a good chance for service, I volunteered for the trip, but Captain Ammen decided that I was wanted on board the flagship, and my application was returned to me disapproved. I had settled the question of being able to do all my duties at sea by this time, and was very anxious to have this cruise on a small, lively vessel to clinch the matter; but it was not to be. I argued and begged hard, but the captain maintained

22. Alexander S. Mackenzie, warranted an acting midshipman on 29 September 1855, was promoted to lieutenant on 31 August 1861, and lieutenant commander on 29 July 1865. He was killed in battle on 13 June 1867.

23. A British crown colony on the southeastern coast of China.

24. Built at the New York Navy Yard, at a cost of $258,408.93, the gunboat USS Maumee was a wooden screw steamer of 593 tons, nine to twelve guns, a top speed of 11 knots, and a 125–56-man complement. She was launched on 2 July 1863, commissioned on 29 September 1864, decommissioned on 17 June 1865, and sold for $31,726.87 on 15 December 1869.

that my services were required where I was. Cushing went after the pirates, and in a few days they began to arrive at Hong-Kong by the dozen. He found, as we all suspected he would, that every Chinese junk was a pirate when it suited the owner to be so. The war junks were the worst of the lot. So Cushing ran in everything that he came across, and only stopped when the authorities asked that he be recalled, as he was capturing the entire Chinese merchant fleet. China had no navy[25] then outside of her fleet of junks, armed with old smoothbore guns and stinkpots. Her ports were all fairly well defended by forts, and on these she relied for protection.

Hong-Kong I found an ideal place for defence. The English certainly showed their wisdom in selecting it as their base of supplies in China. When we arrived there it was garrisoned by two English and several Indian regiments, all excellent troops, and kept up to the highest standard of efficiency. Socially, Hong-Kong was the best place on the station, but only endurable in the winter months; in summer the heat was intense, and all sorts of sickness prevailed, including the plague. The fine race track at Happy Valley and the resort on the signal station hill, particularly the latter, were patronized by all hands. Two Chinamen with a sedan chair would trot you up to this place about as fast as a horse could go, and in a cool evening a visit and dinner here were sure to be enjoyed. There was one hotel in Hong-Kong at

25. During the nineteenth century China was the target of economic imperialism by virtually all of the industrial nations. Her navy, with its reliance on traditional armed junks, was simply no match for Western navies, although small composite gunboats began to be built at Fochow after 1869. An iron gunboat, the *Tien Tsiw,* was launched in 1863, the so called *Kwangtung* gunboats were launched in 1869, as were the wooden sloop *Wan Nien Ch'ing* and *Mei Yuan*-class composite gunboats and the *Peng Chao Hai* composite gunboat. Other wooden and iron gunboats were added in the 1870s, but the Chinese naval renaissance—like many others in the underdeveloped world—awaited wholesale exposure to Western technology via French, British, and German assistance toward the end of the century.

this time, and it was anything but good; but the English Club was excellent, and always open to us. The custom of inviting newcomers to visit the large business houses had not yet died out, and there was, in consequence, no demand for large hotel accommodations. The roads were excellent, as is always the case in places under English control, and I made many excursions in the suburbs either by chair or wheeled vehicle.

The Chinese population seemed happy and prosperous, but given to gambling to an extent that I never saw before. I often visited the gambling shops frequented by the high-caste Chinese, and was much interested in watching the play. Fantan[26] was the game, and it was not unusual to see a Chinaman bet his wife after having lost everything else. Judging from the appearance of the women, the only wonder was that the banker could place a value low enough on them. Like all Chinese coast cities, there was a large fishing population; by that I mean people who lived and had their homes on the water, the women and children not being allowed to visit the shore except at certain specified times. The men were allowed to land where they had employment, but not otherwise, except at stated times and places. When they had landed the boats were shoved off and went about their business until time for the men to embark, when the boats were allowed to come in and take them off. The water police were expected to look after all these people and keep them in order. My observation was that the water population was justly noted as expert boatmen and thieves. You could trust yourself in one of their boats in any kind of weather, and be very certain that they would steal from you every movable thing on your person. On one occasion they stripped the copper off one entire side of a Pacific mail steamer in one night, while she

26. A Chinese betting game in which players lay wagers on the number of counters that will remain when a hidden pile of them has been divided by four.

was lying at her dock, and not a soul on board heard even a suspicious noise.

When bad weather came many of these *sampans,* as they were called, were wrecked, and many lives lost. To prevent the loss of life as much as possible, all the children had small wooden buoys made fast to their bodies. I once saw an entire family driven overboard in a curious way. A Chinese bumboatman brought to our ship a very large monkey, or ape, which he offered for sale. It was a ferocious-looking beast, very wild and vicious; but the maintopmen concluded that they wanted him for the starboard gangway, and so purchased him. He was brought on board at supper time with a short length of chain and a stout leather collar about his neck. Jacky though it well to give him his first lesson in discipline, so he ran the chain through a ringbolt in the deck, and, having pulled the ape's head close down to it, was giving him a good sound thrashing with a broom handle, when the collar broke, and the ape at once ran up the main rigging and took possession of the maintop. Several men tried to get into the top, but it was impossible for them to do it, so fierce were the attacks of the enraged beast. At last he was allowed to remain in charge with the hope that he would be in a better humour in the morning. During the night, however, he cast loose the bunt gaskets of the maintopsail, and at daylight the officer of the deck found the sail hanging from the yard. Of course, this would not do, and several men were sent up to restow the sail. The ape grabbed the first head that appeared in the top and yanked out a handful of hair, nearly scalping the man in the process. The second man was severely bitten, and the others retreated to the deck. At this time Captain Ammen came on deck, having been aroused by the unusual commotion, and, seeing the conditions, ordered the ape to be shot. While the gunner's mate was getting a rifle, however, the ape walked out on the main yard, grinning defiance to all hands. As soon as he was well out of the yard the braces were manned, the yard quickly swung around, and the beast fell overboard. As soon as he came to the surface he swam to a Chinese boat lying near, pulled himself on board, and was soon in command of the craft. The Chinese family of eight or ten persons never disputed possession for a moment, but bolted overboard and swam for the nearest boat. The last we saw of the captured boat as she drifted off to leeward the ape was industriously throwing overboard everything he could lay hands on.

Our stay at Hong-Kong was not a very long one, but we had sufficient time to make a number of very interesting excursions; two of them I recall. A party of us—youngsters, of course—figured out a scheme by which we could beat the Chinese gambling game known as "fan-tan." Our system was carefully gone over, and the more we examined it the more certain it appeared that we had only to play long enough in order to amass great wealth. Finally, we made our plans to go to the Portuguese city of Macao,[27] some fifty miles away, and clean out the gambling shops there first, as they were reputed to be more wealthy than the Chinese dens in Hong-Kong, and wealth was what we were after. Some of our shipmates heard of our scheme, and, being convinced of the soundness of our system, intrusted us with various sums to be invested for their interest—the foundation of their fortunes, as it were. Four of us finally set out on this important excursion, reached Macao safely, and, having secured comfortable rooms at one of the best hotels, began our breaking process on one of the large gambling houses. For a time we did well, and it really looked as if we were going to get the best of the game; but the banker eventually struck the weak point in the system, and we went home at 3 a.m. with just

27. At that time Macao was a Portuguese overseas province comprising Macao Peninsula in the South China Sea, just west of Hong Kong, and two offshore islands. The city of Macao was its capital.

money enough to pay our hotel bill and our fare back to Hong Kong. We did not hear the last of that expedition for many a long day.

Quite a party of us, young and old, went to Canton,[28] and there spent several days looking over that interesting old city. There were no hotels, so we chartered a flower boat, in which we were fairly comfortable at night; the days we spent sightseeing. I was most interested, I think, in the capital punishments as illustrated in the Temple of Horrors by full-sized wax figures. There were hundreds of them, and the authorities had certainly exercised great ingenuity in devising plans for making the victim suffer for long periods of time before actually ending his life. The theory of them all seemed to be that an offender should be made to suffer for his offence, and finally to pay the penalty of his life for the crime he had committed; but the first idea was that he should suffer, and suffer long and cruelly. In carrying out this idea they had certainly shown wonderful ability, and had drawn freely on the experience and practice of all the nations with whom they had come in contact. Among all the punishments illustrated there was not a single one shown that caused instant death to the victim. The one most in use was that by which the suffering was the longest drawn out.

I was also interested in meeting, in the heart of the city, in one of the narrow streets where two chairs could scarcely pass each other, a young man with all the outward signs of a Chinaman except the colour of his skin, and yet who was evidently an Anglo-Saxon. He had the dress of the country and the long pigtail hair of a Chinaman, and was talking fluently with the natives in their own dialect, but he was, in fact, a young Catholic priest. I found afterward that there were a number of them, not only in Canton, but in other Chinese cities, living as this young man was among the people, really one of them. They encountered untold hardships

28. A Chinese city located inland from Hong Kong on the Pearl River.

and privations, but they met with success in their calling, and the progress of so-called civilization in the East is marked by their graves. Their right, moral or legal, to do the things they were doing is a question each man must settle for himself; but that they caused much trouble and the loss of thousands of human lives is a fact that can not be disputed. How many souls they saved is a question that can be settled only at the last roll-call. That the Catholics, however, lived nearer the people and had more influence with them for good or for evil than any other denomination, was plain to me. I am not a Catholic.

Before returning to Hong-Kong we desired to smoke opium Chinese fashion, that we might know from practical experience what the sensation was like. We borrowed a few Chinese experts from the flower boat of a nobleman lying near us, and after due preparation proceeded to smoke. The expert who was giving me his attention prepared a small pill of the opium mixture, and placed it over the pin hole in the pipe, which takes the place of the ordinary bowl. When I had managed to get the large stem of the pipe into my mouth, he applied a red-hot iron to the opium, and the smoking began. I inhaled three whiffs of the smoke, which was all the small pill produced, and then I was very sorry I had done it. All the fine dreams and hallunications which I had been led to expect and did really expect to experience, were missing, and in their stead I was genuinely seasick—nauseated until I could neither eat, sleep, nor stay awake. The sensation lasted for several days, notwithstanding the large amount of strong tea and coffee I drank, not to mention other liquids. I was quickly and thoroughly cured of my desire to smoke or take opium in any form.

After a short stay at Hong-Kong we proceeded on our way up the coast of China, bound to Yokohama, Japan.[29] We

29. A city of southeastern Honshu, Japan, on the western shores of Tokyo Bay.

stopped at Amoy,[30] where I had the pleasure of meeting an old friend, a missionary, who had been my rector in Washington. I called on him and listened to a very eloquent sermon on Sunday. The small chapel was well filled with the foreign element of the settlement, and they appeared to enjoy the sermon; while the native converts, four in number, worked the *punka* from the outside of the building, and fanned us while we prayed. Afterward we dined at a comfortable stone house, on a bluff overlooking the sea, where the converts were again in evidence, this time serving the table in a most beautiful and noiseless way.

30. A city in southeast China located on the southwestern shore of Amoy Island, which is in the Formosa Strait, west of Taiwan.

CHAPTER 11

Stormy Days in Japan

UPON our arrival at Yokohama we found most of the American squadron, as well as a fair number of war ships of other nations, assembled. The Stonewall[1] had crossed the Pacific under command of that excellent seaman Captain George Brown,[2] of the navy, and was waiting to be turned over to the Tycoon;[3] but he was engaged in a deadly

1. The famous rebel ram originally built in 1864 by L. Arman of Bordeaux, France, for Denmark, but ultimately sold to the Confederacy. The only European-built ram to actually reach Confederate hands, she displaced 1,400 tons and carried a 130-man complement. Her most potent weapon was the 20-foot offensive iron ram that projected beyond the bow. Never actually engaged in combat, the CSS *Stonewall* was sold to Japan and renamed the *Azuma,* serving the Japanese Navy from 1867 to 1908.
2. Warranted a midshipman on 5 February 1849, Brown was promoted to captain on 25 April 1877, commodore on 4 September 1887, and rear admiral on 27 September 1893, before retiring on 19 June 1897.
3. A nineteenth-century Western term for the shogun (generalissimo). Evans presumably refers to the last of them, Yashinobu, whose resignation cleared the path to the Meiji Restoration.

struggle with the forces of the Mikado,[4] and no one could foresee how the great revolution of 1867 would terminate. The throne of Japan, and, as it afterward turned out, the fate of the country, hung in the balance, while Japanese soldiers fought in the streets of Yeddo,[5] and unsuccessful officers promptly committed *hara-kiri*.[6] The vessels of the squadron were at once put in condition for active service, owing to the avowed purpose of the Mikado to drive all foreigners out of Japan when he had subdued the Tycoon.[7] Admiral Rowan was not the man to allow American interests or citizens to suffer, and his recent experience in the civil war fitted him admirably for the important position he was filling. Nearly every officer under his command had had war service, and all were ready for any job that might turn up.

We were deeply interested in our surroundings, but found it difficult to take seriously the war performances of the Japanese. Their army was organized as it had been for a hundred years, and commanded, as had been the custom, by the Damios, or feudal lords, each one supporting and leading his particular band of followers. They were armed with every conceivable kind of ancient weapon, and all wore the long, heavy Japanese sword, the officers being each provided with two. The Mikado had one or two batteries of Whitworth field guns,[8] but their use was little understood. All were in the

4. A nineteenth-century Western term for the emperor. Evans is probably referring to Mitsuhito, who inaugurated the Meiji Restoration in 1867.

5. From 1603 this village served as the headquarters of Ieyasa, founder of the Tokugawa shogunate. Restoration of imperial power in 1868 caused Yeddo (or Edo) to succeed Kyoto as the imperial capital, with the new name of Tokyo.

6. Ritual suicide practiced by Japanese samurai and upper classes.

7. A nineteenth-century Western term for the shogun, or generalissimo. The resignation of the last one, Yashinobu, cleared the way to the Meiji Restoration.

8. English-manufactured rifled cannon of various calibers, used in small numbers particularly by the Confederates during the Civil War. Their

ancient uniform of Japan, and presented a curious contrast to the nut-brown Confederates and blue-coated Federals, whose sharp work we had been accustomed to see. The Japanese navy was entirely in the hands of the Tycoon, and consisted of a few old-fashioned sailing craft, under the command of Admiral Ennymoto,[9] a lion-hearted old seaman, who was sure always to give a good account of himself. The officers generally were brave and courteous, but, as military men, about one hundred years behind the European standard. The enlisted men were brave, barbarous, hardy little brown chaps, capable of vast improvement.

Under the circumstances it can be readily understood why the Stonewall, a modern ironclad built by the French for the late Confederate government, was regarded with so much anxiety, and so eagerly sought by each side in the war. It can also be seen why we, fresh from the greatest war of modern times, should feel little concern over this Falstaffian array of Japanese braves. If the Mikado succeeded in securing the Stonewall, his avowed purpose was to drive the foreign ships out of Japanese waters, and we all hoped that he might get her in order to try the experiment—otherwise our sympathies were all with the Tycoon and his brave old admiral.

While the fighting continued in and about the city of Yeddo, a large foreign fleet was kept constantly in Yokohama Bay.[10] When the Tycoon's forces were cleared out of that vicinity, the danger became even greater, and the number of

hexagonal bolt ammunition was easily recognizable; usually 6 to 12 pounders, they were remarkably accurate.

9. Viscount Buyo Enomoto (1839–1909) was the Japanese vice admiral best known as the first Japanese to study naval science in Europe and as the rebellious naval commander who, in 1867, refused to submit to the Meiji Restoration. He proclaimed a republic at Hakodate, but was compelled to surrender and was imprisoned. In 1874 he was chiefly responsible for conducting an agreement with Russia by which Japan exchanged the southern half of Sakhalin for the Kurile Islands.

10. Evans may be inaccurately describing Tokyo Bay.

foreign ships was increased. We were told many times of what the Mikado meant to do to us; but as he had failed to do any of these things, we naturally grew incredulous, and maybe somewhat careless. At last, however, news came through the American minister that sent a thrill of excitement through the entire foreign fleet. The Japs, so the story ran, had prepared a very formidable boat expedition in Yeddo, and were coming down on a certain night to cut out the Stonewall and carry her away. Their preparations were reported to be complete, and there was to be a very large force employed. On receipt of this news most of the foreign ships got under way and anchored well out in the bay, where they would be free to manœuvre when the dreaded ironclad should attack them. Admiral Rowan, who had spent many days within four hundred yards of Fort Wagner[11] in Charleston Harbour, in the New Ironsides, believed in fighting at close quarters; and therefore, after clearing his ships for action, anchored them about the Stonewall in such positions as could best command the approach to her, and at the same time be ready to sink her if the Yeddo force really succeeded in gaining possession of her.

When it was dark all the American ships went to general quarters and prepared for battle. The men stood by their guns ready to open fire, while a sharp lookout was kept for the hostile Japanese boats. An officer was sent on board the Stonewall with orders to remove parts of her machinery, so that she could not get under way, and then to take station on her turret and signal the approach of the boats, when the fleet would open with grape and canister. I remember well how this officer felt as he sat on top of the turret, torch in hand, waiting to make the signal. There was an open scuttle

11. A strong defensive post located on Morris Island, South Carolina, Fort Wagner was important to Charleston's defense. It withstood Union attacks on 7 April 1863 and 9 July 1863 and was finally evacuated on 7 September 1863. Site of the heroic but ill-fated assault by the 54th Massachusetts Colored troops made famous in the movie *Glory*.

near his feet, which he was prepared to use quickly at the flash of the first gun. Fortunately for all concerned, the authorities saw what our preparations meant, and wisely determined to wait until they could gain peaceable possession of the vessel, which they eventually did, after giving suitable guarantees for her conduct.

When conditions permitted, we started for the south, intending to stop at such Japanese ports as we were permitted to visit *en route*. These were Kobé[12] and Nagasaki,[13] and three miles inland was our limit, which rule also applied at Yokohama. From Kobé, our first stopping place, I visited Osaka,[14] a newly opened port, and the place where Admiral Bell had lately lost his life.

Dr. H.S. Pitkin,[15] one of our assistant surgeons, and I obtained three days' leave, and thoroughly enjoyed every hour of it. There was not such a thing as a hotel known at Osaka, but we managed to find two rooms in which we could sleep and store our plunder; the days we spent cruising about over the queer old town, buying such curios as struck our fancy. Lacquered ware, rare and old and valuable, was offered to us at every turn for almost nothing. We were among the first visitors, and the market had not yet been spoiled by the rich globe-trotter. The simple and honest natives offered their goods to us at the same price they sold them to their own people, and I am sure our customs officers would have grown green with envy if they had seen the things we purchased, which, by the way, they never did.

Pitkin was an enthusiastic collector of coins, and during our first day's ramble we came across an old Japanese mer-

12. A southern Honshu Island city on Osaka Bay, Japan.
13. A seaport on the west side of Kyushu Island in southwest Japan on Nagasaki Bay, an inlet of the East China Sea.
14. A city on southern Honshu Island, on Osaka Bay, an inlet of the Pacific Ocean.
15. Pitkin was an assistant surgeon during the Civil War and became surgeon on 28 December 1872. He died on 23 June 1874.

chant who had followed the same line all his life. He showed us his collection with great pride, and well he might, for it was one of the finest in Japan, containing about one thousand coins, a few of them dating before the time of Christ. The old man had no intention of parting with them at any price, but the doctor wanted them and wanted them badly; in fact, had made up his mind to have them. That night we counted up our funds, and found that we could spare one hundred Mexican dollars for the purchase. The next day we made the offer, which was politely refused. Then we stacked the silver dollars up in ten piles, and then in twenty, and then scattered them about, making them ring as much as possible. Meanwhile the merchant eyed the money, and each time we stacked it up we could see a change in his face. In the end the silver won the day, and the coins, case and all, were taken to our rooms, where the old man went over them for the last time, and tearfully left us in possession of what it had taken him a lifetime to collect. We could exchange our silver for Japanese gold, weight for weight, at that time. What we had offered him was probably more money than he had ever seen before at one time. The value of the collection was very great. It is now the property of one of our leading universities.

On our arrival at Nagasaki, which we reached by way of the beautiful inland sea, we found the city crowded with Japanese troops of the Mikado party. The English flagship was present, and there was much excitement over the killing of two of her men. A party of soldiers had found them on shore somewhat the worse for liquor, and at once cut their heads off, left their bodies in the gutter, and put the heads on the curbstone in front of the consul's house. The admiral demanded immediate satisfaction, which he of course received; but as the same thing was liable to happen to any foreign officer or man who was caught on shore at night, the prospect was not pleasing. The governor of the province represented to Admiral Rowan that our officers would be safe if they wore two swords—that all Japanese officers wore two, and that only enlisted men were one-swordmen. The admiral replied that he could arrange matters in a simpler and more satisfactory way, and immediately issued an order that all officers visiting the shore should wear in their belts a loaded Remington breech-loading pistol,[16] and if upon meeting a Japanese soldier he carried his hand to his sword hilt, they were to shoot him at once. This was done because the sword was never unsheathed except for use; a Japanese who drew his sword and returned it without drawing blood was disgraced. A copy of this order, with a letter of explanation, was sent to the governor, and though we remained many weeks in Nagasaki, none of us were ever molested.

The contrast between the Japanese and their neighbours, the Chinese, was at this time very striking and vastly in favour of the former people. Since then it has become even more marked. The leading characteristic of the Japanese was honesty. It was in striking contrast with the trickiness, not to say dishonesty, of the Chinese as a race. During my whole stay in Japan I was constantly tramping about the country, shooting or wandering over strange cities, picking up curios here and there. In all my experience I never had anything stolen from me, though at times I intrusted articles of all sorts to the first small boy I met on the street, to be delivered to my boat or at my hotel, often miles away. Every article was promptly and carefully delivered. If such an experiment had been tried in China, everything would have been stolen.

When out shooting I generally had with me a Japanese lad of eighteen or nineteen years of age, and we frequently went far beyond the three-mile limit which was supposed to fence us in; but uniform kindness and courtesy were what I always received from the people among whom I found myself. A few

16. The model 1867 Navy version was the handgun version of the famous Remington rolling-block rifle. The .50-caliber pistol had a distinctive breech-block arrangement.

words of explanation from my faithful boy always secured such food as they had, and frequently quarters for the night. The houses even of the poorest classes were always scrupulously clean, while those of the Chinese were exactly the opposite. The Chinaman was a dandy in dress, but personally vilely dirty, while the Japanese was plainly dressed, but in person as clean and neat as soap and water could make him. The Chinese had a certain shrewd imitativeness which was much misunderstood, and even taken by many persons for an indication of genius. The Japanese, as a people, had the genius of progress and expansion, with the result that in thirty years from the time of which I am writing they have advanced by steady strides, until they hold a proud place among the leading nations. In that short space of time they have organized an army which is second only to the German in its general staff, and armed as well as the best. Its fighting ability was shown in a winter campaign against the Chinese, which elicited the admiration of all military critics. At the same time their navy became the wonder of modern times in its phenomenal development. It is true that the magnificent ships were, many of them, paid for in borrowed money or bonds; but the way they fight their guns and handle their fleet will prevent any sudden foreclosing of mortgages by foreign countries. To-day they have as fine docks and dockyards as any nation, and can build and arm their own ships. When one thinks that all this has been done in less than thirty years, the conclusion can not be avoided that Japan has broken the record in expansion, and must be seriously considered in any future settlement of the Eastern question.

I had occasion to witness some of the capital punishments of Japan. When we first visited the country the theft of more than thirty dollars' worth of anything was considered sufficient ground for beheading the thief. I saw one of these executions when four men had their heads cut off for various offences. One of them was a young boatman who had often served me in my shooting trips about Yokohama Bay. The execution ground was a cleared space in the edge of a wood on the side of the public road four or five miles from Yokohama, and was in no way screened from the view of the public. When I arrived on the spot, about sunrise, everything was in readiness for the execution. Four small pits were dug in the ground and the earth excavated from them neatly levelled off, and a bucket of water placed near each. The judges who sentenced the men to death sat in a row in front of these pits and about fifteen feet away. The executioner, who had cut off more than one thousand heads, was in attendance, and very proud of his sword, the keen edge of which he examined from time to time. The hilt was carefully wrapped with very fine white linen.

The populace—men, women, and children—stood about the inclosure and conversed in low tones. The four condemned men were brought to the spot, and quickly seated opposite the pits with their legs crossed under them tailor fashion. The executioner advanced to the man on the left of the line, held the heavy, keen-edged sword over his neck for a moment, and then, bringing his left hand up to the long hilt or handle, gave the sword a sharp, quick, downward jerk toward him and the man was dead. The head fell into the pit, the trunk dropping forward; the blood from the body was discharged into the same place. Stepping quickly to the second man, his head dropped off the same way, and so on to the third and fourth. The four men were dead inside of two minutes after they were seated near the pits. Then an attendant stepped up to the first pit, took the head by the hair, dowsed it into the bucket of water, which removed all blood stains, and then held it up, the face toward the judges, who nodded in token that the man was dead. The head was then placed on a post by the side of the road, as were the others after each had been subjected to the inspection of the judges, and here they remained under guard for three days as a warning to others. The bodies were doubled up, placed in coarse bags, and buried on the spot. The whole job was businesslike and quickly performed.

If there is anything in public executions calculated to deter others from committing crime, Japan certainly has the correct method. What I saw on this occasion was in striking contrast to the hanging method as practised in most of the States in America. These poor Japanese convicts were killed as quickly as possible, and that they experienced no pain was evident from a glance at the dead faces, each one of which bore a smile. The mode of execution was meant to be quick and merciful, just the opposite of the Chinese method. I could not help thinking that it was far ahead of our practice, where a poor devil is sung over and prayed over for days, then marched to the scaffold, offered time to address the few newspaper correspondents and prison officials present, and then choked to death. Electrocution, which is now the legal process in some States, is more merciful, but even the electric spark is slow in producing death when compared with severing the spinal column by the keen edge of a Japanese sword in the hands of a man expert in its use. The interval between the time when the man is in full possession of all his faculties and when he is stone dead is inconceivably small. When the men who were executed at the time of which I have just written were brought on to the execution ground, the young boatman who attended me so often looked up at me and smilingly said, "Good-bye." The Japanese have no fear of death, and in this one characteristic alone I found them like the Chinese. This young boatman had, while under the influence of too much *saki,* a Japanese liquor made from rice, overhauled a countryman near Yokohama and pulled him from his chair, which he appropriated for himself and rode in it to the city. He was charged with highway robbery, and though I did all in my power to save him he was convicted, sentenced, and executed.

CHAPTER 12

Hong-Kong and the Philippines

AFTER leaving Nagasaki, which we did with great regret, we anchored in Hong-Kong once more. Our men had not yet been granted shore leave generally, and, as this seemed a favourable place for the purpose, they were sent on shore by watches, starboard watch one day and port watch the next, as was then the custom in the service. Naturally, trouble quickly followed. The American Jacky has no love and little respect for a policeman. The absurd-looking Mohammedan policeman of the Hong-Kong force excited his mirth, and when he had secured a sufficient number of drinks he proceeded to have fun with him. In a short time the turbans and clubs were all in possession of the sailors, and it was not until an English regiment had been put on duty that they were corralled on the dock. Then they fought out their personal difficulties, and were brought on board much battered and the worse for wear, but having had, as they claimed, "a bang-up good time." Five or six months more on board ship fitted them excellently for just such another spree, and they had it when the time came. Fortunately, we do things differently now.

Among my other possessions I was the happy owner of a fine bull terrier—"Jowler"—who could whip any dog in China; at least he had whipped every one that had fought with him. He was a great pet with every one on board ship, from the admiral down, and was really a finely bred, beautifully trained dog. In all the shore riots and pleasures he was an important part. The men would come to the mast and ask for shore leave for him just as they did for themselves. They always saw to it that he whipped everything he came in contact with, man or beast, and the result was that he would tackle a whole menagerie, if the chance offered. After shore leave he generally went into the hands of the doctor, along with Jacky, to have his cuts sewed up and needed repairs made before he appeared on deck.

Our relations with the English military people were strictly official during the earlier days of the cruise, owing to the bitter feeling engendered by the position of the English Government during the civil war; but a hint from their Government changed all this and we became very friendly. They were courteous, hospitable gentlemen, and we enjoyed their mess dinners wonderfully. On their part they always seemed willing to come to us and make a night of it whenever we were ready. On the 22d of February we gave the finest entertainment we had so far attempted, seating over one hundred guests, most of them foreign officers. We broke up at 1 A.M., after a beautiful evening long to be remembered. One of our English army guests jumped overboard and swam ashore, where I delivered his sword and cap to him the next day over a glass of brandy and soda. Long years afterward I met him at the United Service Club in London,[1] old and dignified, and looking as if he had never been young. He did, however, cheer up over

---

1. Also known as the Gothic House on old Devonshire Road, it remains a private men's club whose members are active-duty or retired members of the armed forces.

another glass of brandy and soda and the old Hong-Kong episode.

From Hong-Kong we ran down to Manila[2] to have a look at the Spaniards and their great Eastern colony. Owing to the size of our ship, now named the Delaware,[3] we had to anchor well out in the bay, and visiting the shore was quite an undertaking; but once on shore we found ourselves well repaid for our trouble.

The city was beautiful, and under Spanish military rule very safe, and on the surface clean and orderly. The *cafes* were excellent, and the music of the bands in the afternoon made the Lunetta[4] a favourite promenade. All Manila turned out to look at each other, in which it did not differ from any other city where people had so little to do. The markets were good, there being at all seasons fine fish and splendid tropical fruits in abundance, principal among which was the mangosteen, that queen of all fruits. The tobacco was of that peculiar light quality which grows on a smoker's taste. We were all slaves to cheroots before the cruise was over.

The Spanish authorities gave us a ball, which was largely attended, and added much to the enjoyment off our visit. We, of course, returned the compliment and had the pleasure of meeting on board our ship not only all the officials and their families, but also some of the better class of natives— *mestizos,* as they are called—who danced and behaved generally most becomingly. The ladies were shod with sandals

2. A city of southwestern Luzon Island on Manila Bay, an inlet of the South China Sea. At the time Evans refers to it, it was the capital of the Spanish colony. Manila was captured by Commodore George Dewey and U.S. Army forces as a result of the pivotal Battle of Manila Bay on 1 May 1898.
3. A side-wheel iron steamer, formerly named the USS *Piscataqua*.
4. The site of a powerful Spanish naval battery that guarded Manila. Commodore George Dewey's squadron engaged this defense at the Battle of Manila Bay in 1898. In military engineering, a lunetta is a fortification with two projecting faces and two parallel flanks.

only, which gave one a good view of their beautiful feet. After a delightful visit of two weeks we again sailed down the grand bay of Manila, little dreaming that an American admiral would one day make it celebrated in the annals of naval warfare by showing to the world what destruction modern ships and modern guns could cause when properly handled.[5]

We returned to Hong-Kong, and, as the hot season approached, retraced our way toward Japan and the north. The two leading elements in all efforts to civilize so-called barbarous natives—cards and whisky—were in full blast in all the ports we visited, except Kobé, where they had not yet had time to take root. One had only to stick to the two long enough and he was sure to be ruined, for the card players were expert and the whisky was bad. My tastes ran rather toward out-of-door sports—boating, shooting, and fishing—and I found my amusement in this line; not that I did not drink and gamble somewhat—I could not afford to be so much out of the fashion—but most of my spare time was given to athletics. The shooting all along the coast was excellent; snipe always on the marshes, easy to get at, and delicious for the table. Golden pheasants were in great numbers only a short distance from Shanghai,[6] and a houseboat party after them was one of the pleasantest sprees one could have. We killed them sometimes as many as one hundred to the gun per day. The natives were not allowed to use firearms, and the game in consequence was plentiful and easy to get.

The trapping of all sorts of wild things by both Chinese and Japanese was very skilfully done, particularly so by the Chinese, who would at any time bring us all the teal ducks

5. The famous American victory on 1 May 1898, when the U.S. Navy's Asiatic Squadron under Commodore George Dewey annihilated the Spanish squadron in the Philippines and established American suzerainty over the colony.
6. A city in eastern China at the mouth of the Yangtze River.

or snipe we wanted alive from their traps. They were not yet sufficiently civilized to charge us three prices for things, so that we lived reasonably well at a very moderate cost. The Japanese caught most of their game with a gum which they called *torri-mouchi*. Even deer were caught in this way; any bird or animal that touched it was sure to stick fast until it was removed by cutting off the foot. I never tried the gum, but I certainly had some wonderful days in Japan with my gun. My favourite sport was snipe-shooting, but I sometimes went after ducks and waders, such as curlew and plover, and when such occasions offered, our wardroom table was sure to be good for some days afterward.

Once only did I meet with any mishap. Two companions, officers of the ship, were with me, when one of them, in his anxiety to kill all the plover that were in a flock, got me in range with them and loaded me up pretty well with shot. Fortunately, none of them struck about my eyes, and half an hour's careful work with a sharp knife removed them all. The officer was dreadfully mortified, and I really believe suffered more than I did. On another occasion the marine officer, a very fat, heavy man, walked into a quicksand while we were shooting snipe and came near losing his life. I found him when he had sunk in up to his armpits, and my boatman and I had all we could do to pull him out.

My boating experiences would make a very long story were I to tell them all. The admiral's barge, a fourteen-oared cutter, was built at the New York Navy Yard, and it was soon seen that she was a very fast boat, both under sail and oars. I was very fond of racing, and naturally it fell to my lot to take charge of and train the racing crew. We had plenty of splendid men to choose from, and in a few months I had a crew that could pull six miles from start to finish without distress. I used to say that one could crack walnuts on any of them without marking his skin, and I really believe one could have done so. They were a fine, sandy lot of chaps, and were never beaten while we were on the station, though we

challenged all the ships we met, and raced with all who dared
to accept.

Probably the most notable race we pulled was that in
Hong-Kong on the French emperor's birthday.[7] The French
admiral was determined to take the championship away from
us, and to do so had built a sixteen-oared mahogany barge,
which was light and supposed to be very fast. The crew
trained at night, so that it was impossible to get any idea of
what they were like; but I succeeded at last, by watching
them closely and surprising them in the darkness, in getting
a line on them. I was convinced that we could beat them,
and advised all our people to bet that way, which they did;
and as the betting was at long odds on the French boat, many
of us did not have to trouble the paymaster for months. As
the day for the race approached, the flagships of the different
nations—French, English, American, and Russian—were
moored on the course, where all could have a good view of
the race from start to finish. Six boats were entered—two
French, two English, and two American—and the distance
to be pulled was six miles, three miles away and a turn. I
was lucky enough to draw the position next the starting boat,
which insured my getting off promptly at the word. Next to
me was the French barge, on which so much money had been
bet. She certainly did look very fit and dangerous, but six
miles is a long way, and I knew that I had wind and muscle
in my boat. The day before the race every man in the Delaware drew all the money that was due him, and bet it, of
course. Deck buckets of silver dollars were taken on board
the French flagship, sized up against theirs, and placed under
guard. Everybody was betting, and all, except our crew, were
backing the French to win.

The first mile of the course was packed on either side with
boats crowded with people and covered with flags, and must

7. French Emperor Charles Louis Napoleon Bonaparte (Napoleon III) was
born on 20 April 1808.

Midshipman and Captain

have presented a beautiful sight to those who had time to observe it. I was not able to see much of it. I was busy watching that red-coloured French barge, and occasionally glancing at the fourteen hard-set, anxious faces in my boat. At last we were on the line, oars pointed forward, feet firmly braced against the stretchers, mouths shut like steel traps, and every muscle and nerve tense almost to the point of breaking. "Are you ready?" and then "Go!" came from the starter. With one beautiful flash of the oars we all caught the water together, and were off. I could feel my heart thump in my throat as I saw, with one eye, the light French-built boat shoot out half a length ahead of us, and with the other eye the fourteen faces all turned on mine. Three hard, quick strokes had set us going, and for a moment the red barge seemed to be tied to us, so even was our pace; then I could see my starboard bow-oar slowly, inch by inch, dip out ahead of her. About five hundred yards from the start was a bunch of American boats crowded with yelling lunatics, and as I approached them I spoke a word to the crew, signaled the stroke to rise to forty, and before the Frenchman knew what had happened to him he had our wash, and, barring accidents, the race was won. Then we settled down to our long, swinging thirty-two strokes, which were to last the rest of the distance. The French crew began yelling when we passed them, and I believe they kept it up to the finish.

It struck me as about the worst use I had ever known a racing crew to put their lungs to, but it pleased me immensely to have them do it. At the turning buoy we were thirty seconds ahead, and on the pull in we gained one minute. Crossing the finish line, I tossed oars for a second as the gun flashed, and then pulled to the ship at the same racing speed. As I shot alongside, the tackles were hooked and the boat run up to the davits, crew and all. All hands tumbled out on deck, and when the French barge crossed the line our boat was quietly hanging at the davits, as if nothing had happened. It was only a boat race, it is true, but it was a grand one, and we won it. The boat from the Iroquois[8] came in second, so we had all the honours as well as all the money.

While we were anchored at Hong-Kong news came of the sinking of the Oneida,[9] one of our squadron and the "chum" ship of the Delaware. She had been run down by the English mail steamer Bombay in Yokohama Bay and all hands lost; at least so the story ran. Later and more reliable news was to the effect that the ship and most of her officers and men were lost, but that about fifty of them had been saved. We were under way by daylight the following morning, bound for the scene of the disaster. As we entered Yokohama Bay we stopped and lowered a boat, and I was sent to report what I could make out of the wreck. The main truck, the top of the main royal mast, was just awash, and as I held on to it and looked down into the clear water I could see the yards and the neatly furled sails, but nothing else. The ship was resting on the bottom on her keel, upright, the grave of nearly two hundred as brave hearts as ever sailed under the dear old flag.

The court that followed showed clearly how the Bombay had carelessly cut the Oneida down and sunk her, and how her captain had done a thing most unusual for men of his race—sailed away and left the victims of his carelessness to drown. But in drowning they reflected only credit on their country, for they stood at their quarters and went down like men, without a whimper. We buried some of the poor chaps,

8. The USS *Iroquois* was a screw-propelled wooden sloop of war of eight guns and 1,016 tons. Built at the New York Navy Yard in 1858, she was launched on 12 April 1859, and transferred to Marine Hospital Service in 1899.

9. The sloop USS *Oneida* was a wooden screw-steamer of 1,032 tons, a battery of twelve guns, a top speed of 12 knots, and a complement of 162 to 212 men. Built at the New York Navy Yard, she was launched on 20 November 1861 and commissioned on 28 February 1862. She participated in the Battle of Mobile Bay, and collided with the Pacific and Orient steamer *Bombay* in Yokohama Harbor on 24 January 1870 and sank. The iron-hulled *Bombay* disgracefully did not stop to rescue survivors. The wreck was subsequently sold.

but most of them were never recovered. The Bombay was fortunately not in Yokohama when we arrived; if she had been there, it would have required hard work to control our officers and men and prevent some sort of a demonstration against her. The Oneida was homeward bound when she was sunk, and her loss cast a gloom over the entire squadron.

My promotion to the grade of lieutenant commander came soon after we reached Hong-Kong, during the first year of the cruise. It was thought at first that I would be detached and ordered to some other vessel, but Admiral Rowan believed in keeping both officers and men in the ships in which they commissioned during the entire cruise when possible, and so I was not disturbed. Captain Ammen, who was respected and loved by all of us, was detached, and came home to be appointed chief of the Bureau of Navigation, and Captain Earl English [10] transferred to us from the command of the Iroquois. He was one of the ablest seamen in the navy, and a prime favourite with officers and men. His tastes were for out-of-door sports, and he and I spent many happy hours tramping over the rice fields of China and Japan in search of game. Our cruise, continued until the summer of 1869, was nearly spent when we proceeded to Singapore, there to await the arrival of our relief, the steam frigate Colorado, Admiral John Rodgers. [11]

10. Beginning his naval career as a midshipman on 25 February 1840, Earl English became chief of the Bureau of Equipment and Recruiting on 20 November 1870, and was promoted to commodore on 25 March 1880 and rear admiral on 4 September 1884. Having retired on 18 February 1886, he died on 16 July 1893.
11. Becoming a midshipman on 18 April 1828, Rodgers rose to the ranks of captain and commodore during the Civil War. He was promoted to rear admiral on 31 December 1869 and died on 5 May 1882.

CHAPTER 13

Some Oriental Diversions

THE life in Singapore at this time was simply ideal, and I enjoyed it to the full. The climate was hot, but not unbearable, not even hurtful to those who could and would take reasonable care of themselves. No work was done during the heat of the day. One lived his life at night, so to speak, when the cool sea breeze made existence very enjoyable. The temperature varied only a few degrees—about three—during the year, say from one hundred and seven to one hundred and ten. So also at 10 P.M. the temperature ran from eighty to eighty-five during the year. The mornings were fine for sleeping, and if one remained carefully in the shade until late in the afternoon, he could enjoy the evening and night. Our men were thoroughly well drilled, and the admiral therefore reduced the exercises to the minimum.

The Colorado was much delayed in her passage out, so that we remained at our anchorage four months before she appeared. Every day had its pleasures for me, however. We were all invited to dine out every day, and sometimes had two or more invitations for the same day. We dined with all sorts of people, for every one was anxious to have us; native princes, foreign ministers, military messes, and civilians all asked us, and we went to them all, first and last. The governor was most hospitable, and I enjoyed many pleasant evenings with his charming daughters. One of the military bands furnished music every afternoon in the public square, and here we all met for an hour for the latest gossip, after which we drank tea somewhere and then prepared for dinner, which was the feature of the day.

Five of us hired a bungalow on shore, and regularly set up our establishment, which was a very simple one, but at the same time most comfortable and convenient. It was situated on the edge of the jungle near one of the best hotels, from which we obtained our meals. It was, of course, headquarters for all officers when on shore, particularly for those who had to remain ashore all night. We had only five beds, but they were very elastic, and could be made on occasion to hold a great many men. Cobras and tarantulas were very common "varmints," and no one therefore slept much on the floor or porches. Snake-charmers, jugglers, and fakirs generally abounded, and some of them could always be found near our bungalow.

One morning, as five of us sat taking our morning fruit and coffee, the Chinese attendant broke into the room almost paralyzed with fear, screaming, "Cobra! cobra!" In a moment we had located a large, vicious-looking reptile in the back yard, and the happy thought came to some one to send for a snake-charmer and test his qualities on this specimen, which had evidently just crawled out of the jungle. In five minutes, or possibly less, the charmer appeared, and proceeded to do the neatest trick I ever witnessed. He was a Mohammedan, about forty years of age, stripped to the waist, and carrying a sealskin bag with the fur on the inside, in which he had a large collection of cobras and other snakes. He stood quietly watching the newcomer for a few moments, evidently sizing him up, and then, producing a small reed fife, began blowing it, making a sharp monotonous noise. At the same time an assistant some yards behind him beat slowly on a small tom-tom, or drum. The two advanced slowly to the middle of the small inclosure, and when fifteen or twenty feet from their quest seated themselves quietly on the ground and continued their music, or, more properly speaking, noise. The cobra in the meantime was much excited, and showed signs of fight. He rapidly coiled himself, raised a foot or two of his body vertically, spread his hood, and generally looked very ugly. The monotonous noise of the performers continued, and the cobra shifted his position first to the side, and then directly toward the charmers, always watching them closely with his keen, scintillating eyes. After half an hour of this play he was almost between the feet of the Mohammedan, and as he raised himself and spread his hood we all expected to see him strike and end the performance; but instead, the man reached out his hand, slowly seized the cobra by the neck, and, rising with him, held him limp in the air for a moment, and then deposited him in the bag with his other snakes. The Chinaman had in the meantime bolted; nothing could induce him to stay longer in such a dangerous spot. The assistant took his departure, and the charmer, with his bag of snakes, stepped into our dining room for a parting drink.

The unfortunate thought came to one of our men that it would be a good idea to get the Mohammedan drunk to see what he would do; so he prepared a dose for him that was very effective. He poured a good stiff drink of brandy into a beer glass, and then filled it with gin instead of water. The charmer took kindly to the drink, and in a short time rolled out of his chair on to the floor very drunk, and was soon fast asleep. The bag of snakes had not been thought of up to this time, but it also fell, and the inhabitants quickly spread over the floor. In the meantime five American officers took to the table, and drawing their feet up carefully, remained there until the snake-charmer slept off his dose. He snored quietly while the snakes crawled over and around him, but it was a long time before he finally came to himself, secured his pets, and took them away. We did not repeat that experiment.

I went one Sunday to breakfast with an English officer who was quartered some distance in the country among the hills in a very neat one-story bungalow. I arrived early, found my bachelor friend in his bath, and, lighting a cheroot, sat waiting for him to show up. In a few moments I heard a sharp exclamation from him, and on turning my head saw him in his bath dress looking back into the bathroom, which he had just left. He had discovered a cobra, which had been under the tub while he was in it, and was now reared up and looking into the tub. It was enough to give one the shivers to think what a close call he had had. My friend left me for a few moments, and then came back with a mongoose, or jungle cat, which is the deadly enemy of the cobra. The small cat when released seemed to be all tail, but he knew his business, and did it in a way to excite my unbounded admiration. The fight between the two was short, but very exciting. Several times it looked as if the cobra must win, but the cat managed, somehow, to avoid the lightning-like strokes, and finally fastened on the back of the snake's neck and killed it. I looked carefully under the table as I sat down to breakfast, to be sure that I should not have a cobra coiling himself in my lap before I had finished. The bite of this snake is so absolutely fatal that I never cared to take any chances with it.

While we were cruising in the waters about Java[1] and Singapore we saw hundreds of the salt-water snakes said to be so deadly. Sometimes the sea would be dotted with them, swimming with the head well out of water, and diving always on the approach of the ship. Many tales were told of the ravages of these pests, which climbed up the

1. An island of the South East Indies, lying southeast of Sumatra in modern Indonesia.

chains or into the ports of vessels at anchor and stung people to death. I noticed that all the fishermen about Singapore carried long, heavy knives, which they told me were used in killing the snakes as the fishing nets were hauled in. We never succeeded in catching one, though we saw thousands of them.

Early in August, 1870, the admiral concluded that we had had enough of Singapore, so we said good-bye to all our friends who had entertained us so lavishly, and sailed for Batavia[2] in the island of Java, where we drank no end of gin, and behaved generally after the fashion of the Dutch. I don't think any of us enjoyed our stay very much, as we were expecting our relief hourly, and took little interest in anything else. But the Colorado would not come, no matter how anxiously we looked for her; so the admiral, who was by this time tired of waiting, steamed over to the Straits Settlement[3] in the Straits of Java, where we learned that she had passed in the day before bound for Singapore. Back we went as fast as steam and sails could carry us, and on our arrival found her there waiting for us.

The transfer of commands began at once and was soon completed, but before we sailed we must have one more boat race. The Colorado had brought out a barge which was considered very fast, and our admiral naturally wanted to have the fastest boat on the station to defend the championship we had held so long. I pulled under the bows of the newcomer and challenged, which was accepted, and a race arranged for the following day. Our racing crew had, of course, grown stale from the effects of climate and want of regular practice, but they were better than the Colorado's by long odds. As soon as I saw the boats in the water I felt a warning

2. Now Djakarta, Batavia was the colonial capital of the Dutch East Indies on the Java Sea coast of northwestern Java Island.
3. A British possession, with Singapore as its hub, the Straits Settlement, together with Malay states to the north, became a crown colony in 1867.

of the good licking we got. They beat us twenty seconds in four miles after one of the hardest races I was ever in. The boat did it, for our men were in good shape at the finish, while the other crew was pulled to a standstill. The Daring— that was her name—became afterward the most celebrated man-of-war cutter that was ever in the East. She beat everything she ever raced with, either under oars or sails; even the shell boats of the Shanghai Club could not hold her. When the race was over we pulled alongside the Colorado, and each man shouldered his oar with its silver bands on the blade, marched on board, and deposited it on the quarter-deck as a present to the newcomers. I had our beautiful black gamecock under my arm as a present to the admiral; it was the first time he had ever been in a race without crowing at the finish. Admiral Rodgers ordered a decanter of wine, which was placed on the capstan on the quarter-deck, and my crew drank success to the Daring. The racing days of the Delaware's boat were over, but we felt sure she had a worthy successor.

On August 22, 1870, we broke out our homeward-bound pennant, which was longer than the ship, catted our anchor with three cheers, and stood out of the harbour. Our China cruise was over, and none of us regretted either that we had had it or that it was behind us.

Our run across the Indian Ocean was truly a grand one. We held the trades fresh all the way to Cape Town, where we arrived and anchored without more serious mishap than the loss of a few light sails. After resting a week we again got under way and ran down to St. Helena,[4] and all hands had a chance to see that celebrated and beautiful island. I paid a visit to Longwood[5] and saw the various Napo-

---

4. An island in the South Atlantic off the coast of Africa, it is the site of Napoleon I's exile.
5. The British lieutenant governor's house on St. Helena where Napoleon Bonaparte spent the remainder of his life in exile.

leon relics, which a major of the French army took great
pains to explain to me, not forgetting any of the incidents
which reflected discredit on the emperor's English guard-
ians. Before we left, the mail steamer came in, and the
major, taking one glance at the papers, burst into tears. Sedan[6] had been added to the long list of French defeats. I
could not help thinking as I walked back to my boat how
fortunate it was for Germany that the real Napoleon was
dead.

After leaving St. Helena we reached New York in forty-
seven days, certainly a fine run for a ship dragging a four-
bladed screw. As we entered the Narrows[7] the Guerrière[8]
was made out inside the Hook, bound for Brazil. She saluted
us with seventeen guns, which was the first intimation we
had that Admiral Rowan had been made vice-admiral. Our
officers and crew were wild with delight, and cheered until
the admiral showed himself on deck. It was a splendid reward
for his magnificent conduct during the civil war, and made
solely on his merits. At the time it was done he was at sea,
out of reach of anything like political influence, and not even
where he could be communicated with. Once in our history,
anyhow, the man who deserved it was made vice-admiral.

We anchored off the Battery for a few days, and then went
to the navy yard, where we got rid of our trash—stripped
the ship, put her out of commission, and paid off the crew.
My dog "Jowler" was missing soon after the men left, and I

6. On 1 September 1870 a decisive battle between France and Prussia
resulted in Napoleon III's surrender to the King of Prussia and the formation of the Third Republic.
7. A strait of water southeast of New York between Brooklyn and Staten
Island. It connects Upper and Lower New York bays.
8. Built at the Boston Navy Yard, the USS *Guerriere* was a wooden screw
frigate of 3,953 tons, 350 men, a top speed of 13 knots and eighteen
guns. She was launched on 9 September 1865 and commissioned two
years later. A spar deck was added in 1869–70. The frigate was decommissioned on 22 March 1872.

never saw him again. Many months afterward I received a note from one of the racing crew begging me to forgive him for stealing my dog, and asking me if I ever came to Brooklyn to come and see him at a certain saloon which he mentioned. He said he loved the dog so that he simply had to have him; that he knew I would not sell him, so he had to steal him.

I was granted a short leave after this cruise, and before it was up was ordered to duty in the Ordnance Department of the Washington Navy Yard, where I had interesting work during the winter. Admiral Goldsborough,[9] an officer of the old school, was in command of the yard, which insured a lively time for all hands; and Commander F.M. Ramsay,[10] the inspector of ordnance, was not noted for allowing those under his command to neglect their work or spend many idle moments.

It was in the course of this winter that I became engaged to Miss Charlotte Taylor,[11] of Washington, daughter of Mr. Franck Taylor,[12] and sister of my classmate, Harry C.

9. Born in Washington, D.C., Louis M. Goldsborough entered naval service as a midshipman in 1812. He took part in the Mexican War, was on duty in California during the gold-rush days, and was the U.S. Naval Academy's fourth superintendent. Graduation ceremonies were inaugurated during his tenure (1853–57), the first taking place in 1854. During the early part of the Civil War, Goldsborough commanded the Atlantic Blockading Squadron and later the North Atlantic Blockading Squadron. He rose to the rank of rear admiral following the war, before his death in 1877, and was noted as both a commanding presence and a strict disciplinarian.

10. Warranted both an acting midshipman and a midshipman on 5 October 1850, Ramsay became a captain on 1 December 1877. He was promoted to commodore on 26 March 1889, and rear admiral on 11 April 1894. His name was placed on the retired list on 5 April 1897.

11. The daughter of Franck Taylor of Washington, D.C., Charlotte was Evan's devoted wife of forty-one years.

12. Listed as a bookseller at 402 Pennsylvania Avenue, N.W., in the 1858 Washington, D.C. directory, residing at 17 Indiana Avenue, N.W., according to the 1868 edition.

Taylor,[13] now one of the most distinguished officers of our navy.

13. Henry Clay Taylor was Evans's classmate at the U.S. Naval Academy. Born in Washington, D.C., and appointed to the academy from Ohio, Taylor eventually was promoted to captain on 16 April 1894. He succeeded Alfred T. Mahan as President of the Naval War College in 1893, and served there until 1896. Taylor commanded the USS *Indiana* in the Spanish-American War, and became Chief of the Bureau of Navigation in 1902. He retired that same year. A strong advocate of strategic planning who made wargaming a feature of the Naval War College, Taylor's proposal for creating a general staff organization led to the establishment of the General Board in 1900.

CHAPTER 14

A New View of Annapolis

I N July of the following year I was married, and after
spending the summer at the North, was assigned to duty
at that Mecca of young married people, the Naval Academy
at Annapolis, Maryland. Things had changed wonderfully
since my school days, and during my first year there I found
that I had to study nearly all night in order to instruct the
midshipmen during the day. I say "instruct" the midshipmen, but there really was very little instruction given them.
It required all my time to hear them tell me what they knew
or did not know. The system was afterward changed to a
much better one, under which really valuable instruction was
given. During the second year of my detail I had more lei-
sure, and a fine setter dog and a catboat helped me to bear
the most undesirable duty I have ever had in the navy. Wild
ducks and quail were to be had, and I thoroughly enjoyed
getting them, and did get a good many first and last. I bred
and trained my own dogs, and in this training at least I
was successful.

It was during this year that the first coloured cadet was

appointed to the Naval Academy.[1] He came upon us suddenly, and before we knew it he had passed his examination and appeared in uniform, with a coloured girl as his companion. The place was in an uproar at once, and the excitement among all classes was intense. As I walked along the row of officers' quarters, all the coloured servants were at the front gates discussing the news. When I reached my own quarters my dining-room boy, a small, copper-coloured imp, with his eyes sticking out of his head, said to me, "My Lord, Mr. Evans, a nigger done enter the Naval Academy!" That was what we were all feeling, though we expressed ourselves somewhat differently.

The first consideration was, of course, to see that no bodily harm came to the lad, who had not been wisely advised, and did not behave himself in a way to induce respect from those around him. Our second thought was for the reputation of the naval school, that nothing unworthy its grand record should take place. The great danger was from the system of hazing, which had grown to very deplorable proportions, and which we were bending our energies to destroy. In our efforts to protect the colored boy we ran into the error of favouring him too much, and he soon came to give himself undue importance. He fancied that he was an issue which the authorities of the school dared not meet—which, though a natural mistake to make, was a fatal one for him in the end. After being dismissed several times by court-martial, and each time restored by the Secretary of the Navy, who could not bring himself to believe that politics had nothing to do with the

1. During Evans's tenure as assistant to the Commandant of Midshipmen and instructor in Seamanship, Naval Tactics, and Naval Construction, James Henry Conyers—the first black cadet midshipman—was admitted to the Naval Academy on 21 September 1872. Born in Charleston and appointed from South Carolina, he remained at the academy until 11 November 1873, at which time he resigned because of scholastic deficiencies.

sentence of the court—how should he, poor man?—the boy was really unbearable.

In the same class was a youngster from New York city, a bootblack by profession,[2] who had been appointed to the academy by Mr. S.S. Cox,[3] who represented a district in Congress. Some of us thought that politics might have had something to do with this appointment. At any rate, the two lads, the coloured representative of the great State of South Carolina and the bootblack from the great city of New York, were appointed to room together, with the result that each succeeded in having the other dismissed in a few months. I well remember one night when I was on duty as officer in charge of cadet quarters, that the coloured cadet was reported as missing. It was in the middle of a cold, raw night, and after a long, careful search no sign could be found of him. I was about to report the matter to the commandant of cadets, when I heard a curious barking among some tall trees in the grounds, as if a dog were tied up. On investigation, I found the missing cadet in the top of a tree, very scantily clad, and barking with all his might because some senior classmen had told him to do it. It was the only time I ever knew him to be really hazed, and it was impossible to punish the guilty ones, because the boy himself refused to assist in any way in bringing them to punishment.

We all breathed easier when the two of them, black and

2. It is impossible to confirm Evans's assertion about any bootblack appointment. The second black cadet midshipman listed in Naval Academy records was Alonzo Clifton McClellan, appointed from South Carolina on 22 September 1873; the third was Henry E. Baker, appointed from Mississippi on 21 September 1874.

3. Representative from Ohio from 1857–1865, Samuel Sullivan Cox moved to New York City and became Representative from New York for two terms (1869–85 and 1886–89) before his appointment as minister to Turkey.

bootblack, departed for their homes.[4] The question of colour was one we were not prepared to tackle, and I don't see that we are any better prepared for it to-day than we were in 1872. The antagonism of the two races seems greater now than it was then.

4. Throughout Evan's account there emerges an antipathy toward minorities that undoubtedly stemmed from his Virginia heritage and the climate of the times. Reconstruction of the South was accompanied by decidedly prejudicial feelings toward Freedmen.

CHAPTER 15

On Board the Shenandoah

Two years at Annapolis was all I could bear, and I looked about me for a ship and sea service. The sloop of war Shenandoah,[1] of the Mediterranean fleet, was short a navigator, and the Department was good enough to order me to her in that capacity. I packed up my guns, gave away my dogs, sold my catboat, and with my wife and young daughter sailed on the Cunarder Parthia, Captain Watson. I reported for duty at Gibraltar early in August.

The Shenandoah was a sloop of war built during the civil war. She carried a good battery, could steam about six knots an hour, and roll forty degrees each way twenty times a minute and keep it up for hours at a time. When I joined her she was commanded by Captain Clarke H. Wells,[2] and my

1. This wooden screw sloop of 1,375 tons, nine to ten guns, and a 240-man complement was built at the Philadelphia Navy Yard for $372,879.10. Launched on 8 December 1862 and commissioned on 20 June 1863, the USS *Shenandoah* sold for $18,002 on 30 July 1887 in San Francisco. Her crowning Civil-War duty was searching for the CSS *Florida* in July 1864.
2. Beginning his naval career as a midshipman on 15 September 1840, Wells attained the rank of captain on 19 June 1871, commodore on 22

old classmate McGregor[3] was executive officer. My duties as navigator were light, and the prospects of a pleasant cruise very promising.

The ship was somewhat notorious for the part she had played in the revolution then being fought out in Spain.[4] She was at anchor in Cadiz, when one of the captured Spanish ironclads came in and anchored. The rebellious crew had murdered all the officers, and with the red flag flying, and a new crew of soldiers on board, entered the harbour and threatened all sorts of things under penalty of bombardment. A council of foreign officers was called on board the English flagship, and it was unanimously decided to ask the American captain to blow her up if she should attempt to carry out her threats. Captain Wells accepted this task promptly, as he had himself decided to do it before the council was called. He got his ship under way, and, anchoring close to the ironclad, informed her commanding officer that as he flew no recognised flag he would not permit him either to get under way or bombard as he had threatened, and if he attempted to do so he would blow him out of the water. Wells then opened communication with our minister in Madrid, and actually held the ship under his guns until she was turned back to the Spanish navy.

I found a large English garrison at Gibraltar, and a most hospitable lot they were. Their mess dinners were very enjoyable affairs, and they seemed more than anxious always to

---

January 1880 and rear admiral on 1 April 1884. Retiring on 26 September 1884, he died on 28 January 1888.

3. Born in Cincinnati, Ohio, in 1838 Charles McGregor was warranted a midshipman on 21 September 1860. He attained the rank of lieutenant commander on 12 March 1868, and commander on 5 June 1878. He died on 1 August 1891 in his hometown.

4. The September 1868 revolt by Admiral Juan B. Topete and General Francisco Serrano forced the abdication of the scandalous and despotic Isabella II. The nation then seethed in semi-anarchy while a military junta attempted to keep order.

have our officers as their guests. I attended one soon after I arrived which lasted all night. I reached my ship at 4.20 in the morning. The dinner was given by the officers of the Thirty-first Regiment,[5] whose mess outfit and plate were as fine as any I had up to that time seen. The quarters were comfortable and handsomely furnished, and the service fully up to the standard of the English army. The officers were a well-educated and cultured lot of hard-drinking chaps, who seemed ready for any sort of a job that might turn up. They owned a fine pack of hounds, and rode after them several days each week over the rough country beyond the neutral zone. I was cordially invited to join them, but, not wishing to come to my end in that way, excused myself on the ground that I had neither red coat nor spurs.

Toward the end of August the Wachusetts[6] arrived, with directions for Captain Wells to run up to Cartagena to see what was going on, which we did, stopping at various ports on the way. At Cartagena[7] we found quite a large fleet assembled. The Spanish rebels, who held the place and all the heavy works surrounding it, had seized two steamers, merchant vessels, for some imaginary offence, and declared their

---

5. Nicknamed "The Young Buffs," the Huntingdonshire regiment enjoyed a long history: established in 1702 as Colonel George Villier's Regiment of Marines; after 1711, Goring's Marines; from 1714 to 1782, the Thirty-First Regiment of Foot; and from 1782 until 1881 linked with the 70th (Surrey) Regiment of Foot to form the East Surrey Regiment, as the Thirty-First (Huntingdonshire) Regiment. Principal campaigns included the Iberian Peninsula, the American Revolution, the Peninsula and other Napoleonic-era operations, the northwest frontier of India, the Crimea, and the Far East.

6. The USS *Wachusett* was a wooden screw-sloop of 1,032 tons, a top speed of 12 knots, ten guns, and a 163–212-man complement. Built at the Boston Navy Yard for $212,765.64, she was launched on 10 October 1861 and commissioned on 3 March 1862. A sister ship of the USS *Kearsarge,* the *Wachusett* attacked and captured the CSS *Florida* in Bahia Harbor, Brazil, on 17 October 1864. She was sold in 1887 for $16,501.

7. A city in southeastern Spain on the Mediterranean Sea.

intention of confiscating them. Admiral Yelverton,[8] of the English navy, commanding the Mediterranean fleet, had notified them that on a certain day he meant to take the two steamers to sea and deliver them to their rightful owners, and that they must not be moved in the meantime. In reply, the Spaniards said that if Admiral Yelverton attempted any such move, they would engage him with their forts and ironclad fleet. We were lying in Escombrera Bay,[9] where we could see every move on either side. The forts frowned down on us from a great height, and as the Spaniards shifted gun after gun to bear on the English fleet, and their ironclads prepared for action, it looked as if we might see some exciting work before the episode was closed. The shores near us were bleak and forbidding in the extreme, not a sign of vegetation anywhere. The only buildings in sight were a few silver-smelting works.

Monday forenoon we tripped our anchor and stood down toward the entrance of the harbour, so that we might be in better position to witness the fight, which many expected to see. I was not one of them. I knew what the English would do, and I believed the Spaniards would back down when the time came for action. The English fleet was cleared for action and, as we steamed past them, looked very grim and businesslike. Promptly at noon, the hour set by the admiral for the movement, the fleet got under way, the ironclad division formed around the two merchant steamers, their anchors were broken out, and they steamed away to sea with the English flag flying on each of them. As they were escorted out by the ironclads, and gained some distance from the port, a division of English gunboats stood slowly in toward the forts, turned deliberately, and steamed away after the fast-disappearing ad-

8. Sir Hastings Reginald Yelverton, G.C.B., Royal Navy, was promoted to Admiral in 1875.
9. A small inlet directly south of Cartagena on the southeast coast of Spain.

miral. The Spaniards stood by their loaded guns. The huge ironclads sizzled with steam and smoked viciously from their stacks, but not a shot was fired. Admiral Yelverton had done his work beautifully.

The Spaniards were wise enough to see that it was not well to monkey with such a buzz saw as the sea power of England. This action of the admiral was much questioned at the time, but was finally approved by his Government, which gave it the stamp of right. He claimed, and the Spanish rebels admitted, that the two vessels, seized from loyal Spanish subjects, were to be fitted out as privateers to prey on Spanish commerce. He further claimed, which was a fact beyond question, that they were to sail under a flag not recognised by any nation, hence they would be pirates, and for this reason he seized them. There seems to have been good ground for his action.

From Cartagena we cruised along the Spanish coast as far as Barcelona,[10] where we found the flagship Wabash, flying the flag of Admiral Case,[11] commanding the squadron. Personally we were glad to see the dear old gentleman, but officially we would rather he had been somewhere else. Whenever a number of ships get together there is always a lot of work to be done by surveys, and the navigators seem to be traditionally the men to do it. We surveyed old stoves, carpets, curtains, pans and pots, until I felt myself quite competent to run a shop in Chatham Street. As soon as we arrived we received notice that the admiral would inspect us in a few days, and that meant incessant work until the inspection was completed. We had in our crew representatives of all the

10. A Spanish city on the Mediterranean Sea.
11. Warranted a midshipman on 1 April 1828, Augustus L. Case attained the rank of captain on 2 January 1863, commodore on 8 December 1867, and rear-admiral on 24 May 1872. Retiring on 3 February 1875, he died on 17 February 1893.

nations of Europe, and some from Asia.[12] It was difficult to make one's self understood without the use of at least two or three languages. This was caused by keeping the ship on the station long after the time of enlistment of her proper crew had expired, and was a most unhappy condition. We were moored in Barcelona Harbour between two ironclads, English on one side of us and Austrian on the other, and we could see that our extra work was interesting them. They watched us all the time, and were evidently very curious to see what the Yankes were up to.

Admiral Case was a great believer in torpedoes, and decided that we should fire one on our inspection. The spar torpedo[13]—"a bag of powder on the end of a pole"—was the kind of infernal machine then in favour; but so far none had been exploded in the Mediterranean, and we were to have the distinction of being the first to do it. We had no torpedoes to work with—only an old-fashioned firing machine and a small quantity of insulated wire; the rest I had to make as best I might. After messing myself up with pitch and soluble rubber for three days, I reported that my torpedo was ready, and the inspection began. Our work was fairly well done,

12. Bluejackets of the period were a polyglot mixture of men from all races and corners of the world, seasoned by a few American youth rescued by the recruiting officer from prison, poverty, or boredom. As aged Admiral David Dixon Porter opined, "[they have] no sentiment for our flag; they ship for money." The Navy began employing an apprentice system after 1875, but even by the late 1880s, turnover rates hovered at 60 percent annually. Of the entire enlisted force of 7,900 in 1888, only 46 percent were native born. Gradually, however, by the end of the century some 99 percent of the fleet's manpower were U.S. citizens. At the end of Evans's career, the picturesque men of the old sail and wood navy had been replaced by "sea mechanics" of the steel and steam fleet.
13. A primitive torpedo, or mine, that employed an explosive charge affixed to the end of a long spar. It sometimes proved to be as devastating to the attacker as to the victim. The U.S. Navy was still employing these devices as late as 1888.

considering the crew we had, but our condition in the mind
of the admiral and his official report depended largely on the
success of the torpedo. At the proper moment I received the
order, "Fire the starboard torpedo!" as if we had a dozen on
tap. This was to impress the foreigners, who were watching
us intently. Admiral Case had a fine sense of humour.

My pitched-over water-breaker, containing one hundred
pounds of old black powder, was launched on the end of a
long spar and sunk to a depth of about ten feet. Then I
touched the firing key, and there was a real commotion for
all hands. The explosion which followed instantly shook the
ship—in fact, all the ships in the harbour—quite thoroughly, threw a fine column of water two hundred feet in
the air, and covered the decks of the Austrian, who was to
leeward of us, with very filthy mud blown up from the bottom. The admiral considered it all very successful, complimented me on my work, and ordered that each ship of the
squadron should prepare and fire one torpedo each month. It
is hard to believe, in these days of perfect-running
Whiteheads [14] and Howells, [15] that I am relating what actually occurred on a United States vessel in 1873. Other nations were no better off than we, if as well.

Before leaving Barcelona I determined to witness some of
the shows which amused the people, and as Sunday was the

14. The Whitehead torpedo was a self-propelled, or "automobile," torpedo perfected by British engineer Robert Whitehead during the late
1860s and early 1870s. With a 1,000-yard range, it made the torpedo
boat practical. The U.S. Navy first acquired torpedo boats through a
domestic-production contract with the E.W. Bliss Company in 1891. By
1894 both Whitehead and Howell torpedoes were in the Navy's inven-
tory, although ultimately the Whitehead prevailed.
15. An American-designed flywheel torpedo first constructed for production by the Hotchkiss Company in 1888. Technical and production problems plagued the Hotchkiss effort, leading to the Navy Department's decision to award a contract to the E.W. Bliss Company in 1891 to produce
the Whitehead torpedo, which eventually replaced the Howell torpedo.

great day for that sort of thing, selected it for my outing. I hope I may never spend another such Sunday. First I visited a combination fight—chickens first, then "bull baiting," and finally a dog fight, each more brutal than the other. The bull baiting consisted in tying a bull to a post in the centre of an inclosure by means of a ring fastened through his nose, and then turning loose on him a number of savage bulldogs. The poor beast was unable to defend himself, and soon succumbed to his tormentors. A lean-looking old donkey was then introduced, and the dogs let loose on him. He evidently had more sense than the bull, for he succeeded in killing one dog with his teeth and two with his heels before they finally pulled him down. I regretted very much that it was not men instead of dogs he had demolished. Then came the dog fight, which was a very noisy affair, not on account of the dogs that were fighting, but by reason of the curs surrounding the pit. Almost every cur had a smaller cur under his arm—smaller, of course, and much less brutal and savage than his master. I fittingly wound up the day by visiting a large gambling hell, where I lost a few pesetas, and was chased out on the roof by a gang of thugs, who seemed anxious to put a knife or two in me. When I reached the ship I felt that I had learned something of Spanish customs, and was impressed with the necessity of a bath, both moral and physical.

From Barcelona we hurried down to Alicante [16] to see the bombardment of that place by the rebel ships. We were so slow, however, that we arrived the day after the fight. There were no forts to be seen when at daylight the bombardment began; but the people on shore had mounted some heavy guns in a masked battery and served them so well that the fleet was driven off before sundown, with quite a list of killed and wounded. The town suffered somewhat, but no lives

16. A city in southeastern Spain, south of Valencia, on the Mediterranean Sea.

were lost. The bombardment was caused by the refusal of the authorities to pay the large sum of money demanded of them by the rebel government.

Upon our arrival at Tangiers, Morocco,[17] the American consul, Colonel Mathews,[18] arranged a hunting party for Captain Wells, and I was fortunate enough to be asked to join it. A tribe of Moors furnished the attendants, three camels carried our tents and mess outfit, and we, four of us, followed on horseback. The attendants, cooks, hunters, etc., numbered about fifty. When we had gone some seventy-five miles into the country we struck the hunting ground and the fun began. I had determined to shoot from my horse, as the cover was very thick and the weather hot enough to make the work of getting through it hard for a lame man. Colonel Mathews assured me that the horse, a thoroughbred Arabian, would probably break my neck if I fired from his back, but I had my own views about that. As we were leaving our camp in the morning for our first day's shoot, two partridges got up under my horse's nose and I downed them both, but a second later found myself sitting on the ground. When I fired I took the precaution to throw both my feet out of the stirrups. The horse squatted down and jumped from under me as if he had been greased, and then ran away. He was finally caught, and, after half an hour's training, stood fire like a veteran. I shot from his back every day while we were out, and I am sure he learned to enjoy it. I certainly did. We were shooting the African red-legged partridge, and they were in great numbers. The Moors were spread out like a picket line, with the gunners stationed along at regular intervals. As the line advanced, the flight of birds was almost constant and the banging of the guns incessant, the Moors acting as beaters and retrievers.

17. A city in northern Morocco on the Strait of Gibraltar.
18. A Californian who served as consul to Tangier, Colonel F.A. Mathews was commissioned on 9 July 1870.

Each morning the camp was sent ahead to a spot selected by the colonel, and when we arrived, generally early in the afternoon, we found everything ship-shape and our lunch ready. Our trip was made during the Ramadan,[19] or lenten season, and the Moors neither ate nor drank from sunrise to sunset, but during the night they made merry. Not so with us, however; we ate, drank, and made merry during the day, and slept during the night when the fleas would allow us to. These little pests were in the sand, and in such numbers and so active that we all bore the marks of them for weeks afterward. Colonel Mathews was a real *cordon bleu,* and the stews he made out of English hare, of which we killed a number, and mutton, were beyond criticism. We were all sorry when our week was up and we had to return to work.

The news of the seizure of the Virginius[20] came about this time, and we received hurry orders to proceed to Nice,[21] our storehouse and headquarters. We were off at once and had a fine run until we passed Port Mahon,[22] when a long swell from the Gulf of Lyons[23] and a rapidly falling barometer indicated trouble ahead. The captain had his family on board, and one of his daughters was to be married to an officer on our arrival at Nice; and as we would probably be hurried away as soon as we could take in stores, without much con-

19. The ninth month of the Moslem year, during which a sunrise-to-sunset fast is observed.
20. During the course of the 1868 Cuban uprising, Spanish naval vessels captured a rebel ship, the *Virginius,* and fifty-three passengers, some of whom were Americans. Taken ashore, the prisoners were shot as "pirates." The American outcry could have led to war, but the United States accepted an apology and a money indemnity. The incident was not forgotten entirely, however, festering as part of an overall "Free Cuba" movement.
21. A city in southeastern France on the Mediterranean Sea.
22. A port town on the east coast of Minorca in the Baleric Islands.
23. Gulf du Lion is an arm of the Mediterranean Sea where the Rhône River emerges from the south of France. The French naval base at Toulon and the port of Marseilles are situated on the shores of this body of water.

sideration for the young couple, it was desirable that we should make as much speed as possible. The storm warnings were not heeded, and at sundown we were on our course under all sails and steam. Half an hour afterward I was called on deck to shorten sail, but before I could do anything half the canvas was blown away. We finally got her under storm sails, but she rolled until the side seams were so opened that the water squirted into the officers' bunks in the wardroom. I was on deck, in my double capacity of executive officer and navigator, during the entire night, and I have rarely seen a worse one. The wind blew with hurricane force, and our crew of "dagos" and "rock scorpions" were of little use. Many of the officers had to go aloft to help furl the few sails we had managed to save, most of which afterward blew out of the furling lines and were lost. Our engines were of little use in the heavy sea, barely giving us steerage way, and as a whole the prospect was not pleasing. During the mid watch, about half past one, I was thrown on deck by the heavy lurching of the ship, and had the skin taken off my left knee in a spot just the size of the knee cap. When I had a chance the doctor took a look at it in the wardroom, and before I knew what he was about he clapped a large piece of thick adhesive plaster, which he had melted over a candle, on the raw flesh. It fairly fried me, and caused me intense pain for several days, as well as the use of very strong language.

At daylight the gale blew out, and the ship was really a picture to see. Bits of canvas remained on the yards where the sails had been, and other bits had whipped themselves about the rigging, and all were frayed out, until the Shenandoah looked as if she had been picking cotton. We arrived at Nice, however, after a time, the parson tied the knot for the captain's daughter, amid most beautiful surroundings and distinguished people, and in a few days we reported ready for sea again. War rumours were in the air, and when we said good-bye to our families none of us could even guess when we might see them again. It was a sad time for us all, but the women were so plucky and behaved so well that we were cheered by their example. No weeping and wailing for them—only pale faces and set teeth to show what they were suffering. How proud we were of our American wives!

The admiral sent us to sea as fast as we were coaled and ready to rendezvous at Gibraltar, where we arrived in five days, which was an excellent run for us. The weather tried to make up to us for its hard treatment a few days before, and the wind blew steadily in our favour all the way. Before leaving Nice our cabin party was increased by the arrival on board of the paymaster's wife, who came to look after her sick husband. I shall have more to say about him later on. When we reached Gibraltar war with Spain seemed probable, and orders were received to proceed immediately to Key West.[24] These were somewhat accentuated when the admiral wired to know if there were any further orders, by the answer from the Department at Washington: "Obey your orders at once!" After this the ships got to sea rather promptly, we being the last to start. We ran down to Madeira,[25] where we remained a week, and then headed for St. Thomas,[26] in the West Indies.

The paymaster was very ill at this time and growing worse. Many of us, who knew him well, thought the best thing he could do would be to die—the best for all hands, particularly the wife. The captain, at the instigation of the doctor, purchased a goat, in order that the patient might have the advantage of fresh milk on the passage over. We left Madeira early in the morning, and at eleven o'clock that night the orderly turned me out, saying the captain wanted

24. A city in southern Florida on Key West Island, the westernmost Florida key in the Gulf of Mexico.
25. A Portuguese archipelago in the north Atlantic, west of Morocco.
26. One of the Virgin Islands of the West Indies: that is, islands between southeastern North America and northern South America that separate the Caribbean Sea and the Atlantic Ocean and include the Greater Antilles, the Lesser Antilles, and the Bahamas.

to see me on deck. I was at a loss to know what he could possibly want with me at that hour, but, supposing it to be something of importance, hurried into my clothes and reported to him on the quarter-deck, when the following conversation took place: "Evans, you know the paymaster is very ill, and may die?" "Yes, sir; I hope he will." "Well, he surely will unless he can have some goat's milk. I have sent for you to ask if you won't milk the goat for us. I know you can do it. So far we have not succeeded in getting a drop of milk from the beast, though she seems to have plenty." To this proposition I was naturally disposed to make a sharp reply, but, having a great regard for the captain, I only said, "I was not aware, sir, that it was any part of the navigator's duty to milk a goat." "Of course not, Evans, of course not; I ask you to do it as a matter of humanity, and to oblige me."

That, of course, settled the question, and down I went to tackle Mrs. Goat. I found her in a very excited state of mind apparently, having butted out the captain's steward and a marine orderly who had attempted to relieve her of her milk. One of them had tried to hold her while the other went for the milk. I remembered how the darkies in my young days had treated a cow under the same conditions, and procuring some warm water and exercising a little patience in the premises, soon relieved her of the milk, which was evidently giving her pain. This I sent to the cabin, and went back to my sleep. At breakfast in the morning the whole mess knew what had taken place, and I was, of course, the subject of no end of chaff.

In the afternoon I was again sent for and requested to milk the goat. I declared I would "be jiggered" if I would; but the captain again persuaded me to do it. This time I found the goat standing on her hind legs, snorting at the steward, who was being unmercifully jeered at by the crew because he failed in all his attempt to produce milk. It now looked as if I would have to go on milking the blessed goat all the way to St. Thomas. However, I found a young marine who seemed willing to assume my duties, if the goat would let him, and I succeeded finally in teaching him the trick of milking her successfully. This was my first and only experience with goats. The paymaster lived to reach the United States, where he died a few months later.

On arriving at St. Thomas, we learned that the Virginius trouble was in a fair way of being settled without war. We were, however, to hurry on to Key West, where we had a large fleet assembled ready to fight in case diplomacy failed. The Ticonderoga[27] was in port, just arrived from Brazil, and as soon as coaled we sailed in company and made a good run to the coast of Florida. The force assembled at Key West was the best, and indeed about all, we had. We had no stores or storehouses to speak of at this so-called base of supplies, and if it had not been so serious it would have been laughable to see our condition. We remained there several weeks, making faces at the Spaniards ninety miles away at Havana, while two modern vessels of war would have done us up in thirty minutes. As there was to be no war, the authorities in Washington allowed the foreign *attachés* to come and inspect us, and report our warlike condition to their different Governments. We were dreadfully mortified over it all, but we were not to blame; we did the best we could with what Congress gave us.[28]

27. The USS *Ticonderoga* was a wooden screw sloop of 1,533 tons, a top speed of 10.5 knots, a battery of ten to sixteen guns, and a 270-man complement. Built at the New York Navy Yard in 1861, she was launched on 16 October 1862, commissioned on 12 May 1863, and decommissioned on 5 May 1865 at Philadelphia Navy Yard. She was sold in August 1887 to Thomas Butler and Co. of Boston for $15,900. Her crowning Civil-War duty was searching for the CSS *Florida* in July 1864.

28. American naval officers, particularly younger ones, perpetually noted the obsolete and obsolescent quality of the Reconstruction and Gilded Age navy after the Civil War. A penurious Congress naturally sought to trim military expenses, as was traditionally the American wont in peacetime, in the absence of any perceived national security threat. Certainly a

We had several weeks of fleet manœuvres, which were excellent both for officers and men, and then, as a grand wind up, a landing drill, which for some reason has become the favourite in our service over all legitimate work. On this occasion we landed about three thousand men, and, after spending an afternoon in a temperature running as high as 130° in the sun, returned to our ships and nursed our blisters for days afterward. I had command of the artillery, eighteen guns, which we hauled about seven or eight miles in the hot sun and through cactus so thick in some places that we had to blow it away with the guns in order to get them through. I found one of the men, an old quartermaster, with his shoes hanging around his neck. He said he wasn't going to ruin his shoes by wearing them over that cactus. Finally, we flanked the position of the imaginary enemy, and, with the expenditure of much old, condemned powder, carried it with a rush. Then we had a brigade dress parade, which would have impressed the Spanish regulars if they had seen it. This done, we went on board our ships, and the doctors pulled the cactus thorns out of us.

The time spent on this drill and the money it cost were not entirely wasted. We learned many things besides how to live on turtle steaks. We of the navy knew long before this that our so-called naval force was a sham, and that the country was absolutely without sea power; but if there were any doubters among us they were convinced. The country at large learned something that shocked the people, and they began to take more interest in our floating defences. We tried all the kinds of torpedoes then known to us, and decided that they were good only for newspaper stories, or to scare timid

---

similar problem befell other navies in the transitional period between wooden sailing warships, with their muzzle-loading ordnance, and the naval revolution of iron and steel hulls, steam propulsion, and breech-loading rifled ordnance. In fact, the American Navy may have been quite adequate to "showing the flag" in peacetime, if not altogether first rate in case of an international crisis.

people with. The much-talked-of Harvey towing-torpedo[29] was towed about for days in an effort to make it strike a ship, but it would not do it. Once it did seem to wake up, and jumped over an innocent tugboat, fortunately without killing any one. Then we ran at a large raft, made of many hundreds of oil barrels securely lashed together, and exploded spar torpedoes under it, producing very beautiful fountains, and knocking the barrels about considerably. This was generally done at very low speed, because most of us could not steam over seven knots; some ships undertook the exercise at speeds as high as ten knots, but they always carried away something when the spar was lowered into the water, and before they reached the target the torpedo had swung alongside, where it could not be exploded without disastrous result. Our gun practice was good, and it was found that the officers could handle their ships in a seamanlike way; but the general conclusion was that torpedoes in their then state of development were a very much overrated weapon. Of course, there were enthusiasts who still believed in them. You can find those who believe that "the earth stands still and the sun do move!"

29. An obsolescent torpedo device used in both the British and American navies. The invention of Captain John Harvey and Commander Frederick Harvey of the Royal Navy, it consisted of a case of sheet copper that contained seventy-six pounds of gun cotton, all within a wooden cask. Lines to this device enabled it to be towed at an approximate 45-degree angle from the direction of the course of the vessel from which it was worked. The idea apparently derived from the so-called "otter" contrivance used by Scottish poachers to convey their lines out into midstream.

CHAPTER 16

A Cruise to Africa

W AR with Spain being once more postponed, orders were issued for the fleet to disband, and for the various vessels to proceed to their new stations. The Shenandoah was ordered North to go out of commission for repairs, but as my sea service in her had been very short, I was transferred to the Congress[1] as executive officer. I was considered very young for the job, but I was not responsible either for my age or my orders, and neither gave me any concern. W.T. Sampson,[2] who afterward rendered the country such conspicuous service in the war with Spain, had been her executive, and in relieving him I, of course, found a well-organized

1. A sail frigate of approximately 1,869 tons and fifty guns, the USS *Congress* was built by the government and launched in 1841 at Kittery, Maine. She was sunk in action with the CSS *Virginia (Merrimack)* at Hampton Roads, Virginia, on 8 March 1862, but was raised, repaired, and later sold at the Norfolk Navy Yard.
2. Warranted an acting midshipman on 24 September 1857, W.T. Sampson was promoted to captain on 26 March 1889, commodore on 3 July 1898, and rear admiral on 3 March 1899. Sampson commanded the North Atlantic Squadron at the Battle of Santiago in 1898.

ship. She had a new crew, composed of merchant sailors principally, who had enlisted at Southern ports for the threatened Cuban war, and they were about as tough a lot of Christians as I ever ran up against; but time and discipline did wonders for them. I was again very fortunate in my captain, as my old Delaware captain, Earl English, was ordered to command us. I reported on board early in April, and a few days later Captain English came with orders to hurry things up as much as possible and get off to the Mediterranean without delay. We did not allow any barnacles to grow on us after this, for we knew how many ships would be pleased to take our place. A week or ten days was all we required, after the order came, to report ready, and immediately afterward we went to sea.

Our run to Madeira was made in good time, considering the fact that we did it all under sail. I asked the captain to allow me to drill the men an hour or so each day with sails and spars, as I considered that the best and quickest way to get them in shape. He was good enough to approve the plan I had suggested, and every afternoon we worked ship for an hour, furling and shifting sails, sending up and down yards, and doing the many small things which, if persevered in, tend to make a seaman. Both officers and men thoroughly enjoyed the work, and the improvement in them was most marked. Upon our arrival at Madeira we received orders to proceed to the coast of Africa, where some of the natives near Monrovia[3] had threatened to barbecue our wards, the coloured American colonists. As soon as necessary repairs could be made we left Madeira for the south.

We found the trades good and strong, and running off before them under all sail was the finest going to sea one could have. We enjoyed the perfect semitropical weather to

3. The capital of Liberia, Monrovia is located in West Africa on the Gulf of Guinea.

The Congress

the full, and arrived at Santa Cruz[4] May 13, 1874. The historical old town was well worth a visit, and we all regretted that the service on which we were bound allowed us to remain only three days, during which time we refilled our coal bunkers and made such excursions on shore as were possible. I organized a party of eleven to visit the village of Orotava,[5] which is situated in a valley at the foot of Mount Teneriffe,[6] celebrated as one of the most beautiful peaks in the world. The question of how to get there was solved when I had succeeded in chartering three shabby old hacks and six so-called horses to pull them. We were soon started, and, working laboriously up the steady mountain grade, arrived after a while at an elevation of three thousand feet, where we met the rain in tropical torrents. A convenient hole in the roof of my hack let the water through, and I soon had a small river running down my back and into my shoes, which detracted from the pleasure of the trip, but did not destroy it. The rain soon ceased, and there below us lay the city and the harbour completely inclosed in a perfect rainbow, which touched the water north and south. It was the most beautiful picture I had ever seen, painted by the Master Hand that makes no mistakes.

At the little village of Laguna[7] we halted, wet and tired, to get what lunch we could from the scowling gang of Spaniards who surrounded us. The Virginius affair had not made us popular with these cutthroats. The tavern in which we found ourselves was foully dirty, and the food was in keeping; but we managed to make some sort of a meal on salad and eggs, washed down with very warm Bass ale. After leaving this village we found ourselves on a road winding around

4. Santa Cruz de Tenerife is a city on the northeast coast of Tenerife, the Canary Islands.
5. La Orotava is a town on the northern coast of Tenerife Island, in the Canaries.
6. A 3,718-foot peak that dominates Tenerife Island.
7. La Laguna is a town in the northern part of Tenerife Island.

the side of the mountain, with the sea nearly four thousand feet below us. The scene was wild and beautiful as the sun broke through the clouds which enveloped us. Nature did all she could to make the panorama perfect, but the shadow of Spain was over everything.

Darkness came as we turned into the valley and began the sharp descent to the village, and we saw nothing more until we arrived at the one miserable hotel Orotava at that time contained. After much wrangling and the use of many bad words we succeeded in getting enough cot beds for the party, but it was hours before we were served with dinner, and a very poor one it was when it finally came. When we retired for the night I discovered that one of the sheets for my bed was the tablecloth off which I had dined! This, however, was soon forgotten under the attack of the fleas, which literally swarmed everywhere, and sleep was out of the question. I thought I had seen fleas in Morocco and in Japan, but I was mistaken—it was left for Orotava to show me the real thing. We gave up the beds as a bad job, and wandered about until daylight, when we ascended to the roof of the hotel to watch the sun rise and catch the shadows on the beautiful Peak of Teneriffe. It was a clear morning, fortunately, and as the sun rose we were well repaid for all the inconvenience we had suffered.

After breakfast we strolled for two hours about the village, admiring the splendid flowers, which in their perfection and abundance reminded me of those about Montevideo.[8] The roses were the finest I had ever seen, and I can recall after all these years the appearance of a stone wall which had a cloth of gold climbing over it bearing more than five hundred splendid flowers. After a look at the great dragon tree, which had fallen two years before, having stood the storms of many hundreds if not thousands of years, we started on our return trip. At a point in the road where the view was the most

8. The capital of Uruguay, located at the mouth of the Rio de la Plata.

perfect we halted and looked back over the beautiful valley. It was at this spot that Humboldt was said to have dropped on his knees and exclaimed, "I have found the Garden of Eden!" The view, though very beautiful, had changed much since his time. Then the entire country was one vast vineyard—grapevines everywhere; but now only cactus plants could be seen, and they certainly could not be called beautiful. The people had found that cochineal paid better than wine, and did not require anything like so much labour, so they planted cactus and collected and roasted the small red insects. At the time of my visit aniline dyes had entirely superseded cochineal for colouring purposes, and the cactus plants had consequently been left without care to grow as they pleased.

Our run down to Porto Grande[9] was as pleasant as any I ever made, the weather being perfect. Our drills were kept up constantly, and the men showed the good stuff that was in them. The captain was, unfortunately, very sick all the way, and my work in consequence much harder. There were executives in the service at that day, and I suppose they are not all dead yet, who wanted to be captain as well as executive. I was not one of them. I always wished the captain to back me up in what I did as executive, and I always did what I could to make his position strong and stiff, for I sometimes required a pretty stiff hand to back up some of the things I had to do to make the ship what I knew she ought to be. "To have the captain under your thumb" was one of the fool notions that never entered my head.

Porto Grande was the headquarters of our African squadron, when we had one, and here many officers and men were buried. We were much disgusted to find that the authorities had seen fit to order our cemetery sold, after having levelled the graves and destroyed the tombstones and monuments.

9. A bay on the northern coast of São Vicente Island, Cape Verde Islands, it boasts the archipelago's best natural harbor.

One of our vessels had been sent to look into the matter, and, after she had made a proper row, the governor promised to do what he could to protect the graves. We found that he had stuck up some small posts to mark the boundaries, where before we had a stone wall capped by a proper iron fence; and, not considering this much of an effort, we again made a row, and he again promised to do something; but I am sure he never intended to do more than get rid of us. I was anxious to teach him a lesson, but our orders would not permit it. I found that one of the tombstones from the grave of an American officer was being used for a chopping-block in a private house. Without much ceremony I had this removed to its proper place, and reported the whole matter to the Navy Department. We arrived at this place on May 23d, and, having replenished our coal supply, again started south, bound for Harpers,[10] the American settlement on Cape Palmas, intending to call in at Freetown, Monrovia.[11]

On the morning of June 5th we ran in and anchored off the latter place, where I had my first experience with the native Africans. Their antics were only exceeded by those of our coloured countrymen who had sought homes here in their native land, or rather the land of their ancestors. As soon as we anchored, our minister to Liberia came on board, and was received with all the honours due his high position. I found him a well-educated man, much given to self-admiration and the use of high-sounding words. he was very good-looking, of a commanding figure, very black, and named J. Milton Turner.[12] He wore evening dress and a very becoming high hat. The two Harvard graduates, coloured, who accompanied him were apparelled in the same way. After a short visit, during which he talked incessantly of the call I was to make

10. An American settlement on Cape Palmas and a commercial seaport on the extreme southeastern corner of Liberia, West Africa.
11. The capital of Sierra Leone on the Atlantic coast.
12. Turner was commissioned to the post of consul general to Monrovia on 1 March 1871.

on the President of the republic, he took his departure, and was saluted with seventeen guns. At the first gun he stood up in the stern of his small boat, held his tall hat aloft in one hand, and the American flag in the other. His efforts to balance himself as the boat pitched and tossed about made of him a striking figure.

In an hour or so Mr. Turner was back on board, still in dress clothes, with a message from the President that he would be glad to receive me that afternoon at a stated hour. We had taken on board at Porto Grande twelve Kroomen,[13] trained surfmen, for service on the coast of Africa, to save our men from the effects of the sun. These men were named after the twelve apostles, and were regularly enlisted as a part of the ship's company. They were splendid specimens of the African boatman, and knew their business thoroughly. We also had a very able whaleboat, which I proposed using to land the officers, who, in full dress, were to form my staff in this visit of ceremony. When the boat was manned and ready to leave the ship, Mr. Turner insisted that I should go with him in his small boat, which I finally consented to do, to get rid of his importunities. I sent our whaler in first, and then consigned myself, epaulets and all, to Mr. Turner and his two oarsmen, feeling as I did so that I was taking chances both from drowning and from the vicious-looking tiger-sharks that were present in great numbers.

The bar at the entrance to this harbour was known as one of the worst on the coast, and on this occasion the surf was breaking heavily on it. As we approached it I watched our whaler ahead of us to see how she would behave. The cockswain, a perfect black Hercules, St. Paul by name, handled the steering oar, and at the proper moment sent the boat racing on top of a wave over the bar in the most approved

13. The Kru inhabit Liberia and the Ivory Coast and speak a Kwa dialect. A branch of the Niger-Congo family, they are known on the west coast of Africa for their skills as stevedores.

style. Our little cockleshell also went over beautifully, but
not without wetting all of us pretty thoroughly. When we
landed I asked Mr. Turner why he had insisted on my coming in with him, to which he replied, "You see, sir, if you
had not landed with me, these niggers here would have said
that you considered yourself too good to come in the same
boat with me."

After a walk of five minutes over a bare, sunbaked clay
hill, without one sprig of anything green, where the naked
negro children were playing, unconscious of their nakedness,
we came to the humble home of President Roberts,[14] of the
Republic of Liberia. He had been raised a slave near Petersburg, in Virginia,[15] and I found him a person of pleasing
manners and assured ability—just the man to preside over
the destinies of his fellow-Africans. He had gathered his Cabinet about him, and I was presented to the different members—the Secretary of War, the Secretary of the Navy, the
Secretary of the Treasury, and so on through the list. During
the conversation that followed I heard the rustling of a silk

14. Joseph Jenkins Roberts (1809–76) was the American-born first President of Liberia (1848–56). He was the son of free blacks whose heritage
was more than seven-eighths white. At twenty he immigrated to Liberia
with his mother and younger brothers. Roberts became a merchant and
an unofficial aide to the white governor of the colony, Thomas H. Buchanan, who was a member of the American Colonization Society, which
sought to return American Freedmen to Africa. Upon Buchanan's death
in 1842, Roberts was appointed the first black governor of the colony. In
their efforts to establish the political and economic stability of the colony,
Roberts and other colonists sought treaties with native tribes and recognition from foreign powers. In 1847 they proclaimed the new republic of
Liberia, and elected Roberts the first President. During a visit to England
in 1849, he secured British recognition of Liberia as a sovereign nation;
and in 1852, in another trip to continental Europe, he acquired recognition from other powers. From 1856 on, Roberts served as President of
the new Liberia College and, during a prolonged financial crisis from
1872 to 1876, again as President of the republic.
15. A city of southeastern Virginia, south of Richmond. It was the scene
of a Civil War siege, 1864–65.

dress, and instinctively rose to my feet. There before me
stood a short, neat, very black woman, and, without waiting
for an introduction, I shocked myself by saying, "How do
you do, aunty?" to which she replied, with a courtesy, "Very
well, thank you, sir." I was instantly aware of my mistake
in so addressing the wife of a President, but was relieved of
all embarrassment by the hearty laugh of Mr. Roberts, and
the query, "What part of the South do you come from,
captain?"

Some very warm, sour champagne was served, and after
pledging the high consideration of my Government for the
Republic of Liberia, I took my departure, followed by the
entire Cabinet and half a hundred naked young negroes,
ranging from four to eight years of age. Mr. Turner insisted
that I should call on each Cabinet minister according to his
rank; and, for fear of giving offence, I did so. At each house
or hut I was entertained with such food and drink as the
owners possessed, and everywhere a hearty welcome. I was
told—and it was painfully evident without the telling—that
the people were wretchedly poor, and the revenues of the
republic barely sufficient to pay the salaries of the Cabinet
ministers, and therefore no public improvements could be
undertaken. There was not the first sign of an army or navy,
or indeed a need for either; yet the two secretaries were on
hand and ready at least to draw their pay when the treasury
was in condition to pay it.

After visiting the mayor I returned to the ship, this time
in my own boat, and was most favourably impressed by the
cleverness with which our Kroomen brought us over the
wicked-looking bar. The sharks were snapping at the oars
most of the way, and if we had capsized nothing could have
saved us—at least the white men of the party; the blacks do
not seem a favourite article of food with these sea-tigers. Of
course I had read, as many others had, very glowing accounts
of the missions, churches, and schools of Liberia. I can only
say they were conspicuous by their absence at the time of my

visit. The word "republic" was never more abused and insulted and misused than by applying it to what I saw in Liberia.

During the time we had been at anchor off Monrovia a
particularly large man-eating shark had remained constantly
about the ship, swallowing empty meat cans and such other
trash as suited him. As soon as I had time to spare for him I
prepared a beautiful bait for his dinner, which he took
readily, and it was all twenty good men could do to capture
him after he was hooked. We hoisted him up nearly to the
main yard, and literally "shot him full of holes." More than
a hundred rifle and revolver balls were fired through him,
and, thinking he was dead, I had him lowered on the upper
deck, and allowed such men as had a spite against him to
stick their knives into him, if they could. He was old and
had a very thick hide. Finally, one of the men took a battle-
axe from a gun carriage and struck him a hard blow on the
top of his head, which seemed to wake him up again. He
raised himself as quick as a flash and brought his tail down
with a crack that made all hands stand clear of him in a
hurry. We then killed him "entirely," as the Irishman said,
by cutting his tail off, which of course severed his spinal
column and put an end to him. After decapitating him I
cut out fourteen feet of his backbone and had it cleaned and
preserved, with the head, as a sample of what a man-eater is
like in size.

The stomach contained a curious lot of things: first I took
out a turtle shell, which measured eighteen inches across the
back and was as clear and transparent as the most beautiful
piece one could see in a shop in Naples. Then I took out the
thigh bone of a bullock, and a good large one it was. The
last thing I found was a black flint stone weighing twenty
pounds, which I suppose he had swallowed, or rather picked
up, with the turtle from the bottom. I did not find any gold
watches or diamond rings. When the jaws, which had four
rows of teeth, had been dried and shellacked, I could pass

them over the head and shoulders of the largest man in the ship without their touching his clothing. In other words, he could have swallowed an ordinary man without the trouble of biting him in two. I afterward presented them to the library of the Portsmouth Navy Yard, where they may still be an object of interest to the curious.

From Monrovia we ran to Cape Palmas, which was to be the southern point of our cruise. On arrival we found there was no real trouble with the natives. They had threatened to lunch on some of our missionaries, but had not carried out their threat. A short exercise on shore with a Gatling gun [16] firing at a target, which we left for them to study over, convinced them that they really could get on without eating American missionaries.

The question of coal had now become a most serious one; have it we must, but how to get it was the question. There was none in sight anywhere within our reach. The prospect of beating back under canvas against the trades was not a pleasing one. While on shore one day I made inquiries about the wreck of a large English steamer on the sands, and found that she had been loaded with prepared fuel—coal bricks they were called. On boarding her I found to my great satisfaction that the fuel was still in good condition, and that there was plenty of it. After some trouble I arranged with the owner to purchase as much as we could stow, and then hired enough natives to boat it off to us through the surf, which was always breaking heavily on the beach. We used our own boats for the purpose, but the sun was too hot to risk working our own men, except to stow the fuel after it was delivered on board. For four days we worked away steadily, and succeeded in getting enough on board to carry us back to Sierra Leone. [17]

16. Created by North Carolina physician Dr. Richard J. Gatling in 1862, it was the first successful machine gun.
17. A country in West Africa on the Atlantic coast.

Most of this time I was at work myself, spending many hours on shore and about the wreck, where I had a good chance of observing the native workmen. They were a muscular lot of savages, and, generally speaking, worked well. The lazy ones were stimulated by the head man with a good stout whip which he carried as a sort of badge of office. They were stripped to the skin, and had enormous pads of matted hair on their heads, which apparently was the growth and accumulation of years. I was interested in seeing them feed. When meal time came each would pull a handful of Chili peppers, which were as hot as anything could be; then from the nearest tree he would secure half a dozen fresh limes, which he split open and salted; these, with hard bread and a small portion of dried fish, formed the ration of as hardworked a lot of men as I ever saw. Their work was performed under a tropical sun, where white men could not have done anything. On board ship we were practically living on salt rations, because there was nothing on shore to buy, except fruit, which was very good, and black pigs. Even the pigs in this country were black.

We were glad to point the good ship north again, and when we anchored at Sierra Leone the official calls fell to my lot, as the captain was still on the sick list. The following extract from my journal is of interest:

"On this occasion my staff consisted of young Zeilin,[18] of the marines, an excellent fellow. Wasn't it hot! The house of the governor is on a hill about half a mile high, and when we arrived at the door the perspiration was running over the tops of my shoes. The governor gave us some brandy and soda with *ice,* the first we had seen since leaving Madeira, which had a wonderfully cooling effect. When we left, he invited us to dine the following evening, and we were quick

18. W.F. Zeilin became a 1st Lieutenant in the Marine Corps on 6 December 1879 and died on 4 June 1880.

to accept the invitation—grub has been awful on the coast of Africa.

"After leaving Government House we had to climb about two miles more over the hills before we reached the barracks, where we had more brandy and soda and plenty of time to cool off. The officers and men, part of a West India regiment,[19] had just returned from Ashantee, and had lots of interesting things to show and plenty to talk about. Among other things, the colonel had a couple of young boa constrictors about four feet long and very gentle, but able to give one a good squeeze if allowed to coil around the body.

"On the way back to the ship I called to see the great character of Sierra Leone, one Sibyl Boyle. He had been taken from a slave ship when about eight years of age, and, having no name of his own, was given that of the ship Sibyl and of her Captain Boyle. He was an industrious lad, and gradually worked his way up, until now he is the richest and most influential man in the place, and has a fine family around him. If some of his neighbours would only follow his example we might hope that some day Africa would be developed by her own race, but as things stand now the white race must eventually own the whole outfit."

One of our officers, Lieutenant J.D.J. Kelly,[20] was condemned by medical survey at Sierra Leone, and sent home *via* England. The doctors thought him in the last stages of heart disease, and doubted if he would live to reach London. I knew nothing about such things, of course, but differed with

19. This was a British colonial regiment whose first battalion was raised and used against American colonists (1779–81), as well as in the conquest and policing of West Africa. The 2d battalion (1795–1898) was also deployed in Africa and the Caribbean; this was probably the unit Evans encountered.
20. Warranted a midshipman on 5 October 1864, Kelley attained the rank of lieutenant on 13 August 1872, lieutenant commander on 27 June 1893, and commander on 3 March 1899.

the medical men on principle; there should always be two sides to every question, and I took the only side left in this case. Kelly seemed much cheered up by my assertion that his heart sounded like a music-box to me, and he left us in fairly good condition. Twenty-five years after this I find him in good health, and writing very vigorous articles for one of the leading newspapers of his country.

Having refilled our coal bunkers at Sierra Leone, we put to sea and headed for Madeira; but the coaldealer had done us a dirty trick—the coal would not burn; at least most of it would not, so we had to work up under sail to Porto Grande. On the way up we lost our first man by death since leaving Key West. He was a young chap who had run away from home to go to sea. He showed no concern about dying, and never gave me the slightest clew by which I could find his family, though I used my best efforts to make him do so. We sewed him up in his hammock, backed the maintopsail, hoisted the flag at halfmast, called, "All hands bury the dead!" and launched him overboard with a stand of grape for company on his long trip.

Back once more at Porto Grande, we lost no time in cramming our bunkers full of coal and starting again for Madeira. This time I felt sure that we could not steam directly to our port of destination; I therefore put the ship under sail and stood off into the Atlantic, determined not to get caught again as we were on the coast of Africa. The climate was now suitable, and I resumed the drills, which had been suspended for fear of overworking the men in the tropical sun. The effects of careful training and instruction were beginning to show, and I felt that we should be able to hold our own with the best of them when we finally reached the Mediterranean.

Day by day we gradually gained on the island of Madeira, until I at last felt that I could safely start the engines and do the distance under steam. The sails were snugly furled, the light yards sent down, and the gentlemen of the engine room had us in their hands. We had been a long time in making the last lap of our trip, but on July 16th we ran in and anchored once more off the beautiful town of Funchal,[21] in the island of Madeira. All hands were anxious for news of sweethearts or wives, and as soon as the health officer gave us a clean bill we sent in for our mails, and there came many fat-looking bags. For the first time in five months I had news of my family. In all that time my letters had been accumulating, and not a line had reached me. I had been rattled many times over the thoughts of what might have happened, but now it was all right. Going away to sea is awfully hard at times, but it is no end of fun when you come back again. I opened the latest-dated letter, and found that my people were all well and somewhere up in the north of England. I stowed the others away to be read when I had more time at my disposal.

The captain was much improved since we left Porto Grande, and I was able to get him on shore at once, where I knew he would be comfortable away from the noises of the ship and the smell of the paint I was going to put on her. All hands took hold with a will, and at the end of ten days everything was in fine shape and the ship ready for any service she might be called on to perform, while she was beautiful to look at, and I was not afraid to have any one inspect her. The captain had quite recovered, and was himself again—kind and genial, and a seaman every inch of him. When I had him on board and everything ready, we got under way for Gibraltar, where we arrived safely a few days later.

21. A city located in southeastern Madeira Island.

CHAPTER 17

In the Mediterranean

At Gibraltar[1] I was granted leave, and was fortunate enough to catch a P. and O. steamer[2] the next day, bound for Liverpool.[3] My fellow-passengers were for the most part officers of the English army invalided home from India, where they had been broken down in the Queen's service. They were a fine lot of patriotic men, anxious only to get well enough to rejoin the colours and die in harness. My room mate was a Major McLean,[4] of the Rifle Brigade, who had come to America with the troops sent over at the time the Trent affair[5] threatened to involve us in war with Eng-

1. A British colony located at the northwestern end of this peninsula on the southern coast of Spain.
2. Pacific and Orient Steamship Company.
3. A borough of northwestern England on the Mersey River near the Irish Sea.
4. Henry John Maclean of the Rifle Brigade served as a Special Service Officer in the Ashanti War of 1873–74. He attained the rank of major general.
5. A serious episode in Anglo-American relations that took place in 1861 when the USS *San Jacinto,* under Charles Wilkes, stopped the British mail steamer *Trent* at sea and removed this Confederate commissioners

land. We soon became very good friends, and he gave me much interesting information about his service in different parts of the world. He considered his experience at the time of the Trent affair unique, and it certainly was. When the transport with him and his men reached the mouth of the St. Lawrence,[6] they found the ice so bad that they could not get to Montreal,[7] so they went to a port in the State of Maine, and, by permission of our Government, were sent to their destination to get ready to come back and fight us. He thought it a very dangerous thing for us to have done, but I assured him that one or two brigades of English troops, more or less, would not have made the least difference to us at that time, if we had made up our minds to fight.

I found my family at Carlisle,[8] in the north of England, and from there we journeyed slowly back to London, tarried there a few days, and then on to Paris, and shortly to Italy.

After a delightful drive over the Cornice road,[9] we arrived at Spezzia,[10] where we found comfortable quarters and quite a navy colony at the Croce di Malta, a quiet, well-conducted small hotel, where one could have a charming breakfast in the open air under the shade of the fig trees.

The Congress had in the meantime been docked and cleaned and thoroughly overhauled. I found her lying in the

---

James Mason and John Slidell. Britain claimed that its rights were violated, and threatened war. The Lincoln administration released the men but took satisfaction that Great Britain at last recognized the rights of neutrals on the high seas, one of the principles over which the War of 1812 had been fought between the two countries.

6. A river of southeastern Canada that flows 744 miles northeast from Lake Ontario along the Ontario–New York border and through southern Quebec to the Gulf of St. Lawrence, an arm of the northwest Atlantic.

7. A city of southern Quebec, Canada, on the St. Lawrence River.

8. A borough of northwestern England near the Scottish border.

9. Probably "La Grande Corniche" (a road that runs along a cornice or ledge), which passes from Nice, France, eastward toward Italy.

10. An Italian town on the Ligurian Sea, south of Genoa.

stream, looking smart and ready for work, which the admiral soon gave us with a liberal hand. After a week or ten days we joined the flagship at Marseilles, which was selected as a suitable port for giving liberty to our men, who had been on board steadily since we left Key West. Our three hundred and fifty, added to the eight hundred of the Franklin,[11] kept the police force of the city pretty busy until their money was spent, when they once more settled down to their regular routine life.

Captain English believed in the old custom of giving liberty by watches, and this plan was followed in this case; but it was the last time it was ever done on that ship. It was favoured, I suppose, because the trouble was sooner over. I can't imagine any other reason for it. The idea was that the men would get drunk and raise all sorts of rows whenever they went on shore, and therefore the more we sent at a time the sooner it would be done with. The men certainly justified this opinion at Marseilles.

The captain went to Paris for a week, and so escaped much annoyance; but I had it to face, and it was very bad. I made up my mind that I would do all I could to prevent a recurrence of such scenes as I had witnessed, and, when the captain had had a full description of it all, I prevailed upon him to allow me to arrange the crew in conduct classes. After a reasonable time I found that the men could be relied on to behave themselves decently, and liberty was given them in every port we visited. Of course we had men, and I regret to say some of them the best seamen on board, who got drunk

11. A screw frigate built at the Portsmouth (New Hampshire) Navy Yard, the USS *Franklin* was launched on 17 September 1864, having cost $1,331,236.35. An old seventy-four-gun ship of the line originally built in 1815, she was rebuilt in 1854, mounting thirty-nine guns, displacing 3,173 tons, and having a top speed of 9 knots. Commissioned on 3 June 1867 at Boston, she was put out of commission on 2 March 1877 and recommissioned in 1896 to serve as a receiving ship at Norfolk, Virginia.

and fought the police every time they went on shore. The only reason we had them was because of this: if they could have controlled their taste for liquor they would have remained on shore. I had a very warm place in my heart for these chaps, and always found them leading when there was hard work to be done, and in the right spot when there was trouble. But they certainly were hard to manage. The great majority of our men were quiet, respectable lads, who went and came when they were off duty and had money to spend.

From Marseilles the admiral took us with him for a long cruise, stopping first at Barcelona, and then running down to Port Mahon in the Balearic Islands, where we landed the battalions of the two ships for shore drills. The officers senior to me were either sick or had some other good excuse, and I was therefore detailed to command, much to my disgust, for I have always found soldiering the least desirable part of my profession. We managed to amuse the natives of the island and please the admiral, so the drills were considered a success. The only real good of it all was the physical exercise the men received. In former years, when we maintained a large Mediterranean squadron of sailing ships, Port Mahon was our headquarters, and the people, when we visited the port, seemed glad to see our ships once more, and treated us with great courtesy.

All my life I had heard of two things that came from Port Mahon and from no other place. One was *sobra sada,* a sausage, made in a peculiar way, or rather from unusual ingredients; and the other date fish, a long shellfish much resembling a razor clam, which is obtained from the soft stones of the harbour and vicinity where he makes his home. The stones are broken open, and in the mass is found embedded this peculiar crustacean. I tried the qualities of both of them, and at once became a convert to *sobra sada,* which, broiled and served on toast, is one of the best breakfast dishes I have ever eaten.

On the conclusion of our Port Mahon visit we ran off to
the southward and cruised for some weeks about the island
of Sicily,[12] visiting several ports, and finally anchoring at
Messina.[13] Here we remained long enough to receive and
send mails and get a taste of fresh food for the men, when
we sailed for the Ionian Islands,[14] visiting among other places
Zante,[15] which produced practically the supply of currants
for the world. Then, after a stop in Suda Bay[16] for target
practice, we ran down to the Piræus,[17] and finally to Naples,[18] where we moored in the inner harbour, prepared for
a stay of ten days.

While in Suda Bay I had one day to spare, which I spent
on shore with my gun and an officer companion. We found
very little in the way of game, but I was much interested in
observing the Greek natives, who spend their lives in primitive simplicity. They are herders of sheep, and small farmers,
as they think; but their poverty is beyond anything the farmers of the United States could understand. Even the inhabitants of our poorhouses would consider themselves wealthy
when compared with these excellent, hard-working, simple
people. I stopped at one of their houses in the hills to get a
glass of water to drink with my luncheon at noon. The family
soon assembled about me, and offered me what they had in
the way of food. This consisted of a large wooden bowl of

12. An island off the southwest coast of Italy.
13. A seaport on the extreme northeast corner of Sicily that gave the
name to the body of water that separates the island from the Italian
mainland.
14. Islands off the west coast of Greece in the Ionian Sea.
15. One of the Ionian Islands west of the Peloponnesus.
16. An inlet on the northern coast of Crete near the island's western end.
It is shut in, in the northwest, by the Akoteri peninsula, just east of
Canea. This is the only good harbor on the north coast; it was the site of
a British base captured by German airborne troops on 26–27 May 1941.
17. A city of east-central Greece on the Saronic Gulf near Athens.
18. A city of south-central Italy on the Bay of Naples, an arm of the
Tyrrhenian Sea.

black olives—olives in their natural state allowed to ripen on the tree—black bread almost as hard as a stone, and a cup of goat's milk. They never ate meat, and when I showed them a ham sandwich, which my servant had prepared on board ship, they made me understand that they had never before seen or heard of ham, and the same thing happened when I showed them a piece of cold beef. I wondered at the change that must have come to them since the creation of the Venus of Milo,[19] which had been found in this country.

We were moored near some Italian war vessel at Naples, and soon found friends among the officers, who took great pleasure in arranging short trips for us, frequently going themselves to show us objects of interest. Among these officers I came to know two brothers very well. One morning it was rumoured that a duel had been fought, and one Italian officer instantly killed. Later in the day I learned that these two friends of mine had had a quarrel; that one had drawn a pistol and fired at the other, wounding him, and thinking that he had killed his brother, put the pistol to his head and blew his own brains out. The wounded brother recovered. Not much of a duel about that, certainly.

We had been at Naples but a few days when a gale came on—one of those furious blasts that last only a few hours, but frequently do great damage. The stern chains of the Franklin, secured to the stone breakwater, began to show signs of parting, and the admiral, in order to ease things up, made signal for both ships to send down lower yards and topmasts. The spar drill I had so carefully given our men enabled us to land our lower yards across the rail in twenty minutes, leaving nothing showing above the hull but the bare lower masts, which was fine work, and most gratifying to officers and men. The Franklin was a much heavier-sparred ship than we

19. The Venus de Milo (circa 150 B.C.) was a pastiche of preceding sculptural styles. The Hellenistic statue became the classic that other Romans imitated.

were, and took nearly two hours to get things snugged down in good shape. The following morning, the gale having blown out, the admiral signalled, "Cross royal yards and loose sails to a bowline," as a colour evolution. The whole foreign fleet had their glasses on us, and we received compliments on the smartness of our drill. We felt sufficiently rewarded for all the hard work we had done when the signal, "Well done, Congress," flew from the flagship.

From Naples we cruised along the coast of Syria, and then ran on to Nice. Each ship had an allowance of coal for the year, and the greater part of ours had been expended, so that we could not expect any active cruising for several months. In fact, we remained tied up to a buoy for five months. It looked as if we would ground on our beef bones before we got away from it. Our race boat, in which I took a personal interest, that extended to training the men, won from all comers and held the championship. During the winter the Russian admiral came in with a flagship noted for her smart work aloft. We watched her drills carefully for a few days, and, having learned all her tricks, followed her motions and beat her badly in everything she tried. The decks of the Congress were particularly well suited for quick work, and her crew by this time was in excellent condition. Each man felt that the reputation of the ship depended on his personal efforts, and the result was all we could ask.

Nice, only half an hour away, was crowded with visitors from all parts of the world, among them many of our own countrymen. We were invited, of course, to entertainments of every possible kind, which we had to accept and in some way return. This came hard on many of the officers who had only their pay to live on, and no allowance from the Government for entertaining, such as was given to the officers of all other navies—the "table money" of the English admiral was equal to the whole pay of our admiral; but we had it to do, and we did it handsomely. We established Thursday as our reception day, and our dances were attended and enjoyed by guests from every country in Europe, as well as a great many Americans.

Monaco[20] was only half an hour away by rail, and many of us lost what little money we could spare at this fascinating gambling resort. I always secured a return ticket and reserved a few francs to pay the cab after my humiliating experience, when I had to wake my wife up in the middle of the night to borrow money to pay for driving me home from the station. Everything was done at Monte Carlo[21] to attract people and make them enjoy themselves. The gambling games were fairly conducted, the *cafés* were the finest in Europe, and the music the best that money could furnish. The society was mixed. Most of the people who visited the place went first to the *cafés,* then to the gambling tables, and then listened to the music. Of course, there were some who listened to the music for the love of music, but most of those whom I observed looked as if they wished they had not come. I often felt that way myself. The great interest to me was watching the crowd of gamblers as they lost or won. As a rule, the Americans played the best game, and took their medicine most quietly. Occasionally some foreign chap would lose his fortune, and by way of making up for it blow his brains out; but this was a rare occurrence, as the guards were very clever men, and usually detected such characters in time, and shipped them off by rail to kill themselves somewhere else.

Through the Catholic priest at Ville Franche[22] and my own servants I learned of the great suffering among the poor of the town, and made up my mind to do what I could to relieve them. They were miserably poor, and the suffering was very great. What was left over from feeding our four hundred men and thrown overboard would go a long way

20. A principality in southeastern France on the Mediterranean Seas.
21. The prominent city of Monaco, noted for its gambling casinos.
22. A port in southeastern France, east of Nice, Villefranche-sur-Mer is the principal administrative center of the Alpes Maritime district.

toward providing them with meals if the material could be utilized. I had a number of large tin cans made with proper covers, and these at meal time were placed in charge of the police of the ship, who saw to it that all scraps of bread and meat and meat bones were collected and placed therein. All the coffee and tea left over were carefully saved, and the coffee grounds as well. Our men took an active interest in the scheme as soon as they understood what was intended, and we were able to feed four or five hundred people all the winter through. The Catholic institutions on shore received our cans every evening and returned them early the next morning in time for use after breakfast, and from their contents prepared good, rich soup and plenty of coffee and tea—much stronger than the poor peasants had ever known before. When I went on shore I was kept busy returning the salutes of those who had been comforted by our charity. It was a source of great satisfaction to me to feel that I had done some good to these deserving poor people.

When the winter was over and gone, with all its gaieties, we went to cruising again. At Gibraltar we found many friends among the officers of the garrison. Among others I recall very clearly a captain of a Welsh regiment[23] who was most amusing and witty. He came off to represent his regimental mess, and was prevailed upon to remain to dinner and take potluck with us. In a moment of misplaced confidence he told how the officers of the United States storeship Ino[24] had dined with them during the civil war, and how

23. An unidentified officer of the Royal Welch Fusiliers, or—as styled in the period 1751–1881—the 23rd Regiment of Foot. Organized in 1688–89, the unit served in all of Britain's wars.
24. A double-ended, side-wheel steamer of 974 tons, a top speed of 14 knots, and nine to ten guns, the USS Ino was built by government contract with Larrabee and Allen for the hull, Globe Works, Boston, for the engines. Launched at Bath, Maine, on 20 May 1863, she was commissioned on 26 April 1864 at the Boston Navy Yard. The Ino was decommissioned on 28 July 1865.

they had all gone under the table one after another. One of them, who wore false teeth, had been put to sleep in a large, comfortable chair in the captain's room, and when the morning came there was no end of fun finding his teeth for him. I saw by the look on the faces of our fellows that the captain had sealed his fate by this story. At midnight they carried him ashore carefully, took him to his quarters, and deposited him in the identical chair where the Ino chap had lost his teeth. We saw him again after three days, when he assured us that we had done him up in proper shape. He really had a keen sense of humour.

A new survey of the harbour of Malaga[25] was wanted, so we ran up there, and Elmer, our navigator, soon had it completed. When we arrived we found a regatta arranged for the following day, in which we were asked to compete. Several twelve- and fourteen-oared Spanish boats were to race, so we entered our twelve-oared racing cutter, much to the satisfaction of the Spanish officers. They had never seen our people pull a race, and when we led their boats to the finish line by quite three minutes they never wanted to see them do it again. During our entire stay we were crowded with visitors, which was rather suprising, in view of the relations then existing between the two countries; but they came by hundreds from all directions, and represented all classes of society, from the general commanding to the common labourer with his gamecock under his arm.

On June 18, 1875, we anchored in Algiers,[26] after a pleasant run from Gibraltar under sail. I enjoyed here seeing a balloon ascension, the most successful one I ever witnessed. The balloon had been used in the siege of Paris,[27] and after-

25. A city in southern Spain, northeast of Gibraltar.
26. The capital of Algeria on the Bay of Algiers, an arm of the Mediterranean Sea.
27. The siege of Paris took place from 19 September 1870 through 26 January 1871, during the Franco-Prussian War. German forces were led by Helmuth von Moltke. The French provisional President, Léon Gam-

ward in the Carlist war in Spain,[28] where it was captured,
and the occupants only escaped being shot as spies by the
earnest interference of the French minister. On this occasion
everything worked perfectly, and the party, after sailing out
over the harbour, at a height of about two miles, descended
until they struck a current of air setting toward the land,
when they rapidly disappeared behind a mountain ten or
twelve miles away.

Tunis[29] was our next port, and we anchored there on July
1st. The American consul, Mr. Heap,[30] lived with his
charming family about six miles out of town toward the ruins
of Carthage;[31] and here, after the official visit had been made,
we found a most cordial welcome. Our country was ably represented at this point at least, and I could see the respect in
which our consul was held by all classes.

The Bey of Tunis had expressed a desire, after visiting the
Congress, to see the effect of the fire of one of our Gatling
guns, and requested that we land one and give him an exhibition drill. The captain directed me to take the matter in
hand and make the necessary arrangements, which I did on
July 3d.

I had a small-arm target anchored at a point six hundred
yards from the shore in front of the palace, so that the ladies
of the harem could see the firing, and when everything was

---

betta, escaped from the capital by balloon and organized a nationwide
resistance from Tours.

28. Evans refers here to the renewal of the earlier 1834–39 civil war, or
revolution, led by Don Carlos, brother of King Ferdinand, 1873–76.
This was a particularly brutal civil war against Isabella, with her son
Alphonso XII placed on the throne in 1874 as a compromise.

29. A former Barbary state and seaport of Tunisia, on the north coast of
Africa. The ruler of Tunis circa 1875–76 was Mohamed es Sadok Bey
(1859–82).

30. G.H. Heap was commissioned consul to Tunis on 14 March 1867.

31. An ancient city and state on the north coast of Africa on the Bay of
Tunis, northeast of modern Tunis.

ready, landed the gun with its detachment and quickly went into action. I fired six hundred shots, and in the smoke, before any one could see us, dismounted the gun and placed it and the crew behind a stone wall. When the smoke cleared away there was neither gun nor man in sight. The firing took one minute, and in order to show the Bey the effect, the target was towed in, and he counted fire hundred and thirty hits on it. He was rather stupefied at first, but later on complimented me on the drill of the men and the accuracy of the fire. After I had explained to him fully the working of the gun in all its parts, he directed his secretary to order a battery of six of them, which was done.

The numerous old wells at the ruins of Carthage contained great numbers of bullfrogs of an enormous size, and as I was fond of frogs' legs I started in a boat to try my luck on them. Fortunately, I took for the trip a very able whaleboat, the one we had used on the west coast of Africa. When we were about four miles from the ship we were caught in a sudden furious gale of wind. For two hours we fought hard for our lives, and when we finally reached the ship we were all pretty well used up and of course as wet as rats, and had no frogs to show for our trouble. A great sea was running all about the ship, and it required my best efforts to save the boat and get the men on board without losing some of them. We celebrated the Fourth of July properly at Tunis, and in the evening got under way for Malta.[32]

This key to the Suez Canal had been fortified by the English until one could fairly say that it was impregnable. It was always strongly garrisoned, and the headquarters of the fine Mediterranean squadron. Our arrival was the signal for a round of dinners and luncheons that lasted almost to the hour of our departure. I met, on this occasion, one of the

32. An island that lies in the Mediterranean Sea, south of Sicily.

most interesting men I have ever known—Colonel de la Fosse,[33] of the One Hundred and First Regiment, English army. He was a fine, brave old soldier, full of patriotism and love for his Queen. He had been in Cawnpore[34] at the time of the Indian Mutiny,[35] and was one of the half-dozen officers who succeeded in cutting his way out. We spent many hours together, and I listened while he modestly recounted his experiences. We left this celebrated port and hospitable garrison with real regret, hoping that it would be our good fortune to visit them again.

After leaving Malta we called in at Tripoli.[36] We had orders from Washington to collect such articles as might prove of interest to the Centennial Exposition[37] to be opened

33. Henry George de la Fosse of the Royal Bengal Fusiliers entered the British Army as an ensign in 1854. He served as an artillery lieutenant and throughout the Great Mutiny of 1857–58, being nominated for the Victoria Cross. He served in the Northwest Frontier War of 1863, and was mentioned in dispatches. He became colonel in 1877, went on half pay in 1880, and later commanded the Regimental District of the King's Own Borderers in 1881.
34. A city in northern India on the Ganges River, southeast of New Delhi.
35. The Great Mutiny of 1857–58 occurred among the native armies of the East India Company, which ran the colony. It was brought on by the introduction of the Minie rifle cartridge, which had to be bitten while loading. The cartridge was greased with animal fat, considered unclean by both Hindus and Moslems. Large numbers of British military and civilians died before the mutiny was quashed and the government of India transferred to the British crown.
36. A port in modern Libya on the coast of North Africa. The powerful Pasha of Tripoli effectively controlled commerce in his region in the late-eighteenth and early-nineteenth century, causing American ships to pay tribute before a series of naval expeditions forced him to sign a peace treaty with the United States in 1805.
37. The Philadelphia Centennial Exposition was held in Fairmount Park to commemorate the one-hundredth anniversary of the Declaration of Independence. This gala of glamorous exhibits and celebrations symbolized the Gilded Age in America.

at Philadelphia in the following year. The frigate Philadelphia[38] had been burned by Decatur[39] in this harbour, after falling into the hands of the Moors,[40] and I knew that a piece of her wreck would be considered of interest. I therefore fitted a launch with proper grapnels and tackle, and after a long search located the wreck and was fortunate enough to secure part of a petrified timber which had been charred through. Many of the iron spikes by which the planking had been secured still remained in the piece, and it was curious to note the effect of heat and their long immersion in salt water. They were much softer than when first driven—in fact, were almost like soft lead. I secured one of them and afterward had a set of jewelry made from it for my wife by a jeweller in Geneva. The trinkets were beautifully finished and perfectly burnished, but no amount of care would prevent them from rusting; the moisture seemed to exude from the inside of the metal. The piece of timber was boxed and sent to the Exposition, where I afterward saw it, and it was regarded as an object of much interest.

Upon our arrival at Corfu[41] we were thrown into a state of considerable excitement by the receipt of news that

38. A thirty-six-gun American frigate captured by Barbary pirates on 31 October 1803 in Tripoli's harbor, the USS *Philadelphia* later burned in a daring foray by Lieutenant Stephen Decatur on 4 February 1804.

39. Stephen Decatur was warranted a midshipman on 30 April 1798, and became famous for his daring destruction of the captured U.S. frigate *Philadelphia* in Tripoli Harbor in February 1804. For this action he was promoted to the rank of captain at age twenty-five. During the War of 1812, Decatur commanded the frigate *United States* in her successful action with HMS *Macedonian*. He was mortally wounded in a duel with Commodore James Barron in March 1820.

40. The people of Morocco (Berbers) usually associated with the eighth-century invasion of the Iberian peninsula.

41. One of the Ionian Islands of Greece, situated off the northwest coast of the mainland.

the American consul at Tripoli[42] had been insulted by the
Pasha, or some of his people, and that we were to be sent
there to demand and exact proper reparation. We had lately
been at that port and, having in view the nature of the defenses, wondered how one wooden ship could do much
against them. However, the orders came, and we left at once
to carry them out. When we arrived off the town we found
all hands much excited, and there was great marching and
countermarching of troops about the batteries and through
the streets. An officer was sent on shore to communicate with
the consul, and when his boat approached the landing place
the crowd jeered and spat at him. He promptly returned to
the ship and reported the affair to the captain, who sent a
company of marines and a Gatling gun in to prevent a possibility of trouble. The officer landed without molestation and
soon had the consul on board. The Pasha, having heard of
the conduct of the mob toward our boat, hurried to make
ample apology, which was accepted, and the insult to the
consul was then taken up. He had reported the matter to
the State Department, and our orders from Washington were
positive. We were not to investigate anything, but to demand and exact ample reparation for what had taken place.
The consul insisted that he had been grossly insulted, and
his premises invaded by armed Turkish sailors. The Pasha
insisted that a thorough investigation showed that there had
been no insult to him, but, on the contrary, the consul had
attacked or assaulted a Turkish sailor, and it was only out of
consideration for our Government that he was not fined and
locked up.

Our captain cut the discussion short by stating what his
orders were, and that immediate apology on the part of the
Pasha would prevent serious trouble; to which the Pasha replied by manning his batteries, and stating that he had done

42. Commissioned on 15 August 1876, Cuthbert B. Jones served as
consul to Tripoli.

nothing to apologise for, and that the Sultan would cut his head off if he did it. At this stage of the game we cleared for action; swung our ship around so that the broadside would bear on the town, and sent word to his Excellency that if at the end of four hours we had not received his favourable answer we should open fire on the batteries. Within an hour after this ultimatum was delivered the United States steamer Hartford,[43] on her way home from China, came in, anchored near us, and cleared for action. The Pasha, thinking probably that the entire American navy was coming, decided that he would apologize at noon the next day. An officer of rank was detailed to witness the ceremony, which took place at the American consulate. The Pasha, a very dignified gentleman, did the proper thing in every way, said that he ate dirt in the presence of the offended person, and used many other figures of speech. The consul, a gentleman from the far South and not of a forgiving turn of mind, demanded that the dirt should be actually eaten, but our officer put an end to the business, brought the consul and his family on board for safe-keeping, and we sailed for Corfu, the orders of the State Department having been carried out to the letter. Those of us who knew the real facts in the case were not very proud of the whole performance. The consul was living on the sea-shore, some distance from town, when the Turkish fleet arrived and sent boats in to obtain water. One of the sailors ventured into the kitchen of the residence to obtain a light for his cigarette, where the consul found him, and, having boxed his ears soundly, kicked him out of the inclosure. The other sailors sat on a stone wall and jeered at the consul, who made complaint that the law relating to harems had been violated by this intrusion of the sailor, and hence the deadly insult. This was all there really was to it.

43. A wooden screw-sloop of 2,900 tons, a top speed of 9.5 knots, and twenty-four to twenty-seven guns, the USS *Hartford* was acquired by the government for $502,650.16. Launched on 22 November 1858, the ves-

Upon arriving at Corfu again I was granted a short leave, which I spent with my family in Switzerland. When my leave was up I rejoined my ship at Naples, spending one day and night in Rome on my way there. This trip from Geneva to Naples will always remain in my mind as a horror. The weather was very hot, the cars very dirty, and the customs officers, on the various frontiers I crossed, very officious and trying; but Naples was the same fascinating place. We joined the flagship at Villefranche to have our semi-annual inspection, which was somewhat overdue, and also to submit casually to the "bossing" which flagships always have in store for every one except the flagship. We got through our inspection very creditably, and immediately sailed for Leghorn,[44] where we were to have our decks calked and do some trifling repairs. After dropping both our bower anchors in the stream, we warped our stern in and made fast to the breakwater, in order that we might not take up room in swinging, and also as security against the gales, which at times blew with great fury and did no end of damage. The breakwater was of stone, fifty-seven feet high, and most solidly built.

The gale I had been looking for came at a most convenient time; the captain and his family had gone to Rome, and the calkers had nearly completed their work, when, without much warning, it struck us with hurricane force. I naturally thought that, secured as we were behind the breakwater, we were perfectly safe; but such was not the case. One of our chain sternfasts crushed the iron pipe through which it passed, and in a few seconds ripped a hole in the side of the ship five feet long. This warning was instantly heeded, and in a short time our lower yards and topmasts were on deck, which left only the upper parts of our lower masts above the

---

sel served as Admiral David Farragut's flagship at the battles of New Orleans and Mobile Bay.

44. City of northwestern Italy on the Ligurian Sea, west-southwest of Florence.

breakwater to catch the wind. At the same time our two heavy sheet anchors, which stowed well aft in the waist, were let go and the chains hove taut, which prevented the ship from forging ahead quickly and bringing up on her fasts with a jerk. When all this had been done we found ourselves very comfortable, but in a little while a new danger threatened us: the sea, which rose rapidly as the gale increased, began breaking over the top of the breakwater, and tons of water came pounding down on our decks. In face of this I could only batten the hatches down to keep the water from getting below, and grin and bear it until the gale blew out. It was an annoyance rather than a serious danger. It we had broken loose from the breakwater we would certainly have sunk six vessels as we swung to our anchors, not to mention the prob- able damage to the Congress. The idea of changing our berth was out of the question; we could only hold on to the one we had with all our might.

After the gale had blown itself out, which it did in three days, the fishermen came back in large numbers and began fishing off the sea face of the breakwater, where the loose stone foundation, or riprap, attracted the fish in large num- bers. I had given notice that I would pay a small sum for an octopus, the larger the better, as I thought I might be able to keep it alive until I could send it to Philadelphia. A few days after the gale I heard great shouting on the breakwater, and one of the men came to me with the information that my octopus was caught, or rather *he* had caught two fishing boats and half a dozen fishermen. He made things pretty lively for all hands at first, but some one succeeded in getting a rope around his neck, and by choking him nearly to death we eventually captured him and took him into a large tub, which he filled to the top, and where he seemed satisfied. When the tub was suddenly flooded he would instantly dye the water as black as ink and so hide himself. I found, to my regret, that the rope about his neck had fatally injured him, and he died after I had observed him for three or four days.

His tentacles were as large as a man's arm and ten or twelve feet long. Each one was covered on the lower side with suckers, ranging in size from the body, where they were as large as a silver dollar, to the end of the tentacle, where they were smaller than a ten-cent piece. After he was apparently dead, if I struck my fingers quickly across one of the suckers, it would catch me every time. When he was alive and free to move in the water he could have drowned a man, or indeed several men at the same time, in a very few minutes. I was surprised to find later that the small octopus was largely used for food.

When our repairs had been completed we returned to our winter quarters at Nice. Here we prepared to spend the winter much as we had spent the last one, but the Navy Department had other work for us, and late in November orders came for us to proceed, without delay, to Port Royal, South Carolina, and report our arrival. A few days only were necessary for our preparations and we were off, leaving a forlorn lot of women bravely waving farewells from the docks. Our captain was fortunate enough to be allowed to bring the ladies of his family home with him in the Congress, but the bitter attacks of certain newspapers had had their effect, and the day of the "family ships" was over for all time in our service. The station at Ville Franche was also broken up, and the ships sent cruising in various directions.

As we ran down to Gibraltar for our final coaling the Gulf of Lyons took a last shot at us in the shape of a gale of wind, which blew viciously for two days and then let go. When it was over we drank champagne as well as water out of teacups, for we had rolled pretty much everything loose, and broke all the crockery the mess owned. Two days were spent in coaling at Gibraltar, and I said good-bye to the Mediterranean for some years to come. We left many good friends behind us, and everywhere a record that was a credit to the country we had tried our best to properly represent.

On the run to Madeira the superstitious feelings of our

men, and indeed some of the officers, were much excited by a curious incident. We were under sail and the moon shining brightly, when, for some reason, it became necessary to shorten sail. When the topgallant sails were clewed up there stood a man on the fore-topgallant yard clearly outlined against the flapping canvas of the fore royal. The officer of the deck hailed the officer of the forecastle to know what that man was doing aloft, and was assured in reply that the men were all on deck. But there stood the man in plain sight in the moonlight. The officer then hailed him, but could get no answer. Finally he sent a man aloft to tell the chap, whoever he was, to come down at once and report on the quarter-deck. All hands were by this time much excited, and waited anxiously to see what would happen. Just as the man who had been sent from the deck reached the foretop, the figure on the yard disappeared, as if he had fallen overboard. The watch was mustered and all hands were found to be present. After this sleep was out of the question; the men stood about in groups, watching the fore-topgallant yard, waiting to see the figure reappear, many of them too frightened to reason, and all of them expecting some awful disaster to befall the ship. On the following night, when the moon was about in the same relative position to the ship, the sails were again clewed up, and after changing the course slowly a few times, there was the man again standing in the same position on the yard. The mystery was solved: a shadow from some of the canvas on the mainmast was responsible for the ghost.

Another of our ships had had a very curious ghost experience while cruising in the Mediterranean, which is well worth recording. At about midnight, when over a hundred miles from land and while everything was perfectly quiet about the deck, the sound of a tolling bell was distinctly heard. It could be plainly heard by the officer of the deck as well as the men, and it continued for several minutes. To the crew it sounded like a funeral bell, and they decided that some one was going to die. With much difficulty the men were finally sent to their hammocks and ordered to keep silence. The next morning the story was all over the ship, from the forecastle to the officers' messes. When night came again many had forgotten the incident, but at about the same hour the tolling of the bell was again distinctly heard, and the whole crew gathered on deck to listen in superstitious silence. The officers were much puzzled, and many theories were advanced to account for the strange and unusual noise. The third night found captain and all hands, officers and men, on deck, determined if possible to find a solution of the mystery. At the proper time the sound of the bell came clear and distinct, tolling as if for a funeral. The captain and several of the officers then began a careful investigation, which soon cleared the matter up. The galley of the ship, where the cooking was done, was under the topgallant forecastle, about twenty feet from the ship's bell. The fires in the galley were put out at nine o'clock, and it was found that at a certain point in the process of cooling the contracting of the metal in the galley made it give out a cracking noise which accorded with certain tones in the bell and caused it to ring. The very puzzling ghost story was solved, and the men went to their hammocks, many of them still shaking their heads and predicting that there was trouble in store for somebody.

From Madeira we literally rolled our way across the Atlantic. After coaling at St. Thomas, we reached Port Royal, where we found a few old monitors and one or two small vessels, all in ignorance of the reasons for assembling a fleet at that point, the orders for which had been issued. Captain English was to be the senior officer for a time, and it turned out later that we were assembled for the purpose of drilling the men. It was recognized on all hands that our ships were rapidly deteriorating, and Congress did not seem disposed to give us any new ones. It was the beginning of that long period of neglect of the navy by Congress that made officers' hearts ache. All we could do was to keep the men in good shape, which we certainly did, and hope that a change would come to our rulers.

Admiral LeRoy[45] arrived in February, and took command of the squadron, which consisted at that time of ten or twelve ships. We had been drilling steadily all that time, but now the work was vastly increased. Owing to the length of time we had been in commission and the careful training the men had received, we easily led all the ships except the Brooklyn. She had been flagship of the Brazil squadron, and showed the effect of careful, painstaking work. It required our best efforts to keep even with her. There was much talk of a racing cutter she carried that had beaten everything in the South, and when she challenged us for a five-mile race our chances of winning were considered very poor. Our crew was in excellent shape, but our boat was not as good as the Brooklyn's, which did not prevent our men from betting all the money they had on the result. When the stakeboat was reached, our boat was just two lengths behind, a part of which they made up on the turn; and in the pull in, two miles and a half against a strong tide and stiff wind, they passed the Brooklyn's boat and won at the finish by forty-nine seconds. It was one of the hardest races I ever saw pulled, and condition told, as it always will, in such a contest.

45. William E. LeRoy was warranted a midshipman on 11 January 1832. He rose to the rank of captain on 25 July 1866, commodore on 3 July 1879, and rear admiral on 5 April 1874. Having retired on 24 March 1880, he died on 10 December 1888.

CHAPTER 18

The Centennial and Training-Ship Duty

As the result of an inspection held at Port Royal by one of the bureau chiefs of the Navy Department, the Congress was selected to represent the navy at Philadelphia during the Centennial, and we found ourselves moored off the foot of Arch Street[1] early in May.

The part played by the Congress in the Centennial of 1876 was most creditable to the navy, and very expensive, though gratifying, to her officers. She represented the navy, and was seen and admired by thousands of Americans from all parts of the country. The opening day I landed in command of the crew, who, with a detachment of marines, were the only United States forces in the parade, and therefore held the right of the line. After marching fifteen miles, much of the way in mud halfway to our knees, we were placed in position to receive the President and his party when they had formally opened the Exposition. I waited in the broiling sun nearly

1. Arch Street is near Penn's Landing and Philadelphia's wharves. The USS *Olympia* (a last vestige of the Evans-era navy) lies berthed nearby as a historic shrine.

two hours after the time set, when I was informed that the crowd had walked over the militia and surrounded the President, so that it was not possible to move him. I marched my men through the crowd, extricated the Boston cadets[2] from a very unpleasant position, where they had been placed to do police duty—to which they should never have been assigned since they were visitors—and soon had things moving again. After one of the hardest days I ever knew we returned to the ship, and without a single man straggling or showing the effect of drink, and all because they had pride in their ship and their service.

We remained at Philadelphia until late in July, when we were ordered to Portsmouth, New Hampshire, to pay off and go out of commission. Before sailing, however, the Board of Inspection put us through our paces, and the following letter shows how well we performed. It was written to Admiral Porter, and signed by Commodore John Guest,[3] senior officer of the board:

"PHILADELPHIA, *July 8, 1876.*

"Sir: The board has inspected the U.S.S. Congress this day.

"It is not enough to say that she is in good order in all her departments and an efficient man-of-war. The whole organization and condition is as near perfection as our system will admit. She is admirable.

"To Captain Earl English and his executive officer, Lieutenant-Commander R.D. Evans, great praise is due for the handsome and creditable specimen of the American navy which they have exhibited here at this Centennial period. The board has taken great pride and pleasure in observing the condition of this ship."

2. The famous First Corps of Cadets of Boston, Massachusetts.
3. John Guest began his naval career as a midshipman on 16 December 1837. He was promoted to commander on 16 July 1862, captain on 25 July 1866, and commodore on 12 December 1872. Guest died on 12 January 1879.

This letter was in addition to the regular inspection report, which did not contain a single unsatisfactory answer in the long list of questions. I mention this as a tribute to the officers and men who made up the splendid crew of the Congress.

When we reached Portsmouth and were ready to haul down the flag over what had been such a happy home to us all, I was shocked at the number of boarding-house sharks that flocked about the ship, ready to relieve the men of all their belongings. I made up my mind to "do" those same sharks, if I could; and I did. I arranged for a special train to run through to New York and Philadelphia, which backed into the navy yard, and when the pennant came down the whole crew, with their bags and hammocks, marched into it instead of the boats which were waiting to land them in the rum mills. I went through on the train myself, and when I saw the men land clean and sober near their homes it gave me a very lasting thrill of pleasure.

After the Congress I enjoyed two months' leave, getting acquainted with my family again. I was then ordered to signal duty in the Navy Department in Washington, where, with the able assistance of Lieutenant Maxwell Wood,[4] I developed and patented a signal lamp for long-distance signalling, which performed its functions very satisfactorily. When winter came, however, I found myself looking about for a ship, and, owing to the good reports about the Congress, I was ordered to command the training-ship Saratoga,[5] one of the old sailing sloops of war. She had been lying in reserve

---

4. William Maxwell Wood was warranted a midshipman on 20 July 1865, and rose to the rank of lieutenant on 11 December 1877. He died on 16 December 1897.

5. A wooden sailing sloop of 882 tons, a top speed of 8 knots and twenty-two guns, the USS *Saratoga* was built by the government at Kittery, Maine, whence she was launched on 26 July 1842. She was commissioned twice—5 November 1860 and 24 June 1863—at the Philadelphia Navy Yard for the African Squadron and South Atlantic Station, respectively.

as a gunnery ship at Annapolis, and required a complete overhauling and refitting, which we gave her at the Washington yard. In the spring I sailed in her, and for four years commanded her, doing the pleasantest duty that has fallen to me in peace times during my naval career.

My duty was to enlist American-born boys between the ages of fifteen and eighteen years, and drill and educate them for the naval service—not to serve as officers, but as enlisted men, to man the ships and fight the guns. The first crew I enlisted came from the section of country about Washington and Baltimore, and a fine, hardy lot they were. The pleasure of watching them grow up and develop into strong, self-supporting men was very great. One unforeseen trouble met me from the start. I could not hold the boys back. They would learn more than was required of the ordinary deck hand, and during the first year of my command I placed quite a dozen of them on merchant vessels as mates. I finally concluded that I had gone too high in the social scale for the material to start with, and, though I was doing a splendid work, I was not getting the men we wanted. Then I tried what is called the "gutter snipe," and there I found just what I was looking for. When caught at the right age, and then properly educated and treated, the boy of this class made his home in the navy, and was willing to spend his life there.

During my four years in command of the Saratoga I had many interesting experiences. I enlisted boys from all parts of the country, and necessarily saw the conditions surrounding the lives of the poorer classes in many different cities. After one trip to Boston, where I enlisted several hundred boys, I was satisfied that education, or rather over-education, was doing great harm in New England. Book schools were not doing what industrial schools would have accomplished. Because a tailor or a shoemaker had been President, every tailor's and shoemaker's son was being educated to fill that high office, and the result was bad—in many cases very bad. Over-training of any kind is not good, and I found mental over-training the worst of all. My experience—and I had plenty of it—was the same over and over again. Each morning when I went to my office at the navy-yard gate I found a long line of fairly well-dressed boys with very shabbily dressed parents. In every case the boy had spent his life at school, winding up in many instances in the high school, and after that finding nothing to do. The parents were striving hard and stinting themselves that the boys might appear well and dress like gentlemen, while the lads were growing more and more ashamed of their surroundings and their honest fathers and mothers, who had been and are to-day the bone and sinew of this great republic. To save them from pool rooms and worse, they begged me to enlist them as apprentices in the navy and begin anew their educations. I almost had it in my heart to wish that every high school in Boston would burn to the ground, and that every boy and every girl should be taught to work with their hands and make a living, as their honest parents had done before them.

While commanding the Saratoga I crossed the Atlantic four times in her, each time with a crew composed in most part of boys. On one trip I ran a line of soundings from Cape Hatteras to Horta, in the island of Fayal,[6] and thence over some supposed shoals to the southward of that island, and then to the coast of Africa. This duty was wonderfully interesting, particularly when, after two hours' hard work, I was rewarded by holding in my hand a specimen of the bottom, which had been hauled up in some cases through over two miles of water. The microscope showed beautiful lacelike shells, which I afterward found extended in a belt from Petersburg, Virginia, to the vicinity of the Western Islands, where they became covered with volcanic ooze. On this trip

6. The westernmost island of the Azores in the north Atlantic.

I had with me Mr. F.B. McGuire,[7] of Washington, who acted as agent of the Smithsonian Institution, and made a large and very valuable collection of fishes, which was highly valued by Professor Baird[8] and his associates. Upon my return I was able to make a good report of work done, not only in the way of training boys, but upon deep-sea soundings and the food fishes of the Western Islands.

I had expected to have many accidents among the green boys, from the constant drills aloft with spars and sails; but when my time was up a careful examination showed that I had no fatal accident, and only a very few serious ones. The rivalry among the boys was very great, and once I had the whole crew betting as to which one of two boys could beat the other over the royal yard. To decide the question I started

7. Frederick B. McGuire appears in the 1860 Washington, D.C., directory as an employee of James C. McGuire and Co., commercial merchants at 10th and D streets, N.W. He resided at 445 E Street, N.W. (according to the old numbering system). He is listed in the 1872 edition as a real estate agent and auctioneer with an office at 1306 F Street, N.W. He resided at 614 E Street, N.W. (according to the new numbering system). In 1890 McGuire was vice president of Columbia Fire Insurance Co., living at 1333 Connecticut Avenue, N.W. In 1894 he was president of the company, and from 1905–19 he served as director of the Corcoran Gallery of Art.

8. Spencer Baird (1823–88) was a zoologist who graduated from Dickinson College, in Carlisle, Pennsylvania, and became a professor of Natural History there in 1846. He moved to the Smithsonian Institution in 1850 as assistant secretary to the venerable physicist Joseph Henry. Baird succeeded Henry as secretary of the institution in 1878. He constructed a network of acquisition agencies in order to build the Smithsonian into a great museum. The center of his work was ethnology, as well as zoology and botany. An ornithologist who wrote prolifically on birds, his career with the United States Commission of Fish and Fisheries dated from 1871, and he became involved in all forms of ichthyological knowledge and fish protection. Robust in statue, indefatigable in his professional work, Baird ranks as one of the ablest teachers and administrators in the realm of natural history.

The Saratoga

them aloft one evening just before sundown, as we were fanning along under full sail before a light breeze on the edge of the Gulf Stream. They were both as active as cats, and went aloft very rapidly, but one, in passing the maintop, unfortunately lost his grip on the rigging and pitched over backward. I was standing on the deck watching them, and as the lad fell, I distinctly heard his head strike the projecting muzzle of a gun, and I supposed he was instantly killed. One of the officers whipped off his coat, and was in the act of jumping overboard to his rescue when the boy called out that he was all right. In a few minutes he came up over the stern, having caught one of the trailing life lines, and was apparently none the worse for his ducking; but the moment he saw the blood which was streaming from a wound in his head he fainted dead away. His scalp was pretty well torn from one side of his head, but in a few days he was running aloft again as smartly as ever.

On one of my trips I ran up the Mediterranean as far as Naples, and on my way back fell in with the English fleet, commanded by Admiral Sir Beauchamp Seymour,[9] who afterward bombarded Alexandria.[10] We were all anchored together for ten days at Ville Franche, and my sailing ship was closely watched by the captains of the splendid ironclads. The work of my boys pleased them greatly, and the admiral paid us many compliments on the smartness of our drills. Captain George Tryon[11] commanded the Mon-

9. Sir Frederick Beauchamp Paget Seymour was promoted to the rank of rear admiral in 1870 and vice admiral in 1876.
10. A city in northern Egypt on the Mediterranean Sea.
11. Sir George Tryon (1832–93) entered the Royal Navy in 1848 and served in the Crimea on board the royal yacht. He commanded HMS *Warrior* of the Channel Fleet in 1861, the first British seagoing ironclad. Rising rapidly in the service through command of HMS *Raleigh* and HMS *Monarch*, he also assisted in revising the Royal Navy's signal book. Tryon served as secretary to the Admiralty from 1882 to 1884. Appointed rear admiral in 1884, he commanded the Australian station and helped formulate colonial defense there. He received the Knight Commander of the

arch,[12] and he and I had so much in common over our shooting and fishing yarns that we formed a friendship which continued until he found his grave in the unfortunate Victoria.[13]
I always regarded him as one of the best of our cloth, and a
great credit to the British navy. In the same fleet was a jolly
young lieutenant, Hedwith Lambton,[14] who afterward performed such gallant service in South Africa. I knew him
again in Chili when I commanded the Yorktown[15] and he
the Warspite.[16] Our acquaintance ripened into a warm
friendship, which I value very highly. Among other com-

Bath in 1887 and was named vice admiral two years later. Tryon commanded the Mediterranean station in 1891, and was lost two years later
when HMS *Victoria* collided with HMS *Camperdown*—a result of his error—off Tripoli.

12. A steam and sail steel-masted turret ship of 8,322 tons, seven guns,
a top speed of 15 knots and a 575-man complement, HMS *Monarch* was
laid down at Chatham Dockyard on 1 June 1866, launched on 25 May
1868, and completed on 12 June 1869. Broken up and sold in 1905, the
Monarch had been the first seagoing turret ship and first warship to carry
12-inch guns.

13. HMS *Victoria* was a steel turret ship with a top speed of 17 knots, a
standard displacement of 10,470 tons, a battery of thirty-six guns, four
torpedo tubes, and two torpedo-launching carriages, and a complement
of 550 men. Laid down on 23 April 1885 and launched on 9 April 1887,
she was completed in March 1890. First of her class, *Victoria* served as
the flagship of the Mediterranean Fleet. She sank on 22 June 1893 during
maneuvers as a result of a collision with HMS *Camperdown*.

14. Sir Hedworth Lambton was promoted as follows: captain in 1889;
rear admiral in 1902; vice admiral in 1907; and admiral in 1911.

15. A steel and steam patrol gunboat of 1,710 tons, eight guns, and a
top speed of 16 knots, the USS *Yorktown* was constructed at Cramp &
Sons Shipyard in Philadelphia. She was laid down on 14 May 1887,
launched on 28 April 1888, completed on 23 April 1889, and sold in
1921.

16. HMS *Warspite* was a steel and steam armored cruiser of 8,500 tons,
a top speed of 17.75 knots, a battery of eighteen guns and six torpedoes,
and a 555-man complement. She was laid down at Chatham Dockyards
on 25 October 1881, launched on 29 January 1884, completed in June
1888 and sold on 4 April 1905.

manding officers of Admiral Seymour's fleet I was glad to meet Captain Freemantle,[17] of the Invincible,[18] who had recently performed an act that did him great credit. He was on the bridge of his ship when one of his men fell from aloft and struck the water with such force that he was disabled and rapidly sinking. Without a moment's hesitation, and with all his clothing on, the captain sprang into the sea, made a long dive, brought the disabled man to the surface, and saved his life.

My pleasure was much enhanced during my last cruise in the Saratoga by having on board, as my guests, three officers of our army, Colonel Warner[19] and Majors Randolph[20] and Taylor,[21] of the artillery. They saw much to interest them in the various ports we visited, and were lavishly entertained at the different garrisoned towns. The following extract from my journal will give an idea of what our life was in port:

17. Sir Edmund Robert Fremantle attained the following ranks: captain in 1867; rear admiral in 1885; vice admiral in 1895; and admiral in 1896.
18. HMS *Invincible* was a second-class, central-battery ironclad of circa 6,000 tons, twenty guns and a 450-man complement. Intended for service on foreign station, she took part in the famous bombardment of Alexandria in 1882.
19. Edward Raynsford Warner served as a captain with the 3d Artillery; a major with the 1st Artillery; and a Civil War volunteer officer. He retired in 1887.
20. Wallace F. Randolph was a major in the 3d Artillery; a Civil War and Spanish-American War officer; and chief of artillery from 1901 to 1903, with the rank of brigadier general.
21. It is unclear if this was Asher Clayton Taylor, a lieutenant in the 2d Artillery, and Civil War veteran of service with the 3d Wisconsin Volunteer Infantry, in which he advanced from corporal to 1st lieutenant. He reentered the regular service as a 2d lieutenant with the 15th Infantry in 1867 before being reassigned to the 2d Artillery in 1871. Taylor graduated from Artillery School in 1876, and was promoted to lieutenant colonel of the Artillery Corps in 1902. Or it may have been Sydney Wentworth Taylor, a lieutenant in the 4th Artillery—promoted to major in 1901—who was cited for gallantry in the Modoc War of 1873.

"Of course, beating a sailing ship through the straits is no fun, and even dangerous at night, owing to the number of steamers running through, and the danger of collision; but we had a fair night, and of course I had to be on deck all the time. As I had not had my clothes off since four o'clock Monday morning, I required numerous cups of coffee to keep my eyes open.

"Mr. Sprague,[22] the consul, came on board at ten o'clock, and at noon we all started in full feather to call on the officials. We found Lord Napier[23] of Magdala most polite and agreeable and thoroughly interested in America, and a great Grant man. After our call on him, we paid our respects to the naval authorities and the officers of one of the regiments, and when we came home found an invitation from the consul to dine with him; also a notice that an English officer would show us through all the galleries at 10 A.M. to-morrow. While we were at dinner two cards came from Lord and Lady Napier of Magdala, one for an 'At Home' for to-day, the other a formal invitation for dinner on Thursday. We also had an invitation from the mess of the Forty-sixth Regiment[24] for Friday, all of which we have accepted. We have our hands full.

22. Horatio J. Sprague was consul at Gibraltar from 12 May 1848 to 18 July 1901.

23. Sir Robert Cornelius Napier, 1st baron of Magdala (1810–90), was a British field marshal. After distinguished service in the Indian Mutiny, 1857–58, he commanded the British Army in the Abyssinian War of 1867–68, which culminated in the capture of Magdala, the capital of Abyssinia.

24. Originally the 57th Regiment of Foot upon its formation in 1741, it was renumbered the 46th (South Devonshire) Regiment of Foot in 1748. In 1881 it became linked with the 32d, or Cornwall Regiment, Light Infantry, to form the Duke of Cornwall's Light Infantry. Nicknamed "Murray's Bucks," "The Surprisers," "The Lacedemonians," and "The Red Feathers," the regiment saw action in North America, the Caribbean, and the Crimea. Transferred to Gibraltar from Bermuda in 1881, the unit remained there until July 1882.

"*Gibraltar, 12th June.*—Wednesday we had a delightful dinner with the consul, after having visited all the galleries and the signal station on the top of the rock.

"Thursday we dined with Lord and Lady Napier. No end of style. The ladies were all charming, after the fashion of English women. The gentlemen left the table with the ladies, and did not return to their wine, which is a new fashion brought here by Lord Napier from India. It has many good points, I think, but the English do not fancy it much.

"Yesterday we went through the town, made some purchases, and in the evening dined with the Forty-sixth Regiment—and a most delightful dinner we had—returning to the ship at midnight. I like the way these English regiments hold on to their traditions. The Forty-sixth during our War for Independence were in America, and on account of some bad conduct of their men our general issued an order that no quarter should be shown to them; that any one of them caught should be at once executed. The colonel of the Forty-sixth thereupon had a red pompon placed in the hats of his officers and men as a part of their uniform, and sent word to our man that they were the only people in the British service who wore red pompon, and he could with safety execute any one found with it on. The pompon can be seen in the crest of the regiment, and they are having just now a bitter fight about it. When the Forty-sixth came here, Lord Napier noticed the red on their hats and could find no order permitting it, so he directed its removal; but the colonel and officers have petitioned the Queen to allow them to use it. After dinner they showed us the Bible on which General Washington was made a Mason.[25] One of our army officers offered a

25. Masonic historians have puzzled over this story of George Washington's Bible for some time. Irrefutable documents in the possession of Fredericksburg Lodge Number 4, in Fredericksburg, Virginia, show that Washington became a Freemason on 2 November 1752 at the age of twenty. That lodge possesses the Bible. The 46th Regiment, to which a Canadian lodge was attached, has perpetuated the claim alluded to in the

thousand guineas for it, but the colonel replied that they had
already refused forty thousand dollars for it. It was once captured by our people and returned to the regiment; and the
French got it twice, but each time sent it back.

"*Sunday*, P.M.—We have been up to our eyes in Englishmen. Yesterday morning we were engaged to breakfast
with the Forty-sixth. Our breakfast was an entire success,
and when we went to the range our friends of the Forty-sixth
met with a most crushing defeat. After we had beat them
with our own gun we took theirs—the Martini-Henry[26]—
and beat their best score. About four in the afternoon Colonel
Bennett[27] turned out his regiment and gave us a drill which
was beautiful to see. We got back at seven and dressed for a
dinner at the engineers' mess, for which we had accepted an
invitation. We had a beautiful dinner, and got on board at
midnight. I had intended going to sea to-day, but when we
got on board found a note from Lord Napier, saying that he
had ordered a target put out, and would have the thirty-
eight-ton gun fired for us Monday afternoon. As each shot
costs fifty guineas (!), of course we had to stay, and so shall
not get away until Tuesday. I was shocked on our arrival here
to get a telegram saying that Zeilin had been killed. Poor
Billy! He must have been thrown from his horse. Before we

Evans account from the nineteenth century, but since the 46th Regiment
did not arrive in North America until after 1757, the claim is considered
an impossibility.

26. A product of Swiss inventor Frederick von Martini, who joined a
lever-action, self-cocking mechanism to an English Henry rifle barrel to
produce the official British Army firearm of the late-nineteenth century.
A .45-caliber model was adopted in 1871.

27. Robert Bennett was a veteran of the Crimean War, where he secured
several medals and was severely wounded at Inkerman. *Hart's Army List*
of 1881 confirms that he was a lieutenant colonel of the 46th Regiment,
South Devonshire, from 26 July 1876 to 1 July 1881, when he went on
half pay as his regiment merged with the 32d Regiment to form the
Duke of Cornwall's Light Infantry. In July 1882 he became colonel of
the Regimental District of the Royal Inniskilling Fusiliers.

left home he had been riding in a very desperate sort of way, and his friends had predicted that he would come to grief. Now I must get to bed and try to make up the lost sleep of the last three nights.

"*At Sea. Off Cape de Gatte,*[28] *18th June.*—We managed to get away from Gibraltar Tuesday morning, and I flatter myself we did it handsomely—much better than our New York affair, of which so much was said. The night before we left we had an awful 'ranky' dinner with the artillery, which was very enjoyable. We had much scientific talk, but managed to pull through.

"Tuesday afternoon Lord and Lady Napier and all the swells turned out to see the thirty-eight-ton gun fired, and it was evident from the first that we were to be immensely impressed. After the gun had been cast loose and run into battery, we were shown how easily it would work, and with what perfect accuracy it could be controlled. Just as the colonel in charge was telling me this, the monster got away from them, and out it went with a bang that almost upset the carriage! Of course, all hands caught the mischief, though it was simply due to a lack of knowledge of the complicated machinery. It took over ten minutes to load the gun, and when it was fired at a target, about a mile away, the shot struck seventy yards short and bounded heavenward. When it was loaded the second time and all ready, the order was given to fire, but the primer failed, and they continued to fail for four or five minutes, when, by pouring powder into the vent, they managed to get it off. This shot struck fifty yards over. The third and last shot stuck in the gun, so that it took some fifteen minutes to load it, and when it was fired the projectile went one hundred and twenty yards wide of the target. Lord Napier was awfully disgusted, as well he

28. In Spanish, *Cafo de Gata.* It is the cape at the southeastern tip of Spain on the east side of Golfo de Almeria, where the Alboran Sea joins the Mediterranean.

might be, and we were not in the least bit impressed or frightened."

We made a new record for sailing vessels from Gibraltar to Naples, and I was much gratified at the comments of the Italian officers when we entered the latter port. We ran in under all sail and picked up our buoy without lowering a boat, and then furled everything very smartly, which, in that day of mastless ironclads, attracted much attention.

After several weeks of interesting cruising I reached Villefranche, where I found that I had not been forgotten. The following from my journal shows that my kindness to the poor, when executive officer of the Congress, had made a lasting impression:

"*Villefranche Sur Mer, 17th July.*—Night before last I was, as I had expected to be, up all night. In the morning at daylight we were in the mouth of the harbour, but not a breath of air; so we hoisted out the boats and towed her in. The placed looked as natural as possible, but I missed the face of the old pilot, who used always to get thirty francs when one of our ships came in. The same old one-gun battery returned our salute, taking about half an hour to do it. As soon as we were anchored I sent for the mail, and before long my old friends began to pour in. First came the bumboat people, and then the washerwomen. I could not remember the name of one of them, and was really ashamed when they all knew me and were so glad to see me, and asked after my children. I suppose a dozen or more of them had interviewed me, when Carolina (my former cook) came and wanted to cry at sight of me, but I talked too fast for her. The poor soul has had great trouble, and her husband has deserted her, leaving her with three children to support. I sent for my steward, and gave orders that she should have plenty for them all to eat while we remain here. Carolina had not gone, when Antionetta Allari came rushing at me past the orderly, who had by this time made up his mind that it was no use trying to stop them. Antionetta is fat and lovely, and was disposed to kiss me, and with tears in her eyes asked after my wife and children. Then came Angelica in the same way, and I don't know how many more, all asking after my family."

On one of my trips to Tangier my old friend Colonel Mathews arranged a wild-boar hunt for me, which I enjoyed very much when it was over. After riding on horseback about fifteen miles over a very rough country we came to the jungle where the first drive was to be made. A tribe of Moors, under their venerable old chief, were to do the driving, and I was to do the shooting. The chief inspected my gun, a Hotchkiss magazine service rifle,[29] and suggested that I take a double-barrelled shotgun and load it with balls; but I preferred to work with the tool I had selected, with which I was familiar. He explained to me that the cover was very thick where I was going to shoot, and that the pig would be close to me before I saw him; and that I would only have time for two quick shots before he charged and was on top of me. I was not over well pleased with this description of what I had to face, but decided that I would kill with my magazine rifle or let the pig go. I had not the least intention that he should get me.

When we had penetrated the jungle half a mile or more we found a well-beaten pig-track, and, selecting a favourable point, I took my station. The chief explained that I would first hear the dogs, of which they had a large number, give tongue; then I would hear the men shouting as they drove the pig in my direction; and, finally, when sure that he was coming to me, they would fire blank cartridges in their guns to keep him moving. The old man took his departure and left me alone with my gun. I looked about me for a conve-

29. Patented by B.B. Hotchkiss—an American living in France—this five-cartridge .45-caliber magazine rifle first came to attention during the Centennial Exposition in 1876. It was adopted by the U.S. Army and Navy as the first official bolt-action magazine arm in service, but by the 1890s it was succeeded by the Lee magazine rifle.

nient tree up which I might climb in case of necessity, and
having found one a few yards from my station, felt decidedly
more comfortable. Then I waited while the flies buzzed about
my head and the mosquitoes stung me wherever my skin was
exposed. I was almost on the point of giving up the job when
I heard the far-away barking of a dog, and then a dozen or
more joined in, and the sound came rapidly my way. I examined the gun to make sure that it was ready, and while doing
so found that my hands were shaking just the least bit. However, I was out for pigs, and it sounded as if a whole drove
were coming my way, and I must have one at least. The
baying of the dogs was now mixed with the shouting of the
Moors, and in a few seconds I heard the guns begin. About
thirty yards from where I was standing, and in the direction
of the dogs, there was a slight rise in the ground, and while
I was intently watching for the pig I saw his head come above
the weeds and grass on this rise. He stopped for a moment,
and, with his head partly turned from me, was apparently
trying to judge the direction in which the beaters were coming. I considered him quite close enough for comfort, and,
throwing the gun to my shoulder, fired at a point about
where I supposed the point of his shoulder-blade to be. Then
I stepped nearer my tree and, with the second cartridge ready
to fire, waited to see what would happen. Everything was
quiet where the pig had been a few minutes, then the dogs
and men were upon us.

When I found there were no pigs coming, I walked out
and met the chief, and showed him about where one had
been when I fired at him. On approaching the spot, there he
was, sure enough, and as dead as a herring. He was a vicious-
looking beast, with tusks seven inches long, and weighed
over five hundred pounds. At close quarters he would have
used a man up in very short order. A second drive was decided on, and this time I fired at something I saw moving in
the bushes and killed a jackal, which pleased the Moors better than the killing of the pig, as this animal destroyed many

of their sheep. Before I left Tangiers, I secured a young wild pig, which became a great pet on board ship. She finally came to an untimely end from eating too many live-oak acorns at Fortress Monroe. Like all pigs on board ship, male or female, she was named "Dennis," and soon learned to chew tobacco and drink strong hot coffee.

On the way home I stopped at Madeira, and then, taking the trades, ran to Fortress Monroe in twenty-six days. After transferring my crew of boys to ships in service, I proceeded to Baltimore, moored to the dock, and prepared to ship another crew of green lads and be ready to take them to sea in the spring. My time was up, however, and I could not object to my detachment, which came in the early winter. I had been in command four years, and had thoroughly enjoyed the work, which was of vast importance to the country and the service, and to me personally most attractive and interesting. Most of the boys who came under my care have advanced to warrant or petty officers. Those who left the service have good positions on shore; scarcely a week passes that I do not meet some of them, and they are always glad to speak to me and say a good word for the old ship. When war comes, they all flock back to us and do most excellent service. It would be a good thing for the country if we had twenty Saratogas always in commission, making better men of those who sail in them, whether they follow the sea or find their places on the land.

CHAPTER 19

Metallurgy and Lighthouses

F ROM the Saratoga I was transferred at once to the position of equipment officer of the Washington Navy Yard, where in a few weeks I found myself deeply interested in the manufacture of chain cables for the navy and gun forgings for the ordnance. Seamanship, with all its pleasures, had to be set aside for the time, and hard thought and work given to metallurgy. The change was very sudden, but only what every officer has to be prepared for, and the effect was undoubtedly good. We were on the edge of the experimental period, during which the navy was to shake off the mould that had been accumulating since the period of the civil war and once more occupy the proud position it had held in former years.

While I was busily engaged in making experiments on steel cables and anchors, and trying to find, with a new fuel (vaporized petroleum), a satisfactory means of welding steel, Secretary Hunt[1] organized the first Advisory

1. William Henry Hunt (1823–84) was a Louisiana lawyer and Unionist who nevertheless served in the Confederate Army. He entered politics during Reconstruction and became President James Garfield's Secretary of the Navy in 1881. Garfield's successor appointed him minister to Russia.

Board[2] for the rebuilding of the navy. The board was composed of able officers of the line, engineer and construction corps, and was presided over by Admiral John Rodgers, who was probably the best-equipped officer in the service for the position. I was fortunate enough to be ordered as a member of the board. We sat during the entire summer of 1882, and our report was submitted to the Secretary, who recommended action by Congress. This was the first step taken toward rebuilding the navy, but it was many years before the actual work was begun.

A short time after the board was organized I submitted a resolution, to the effect that all vessels recommended by the board should be built of steel. This precipitated a discussion which lasted many months and caused much comment both in and out of the service. I state the fact of having offered the resolution only because I wish to assume the responsibility that necessarily attached to it. The line officers, as a body, stood with me, as did several of the engineer officers, but the officers of the construction corps were solidly against the proposition, on the ground that we could not make the mate-

---

During Hunt's brief tenure he persuaded the administration and Congress to undertake a program that led in 1881 to the construction of the first steel vessels of the new navy—the "ABCD" ships.

2. Formed at the suggestion of senior Admiral of the Navy David Porter, this first advisory board consisted of fifteen line officers and constructors under the chairmanship of Rear Admiral John Rodgers. The group was to determine the size and composition of a suitable peacetime navy and to recommend equipment and hull material for its units. Reflecting the traditional commerce-raiding naval strategy, they recommended an immediate building program of eighteen unarmored cruisers, twenty wooden cruisers, ten torpedo boats, and five rams, plus a phased eight-year expansion program of twenty-nine additional cruisers (twenty-one of which would be armored) and twenty-five torpedo boats. A widely touted recommendation to use steel for the hulls (reportedly Evans's suggestion) was offset by the caveat that wood was necessary for some of this fleet. (For the complete report, see "Report of Advisory Board" in *Annual Report, 1881,* U.S. Navy Department, Washington, 1882.)

rial, and that American ship builders could not build steel ships. The issue was clearly drawn, and the discussion, which covered a wide field, became at times heated. Finally, the Naval Committees of the two Houses of Congress were asked to meet the board in the office of the Secretary of the Navy to hear the finish of this important matter. The meeting was held, and those favouring steel as the material for all naval constructions won the day. It was this action of naval officers that opened the way to the steel industry of the United States, to outstrip all its foreign competitors, as it has undoubtedly done.

At the time this action was taken, it was true, as claimed by the constructors, that we could not manufacture steel plates in this country; but it was only because there had been no demand for them. Once having the demand, the supply followed promptly, and it was of the best quality. We were buying steel gun-forgings and shafting abroad only because we demanded them in such small quantities. When we wanted enough of them to make their manufacture a paying venture, our own people produced them in any desired quantity and of any specified quality. I shall always feel proud of the work, small though it was, that I did in connection with the Advisory Board of 1882.

When I had served less than two years as equipment officer of the Washington yard I was detached and ordered as inspector of the Fifth Lighthouse District, with headquarters at Baltimore, Maryland. The change from metallurgy to a disbursing officer under the Secretary of the Treasury and the care of buoys and lighthouses was radical, but it was a part of my profession and therefore to be done. Being a disbursing officer without bond frightened me somewhat at first, but I soon found that it was easy work, requiring only care and honesty. The duty was pleasant and congenial, and kept me very much in the open air, with fine opportunities for shooting and fishing, which I did not neglect. My district extended from Havre de Grace, Maryland, to Beaufort, North

Carolina, and included all the buoys and lighthouses in the navigable waters within those limits.

The condition of the lighthouse service at that time was far from satisfactory. The appointment of the keepers was in political hands, and though the inspector had the examination of the men, it was practically impossible to prevent the appointment of those who rendered political service. An attempt to do this was the cause of serious trouble to me long before my tour of duty was completed. I found that the light-keepers were being assessed a portion of their pay for political purposes, which was clearly illegal, and when I directed them to refuse to pay such assessments I became *persona non grata* to a certain class of men having political power but nothing else to commend them. They were quite honest with me, however, and served notice on me that unless I changed my ways I would come to grief, which I eventually did.

A certain fellow, who had been elected a delegate to a political convention, was nominated to be light-keeper as a reward, but was found so disreputable on examination that I refused to pass him. I would not submit to dictation in my duties by a set of men quite as disreputable as the suggested keeper, and on this issue I was detached and placed on waiting orders. Report was made to the Secretary of the Navy that I was interfering with political conditions in the Fifth District, and, without asking a word of explanation from me, I was punished by being relieved and placed on reduced pay. It was, of course, a gross injustice, and caused no end of comment in the newspapers; but I took it as quietly as possible, and have always felt contented that I was not personally known to the man who could so far degrade the high office he held. The navy had in some ways degenerated into a job lot, at least in the eyes of those who used it for their own purposes, and was sometimes let to a very low bidder.

Finding myself on the beach, as it were, because I would not take a hand in politics, rather than because I had done so, and knowing that I would not have employment again

during the time of the Administration then in power, I asked
for leave for a year, with permission to leave the United
States. In the absence of the Secretary of the Navy the request
was granted, and I was busy making preparations to enjoy it,
when a telegram came from the Secretary revoking my leave
and again placing me on waiting orders. I was really of more
importance than I had considered myself, and I must be
made to feel my punishment. However, I had felt the sting
of insects before in my life, and did not consider them of
much importance.

The Baltimore and Ohio Railroad Company was about to
build a large steel bridge over the Susquehanna River at Havre de Grace, and Colonel Henry T. Douglas,[3] the able chief
engineer of the company, offered me a position as inspector
of material, which I was glad to accept. In a few days I was
installed in my office in Pittsburg, and had charge of the
inspection of all bridge material for the Baltimore and Ohio
road. It proved most congenial work to me, and thoroughly
occupied all my time, giving me an insight into the manufacture of various kinds of steel and the working of the mills
that was to prove of great benefit to me personally as well as
to the Government. The bridge in question was the first one
in this country constructed of Bessemer steel,[4] and caused

3. Evans's reference here is unclear. One possibility is Henry Trovert
Douglas, Jr., a civil engineer. Born in Richmond County, Virginia, on
16 June 1863, he was educated in public schools and by private tutors.
He began as a civil engineer in Baltimore, Maryland, in 1883. From
1902 to 1912 he was chief engineer for the Wheeling and Lake Erie
and Wabash and Pittsburgh Terminal railways. Other career promotions
included serving as: chief engineer for the Chicago and Alton Railroad;
vice president of the Joliet and Chicago Railroad; director of the Mississippi River and Bridge Company; and major in the Engineer Reserve
Corps in World War I.
4. A steel made directly from molten cast iron by drawing currents of
air through it to oxidize and carry off the carbon and impurities. The
process was developed independently by William "Pig Iron" Kelly of
Eddyville, Kentucky, and Sir Henry Bessemer of England. Bessemer's

much trouble before it was finally completed. The Carnegie firm had the contract, and its familiarity with steel rails led its members into the error of supposing that a bridge could be built of the same sort of stuff. The process of convincing them that this was not the case caused serious delay and much friction, but in the end Mr. Andrew Carnegie[5] showed his admirable qualities, and carried out his contract to the satisfaction of all concerned. The bridge was completed, and proved to be all that Colonel Douglas claimed for it. In the meantime I had learned, from hard experience, many things about the manufacture of steels that I could not have learned in any other way. It was on my suggestion that Mr. Carnegie first seriously considered the question of starting a plate mill for the manufacture of ship plates. Aside from what I had actually learned, the acquaintance I had made among men engaged in the steel industry was to be of vast importance to me in the years to come.

When the Administration had changed, and Mr. W.C. Whitney,[6] the prince of secretaries, had taken his place as

patent was issued in 1856; Kelly applied for a patent a year later, although he was able to prove he had worked on the idea as early as 1847.
5. Born in Dunfermiline, Fifeshire, Scotland, on 25 November 1835, Andrew Carnegie emigrated to America with his family in 1848, settling in Pittsburgh, Pennsylvania. Having served as the superintendent of military railroads and government telegraph lines in the East during the Civil War, Carnegie engaged in steel making and introduced the Bessemer process in 1868. He was the principal owner of Homestead and Edgar Thomson Steel Works, Carnegie Phillips and Co., and Carnegie Bros. and Co. The three companies consolidated in 1899 as Carnegie Steel, and merged as U.S. Steel when Carnegie retired in 1901. He was a benefactor of libraries and educational institutions and the author of several books, including *The Gospel of Wealth* (1900) and *Empire of Business* (1902). He died on 11 August 1919.
6. William Collins Whitney (1841–1904) was a wealthy New York lawyer whose role as a corporation counsel and streetcar magnate moved him naturally into politics. He served in the Democratic administration of Grover Cleveland as Secretary of the Navy from 1885 to 1889. Whitney introduced a second generation of steel warships, including the *Maine* and

Secretary of the Navy, there was a sense of relief among us all. His business methods soon began to show excellent results, and his fair treatment of those under him made officers and men alike feel that he was their friend. After he had been in office but a few weeks he sent for me, and, telling me frankly what the reports against me as inspector of the Fifth District had been, heard what I had to say in reply. I was immediately ordered to resume my duties in Baltimore; but, in view of the large amount of work I had on hand in Pittsburg, I was allowed to delay one month in order that I might complete it.

Once more in the lighthouse service, and this time with the assurance that my side of any controversy would be heard, I felt that I could do many things to the benefit of the service. The change of Administration brought with it a desire on the part of the smaller politicians for a complete change in the keepers of all lighthouses, as well as in other Government places. The Secretary of the Treasury and the Lighthouse Board decided that political opinion was not a sufficient cause for removal. If a keeper was found neglecting his duty he was to be removed at once; but in all cases where charges were preferred against them keepers were to have a fair investigation, and justice was to be done them. Charges were written against nearly every keeper in the district, and many of these documents were worthy of Thomas Jefferson[7]

New York, but it was his administrative improvements that were of major importance. Evans and other traditionalists regarded him very highly, possibly because of Whitney's lenient manner toward old-line naval professionalism. He harshly criticized shipbuilder John Roach and the "ABCD" ships, possibly more through political carping than anything else.

7. Lawyer, author, and scientist, Jefferson was born in 1734 at "Old Shadwell," Goochland (now Albemarle) County, Virginia. He graduated from the College of William and Mary in May 1762; became a member of the Continental Congress in both 1775 and 1783 (for one-year terms); participated in the Virginia House of Delegates, 1776–79 and 1782; and was elected governor of Virginia, 1779–81. Jefferson was minister to

or Henry Clay.[8] I carefully investigated every case, and, after hearing all the evidence, sent in my report. Out of over four hundred keepers I found it necessary to recommend the removal of one, and one only, for neglecting his duties to do political work.

One case on investigation amused me very much; it is a fair sample case. The keeper of a light on the western shore of Chesapeake Bay was charged with offences enough to have hanged a dozen men. The language of the report against him was, as I have stated before, worthy of Thomas Jefferson. I notified all the witnesses to be at the station on a certain day to give testimony in the case. After a long hearing the lawyer who represented the side of the complainants admitted that he had failed to show cause for removal; but the charge of drunkenness still had to be heard. The witness to this charge was a fisherman who had been playing cards with the accused keeper, and upon being sworn testified that he, the keeper, was undoubtedly drunk—very drunk. I asked what the indications of drunkenness were. "Well, sir, the accused was playing 'seven up' with me, and had only two to go when I

France from 1785 to 1789; first secretary of state under the new Constitution, 1790–93; and third President of the United States, 1801–09. The principal founder of the University of Virginia and president of the American Philosophical Society from 1797 to 1815, Jefferson was buried in 1826 at his home, Monticello, in Charlottesville, Virginia.

8. Lawyer and statesman, Clay was born in 1777 in Hanover County, Virginia, then moved to Kentucky in 1807. He served as a member of the Kentucky legislature from 1803–06; was a U.S. Senator, 1806–07, 1810–11, 1831–42, and 1849–52; a U.S. Congressman, 1811–21 and 1823–25; and was Speaker of the House of Representatives, 1811–20 and 1823–25. Clay was also a member of the Ghent Peace Commission and author of the "American System" of internal improvements. He was called the "Great Pacificator" as a result of the Missouri Compromise of 1820. Secretary of State under President John Quincy Adams, 1825–29, Clay himself was an unsuccessful Whig candidate for President in both 1832 and 1844. Clay was the principal author of a series of resolutions—known as the Compromise of 1850—by which he sought to avoid civil war. He died in 1852 and was buried in Lexington, Kentucky.

dealt him the Jack and deuce, and he begged; now, you can't convince any man in Matthews County, Virginia,[9] that a man who would do that wasn't drunk; certainly he was drunk, sir, and ought to be turned out." I sent to the Treasury Department many cases where the evidence wasn't even as incriminating as the above.

I found most of the keepers of lighthouses in Virginia waters were coloured men put in office by General Mahone [10] and his followers. Many of them had to be removed, generally because they would go to sleep and neglect their lights. One of them I had to remove for a very curious offence, or rather he removed himself when he found I was going to do it. I visited the station where he was on watch, and was inspecting, when I noticed that he followed me about, spitting frequently when he thought I was not observing him. I learned from the principal keeper, a coloured Methodist minister, that the fellow was chewing herbs and spitting around me as a hoodoo to prevent me from reporting the various irregularities I discovered. When he found that I had reported them all, and asked his removal as well, he jumped overboard and was not seen again.

When Congress had appropriated money for new ships, Mr. Whitney detached me from lighthouse duty and ordered me as chief steel inspector, with an office in the Navy Department. The rebuilding of the navy had begun in earnest, and the work could not have been in the hands of a man who understood better how to handle it. In addition to being an able business man of broad gauge, Mr. Whitney knew how to select his subordinates and get the best work out of them.

9. A small tidewater county jutting into the Chesapeake Bay near the mouth of the Rappahannock River.
10. Born in Southampton County, Virginia, in 1826, William Mahone graduated from Virginia Military Institute in 1847, and was involved in railroad development, including construction of the Norfolk and Western. Elected to the U.S. Senate in 1880 as a Republican, he died in 1895.

I went to work at once on the specifications for the material for the new ships, and it was at this time that I felt most the advantages my Pittsburg experiences gave me. I was confident of what the steel men could do, and I therefore made the specifications harder than those of the British admiralty, which had, up to this time, been considered quite difficult to fill. When I had secured the services of a sufficient number of line officers to look after the inspection of the material, I went with them to the different mills and showed them just how the work was to be done. In a wonderfully short space of time everything was working smoothly, and the shipyards were being supplied as rapidly as they could use the material. This was not accomplished, however, without much complaint from certain steel mills. They thought the specifications too severe, and declared that they could not fill them; but I knew better, and was able to convince the Secretary that it would be bad policy to change. I knew, of course, that pot metal was cheaper than steel, and that our people would go on making pot metal until we forced them to do something better. Men were not in the business for their health, and if they could get steel prices for pot metal, so much the better. Many of the leading firms saw the advantage of working to a high standard, and they admitted afterward that our specifications and inspection had been the very best thing for them in the end. It was marvellous to see with what rapid strides our people went ahead, until in a few years we could make better stuff than any of the celebrated foreign concerns. Eventually the United States became a dangerous rival in the steel markets of the world. It is a pleasure to know that I lived to see it, even if I had so little to do with accomplishing the result.

When everything was running smoothly and the steel being supplied satisfactorily, the Department found a new job for me. I was ordered as naval secretary of the Lighthouse Board, and at last I was in position to do many things I had long hoped to accomplish. Mr. Fairchild,[11] the Secretary of the Treasury, was a most progressive and able business man, and saw the good to come from many of the things I proposed. With the approval and assistance of the board, I succeeded in having the lighthouse keepers put into a proper uniform, and their appointment entirely removed from any chance of political interference.

I had long felt the necessity of some system of lights by which large vessels, particularly the ocean liners, could enter the harbour of New York during the night instead of lying outside and waiting for daylight. Captain Fred Rogers,[12] the able inspector of the Third District, and Lieutenant-Commander Mackenzie,[13] his assistant, gave me their cordial assistance, and by united effort we worked out and installed the system of electrically lighted buoys now in use. I supplied the money and they the brains, and between us we scored a great success. New York was the first place in the world to be supplied with such buoys, and from the day they were put down vessels came in at night as readily as in daytime.

In my efforts to aid the seafaring people, knowing well

11. Born in Cazenovia, New York, on 30 April 1842, Charles Steffins Fairchild attended Harvard in the early 1860s and earned graduate degrees there and at Columbia in the late 1880s. He served as the attorney general of New York, 1876–77; as assistant secretary of the Treasury, 1885–87, then as secretary of the treasury in Grover Cleveland's cabinet, 1887–89. Fairchild was president of the New York Security and Trust Co., 1884–1904, and later president, Atlantic and Charlotte Air Line Railroad Company, and a director of the Erie and Pittsburgh Railroad Company. Fairchild died on 24 November 1924.
12. Beginning his naval career as an acting midshipman on 25 September 1857, Rodgers was promoted to captain on 28 February 1890, commodore on 25 December 1898, and rear admiral on 3 March 1899.
13. Morris R.S. Mackenzie graduated from the U.S. Naval Academy in June 1866 and rose to the rank of lieutenant commander on 26 December 1884. He subsequently was promoted to commander on 16 April 1894, and captain on 1 July 1900.

their necessities, I sometimes encountered very curious opposition. A whistling buoy was placed in the entrance to Newport Harbour, where the dense fogs made navigation very dangerous for the thousands of passengers who entered and left Narragansett Bay. The captains and officers of vessels on that part of the coast were very grateful, but in a few weeks one of the leading landed proprietors on Bateman's Point, a man of wide scientific reputation, complained of the buoy as a nuisance, and brought every possible influence to bear on the Lighthouse Board to have it removed, regardless of the interests of commerce. He finally asserted that the noise made by the buoy was so dreadful that it turned the milk sour in his fine herd of Jersey cows. When we had secured a proper site and built a lighthouse and fog signal to protect the dangerous point the whistler was removed, and the professor again had sweet milk for his breakfast.

After getting my work in the Lighthouse Board in good shape, I was given a job in shipbuilding in addition to my other duties. Congress had made an appropriation for building two armoured cruisers in Government dockyards, and one of them was to be constructed at the New York yard. For some reason there was great delay in starting the work, which did not meet with the business views of Mr. Whitney. He sent for me and, after discussing the case somewhat, said to me: "We have everything that the Cramps[14] have—engineers, constructors, draughtsmen—everything except Cramp; yet we can't get the ship started. I want you to be Cramp,

14. Cramp Shipyard was owned and developed by Philadelphia's venerable shipbuilding family, William Cramp and Sons. They became the principal supplier of the U.S. Navy's steel warships under the tutelage of Charles Henry Cramp (1828–1913), who assumed presidency of the yard in 1879. Engaged in ship design and construction, William Cramp and Sons promoted the notion of maritime and naval supremacy. They built vessels for the American as well as Russian, Turkish, and Japanese navies, among them the USS *Indiana, Massachusetts, Iowa, Alabama, Maine, New York, Brooklyn,* and *Columbia.*

and get things moving." So I went to New York, and in my very limited way tried to play the part of the great ship-builder Cramp, who has no peer in his line of work. The keel of the Maine[15] was promptly laid and the material rapidly procured, but, owing to the lack of proper machinery and the vast amount of red tape encountered under the monstrous bureau organization of the Navy Department, progress was very slow. I well remember striking a small water pipe while placing the foundations for a plate-bending machine, and the month and more of anxious work to find out which bureau owned it, and then to get it moved a few feet. I generally left Washington on Monday, spent Tuesday and Wednesday with my able assistants in the New York yard, and on Wednesday night returned to my work in the Lighthouse Board. I had always held that it was better for an officer to wear out rather than rust out. About this time I was confident that I was not in danger of rust.

When the Harrison Administration[16] came in I felt the need of rest, and at once applied for a year's leave, which was granted. I intended to take service with the newly organized Nicaragua Canal Company,[17] but finding that undesirable, was employed by a New York syndicate, which was to en-

15. A second-class battleship originally rated an armored cruiser, the USS *Maine* was authorized under an act of 3 August 1886. Displacing 6,682 tons, having a top speed of 17 knots and a 374-man complement, and mounting twenty-five guns and seven torpedo tubes, she was laid down at the New York Navy Yard on 17 October 1888, launched on 18 November 1889, and completed on 17 September 1895. When she was blown up in Havana Harbor on 15 February 1898, the United States went to war against Spain.

16. This single-term (1889–93) Republican administration of Indiana Governor Benjamin Harrison introduced major naval rearmament and overseas expansionism to the American political and economic scene. His able subordinates Secretary of State James G. Blaine and Secretary of the Navy Benjamin F. Tracy—together with the newly formed government-industry team—played major roles in the naval renaissance.

17. Organized in 1887 to build a trans-Nicaraguan canal.

gage in the manufacture of wood fibre under a new process. This opened to me a new field of study, and I was busily engaged looking over the various water powers in Maine and examining the supply of spruce wood, when suddenly, without warning, I was ordered to command the United States steamer Ossipee,[18] at Norfolk, Virginia. I was to sail as soon as possible, and take Mr. Frederick Douglass,[19] our minister to Hayti,[20] and his family to Port au-Prince.[21] The ship was reported by the yard officials as unfit for sea on account of the condition of her boilers. Certain newspapers assumed that I did not fancy the job, and had therefore, in some mysterious way, disabled the ship, to avoid obeying my orders. As the ship had plenty of canvas, I was confident that I could sail her to Hayti, and I was very sure she would drift back with the Gulf Stream when I had landed the minister; so I wired the Secretary that, notwithstanding the report about the boilers, I was prepared to carry out the orders he had given me. At the same time I assured him that I had no feeling as to the cargo he might order carried in a Govern-

18. A wooden sail and steam screw sloop of 1,240 tons, a top speed of 10 knots, eight to eleven guns, and a 214-man complement, the USS *Ossipee* was built at the Portsmouth Navy Yard for $272,971.25. Launched on 16 November 1861 and commissioned on 6 November 1862, she participated in the Battle of Mobile Bay. The sloop was sold in 1891.
19. Born to slave parents in Tuckahoe, Maryland, in 1817, Frederick Douglass escaped in 1838. He became prominent in Massachusetts and New England antislavery societies and established the Black American newspaper *North Star*. Douglass assisted in raising the 54th and 55th Massachusetts Colored regiments for the Civil War. He was secretary of the Santo Domingo Commission, 1871; marshal and recorder of deeds, District of Columbia, 1877–86; and U.S. minister to Haiti, 1889–91. A strong supporter of the women's suffrage movement, Douglass died in 1895 in Washington, D.C.
20. A country of the West Indies on the western part of the island of Hispaniola.
21. The capital of Haiti, on the southwestern shore of the Gulf of Gonaives.

ment vessel, be it ammunition, ministers, dynamite, or mules. I had known Mr. Douglass all my life, and entertained the highest respect for him. Another vessel was ordered to convey him to his station, and the Ossipee, on closer inspection, was found too rotten even to permit of repairs. After being in command two weeks, I was again granted leave and allowed to go on with my outside work.

When I had fairly mastered my subject I was directed to erect a sulphite-fibre mill[22] at Appleton, Wisconsin,[23] which I did, and in nine months had it completed and turning out first-class sheets of wood fibre. During the winter I was engaged on this work the thermometer frequently went as low as 30° below zero, and once touched 39° below; but the air was very dry, and I enjoyed every hour of the time. My water power was at last harnessed, and when all the water wheels were running and the vast mass of machinery doing its work, I felt well repaid for my labour. The knowledge I gained was of great benefit to me afterward when I found myself in command of a ship with her seventy-odd engines of various kinds.

22. Undoubtedly the one owned by the Manufacturing Investment Company under the presidency of W.C. Whitney, erstwhile Secretary of the Navy, to whom Evans owed his leave of absence. It was located on Maple Grove Street near the John Street bridge in Appleton, Wisconsin.
23. A city in the eastern part of the state, southwest of Green Bay.

CHAPTER 20

The Yorktown's Cruise to Chile

I N August, 1891, I was ordered to command the gunboat
Yorktown, then in the North Atlantic Squadron,[1] known
as the "White Squadron," from the fact that the ships were
all painted white. I joined her in New York, relieving Commander F.E. Chadwick,[2] who had commanded her since she
was first placed in commission. She had the reputation of
being a strong, well-built ship, very fast in smooth water,

1. The so-called "White Squadron" consisted of, at this point, the first
steel ships of the "New Navy"—the *Atlanta, Boston, Chicago,* and
Dolphin.
2. French Ensor Chadwick was warranted an acting midshipman on 28
September 1861. Attaining the rank of commander on 12 December
1884 and captain on 7 November 1897, he was the first U.S. naval
attaché to London, 1883–89. Chadwick headed the expanded Office of
Naval Intelligence, 1892–93, and was chief of the Bureau of Equipment,
1893–97. He succeeded Evans as skipper of the *New York* (1897–98),
and was Sampson's chief of staff during the Spanish-American War.
Chadwick was president of the Naval War College from 1900–03, and
commanded the South Atlantic Squadron before retiring in 1906. A
member of the progressive reformer element in the new steel navy, he
also wrote on naval intelligence, diplomacy, history, and science.

but a little tender in a heavy sea. Her officers were able men, and her crew very smart and well up in their drills and exercises. Ten days after I assumed command the squadron, under command of Admiral Walker,[3] got under way and passed up through Hell Gate,[4] the flagship Chicago[5] leading. We visited a number of New England ports where fairs and shows of various kinds were being held, and where the presence of a number of war ships would add to the attractions of such gatherings. It was not very exciting work, and was in many ways unpleasant duty, but the ships belonged to the people, and we were only too glad to show them how their money was being used. In return for what little courtesy we could show them the people were kind and generous in their treatment of us, and entertained us with true New England hospitality.

At the end of September I was ordered to New York to prepare at once for foreign service. A few days later orders came for us to proceed without delay to Valparaiso,[6] Chile, and report to the admiral commanding the Pacific station for duty. The Chileans had for a year past been fighting among

3. A top graduate of the U.S. Naval Academy Class of 1856, John Grimes Walker served with distinction under Admiral David Porter in the Civil War and thereafter as chief of the Bureau of Navigation (1881–89). He commanded the new Squadron of Evolution in 1889 and subsequently the South Atlantic, North Atlantic, and Pacific squadrons before retiring in 1897. An effective administrator and commander, Rear Admiral Walker was profoundly disliked by younger progressives because of his rigidity, conservatism, and authoritarianism.

4. The confluence of the Harlem and East rivers in New York City.

5. A sail and steam protected cruiser authorized under an act of 3 March 1883, the USS *Chicago* was the third so-called "ABCD" warship—the first steel warships of the "New Steel Navy." Begun by John Roach (and completed by his successors), this ship of 4,500 tons, a top speed of 14 knots, eighteen guns, and a 409–71-man complement was launched on 5 December 1885 and completed on 17 April 1889. She served until 1935, having been renamed the USS *Alton* in 1928.

6. A city of central Chile on the Pacific coast, west-northwest of Santiago.

From a copyrighted photograph by Enrique Muller.

Gunboat Yorktown

themselves, and unfortunately much bad feeling had been
shown toward us, particularly toward our navy, by the revolutionary party in this war. The friction between the two
countries had become acute, and the prospect of active service, possibly war, gave great interest to our cruise. We
worked incessantly night and day, and on October 8th I
hauled out from the navy yard and that evening put to sea.
As we passed Sandy Hook the storm signals were flying, and
everything indicated a northeast gale; but for the time being
the wind was fresh from northwest, and we ran for Hatteras
with all sails set and a fair wind. The long northeast swell
that was felt all the next day warned me not to lose any time
in getting across the Gulf Stream if I wanted to avoid trouble. Owing to the reputation the ship had of being tender
under canvas, I did not drive her hard for the first day or
two, but gradually, as we learned her tricks, we gave her all
she could stand, and I found to my surprise that she was as
stiff as a church, and could easily carry all her canvas.

We ran just ahead of the northeaster until we reached the
latitude of Bermuda,[7] where we found beautiful weather,
which we held until we arrived at St. Thomas. We made the
land in the afternoon just before dark, and were fortunate
enough to get in in time to avoid a hurricane which passed
to the south of us during the night. We coaled in eight
hours, and by noon of the following day were off again,
bound for Bahia, in Brazil,[8] which was to be our second coaling port. As we passed through the beautiful West India
Islands the marks of the recent hurricane were all about us in
the shape of trees and *débris* blown off from the land. These
Windward Islands are certainly as grand in scenery as any in
the world. I did not wonder at the enthusiasm of Columbus

7. A British colony in the Atlantic Ocean, southeast of Cape Hatteras,
that comprises an archipelago of 350 islands.
8. Modern Salvador, Bahia is a city in eastern Brazil on the Atlantic
coast.

and his rascally crew of thieves as they sailed about there in search of the yellow metal and slaves. For the first few days out of St. Thomas the Yorktown raised Cain, because she had a heavy following sea which made her roll very badly. I had my chair lashed, and so managed to hold on, but I was about the only thing in the cabin that did. One minute she was down on her beam ends apparently, the next second she was down on the other side, and in the interval she had done more different kinds of things than any ship I was ever in before; but she did them all very easily and with comfort to her crew. Writing in the cabin was impossible, and there was not much sleep to be had, owing to the constant throbbing of the screws. The weather grew hotter as we ran south, and the fireroom force suffered severely before they became seasoned to the heat. We crossed the line in fine weather for Neptune,[9] who came on board for a visit. We gave the afternoon to him and his antics.

During the night of October 28th the wind suddenly whipped around to the south and blew a hard gale from that quarter. We drove head into it all night, and at daylight had the land in sight ahead and on both bows, but nothing that we could recognise. My cabin had been flooded during the night, and I had spent my time on the bridge, so was well pleased when the navigator found something he could swear by. We had been set out of our course eighteen miles during the night, but now we had the entrance buoys in sight, and in a short time were anchored in the harbour, eleven and a half days from St. Thomas—not a bad run for the little ship. It was my first visit to Bahia, and I found the city, as viewed from the water, very pleasing. The health officer, a much-begilded dago, paid his visit and assured me that there was no fever on shore, the health of the place in his opinion being

---

9. A traditional nautical ceremony upon crossing the Equator whereby Neptune, the God of the Seas, initiates everyone on board who is crossing the latitude for the first time.

perfect. I took this with many grains of salt, and gave the necessary orders to guard against infection if possible. The coal [10] men, bumboat [11] men, and various other sharks were soon on board. Coal was twelve dollars a ton, but have it I must, no matter what the cost, and arrangements were made to fill my bunkers at the earliest possible moment. The American consul soon came on board, and from him I learned that the Chileans had killed several of the crew of the Baltimore [12] and wounded many others in the streets of Valparaiso; that the Boston [13] and Atlanta [14] had been ordered out, and that other vessels were soon to follow. Of course, we were much excited over the news, and most anxious to hurry

10. The use of coal (and later oil fuels) naturally involved securing overseas bases for refueling. This was one rationale for U.S. territorial expansion overseas in the late nineteenth century.

11. A seafaring peddler who catered to the enlisted ranks.

12. The USS *Baltimore* was a sail and steam, steel protected cruiser authorized under an act of 3 August 1886. She displaced 4,413 tons, had a complement of 386 men, a top speed of 19 knots, and eighteen guns. Laid down by the Cramp Shipyard on 5 May 1887, she was launched on 7 October 1888 and completed on 1 July 1890. The *Baltimore* served as a receiving ship at Charleston from 1911 to 1912 and was converted to a minelayer, 1913–14, to participate in laying the Northern Mine Barrage in World War I. Decommissioned at Pearl Harbor in 1922, she was not sold for another twenty years.

13. The second of the so-called "ABCD" cruisers, this sail and steam steel protected cruiser displaced 3,189 tons, mounted fourteen guns, and had a 284-man complement. Built by John Roach (and completed at the New York Navy Yard), she was laid down on 15 November 1883, launched on 12 April 1884, and completed on 2 May 1887. The USS *Boston* served with the Oregon naval militia, 1911–16, and was a receiving ship at Yerba Buena, 1918–46. Renamed the USS *Despatch* in August 1940, she was scuttled on 8 April 1946.

14. First of the "ABCD" warships, and sister ship to the USS *Boston* in size, armament, and complement, the USS *Atlanta* was laid down by John Roach on 8 November 1883, launched on 9 October 1884, and completed on 19 July 1886. From 1903 on she served as an accommodation ship for torpedo boat crews until being sold in 1912.

on our way. We drove the coal men to their limit day and night.

I had lost so much sleep during the last days of the run from St. Thomas that I found myself quite done up; but a few hours' sleep, a fine fresh lettuce salad, a pineapple, and many glasses of iced water quite put me on edge again, and I was ready for whatever might come my way. In the late afternoon a German steamer from Santos, Brazil,[15] came in and anchored a short distance astern of us. The health officer visited her and then came to inform me that she had six cases of yellow fever on board, and had lost her chief engineer and four men of the crew from the same disease on her way up the coast. It was only after I had used some very strong language that this brass-bound individual returned and shifted the steamer's berth to the quarantine ground. He had assured me that there was no yellow fever on shore, but I did not believe a word he said, and never went on shore myself nor allowed any one else, except those having important business, to go. On October 30th I received a telegram from the Secretary of the Navy to proceed to Montevideo and there await further instructions. This, of course, might mean anything—change of orders, or to await the arrival of more ships before proceeding. One thing I was sure of, however, and that was that I was to lose no time in getting to the point indicated; and I did not. As soon as the coaling was completed and mess stores taken in I put to sea. The caterer of the wardroom mess complained of the difficulty of getting necessary articles, and the loss of one very important one in the shape of a black pig. The pig had been brought on board, but disappeared in a very mysterious way—it was supposed that he had gone overboard through one of the ports.

When once more outside and heading for Montevideo, we found the sea very heavy, caused by a strong southwest

15. A city in southeastern Brazil on the Atlantic coast, east of São Paulo.

breeze. About six o'clock in the evening of the third day out the clouds began to bank up a little in the southwest, and occasional flashes of lightning could be seen, which gradually increased, until by half past eight it was one vibration of light. The effect was most alarming, but at the same time grand and beautiful. The brain was stunned and the eyes blinded by it. As yet not a sound of thunder could be heard, though the storm was evidently approaching us with great rapidity.

I stood on the deck aft watching it, and when, at about 9:30, it struck us, I was blown down as if by some heavy weight. Our sails, though furled, were snatched off the ship in a second, and went whirling through the air like great birds straight up over the mastheads. At the same moment the thunder broke over us like forty batteries of artillery, and the electric fluid running down our conductors was sufficient to make the whole deck as bright as noonday. It was the most awful, grand, and beautiful sight I ever saw. Of course, I realized that a whirlwind had struck us. Nothing could be done to save our sails—they were gone; but I could do something to ease the little frigate and help her out of the scrape. I rang full speed ahead, and pointed her up to the wind so that I passed through the blessed whirlwind in the shortest possible time. Just ten minutes after it struck us it was gone, and so were all our sails and much of our rigging; but I was satisfied to get off as well as we did. It was the beginning of a nasty, hard, southwest gale which blew all day, and, in fact, at intervals in various directions for several days afterward.

All day Wednesday we had to head her up to the sea and slow her to six knots, as she was taking in too much water over the bows; but with it all she proved herself a perfect beauty, and one of the best sea boats I was ever in. I was on the deck constantly, of course, watching everything, increasing speed whenever practicable, and so managed to plug

along, and on the morning of November 7th, at three
o'clock, made Maldonado Light,[16] and anchored at Montevideo in the forenoon. What a difference—October 8th in New
York, November 8th in Montevideo! We certainly had made
a good run, doing the distance, including stops, in thirty
days, which, I believe, was the best ever done by a vessel
of war.

The usual calls were made on me at once, and in returning
them I got a good wetting, as there was a heavy sea running,
and the place was totally unprotected by anything like a
breakwater. The whole South Atlantic came tumbling in
when the wind was in the right direction, and made it very
nasty. Captain Lang,[17] of the Cleopatra[18] (English), came on
board in a driving rainstorm to call. He had been in command of the Chinese navy at one time, and I found him a
most interesting man to talk to. Soon after he left me the
rain turned into a southeast gale, and by night it was howling at a great rate, the ship pitching as if she were at sea.
This was not promising for taking the coal, which I had
ordered to be alongside at daylight in the morning. However, I went to sleep, hoping that it would pass off as suddenly as it came. I knew that everything in that part of the
world, from the form of government to the rise of the tide,
changed with great rapidity. In this, however, I was mistaken; the weather grew worse rather than better, and the

16. A lighthouse in the small coastal town of Maldonado, east of Montevideo, where the Rio de la Plata empties into the Atlantic.
17. William M. Lang was promoted to captain in the British Royal Navy
in 1884.
18. HMS *Cleopatra* was a sail and steam, iron and steel corvette of 2,380
tons, fourteen guns, a top speed of 13 knots, and a 265-man complement. Designed by Nathaniel Barnaby and built by Elder of Glasgow,
she was laid down in 1876 and launched on 1 August 1878. The *Cleopatra* was quickly rendered obsolete by the spate of naval construction authorized by Britain's Naval Defence Act of 1888.

ship began walking away with her anchor. A second anchor brought her up, and she rode it out, pitching bows under in the heavy seas which were breaking clear over the Cleopatra.

As soon as I arrived I wired the Navy Department the fact, stating that I would leave in five days, that time being necessary to complete the new sails which had been ordered, and some of the canvas cut in two hours after my anchor was down. The following day I had a cable from the Secretary of the Navy directing me to proceed to Valparaiso, which was very satisfactory. I got under way at once from the outer anchorage and took the ship inside, where I ran her on to the mud so that we might coal. She was soon a mass of coal dust from stem to stern.

On the way down from Bahia, and when five days out from that place, I had a curious experience with the pig the wardroom mess had lost. At two o'clock in the morning I was aroused by my orderly, who announced, "Sir, Dennis is found." "Who the devil is Dennis," I replied, "and why do you disturb me?" He explained that Dennis was the lost pig, that he had been found in a coal bunker, was very weak and ill, and they wanted the captain to come out and see if anything could be done for him. So out I went, and found the ship's cook with the pig in his arms feeding him condensed milk out of a teaspoon. One of the coal passers, an Irish lad, had gone into the coal bunker to pass out coal for the furnaces. After a few shovelfuls had been taken out he felt something move about his feet, and in a moment heard a faint squeal, which in the black darkness of the place was too much for his nerves. Dropping his shovel, he made at top speed for the fire room, thinking the devil was close at his heels! Upon investigation, Dennis was found, so thin that one could almost read a newspaper through him. He had fallen into one of the coal chutes while coal was being taken in, and, becoming packed in with the coal, had remained in that position without food or water for five days, until released by the coal heaver as I have related. He recovered entirely, became the pet of the ship, and cruised with us clear up into the ice of the arctic regions.

When the coaling was fairly under way I went on shore to call on our minister and stretch my legs. Afterward I took a cab and drove about three and a half miles to call on a Mr. Evans, who had sent me his card, and was well repaid for my trouble and time. On the way to his *quinta* (country place) I passed through the main portion of the city, which was clean and comfortable and well paved. Mr. Evans had quite a history. He had gone to Montevideo forty-eight years before, a boy from Pennsylvania, as a sailor on a brig, and, being steady and of a practical turn of mind, thought he would try his hand at supplying ships. From the first he made a success of it, and when the civil war broke out he had amassed a considerable fortune, which he had well invested. The time soon came when our credit was down and our vessels could get neither money nor credit, and at this moment Mr. Evans stepped in and put his entire fortune and all he could borrow at the disposal of our people, saying that he would back the United States for all he was worth. After the war was over he received his money back with a good interest, and he at once invested in real estate, which went up with a boom, and he was immensely wealthy. Then he bought two blocks of land in the edge of the city and proceeded to make his home, which was like fairyland. Not having a wife, he sent home for a widowed cousin, who came out to him and had always been his housekeeper and mainstay. When I was there she was very ill, not expected to live, which threw a gloom over the fascinating place. She must have been a wonderful woman, for the house was full of her work—such embroidery as I never dreamed of, pictures by the dozen so finely done that I was persuaded they were oil paintings, and such a collection of bric-a-brac!

But what pleased me most were the flowers—thousands of such roses as we see in the rose catalogues, American Beauties, as large as a dinner plate, and Maréchal Niels so perfect that I just stopped and stood lost in admiration. I don't exaggerate when I say that one could have filled a freight car with the most perfect flowers I had ever seen without making perceptible impression on the mass. When I went back to the ship I had two large baskets of the beautiful things, and one of lemons which I had helped to pull, and both hands full of choice buds; the cabin was beautiful as a result. When Mr. Evans first started in business he had had built in Baltimore a very able boat, which was brought out on the deck of a vessel, and with her his fortune was begun. She was now hauled up in his yard, painted and gilded and surrounded with flowers, and as they would not allow him to fly the American flag here, he had it painted on her mast, wrapped round and round from one end to the other. He had known every naval officer in these waters for forty years, and many of his stories were most interesting.

During my stay at Montevideo I had many cables from the Department regarding the new Chilean cruiser Errazuriz,[19] which for some reason was causing them much anxiety. I found that she was undergoing repairs at Buenos Ayres,[20] and promptly sent an officer in plain clothes to have a look at her. He succeeded in getting on board, and remained more than an hour before he was suspected and invited to leave. During that time he had found out all I wanted to know, and after he had made his report I wired the Secretary her condition, and that he need not worry about her, as I could do her up with the Yorktown in thirty minutes if it became necessary. The news from Valparaiso at this time was alarming. The tension between the two Governments was great, and war might come at any moment.

19. A steam-powered steel protected cruiser of 2,047 tons, ten guns, three torpedo tubes, a top speed of 25 knots, and a 170-man complement, the *Errazuriz* was built in France by La Seyne and launched on 4 September 1890. The cruiser was discarded circa 1910.
20. The capital of Argentina lies in the eastern part of the country on the Rio de la Plata.

The instant our new sails were on board I again put to sea. I find in my journal the following:

"*Friday Night, November 20th.*—We are at anchor inside Cape Virgin in the Straits of Magellan,[21] the most desolate spot God ever made; but glad to be here, for it is a frightful night at sea—blowing a howler from northwest, and so bitterly cold! . . .

"The day before we left Montevideo the Philcomayo,[22] a Chilean gunboat, came into port and anchored near us for the purpose, no doubt, of advising the Errazuriz at Buenos Ayres of our movements, and the latter may make an effort to beat us to Valparaiso; but she will have to 'dust' if she does it, for we have averaged twelve knots since leaving the river, and won't let any grass grow on our ship's bottom until I report to the admiral. I wish we could have a scrap with the Errazuriz, for I feel confident that we could take her into camp in forty-five minutes by the watch, notwithstanding all her new French rapidfire guns; but no such chance will offer, I fear.

"Within a mile of us, on the point of Cape Virgin,[23] lies a magnificent great iron ship smashed to pieces and turned upon her beam ends. It was a painful sight as we came by; some poor fellow, no doubt, running in a gale and thick weather, and two hundred yards more could have taken him clear."

At early daylight I was again under way, standing for Sandy Point, where I anchored at 4 P.M., thoroughly worn out and nearly frozen to death by a gale from such awful snow-clad mountains that I was nearly congealed, and unfit for work. I could see the great glaciers forty miles away glint-

21. A 350-mile channel that separates southern South America from Tierra del Fuego.
22. Built on the Thames in Great Britain, the *Pilcomayo* was a wooden gunboat of 800 tons, four guns, a top speed of 11 knots, and a 130-man complement. Launched in 1874, she was discarded circa 1910.
23. *Cabo Vírgenes* lies at the northeastern mouth of the Strait of Magellan.

ing in the sun. Our recent run through the tropics had un-
fitted us for this sort of weather, and our suffering was very
considerable. I remained at Sandy Point only from sundown
one day until 3 A.M. of the next, when it was light enough
to see, when I again drove ahead at thirteen knots speed,
fearing that the Errazuriz might be trying to get ahead of
me.

The scenery was grand beyond anything I have ever seen,
but it was so fearfully cold and blowing such a howling gale
that I could not enjoy it as I would if I had not been compelled to face it all the time. That first night we found an
anchorage in a sung little hole in Smythe's Channel,[24] and
had a comfortable night surrounded by such mountains of
snow and ice as Switzerland never dreamed of. Directly east
of us was a magnificent mountain, as large as all Switzerland,
and a pure clear white to the very top, where the outline was
as sharp as broken glass; and in the very front, facing us, a
glacier thirty miles long. As the sun set, the light on the
blue crystal ice was a sight to be remembered, and the silence
most delicious—one could have cut it with a knife, it was so
dense. In the early morning, 2 A.M., daylight, we were under way and again driving north through Smythe's Channel,
which was much more beautiful than the Magellan Strait.
There was hardly a moment when we were out of sight of a
glacier as we twisted and turned through this tortuous channel, but always the same biting, bitter cold.

Our second and last night in this inland sea we found a
most beautiful spot for the night about sixty miles south of
the English Narrows,[25] which are the terror of all navigators.
When our anchor was down we could just swing clear of the

24. Should be Smyths Channel. One of a succession of channels approximately 338 miles long between the Chilean mainland and a number of
archipelagos just north of the Strait of Magellan. Together, they form a
relatively safe, inside passage for small steamers.
25. Lies between the Wellington Islands and the Chilean mainland,
north of the Strait of Magellan and south of the Gulf of Penas.

rocks, which rose sixteen hundred to three thousand feet straight up and down all around us, with a magnificent waterfall almost on our stern. It was as if we had been dropped into a well—only our surroundings were perfect. At each of our stopping places the men landed and put up our headboard bearing the name of the ship, date, etc. This is a custom which has always prevailed, and some of the anchorages in the Straits of Magellan looked like graveyards. We found the Trenton's [26] mark at one place. I wish I could have had some photographs of the scenery, for no one can ever comprehend the utter wildness and magnificence of it from mere description.

From this last anchorage we got under way at 2 A.M., and before seven were approaching the Narrows. As we came up it seemed impossible that a ship could get through; indeed, there seemed no opening, the turns were so short. But she went through, running thirteen and a half knots, and it was a beautiful sight to see her do it—at least the officers told me it was; I did not see much of it myself, for I had taken charge, and my blood was rushing so that I was warm for a few minutes anyhow. I remembered afterward that every face—all the men were on deck—was turned to me. We were in the Narrows scarcely six minutes, and yet in that short time we had made nearly two complete turns. After we had passed the Narrows it was all plain sailing, and by four in the afternoon we were out into the Gulf of Peñas [27] and the nasty Pacific was about us. And such a gale, and the most terrific sea I have ever met! It was running from the south-

26. The USS *Trenton* was a wooden sail and steam screw-frigate of 3,900 tons, a top speed of 12.8 knots, fifteen guns, and a 416-man complement. Laid down in December 1873 at the New York Navy Yard, she was launched on 1 January 1876 and commissioned the following year. The *Trenton* was wrecked by a typhoon at Apia Harbor, Samoa, on 16 March 1889.
27. A gulf formed by the Peninsula de Taitao to the north and the island of Campana to the south, north of the Strait of Magellan.

west and the gale blowing from the northwest, which was our course up the coast, and the little Yorktown was like an eggshell in the whirl of waters. We had to run slowly all night, but in the morning I gradually increased her speed and for two days did very well, notwithstanding the gale continued; but then the chief engineer reported that by some miscount we were forty tons of coal short, and I was counting on that forty tons to bring us to Valparaiso.

I put her under half power at once, and on Saturday night at midnight ran in and anchored at Lota,[28] two hundred and sixty-five miles south of Valparaiso. Early Sunday we took in seventy-five tons of coal, and Monday we anchored at Valparaiso at 5 P.M., fifty-one days from New York. Every one said we had made a wonderful passage, but I did not think so. If we had not lost our sails on the coast of Brazil and thus met with delay at Montevideo, and if we had had the coal I had counted upon, we should have made a good passage, but as it was I was not any too well pleased.

28. A city of south-central Chile on the Pacific coast, south-southwest of Concepción.

CHAPTER 21

Chilean Hostility

W E found the Baltimore looking warlike and ready for business. The harbour was full of war vessels, and we anchored nearly two miles from the landing; but at that season it made no difference. All the inshore port was filled with the Chilean navy, and a sorry-looking lot they were. The story of the killing of the two men of the Baltimore and the wounding of eighteen others showed it to have been about the most cowardly and brutal thing I ever heard of. The men, to the number of say one hundred, went on shore on liberty at 2 P.M., and at six or half past a mob of two thousand, assisted by the police to the number of fifty, armed with carbines and bayonets, attacked three of our men in a street car, pulled them out and stabbed them in the back; one of them, Reagan, while being supported in the arms of a shipmate, was shot and instantly killed by a policeman. I don't think the shot was meant for him, however, but for the man who was holding him. Reagan was already, to all appearances, stabbed to death, and they meant to kill the other man; but the ball passed through his shirt and neckerchief and through Reagan's neck, killing him instantly. Whenever

half a dozen of our men got together they would fight their
way through the cowardly mob, but as they were completely
unarmed, of course they had no show, and so were gradually
cut down, one after another, and dragged off, in some cases
by horses, to the prisons. Of all the wounded men of the
Baltimore not one was cut or marked in front of his body; all
wounds were in the back, which tells its own tale.

When I had called on Captain Schley,[1] commanding the
Baltimore, and reported for duty, I paid my visits of ceremony to the authorities on shore and the senior Chilean naval
officers afloat. They were all scrupulously polite to me, but
everywhere there was intense hatred for the Baltimore and
her crew. At this time I think the feeling was confined to
them, and did not extend to us as a nation; but later on it
changed and involved everything North American. Captain
Schley informed me that he was going north in a few days,
probably as soon as the Boston arrived, which I regretted, as
I thought he should remain until the trouble about his men
had been settled. He was in the midst of a correspondence
with the intendente, conducted in the most perfect Castilian,
to show, or prove, that his men were all perfectly sober when
they were assaulted on shore. I did not agree with him in
this, for in the first place I doubted the fact, and in the

1. Winfield Scott Schley (1839–1911) attained the rank of captain on 31
March 1888, commodore on 6 February 1898, and rear admiral on 3
March 1899. A graduate of the Naval Academy Class of 1860, Schley
served in the Civil War and in the Korean punitive expedition of 1871.
He commanded the Greely relief expedition of 1884, and as captain of
the USS Baltimore became involved in the Chilean imbroglio of 1891.
Succeeding Evans as skipper of the New York, Schley was commander of
the Flying Squadron during the Spanish-American War. As such—and
senior to Evans—Schley sustained a tenuous relationship with Evans that
stemmed from their Valparaíso days and was fed by Schley's controversial
handling of the Flying Squadron, as well as his tactical conduct of the
Battle of Santiago. His popular credit for the victory came under attack
in 1901, and a subsequent court of inquiry was equally critical of his
actions. He retired as a rear admiral in 1901.

second it was not an issue worth discussing. His men were probably drunk on shore, properly drunk; they went ashore, many of them, for the purpose of getting drunk, which they did on Chilean rum paid for with good United States money. When in this condition they were more entitled to protection than if they had been sober. This was my view of it, at least, and the one I always held about men whom I commanded. Instead of protecting them, the Chileans foully murdered these men, and we believed with the connivance and assistance of armed policemen. That was the issue—not the question of whether they were drunk or sober. I find the following notes from my journal, made at that time, of interest:

"*Valparaiso, December 4, 1891.*—My time has been about all taken up with official calls without end. . . . I found here, when we came, three German ships, with an admiral, three Frenchmen, and the whole Chilean navy; and in addition to calls on each of them, I had to call on our consul, and the intendente of Valparaiso, and the senior naval officer on shore. All hands have been exceedingly polite to me. They all hate the crew of the Baltimore as a whole, but against us, as a nation, I don't think they have any feeling. It is not my business to make trouble here, and I don't intend to give offence to any one until I have orders from home, and then I shall do it with my guns and not with my tongue. I am giving all the time I can to get at the bottom facts about the trouble on hand. As far as I can now see, the mob that set upon the Baltimore's men and brutally murdered them was made up of the worst element of the city, and included discharged sailors from the Chilean fleet and probably soldiers; but it is plain that some of the Chilean sailors helped our unfortunate men in every way they could, and it is known that one officer, a lieutenant of artillery, cut down and generally knocked out seven or eight leaders of a crowd who were trying to get at some of our men in a restaurant. In fact, he drew his sword and defended the door until our men had escaped.

"My position is that even if our men were all drunk that does not justify the police in shooting their heads off. If such be the law, we must either make them change it or stay away from a country where drunkenness is so severely punished. The Government of the United States must have ample apology for this affair, and the families of the men hurt must be paid, or we had better pull out every American from Chilean soil, for their lives won't be worth having. Strongly as I feel on the subject, I can not see any good reason why I should not be perfectly civil and polite to them, even if I have to shoot them tomorrow.

"As soon as my anchor was down the senior officers sent at once and made proper calls, and I, of course, returned them; and then, being the last comer, I called on them all in succession—first the Cochran,[2] then the Esmeralda,[3] then the Huascar,[4] then the Lynch,[5] and then the Condell.[6] On each I was most pleasantly greeted, and the officers were cordial; the men, on the contrary, scowled at me, and looked as if they would be glad of a chance to cut my throat.

2. An iron-hulled barque-rigged central-battery ship of approximately 3,560 tons, a top speed of 12.75 knots, armed with nine guns, an iron-rim bow, and a 300-man complement. Built by the British firm of Earle, the *Admiral Cochran* was launched in 1875.
3. Built by Armstrong, this sail and steam steel protected cruiser displaced 2,950 tons, was armed with ten guns and two torpedo tubes, and had a ram bow, a top speed of 18.3 knots, and a 296-man complement. Launched on 6 June 1883, she was sold to Japan on 15 November 1894.
4. An armored turret ship of 2,030 tons that was captured from Peru on 8 October 1879. The *Huascar* was rebuilt to mount nine guns and have a 170-man complement and a top speed of 12.3 knots. Launched on 6 October 1865, she was later fitted as a gunnery ship and naval museum.
5. The *Almirante Lynch* was a sail and steam steel torpedo gunboat of 713 tons, a top speed of 20.3 knots, seven guns, five torpedo tubes, a ram bow, and an 87-man complement. Laid down in 1889 and completed in 1890, she was renamed the *Tome* in 1910 and discarded in 1920.
6. The *Almirante Condell* was identical to the *Almirante Lynch* except for speed. (She was capable of 20.65 knots.) The gunboat was renamed *Alcahuairo* in 1910.

"Saturday, December 5th.—To-day we have papers up to October 31st. . . . It is curious to sit in this quiet place and read in the home papers of the excitement over Chilean affairs. . . . One paper has it that the Newark[7] and Philadelphia[8] are to come with the Atlanta, and that Gherardi[9] will command; while another, of the same date, says that he goes at once to the West Indies for the winter. There is a telegram published here this afternoon that Walker is ordered to Brazil with the Chicago, Atlanta, and Bennington;[10] and so it goes. One thing, however, I am certain of, and that is that the Yorktown is here without any question, and ready for any sort of business.

"December 6th.—. . . At a dinner the other day we had much talk about the recent war in this country, and after-

7. Authorized under an act of 3 March 1885, the USS *Newark* was a sail and steam cruiser of approximately 4,592 tons, twenty-two guns, a top speed of 18 knots, and a 384-man complement. Laid down on 12 June 1888 and launched on 19 March 1890, she was commissioned on 2 February 1891. The *Newark* was stricken from the Navy List in June 1913, but she served as a quarantine hull at Providence, Rhode Island, and temporarily as a naval hospital annex until being sold in 1926.

8. A sail and steam steel cruiser authorized under an act of 3 March 1887, the USS *Philadelphia* had a top speed of 19 knots, mounted twenty-two guns, displaced approximately 5,305 tons, and carried a complement of 384 men. Laid down on 22 March 1888 at the Cramp Shipyard, she was launched on 7 September 1889 and commissioned on 28 July 1890. The cruiser was sent to the Puget Sound Navy Yard for extensive repairs in August 1902. She was housed over as a receiving ship in 1904 and as a prison ship until being sold in 1927.

9. Bancroft Gherardi rose in his naval career as follows: midshipman, 26 June 1846; commander, 25 July 1866; captain, 9 November 1874; commodore, 3 November 1884; and rear admiral, 25 August 1887. He retired on 10 November 1894.

10. The USS *Bennington* was a sail and steam steel gunboat of 1,710 tons, ten to sixteen guns, a top speed of 16 knots, and a 187–201-man complement. Authorized by an act of 3 March 1887, she was laid down in May 1888 by the Delaware River Iron Works. Launched on 3 June 1890 and commissioned on 20 June 1891, the *Bennington* suffered a disastrous burst of two boilers in 1905 and was never recommissioned.

ward went out to look at some of the places where the fighting was done. The idea prevails in the United States that
the Chileans, and particularly their navy, fought with great
bravery; but I find on investigation that such is not the case,
at least not according to our standard. Balmaceda's [11] men all
seem to have been a miserable lot of traitors, and when the
time came to fight they all either ran away or went over to
the enemy. To-day I have been on board the Cochran to a
dance. The captain invited us. The people were very cordial
to us, and we stayed about twenty minutes and then went on
shore for a walk.

"*Monday Night, December 7th*—We are all anxious to-night
to know what Congress has done, and what President Harrison has advised about Chile. I do hope it has been so strong
and plain that there may be no mistake about it. The feeling
on shore is very uneasy, and I could see to-day when walking
through the main street with Schley many anxious faces. The
mob is all for war with the United States, or any one else as
far as that goes; but the sensible men know it would be suicide and nothing else. The Baltimore and Yorktown would
give their navy a drubbing in two hours, and when the Boston comes we could shell the town into ruins and never be
hurt. Everything to-day looks bad for Chile. The discontent
of the army over the preference shown the navy has gone so
far that there is great alarm and fear of another revolution,
and all the soldiers have been taken out of the forts around

11. Jose Manuel Balmaceda (1840–91) was a liberal reformer and President of Chile (1886–91) whose conflict with his legislature precipitated
civil war. He was elected to the Chilean Congress in 1870. While serving
in the cabinet of President Domingo Santa Maria (1881–86), he pushed
anticlerical measures and promoted public works. As President he advanced public education and railroad construction but inherited the legislative revolt against the executive begun in the 1860s. Balmaceda's attempts to prevent congressional limitation of presidential powers led to
civil war in 1891. With naval support, the Chilean Congress defeated
Balmaceda's forces within eight months. His defeat and subsequent suicide left parliamentary government entrenched until the mid-1920s.

the harbour and men from the fleet put in. News from Santiago is also alarming. Fifteen hundred rifles and two thousand revolvers were yesterday stolen from the Government arsenal at that point, and are now supposed to be in the hands of the Balmacedists. Several of the Chilean naval officers have intimated to me very plainly that they would not stand any nonsense, and I don't hesitate to say that I would not be surprised to see another revolution in a month. Recently some officers of the army, who had been promised promotion, received commissions which did not suit them, so they tore them up, put the pieces in a bag, and sent it to the Secretary of War. How is that for military discipline?

"*Tuesday Night.*—No news yet of the President's message nor what Congress thinks of affairs in Chile. The Baltimore received orders to-day to proceed to Mare Island,[12] and in a few days I shall be here alone to face the music until Wiltse[13] comes in the Boston.

"*December 11th.*—The Baltimore sailed away for Mare Island at 9 A.M. to-day, cheered by all the foreign ships except the Chileans. First we gave them three times three, then the French cheered them, and the Germans followed suit; both nations had up the signal, 'Wish you pleasant trip,' to which Schley answered, 'Thank you.' The senior Chilean ship, the Cochran, hoisted a signal, but we could not make out the flags, and the Baltimore did not answer, so I suppose they could not read it. The signal was kept flying until the Balti-

12. Mare Island Navy Yard is located thirty-five miles northeast of San Francisco in the San Francisco Bay. This first U.S. naval base on the Pacific Ocean was established in 1853. Some 513 warships have been built at this facility to date, although it played only a small role in the Civil War and expanded slowly during Evans's period. It did outfit many of the ships that fought with Commodore George Dewey at Manila Bay in 1898.

13. Gilbert C. Wiltse was warranted an acting midshipman on 20 September 1855, and was promoted to commander on 8 November 1873. He made captain on 26 January 1887, and died in that rank on 26 April 1893.

more was out of sight, when they hauled it down. I suppose we will now be told that Captain Schley did this as an insult to the Chilean flag. For all official purposes I shall assume that the signal was not read, and could not have been, because the officer of the Cochran waited too long before hoisting it. . . .

"I have followed strictly the regulations and customs for intercourse with foreign ships of nations with whom we are at peace, and the result is that the Chilean officers have been most careful in observing toward me the greatest courtesy; they were smart enough to see that while I had no 'chip on my shoulder,' yet I would yank up the first man who ventured to neglect the least point of etiquette. People on shore are very generally saying that the presence of the Yorktown has done much to produce a proper and friendly feeling, and at the same time some of the long heads are saying: 'Commander Evans is smart; he is learning all about the Chilean ships.' which is a fact; and none of them know just how much I have found, nor will they ever, unless we have war with them, when they will find my shells searching out their most vital points. I am quite prepared to have some people say that I am leaning too far toward a friendly solution of the trouble between the two countries. They little know how hard I have to hold myself. One of the Chileans came on board to-day and sat in my cabin fully an hour, giving me an account of his exploits during the war. He was most entertaining with his bad French, and I got from him some very valuable professional information, and he went away much impressed with the friendly way in which I had received him. All I did was to give him a glass of champagne and let him talk. We have news that the Boston left Montevideo to-day, and Walker and his ships sailed from Hampton Roads yesterday for Brazil.

"*Saturday Night.*—The President's message, at least the portion of it about Chile, is published here to-day, having been wired through, and Mr. Matta,[14] the Chilean Secretary of State, has sent a most insulting message to their minister in Washington to be delivered to the State Department. He says, in so many words, that Egan[15] and Schley have lied all the way through, and that President Harrison has knowingly used false information in his message to Congress. And all this is given to the press here before it reaches Washington. I don't see how Mr. Harrison can help sending a fleet down here to teach these people manners. Among other things Mr. Matta says, in relation to the Baltimore matter, that Chile is prepared to administer justice without the advice or interference of the United States. No doubt there will be great excitement when this is all published, which it probably is in the New York papers to-day, as it was all wired through this morning. I certainly would like to hear what Mr. Blaine[16] has to say in reply.

"*Sunday, December 13th.*—I have been on board the Chilean flagship to-day to attend a dance, and was struck with the cordial way in which all their officers came forward to greet

14. M.A. Matta, the vehemently anti-American Chilean minister of foreign relations, was a leader among Chilean Radical and Liberty Party politicians.

15. Patrick Egan served as minister to Chile from 30 March 1889 to 4 July 1893.

16. James Gillespie Blaine (1830–93) was editor of the *Kennebec Journal* from 1854 to 1860, and a founder of the Republican Party in Maine. Speaker of the U.S. House of Representatives from 1864 to 1875, Blaine became a leader in the so-called "Half Breed" wing of the party. Elected Senator from Maine from 1876 to 1881, he served as Secretary of State under President James Garfield, March–December 1881. Blaine made an unsuccessful bid for the presidency in 1884, then served as Secretary of State under President Benjamin Harrison, 1889–92. Blaine organized and presided over the 1st Pan-American Congress; promoted the theory of reciprocal tariffs; secured a treaty with Great Britain concerning seal hunting; and was known as the Plumed Knight, being the author of *Twenty Years in Congress* (two volumes, 1886) and *Political Discussion* (a collection of speeches, 1887).

me and my officers. Many ladies asked for introductions, and I was assured that the Yorktown was becoming most popular on shore, and that people thought very highly of me. I took it all in very quietly until I was introduced to a young woman who proclaimed that she was a Yankee. She proceeded to tell me what a splendid man I was, and so different from Captain Schley; she hated him and all the officers of the Baltimore. Her cheek and insolence were so massive that she staggered me for a moment, but only for a moment. Then I said to her, very slowly: 'We are all the same in our service; the officers of the Yorktown and the Baltimore are as much alike as eggs in a basket, and you must not say disagreeable things about any of us.' She replied that she was ashamed to be known as an American, to which I answered that I did not think she would ever be recognised as one, and immediately returned her to the captain of the ship, who had introduced her to me at her request, and then I left her. It is easy to imagine how angry she made me. . . . The feeling today is very unsettled, owing to Matta's foolish and insolent letter published yesterday, and no one can tell what the result may be.

"*Monday, December 14th.*—The press of Valparaiso has to-day begun publishing the correspondence about the Baltimore row, and editorially they demand satisfaction. They say we owe them a large sum for stopping the Itata [17] and thus prolonging their war; that our ships and men acted as spies for Balmaceda; that our sailors landed and raised a riot in their streets, that the United States must apologize and pay a heavy sum as indemnity, and that Egan must be at once recalled. They also published to-day a story wired from Montevideo that the Boston's men landed there, fought and killed

17. A Chilean insurgent steamer engaged in a gunrunning incident that led to her capture—at the State Department's insistence—by the U.S. Navy. The incident caused an imbroglio with Chile and inflamed anti-American sentiments there in 1891.

some of the police, and in fact held the town. I don't of course, know how much truth there may be in all this, but these people are using it for all it is worth. The trouble seems further from a settlement to-day than at any previous time.

"*Wednesday, December 16th.*—There is no change in the situation on shore—still very bitter and haughty. We are coaling ship, to be ready for anything that may come. *Later.*—I am somewhat worried to-night as to what I shall do in a matter, small in itself, but possibly annoying in its results. There is a correspondent of a New York paper here for whom I do not much care. Last Thursday he went to Santiago de Chile [18] to interview President Montt, [19] and when he returned came to me with the story that Montt wanted to see me, and asked that I would come to Santiago for the purpose. Of course, I do not believe this, nor that Montt ever sent any such message, but I am not certain of it. Such an invitation ought to come through the United States minister. This was before the publication of Matta's insolent letter to the Secretary of State, which, with other things that have occurred,

18. The capital of Chile, Santiago is also called the "Andean City of the Snow White Crown." It survived flooding of the Mapocho River and a revolution in 1891 to become one of South America's premier cities.
19. Pedro Montt was President of Chile from 1906 to 1910. His conservative government, which furthered railroads and manufacturing activities, ignored pressing social and labor problems. Son of former Chilean President Manuel Montt, Pedro graduated in law from the *Instituto Nacional* in 1870. He was elected a member of the Chamber of Deputies in 1861 and became its President in 1885. He held two posts in the cabinet of President Jose Balmaceda but in 1891 took an active part in the revolution that overthrew him. He then went to the United States, first as an agent of the revolutionary junta and later (after U.S. recognition) as minister from Chile. Unsuccessful in his first bid for the presidency in 1901 as the candidate of the National Union ticket, he was finally elected in 1906. His first action was to call out the Army to suppress large-scale strikes (1907). His administration supported the construction of a railroad that ran the length of the country and stimulated the production of nitrates and copper. In 1910 Montt left Chile for medical treatment in Germany, where he died.

has determined me not to have any intercourse of an official character with any of them unless I am ordered or forced to do so.

"Well, to-day Mr. Egan telephoned down from Santiago to say that he wanted to 'chat' with me over the telephone, and as I was not on shore he asked the naval *attaché* to come aboard and ask me if I did not think that I ought, in view of the turn things had taken, to telegraph Schley at Callao[20] to come back here with the Baltimore, and would I come to Santiago to consult with him (Egan). My answer was that Secretary Tracy[21] was at one end of the wire and Schley at the other, and I had no doubt the Secretary would send the Baltimore back here if he considered her presence necessary; also that I saw no good reason why I should leave my ship to consult with him about matters over which I had no control and could take no action. I am quite determined to attend to my own business and not get mixed up with the political part of this muddle. If I should go to Santiago, and if Montt did send me that message, he would be offended if I declined to call on him except in company with our minister—which I undoubtedly should do—so the best thing is to stay where I am. But it worries me, and I may have to give in and go.

"The papers here grow more and more insolent, and I

20. A city of west-central Peru on the Pacific coast, near Lima.
21. Dubbed the "Father of the Modern American Fighting Navy," Benjamin F. Tracy (1830–1915)—a New York lawyer and Civil War hero (he received the Medal of Honor)—served as district attorney in New York City before becoming a political appointee in Benjamin Harrison's administration. An ardent nationalist and navalist, Tracy embraced the sea-power doctrine of Alfred Thayer Mahan, successfully proselyted the naval renaissance before Congress, introduced construction of fighting vessels such as battleships, and forged the naval-industrial relationships necessary for the production of armored steel and heavy ordnance. His role in the expansionism of the period was robust and countered the often more pacific diplomacy of Secretary of State James Blaine. Tracy was also instrumental in advancing naval organizational and educational reforms during his tenure.

don't see how Mr. Harrison can avoid sending an ultimatum at a very early day. In the meantime the Chileans are working like beavers to get their ships ready, and in two weeks from now the whole fleet will be ready for service. My relations with them all are in accordance with the strictest etiquette, and will remain so until the shooting begins—and even after.

"*Thursday, December 17th.*—I had to go on shore to-day, *nolens volens,* as Mr. Egan *must* talk with me through the 'phone. He did about all the talking, and I listened. Yesterday he discovered that they had fifteen men—ten soldiers, disguised as policemen, and five spies—around his house; and he also thinks he has discovered a plot to burn his house, by setting fire to the house next to his, and thus get possession of the refugees now under his protection. Five persons were arrested as they left the Spanish legation in the evening, and one of them, ex-President of Ecuador,[22] was detained several hours in the common jail. Egan is much excited, evidently expects trouble, and, I think, rather hopes to see it, but I can't join him in that.

"The afternoon papers publish a telegram from San Francisco, saying that the San Francisco has sailed with sealed orders, probably for Chile. I shall be glad when the admiral arrives, as I am not in the least pleased with the present outlook here.

"After I had done talking with Mr. Egan I went for a walk, and was scowled at by no end of cutthroat-looking chaps."

On Friday, December 18th, came a long cipher cable from the Department, which required four hours for its translation. The contents were not of the most peaceful nature. My reply gave the information wanted in something like two hundred words. It took me all night to put it into cipher.

22. Evans is possibly referring to Dr. Placedo Caamano.

CHAPTER 22

Strained Relations

O N the following morning the Valparaiso papers said the trouble between the two countries was about settled; that there would be no war, and that we had found out that Chile was in the right all the time. If the editors had seen the message I had received and my reply I think they would have changed their minds somewhat. Press reports from the United States published the same morning indicated great activity in the Navy Department. One of the papers had, in large headlines, "What we may expect when the Boston arrives." The article then went on to state that she had landed ninety-five men on liberty in Montevideo, and ninety of them were arrested. I felt sure that the Boston's men were not in any such condition as this indicated, and I was confident at the same time that the article and many more like it were meant to influence public opinion against us and prepare them for more riots and bloodshed.

Monday, December 21st, brought me a telegram to keep my ship filled up with coal, which led me to wonder if they regarded me at the Department as some kind of an idiot. Of course I was full of coal and everything else I should need when the time for action came. All my plans were made down to the smallest detail, and my mind made up as to what I would do under certain conditions. The head of the house of Grace & Company [1] must have had some serious telegram from New York on this day, as he said to me in the afternoon that things looked bad for a settlement. Mr. Egan 'phoned me in the evening that his son had been arrested in Santiago the previous day as he came out of the legation, and later two other persons had been arrested in the same way and held for two hours or more. The situation was becoming very critical, and the conduct of the authorities seemed like madness to me—almost as if they intended to force us into war. I was quite ready for it if they said the word.

I was determined to meet the Chileans halfway in any proposition they had to make, and therefore, when I received an invitation for a Christmas tree [tea], I accepted it and presented myself at the proper hour. It was pleasant to see some fifty-odd children enjoy themselves, but the grown people were as nasty a lot as I ever met. I was introduced to them all and tried to talk to them, but one after another had something disagreeable to say about the United States. One and all of them hated the officers of our navy who had been there before us, and they did not hesitate to tell me so. My visit was cut very short, and I returned to my ship feeling as no Christian ought to feel on Christmas eve.

Our surroundings naturally drew all of us closer together, and I gladly accepted the invitation of the wardroom officers to take my Christmas dinner with them. They had also, as

1. William R. Grace & Company was the influential New York commercial house whose role in the Chilean controversy and American overseas commercial expansionism of the Benjamin Harrison administration was conditioned by its president. A former New York mayor and Republican supporter, Grace served as a confidential adviser to Secretary James Blaine and sometime supporter of the Chilean insurgents, providing them with arms and ammunition.

their guests, the consul and several of our countrymen from
shore. We had a charming dinner over "sweethearts and
wives," and forgot for the moment the troubles threatening
us. The following from my journal gives an accurate account
of incidents at this time:

"Events crowd on rapidly now, and our troubles here must
soon be settled one way or another. The Boston came in yesterday, and I was glad to see her, but to-day she is ordered
north, leaving me alone again to face the music here. It is a
great surprise to every one. Wiltse signalled me this afternoon at five to repair on board, which I at once did, and
found him up to his eyes in a cipher telegram which was too
much for him. We soon unravelled it, however, and it was,
'Proceed north immediately with the Boston,' etc. He will
be off to-morrow, and the Yorktown will again hold the fort,
which shows a gratifying confidence in me on the part of the
Secretary. I feel the weight of responsibility which rests on
my shoulders. The Boston will be off to-morrow, and in the
meantime I have information that a riot is threatened here,
and that two regiments of artillery came here to-day from
Santiago. Of course, they would not have sent them unless
they feared another row, and if it comes my duty will be a
hard one. There will be only two ships here, one French and
one American—except, of course, the vessels of the Chilean
fleet, which can not be counted on at such a time. If trouble
comes, the English and Germans here will call on us for protection, and I shall have them on my hands as well as our
own people. So I am not yachting in the real sense of the
word.

"*Saturday Night, December 26th.*—The Boston has gone,
and we are once more the only Yankee here. Wiltse called on
most of the officials, and the newspapers give him a good
send off. One paper says that his politeness, following so soon
on the courteous conduct of 'Señor' Evans, commanding the
Yorktown, had gone far toward removing the bad impression
made by the Baltimore. Another paper copies a long article

from the London Times, showing how easily the Chilean navy could clean us up, capture San Francisco, and do no end of awful things. Still another says that the Chicago, Concord,[2] and Wilmington[3] will soon be here, and when they have gone north the people of Valparaiso will have had two thirds of the Yankee navy passed in review. Such insolence!

"Mr. Egan 'phoned me to-day that he had not attended the inauguration of President Montt. I suppose the press will make all sorts of a row over that. I am sure that if he had gone he would have been insulted, and it is likely that some attempt on his legation would have been made in his absence. His position and that of the United States is much strengthened by an incident which occurred day before yesterday, the arrest of General Velasquez. He was Secretary of War under Balmaceda, and about two months before the collapse of that government was thrown from his horse and had his leg broken. He had been arrested by the Junta government[4] and bailed for ten thousand dollars, but day before yesterday was again arrested, on the ground that he was organizing a revolution, because arms were found in his house. A mob gathered and demanded his blood, but enough of a

2. This sail and steam, steel patrol gunboat was a sister ship to the *Yorktown* and *Bennington* in all particulars except that she was constructed by N.F. Palmer. Laid down in May 1888, the USS *Concord* was launched on 8 March 1890 and commissioned on 15 February 1891. She served as an accommodation ship from 1909 to 1914, and then as a quarantine station vessel under the Department of the Treasury until being sold in 1929.
3. Authorized under an act of 2 March 1893, the USS *Wilmington* was a steam-powered steel patrol gunboat of 1,397 tons, a top speed of 15 knots, sixteen guns, and a complement of 183–199 men. Laid down on 8 October 1894 at the Newport News Shipbuilding Company, she was launched on 19 October 1895 and commissioned on 13 May 1897. The *Wilmington* was used later as a training ship and renamed *Dover* in World War II. She was sold in 1946.
4. Elected by the Chilean Congress, the Junta government consisted of Don Ramon Barros Luco, Admiral Don Jorge Montt, and Don Waldo Silva.

guard was on hand to drag him away and place him in confinement on board the Magallanes, one of their receiving
ships. I am told to-day that he was shot to death on board
that vessel at midnight last night, and the authorities do not
deny it, but say that if he has not been killed he will be, and
that his friends will never know how or when. Now this is a
find prospect for the gentlemen who are refugeed in the legation at Santiago! If they are given up, every one will undoubtedly be killed, and the nations of the earth will justly
hold us responsible. While I do not believe in the right of
asylum, and would not permit our legations to be used for
that purpose, still, having once received these men, we must
stand by them even if it leads to war. Just at this point I was
called on deck by some quick volleys fired on shore near us,
followed by a few straggling shots. One of these fine nights
they will send some of their bullets over us, and then they
will have a surprise party.

"*Sunday Night.*—I found out this afternoon in a curious
way about the firing last night. It was continued at intervals
all night. This morning early the Esmeralda came in with
colours at half mast, having on board the fragments of patriots killed at Iquiqui[5] and Caldera Bay.[6] She was draped in
black, and looked as if she had not been scrubbed for a
year—quite the most grief-stricken craft I ever saw. Just at
four o'clock a boat came to us from the senior officer afloat
to ask us to participate in the ceremonies afloat tomorrow,
when they are going to bury the remains of some naval patriots. So little could be made out of what the young officer
was trying to tell us that I took my boat and went on board
the Cochran to get things straight. Captain Vial, who commands her, . . . when I assured him that we should be glad
to join in honouring their dead, did not know where to put

5. A city of northwestern Chile on the Pacific Ocean.
6. Named for the town of the Chilean coast north of Capiapo between
Valparaíso and Iquiqui.

me. He told me he was much gratified by my acceptance, but had feared that I would decline because these officers had been killed during the war. In other words, we were on the Balmaceda side, and would not even go to the funeral of the other party. I was not to be caught by such stupid trash. I told him that in my country we knew no difference among Chileans, alive or dead; that we never in any case carried our feelings beyond the moment of dissolution, etc. When I asked him what the firing was about last night, he said the men in the naval battery on shore thought some smuggling was going on and fired, and some soldiers in adjoining works, to give the idea that they were ready, took it up, and hence the row. While he was telling me this plausible yarn I was observing his decks and wondering if the smuggling racket would account for all the ammunition I saw piled ready for use. The truth is, they expected an attack, and no doubt shot some of the suspects just to keep their hands in. I shall go to their wake tomorrow, as I told Captain Vial, on the water; but, as I also told him, I will not allow one of my men to land.

"No news from Santiago to-day, except that Montt was inaugurated and that the Chambers could not agree on a Cabinet, which is unfortunate, as the present lot will have to hold over, and they will continue to menace our legation and thus make matters worse. As to Egan, he has done only what he was instructed to do from Washington, and he has done it capitally well. The Chilean Secretary of State has found himself outclassed every time he has tackled the little Irishman, who really writes clearly, forcibly, and beautifully, and so far they have not scored one point against him.

"The whole diplomatic question in dispute is a simple one: 1. 'The right of asylum in foreign legations.' 2. '*Salvo conducto*,[7] for such refugees, to a neutral territory.' In 1866,

7. Literally, safe conduct.

during a revolution in Peru, the Chilean Government directed its minister in that country to insist on both principles, and they were enforced, and *salvo conducto* furnished to neutral territory. In 1888, at a Congress of the South American Republics, the Chilean representative presented and had embodied in a treaty, which was afterward ratified by all, a clause that refugees should be protected when sheltered in foreign legations, and charged only with political offences; and that *salvo conducto* should be demanded and furnished all such refugees, reserving to the Government in whose territory the legation is located the right to demand the speedy removal of the parties from its territory. Thus this practice became international law as far as the parties to the treaty are concerned, but the Junta government, through Mr. Matta, now says the Government of Chile has changed. Mr. Egan replies that local changes and edicts of Chile can not change international law and practice. The Chileans are knocked out and refuse to continue the discussion. Having admitted his right to give them asylum, their present attitude is absurd, and only makes a permanent prison of the legation; the men would undoubtedly be killed the moment they were turned out.

"*Monday,* P.M.—We helped to bury the patriots to-day, or rather we escorted them to the shore from the Esmeralda, and then returned to the ship. Of course, I would not go on shore for the funeral, but I did go later to call on the senior officer in command of the naval station, to get what news I could out of him, and was moderately successful. He let it out that they would send four of their vessels to Iquiqui, some time in January, at the suggestion of President Montt. Of course, their idea is to defend that place against us and rely on the rest of the fleet and the forts to hold Valparaiso. He had no idea of the value of the information he was giving me, or he would not have talked so freely. Afterward he said many things which lead me to believe that they expect an attack every night, and I should not be surprised to see it any hour.

"When I left him I met the head of the house of Grace and Company, and he showed me a long telegram from W.R. Grace, dated in Washington yesterday, of the most alarming character. Grace has been in Washington for the past ten days trying to convince Secretary Blaine that we must not have war. He wires that Harrison is for war, that the Navy Department is making every preparation for war, and that Blaine, while in favour of war under certain conditions only, can not stem the tide, and that unless Chile makes ample apology at once nothing can prevent war. The message is to Grace's business house, and therefore can be relied on as giving his best information; and he is a warm personal friend of Mr. Blaine. Taking all this into consideration, the crew of the Yorktown will sleep at the loaded guns to-night, and every night until I get some better news. While I can not deny to myself that things are on the 'ragged edge,' so to speak, yet I can not conceive of the Chileans being stupid enough to allow it to come to blows—it seems incredible folly. And yet it may come. News from Santiago to-day is to the effect that President Montt is still unable to form a Cabinet. If this condition continues much longer, it alone will bring revolution.

"*Tuesday*, P.M.—After the alarming telegram I saw yesterday I went on shore again to-day and found that the English minister had long messages from his Government, which he had shown to Mr. Egan, and here again I was much surprised. The despatches say, in plain language, that the English Government considers that war between the United States and Chile is inevitable; and yet I have not one word from the Department to put me on my guard. I certainly do not understand it in the least.

"*Valparaiso, Chile, December 30th.*—The steamer has just

gone out. Every one that goes I hope may be the last until we go. While I was ashore, walking up the street with Fred May,[8] three *rotas*,[9] the most villainous-looking scoundrels I ever saw, crossed over and followed us some distance, muttering about 'damned Yankees.' I saw Fred get a fresh grip on his stick, and I did the same, and, keeping one eye over my shoulder, just as they were close behind us we suddenly turned and walked through them, as it were, before they had time to do anything. We were in the main street of town, otherwise I have no doubt they would have attacked us, and if they had we surely would have pounded the life out of two of them at least.

"There is a rumour to-day on the street that Chile has offered thirty thousand dollars as a settlement of the Baltimore affair, but I can not learn that it is true.

"*December 31st, Night.*—There is to be a row at midnight and I have been asked to join in it, but declined. The Chileans are going to fire twenty-one guns and burn fireworks to usher in the new year, which seems an odd thing to do, but these are odd people. The war feeling is about the same to-day, and the papers publish a telegram in which Admiral Brown[10] is made to say that there will be no war with Chile, and that he is not coming back with the San Francisco; and, further, that the affair of the Baltimore will be submitted to arbitration, which seems too silly to notice. When the United States is willing to submit the question of the murder of her sailors in uniform to arbitration, I must look for other

8. Sidney H. "Fred" May graduated from the U.S. Naval Academy on 4 June 1869 and rose to the rank of lieutenant on 9 May 1878. He died on 20 July 1892.
9. The term refers to the Chilean urban working class. Evans has the wrong gender, however. *Roto* is masculine; *rota,* feminine.
10. George Brown ascended during his naval career as follows: midshipman, 5 February 1849; commander, 25 July 1866; captain, 25 April 1877; commodore, 4 September 1887; and rear admiral, 27 September 1893. He retired on 19 June 1897.

employment—the navy won't any longer suit me. They can arbitrate 'till the cows come home' about the people in the legation at Santiago, but if they ever hint at such a thing about the Baltimore's men, then I think the voice of the American people will be heard in no uncertain tones.

"*January 1, 1892.*—Just before midnight last night we ordered champagne, and each one stood with his full glass until the bell struck, when we all drank to our friends at home a 'happy New Year.' Then we went on deck, whence we could hear and see the Chileans making their row. The whole city of Valparaiso was red and green with lights, presenting one of the most beautiful sights imaginable.

"The Chilean vessels added to the effect by flashing their electric lights in every direction, and everything that could make a noise was doing its best, but not a sound came from the Yorktown except the low murmurs of the men as they stood around the guns. It was an impressive sight."

As the Cochran fired the first gun of her salute she sent off a flight of rockets; one of them, a war rocket, just missed the Yorktown. We were in plain view on account of the beams of the numerous search lights from the Chilean war vessels, and it seemed that the rocket must have been purposely aimed at us; but there was room for doubt, and as it had not struck us I assumed that it was an accident. I at once hoisted a large American flag and turned both my search lights on it, so that if any one really wanted to hit me he could know just where I was. I was determined, if trouble came, there should be no ground for saying we had been accidentally struck in the dark. When the search lights, a few moments later, again lighted us up, they showed the crew of the Yorktown standing at their quarters and the guns all ready for business. The second war rocket from the Cochran went through the rigging of a German steamer some distance away from us, but no more came our way. I again quote from my journal:

"*January 1, 1892.*—The telegrams in the morning papers

from Washington are most warlike. Before I was through with my breakfast a long cipher message came from the Secretary, directing me to keep him posted on all movements of Chilean warships; and one from the President, to proceed to Santiago and confer with our minister, ascertain present situation, and especially the sentiment of Chile toward the United States. It is extraordinary to send a naval officer to find out the sentiment of the country, and I have a job on my hands. The responsibility of the position almost frightens me. I could wire back a message to-morrow that would cause a declaration of war in twenty-four hours. I shall leave for Santiago in the morning and spend two days there, getting such information as I can, and looking at the actual condition of things, that I may give the President such an answer as will enable him to lay the matter before Congress. Of course, I shall be uncomfortable and much worried all the time I am away, but that is what I am paid for.

"*Later,*—This afternoon the most important part of the finding in the Baltimore case is published. The judge finds that two Chileans are implicated; that the row was begun by the Baltimore's men, who were drunk, and that their testimony was of no value; that Reagan was killed by a revolver shot from some party unknown. He does not seem to see the absurdity of two Chileans having stabbed over a dozen men in a fight which went on at the same time in half a dozen different places covering a space of more than half a mile. I am curious to know what Mr. Blaine will say when he gets the news.

"*Monday, January 4th.*—Glad to get to the little ship once more last night at midnight. I have been making out a cipher message of one hundred and seventy-eight words to the Secretary, and it consumed the entire day, so that I have not been on shore; but the message has gone, and by now the Secretary and probably the President knows just what I think of the situation at Santiago. My message gave the decision in the

Baltimore case and some news of the Chilean navy, and then I said substantially that the United States legation at Santiago, containing many refugees, was virtually a prison watched by uniformed police and spies in plain clothes—the latter removed during my visit. General sentiment of Santiago and Valparaiso brutally hostile to the United States. New Chilean Secretary of State expresses friendship, and hopes matters will be promptly arranged. . . . I was too anxious and full of business to enjoy the trip. . . .

"Santiago is a large, straggling city in a great dust-covered plain surrounded by brown mountains topped with snow. The minister met me at the station, and we drove a mile or so through very rough streets to a very dirty hotel. I started with Mr. Egan and the three officers who were with me, to walk to the legation, a distance of about ten blocks, and I was amused at the scowls the party received from the people on the way. When we came in sight of the legation I counted eight uniformed police and five of the worst-looking devils of *rotas* in plain clothes that I have ever gazed on, all guarding the place. I walked around, counted these brutes, and looked them over, and they were very uncomfortable under the scrutiny. In the afternoon the spies were withdrawn, leaving only the police in uniform.

"After I had paid my respects to Mrs. Egan I was introduced to the party of refugees, and was really impressed with the scene. Our minister, an Irish agitator representing a great Government, and under his protection many of the finest men of Chile, blue-blooded and aristocratic, treating Mrs. Egan like a queen, and looking to the self-made, brave little Irishman for their lives. The whole thing was impressive and curious. I managed to say a few words to each of them, but with General Gana, formerly Secretary of War, I had a long conversation; his French was awful, but perhaps he thought the same of mine. He is seventy years old, and was an intimate friend of Admiral Dahlgren,[11] for whose memory he entertains a high regard. In fact, he considers all Americans superior people. He was for many years general of the army, and gave his whole life to the service of his country; and yet they would tear him to pieces were it not that the American flag protects him.

"I also had some talk with Señor McKenna, who was President of the Balmaceda Senate, a most thoroughbred, delicate-looking gentleman. He is enormously wealthy. His position and surroundings are most irksome, and the confinement is telling on his health. It was pathetic when he told me that if his countrymen did not kill him he would make his home in North America, where he could rear his children with the advantages of civilization."

The sacking of Santiago by the rebels after its surrender probably has no parallel in history for wanton waste and destruction. The houses to be sacked were all placed on a list, which was given to a regiment of half-breeds from the mining districts, and they were ordered to do the job. I can certify from personal observation that they did their work very thoroughly. I stood in front of what had been the beautiful home of Mr. John McKenna, and wondered how human beings could be found to do such work. Every article of value had been stolen or destroyed, and the floors and woodwork, even to the window casings, torn up and broken to pieces or carried away. It was a fearful picture of what civil war might mean at its worst. I again quote from my journal:

"On Sunday Mr. Egan gave me a breakfast at Santa Lucia,

11. John A. Dahlgren was warranted a midshipman on 1 February 1832. He was promoted to commander on 14 September 1855, captain on 16 July 1862, and rear admiral on 7 February 1863. He died on 12 July 1870. The Navy's foremost ordnance expert of his day, Dahlgren was most noted for his development of the soda-bottle-shaped Dahlgren gun. He served as chief of the Bureau of Ordnance, 1862–63 and 1868–69, and as commander of the South Atlantic Blockading Squadron from 1863 to 1865.

a rock which rises some hundreds of feet in the heart of the city, and on top of which is a fair restaurant, and whence the view is fine. The party was mixed, which for my purpose suited very well, and I got much valuable information from them, especially from a Chilean army officer, who had been a junior officer in the British army. He resigned, to find employment about Iquiqui, where he was when the war came, when, believing the rebels to be right, he joined them, fought well, and after the fall of Balmaceda was promoted and is now on duty at Santiago. I got a lot of information from him. When the Baltimore row took place he was sent down to Valparaiso to investigate the matter privately and report to the authorities in Santiago. He was soon satisfied that the police shot Reagan, but in order to decide the point fully he demanded such orders as would compel the authorities here to give him the witnesses he wanted. He went to Santiago and reported his conviction that the police had done the killing, for which the authorities jumped on him and 'gave him the devil,' and would not let him return here. Now he has given them notice that if they have any trouble with the United States he will leave their service. The day we left Santiago the minister saw me off, and we had the same salute of scowls from the people. On my way to Santiago I am sure I was guarded by two very nice-looking officers in uniform, who observed my every movement, and on my way down I had a similar escort, probably sent by the authorities to see that no harm was done me.

"*January 5th.*—To-day I have been on shore for an hour and saw the consul's son, who has come out as secretary of legation. He left Washington on December 10th, and tells me that the war talk here was very strong—that Harrison was wild over the Baltimore matter, and it was all Blaine could do to hold him back. I don't wonder. To-night I have been reading up the papers, and find the tone of our Administration very dignified, though savage. I don't see how war can now be avoided. Sorry to see that Jack Philip [12] was detached from the Atlanta if she is to come here; but he will have a beautiful command in the New York, and do the service credit anywhere.

"*January 6th.*—This afternoon I went for a few minutes to a grand ball on board the Cochran, and when I came back found awaiting me a half-tipsy chap who had come to tell me, confidentially, that my ship was to be attacked to-night or to-morrow night by the Chileans, and he warned me to make every preparation, as they were in earnest, and would begin the war with the United States by sinking or capturing the Yorktown. Nice information for a fellow to sleep on! The chap said he had been well treated by the Americans and would stand by them. Of course, I don't place much confidence in the story, but I am on my guard all the same, and to-night we have steam up and the men sleeping at the guns among the ammunition.

"The captain of the Cochran has just sent an officer on board to say that he will fire a salute of twenty-one guns at one o'clock in the morning, as that will be the anniversary of their revolt. Such idiots! I don't think I shall sleep much *este noche.*

"*January 8th.*—The Chileans certainly did celebrate night before last, to the annoyance of all quietly disposed persons. The harbour was ablaze and salutes were fired until midnight, and I was not certain that they would not take a shy at us, so I watched them closely, and am thankful that nothing unpleasant happened. I am equally sorry that something very unpleasant did happen to-day—nothing less than the stoning of my gig while she was lying off the landing-place, waiting to bring me off. When I landed I noticed that the people

12. John W. Philip was warranted an acting midshipman on 20 September 1856. Captain of the battleship *Texas* in the West Indies campaign, Philip was promoted to commodore on 10 August 1898 and rear admiral on 3 March 1899. He died on 30 June 1900.

scowled at me rather more than usual, but it passed out of my mind until a party of young fellows on a street car made themselves offensive.

"After I had attended to my business I came down and called my boat in, and while waiting for her to get alongside I became aware that there was a crowd of rather larger proportions than usual on the mole, and they seemed excited by something. Just as I stepped into my boat one of them advanced quickly toward me, and the cockswain said, 'Look out for that fellow, sir!' I said, 'He won't trouble me,' stepped into the boat, and shoved off, and then discovered that the crew were all fighting mad. On inquiry I learned that a lot of toughs had amused themselves by throwing stones at the boat and daring the men to come on shore. I was hot all over, and without going to my own ship I pulled straight for the Cochran, whose captain, Vial, is senior officer in command of the city as well as the fleet. I could hardly hold myself down while I told him of it; but I did, and then read him the riot act. I demanded of him immediate and efficient protection by the police, and served notice on him, then and there, that a repetition of the offence would be sufficient evidence that they could not control their people, and that I should arm my boats and shoot any and every man who insulted me or my men or my flag in any way. Vial was greatly shocked, or pretended to be, turned as white as a sheet—my manner was not very mild, I fancy—swore and damned the discharged soldiers, and said they were doing all they could to involve the country in war with the United States, while he and the navy were determined that it should not be; and then, in his excitement, he gave away something I am sure he was very sorry for: he said, 'We have just discovered to-day a plot to attack the American legation at Santiago, and we have the men under arrest.' What a set of savages we have to deal with! After a few moments Captain Vial hastened on shore to jump the police, assuring me that I should have an ample apology to-morrow, and assurances of protection. Of course, I shall wire the affair to the Department after I have settled it, but in the mildest way I can. I don't want to be sensational, and I hope the papers won't get hold of it.

"If they bother us again I shall consider that the time has come to shoot. The anxiety of the position here is very great; it interferes with my sleep, and is telling on my temper.

"*Valparaiso, January 9th.*—Lots of things have happened since last night. Just at midnight I heard a sharp hail, 'Boat ahoy!' and the answer, 'American consul.' I was out in a minute, and there the consul was, as large as life, and evidently with something important on his mind. When we reached the cabin he said Mr. Egan had just telephoned to ask me to have my steam launch at a certain point about five miles from the ship at six sharp this morning, as he was coming unexpectedly to pay me a visit. Of course, I knew what that meant, and everything was made ready, and at about 2 A.M., after providing the consul with a shakedown, I went to bed. We were up at four, had some coffee and eggs, and the executive officer shoved off in charge, with the consul to show him where to go, and half a dozen revolvers, with cartridges, etc.

"At 7:30 I saw the boat returning, and was much relieved when she came alongside.

"The first man out was Mr. Egan; then came Mr. Mc-Kenna, [13] formerly Minister of Foreign Affairs, then President of the Chilean Senate, and lately a refugee in the American legation. After him came his cousin, William McKenna, late Governor of Santiago under Balmaceda; and then their wives and servants. My heart sank into my boots when I saw the women, but fortunately they went on shore afterward; and their husbands, who would be torn to pieces if they were caught, are now sleeping as calmly as two children, within twelve feet of me. The American flag is a wonderful thing

13. Juan McKenna was President of the Chilean Senate during the Balmacedist regime.

when all is said and done. Here are these two men with no claim on us beyond our sentiment of right and humanity, whose lives have not been worth a nickel for months, now resting quiet and secure in the midst of the Chilean fleet, and under the guns of ten heavy forts; and all because a small gunboat flying the American flag has them in charge.

"Other important things have happened: Captain Vial has been on board to apologize for the stoning of the gig yesterday and to assure me of protection, and the English admiral has arrived in the Warspite.

"*January 10th, 11* P.M.—Just back from a conference with the English admiral on board the Warspite, and more tired than last night, but must write a few lines, because if I do not set down things as they happen I shall forget them.

"Admiral Hotham, R.N.,[14] is disposed to be very nice. Mr. Egan, who went back to Santiago last night, wires me to-day that he has a long message from Mr. Blaine, directing him to *ask* the Chilean Government: (1) 'If they will give *salvo conducto* to those who still remain in the legation at Santiago'; and (2) 'Do they want to withdraw the letter of Mr. Matta, Secretary of Foreign Affairs, which was so insulting to our Government?' This looks to me very much as if it were going to rain in a few days in Chile.

"To comprehend the situation we must consider that Mr. Egan brought the men, now on board, without written *salvo conducto,* but with the tacit permission of the authorities. They refused to give a written permit, thus hoping to dodge the question, but Mr. Blaine is nailing the matter, and will make them settle the *salvo conducto* question at once. Egan will not now allow any more refugees to leave the legation without written permits. This is the beginning of the end of the Chilean trouble.

14. Evans is referring to Sir Charles Frederick Hotham, once Commander-in-Chief, Pacific Station, Commander-in-Chief, Portsmouth (1902), and Admiral of the Fleet (1903).

"*Monday Afternoon, January 11th.*—Yesterday evening came more cablegrams, and to-day I have news from Egan that the Chilean Government pledges safe conduct to the refugees now in the legation out of the country, and to-morrow night they will be down on me to the number of six or eight—not only those in the legation, but others. There is no Spanish vessel of war in the harbour, and at the request of the Spanish and American ministers I have consented to take on board the refugees now in the Spanish legation. I wish they were all clear of the country and we with them.

"This ship is constantly overrun with the wives, daughters, and cousins of the men now on board, and I suppose, when the others come, things will be much worse. A large party has just gone away, among them a beautiful daughter of Mr. McKenna, who said to me as she left, 'I love zis plaice'—and much they may love it!

"Mr. Egan also tells me that the police have been removed from around the legation, but the Chilean Government is not prepared to withdraw the offensive note of Mr. Matta. It is willing to say that no offence was meant, but will not withdraw the note. Egan replies that ours are a thinking people, and, given the language of the note, they can decide for themselves as to its offensiveness. After it is withdrawn we will settle the Baltimore affair. All the refugees once out of danger, we shall then be in a position to say what we propose to do, and then go ahead and do it; but up to this time we have been heavily handicapped by our wards, who would undoubtedly have been killed at the first warlike demonstration.

"*Tuesday, January 12th.*—Last evening I dined with Admiral Hotham on board the Warspite, and had a good dinner and friendly treatment. To-day I am notified by Mr. Egan that he will be down to-morrow with more refugees—all that are left in Santiago, it seems. They will be escorted by the Spanish and Italian ministers, who are all coming on board the Yorktown, and will probably spend the day with us. I have no idea what I shall do with so many people, but one thing I am sure of, and that is that I shall salute all these ministers; and when I have fired my forty-five guns the people of Valparaiso will know that the question of *salvo conducto* is settled, for the present at least. Egan has come out of the whole business with flying colours, and were it not for what might be said I would wear a green ribbon in my buttonhole tomorrow simply to show my respect for the sandy little Irishman. The consul is on board for the night, and will go with my boats to-morrow morning to show them just where to find Egan and his party, and after they come the cabin will be more crowded than it is now.

"I shall do all in my power to send the refugees away in the first steamer that leaves here.

"*January 17th.*—It is some days since I last wrote, but the cabin is so crowded that I can only write late at night. Four days ago, early in the morning, I sent in two boats, met the train, and brought off the whole lot of refugees from the United States and Spanish legations, accompanied by the United States, the Spanish, and Italian ministers. I made them as comfortable as I could, being assured not only that they came by permission of the Government, but that they would leave on Saturday (yesterday) in the steamer John Elder, of the P.S.N. Co., for Europe. Tickets were bought and everything made ready. In the meantime, when the ministers were about to leave the ship, the one from Italy asked that I would not fire him a salute, and I did not. The Spaniard, Count Brunetti, had requested me to take two refugees from his legation, which I did, and therefore (if for no other reason) saluted him when he left. On Friday Mr. Egan wired me that the Santiago authorities had changed base, and would not give safe conduct to the refugees, and that they would arrest them when the John Elder touched at a Chilean port—all because we had saluted the Spanish minister, and thus called attention to the fact that they had permitted the refugees to leave.

"I promptly requested Mr. Egan to say to the Minister of Foreign Affairs that I was responsible to my own Government and not that of Chile for my conduct, and that I considered his remarks about my salute to the Spanish minister offensive and would not submit to them; also that I should cable the matter to my Government, which I did, and, as they have not said a word about it, I assume that they approve of my action.

"Of course, the refugees could not go on the John Elder, and we now have them quartered on board. The bother and discomfort are very great, but the expense is the more serious matter to me. The John Elder put to sea at 2 P.M., and at four this afternoon we had news of her total loss on the rocks at four this morning—all hands saved. What an escape the refugees had! If they had gone in her they would all have been shot by this time.

"The English cruiser Melpomene [15] has gone to the scene of the wreck. Of course, I have wired the Secretary very fully, and he and the President know the whole situation. I have wired for permission to land my passengers at Callao, twelve hundred miles away, but fear he will not permit it. A Chilean squadron will leave here to-morrow, bound south, and I have information that they will attempt to stop Walker in the Straits of Magellan. I have wired it to Washington."

From the time I received the refugees on board I was in constant anticipation of trouble. The morning they came I had my ship cleared for action, and fully expected to have to use my guns before the affair was concluded. Threats had been openly made that if I took the refugees on board, the Chilean ships would take them out again. The excitement

15. A second-class steam-powered steel cruiser of approximately 2,950 tons, nineteen guns, two torpedo tubes, two torpedo carriages, and a 218-man complement. HMS *Melpomme* was laid down at the Portsmouth Dockyard on 10 October 1877, launched on 20 September 1888, and completed in 1890. She was sheathed in wood and copper for tropical service. The cruiser was sold in 1905.

was very general, and feeling ran high. While Mr. Blaine had not insisted on written *salvo conductos,* he had exacted verbal ones; and the Chilean Government was not aware of what was going on, but anxious to get the parties out of the country. But Santiago could not control Valparaiso, and in the latter port, with its turbulent population, lay the danger.

During the first few hours after their arrival I noticed that none of the refugees would show themselves above the rail of the ship, notwithstanding I had chairs on the poop deck for them. Senor Ibaños, formerly minister to the United States, was among the last lot that had arrived, and when I asked him what the trouble was he showed me a letter from a friend on shore warning him and his friends that if they raised their heads above the rail they would be shot, and that boats were lurking about my ship for the purpose of shooting them. Up to this time I had allowed the fishing boats to fish close alongside the Yorktown, but I now gave orders to keep them away and to double our sentries. The orders the sentries had would have made it serious work for any boatman to show anything that looked like a gun anywhere near us.

I had my boat manned, and with the letter spoken of, and several others of the same tenor, called on Captain Vial, of the Cochran, and gave him tersely my views of the situation. I pointed out to him that I did not command a prison ship, but that his countrymen, who had taken refuge on board of me, were the guests of the United States, and that they were there with the knowledge and consent of the Chilean Government. I assured him that I would protect them to the last extremity, and warned him to keep all boats away from the immediate vicinity, or they might come to grief. At the same time I notified him that I would only allow boats from men of war showing the Chilean flag to come alongside the York-town, so that in case anything unpleasant happened I should know whom to hold responsible. After this there was no more trouble, but I was constantly on the lookout and pre-pared for it.

CHAPTER 23

A Welcome Departure

About January 20th I received telegraphic orders permitting me to land my passengers at Callao, Peru, at my discretion. I at once notified the Chilean authorities that I would leave Valparaiso in six hours. I also visited the English admiral and gave him the same information. He called my attention to the fact that four of the Chilean ships had steam up, and to the further fact that it had been announced in the Valparaiso papers that when I went to sea their ships would go after me to see that I did not land the refugees and get up another revolution. I told the admiral very plainly that if any ship or number of ships followed me to sea and undertook to follow my motions I would regard it as an act of gross discourtesy and insult to my flag, and would resent it on the spot. I never learned whether he communicated with the Chileans on the subject or not, but when I got under way at the time I had fixed and steamed out, nobody pursued me, or attempted to do so. The condition in Valparaiso had become almost unbearable, and it was with a sense of great relief that I found myself at sea.

During the early part of the first night out, while running

at very high speed, a suspicious noise was heard in the high-pressure cylinder of one of the engines. When the cylinder head was taken off I found two hardened steel wedges, which had been placed in the valve chest, no doubt, when we first arrived at Valparaiso by some evilly disposed person, with the intention of sending us all to the bottom. It could easily have been done when we first arrived, and before we knew what kind of people we had to deal with. It was simply a miracle that I escaped a serious disaster, for if the cylinder head had been knocked out with the pressure of steam I was carrying, the side of the ship would have gone with it. As I stood watching the group of machinists and firemen working about the engines I could see the blood come into their faces until the whites of their eyes were bloodshot. I knew pretty well what they were thinking, and was very careful that all parts of the ship were thoroughly guarded until my refugees were landed in Peru, safe and happy.

One of the performances that had most tried my patience and temper at Valparaiso was the way they ran their torpedo boats about my ship, using her apparently as a target. At first I considered it only as an exhibition of bad manners, but, in view of the various warnings I had had, I concluded that there might be something more serious in it. It was plain to all hands that an effort was being made to impress the officers of the foreign ships in port, who watched closely with their glasses. I was unwilling to play the part which had apparently been assigned me. When they ran at me the second time one of the boats missed my stern by less than six feet. I went to quarters at once and gave orders, if one of them even scratched the paint on the Yorktown, to blow the boat out of the water and kill every man in her, so that there could be no question of an accidental collision. I then saw the officer in charge of the drills, and told him that he certainly had great confidence in the steering gear of his torpedo boats; that if anything should jam so that one of them struck me I would blow her bottom out. He replied that the water

in the harbour belonged to his Government, and that he proposed to use it for the purpose of drilling his boats. I answered that I was fully aware of the ownership he had stated,
but that the Yorktown and the paint on her belonged to the
United States, and that neither must be defaced by his torpedo boats. After this incident they did not run at us so
much, though the newspapers encouraged them to do so.

Before the refugees were well clear of me at Callao I had
coal lighters alongside, and in a few hours I was ready to
start back to Valparaiso to see the trouble out. In answer to
my telegram saying that I was ready to sail, I was directed
to await further orders at Callao. The following from my
journal is of interest, as showing my feelings at the time:

"*Saturday Night, February 6th.*—A mail is in, and I have
nice letters from friends commending my course at Valparaiso; very satisfactory, but I wish the newspapers would let
me alone. Why should they call me 'Fighting Bob'? Some of
them say they must take my statements with 'very large
grains of salt.' But generally they seem to commend me,
which, if one must figure in them, is the best way; but as I
see my duty I shall do it, hoping for the approval of the
Government. When they send me orders I shall try to follow
them. Some of the letters say, 'We are waiting for you to stir
up the war,' and the writers will never know how near I came
to doing it. Looking back at it now, I am glad I did just
what I did, and in the way I did it. I would not change it if
I could. Of course, I could have 'stirred up the war,' and it
may be that people would have justified me, but I could not
justify myself. In the discharge of my duty I gave the Chileans a fine chance to fight if they wanted to, and the odds
were enough in their favour—nine ships to one. But they
backed water every time, and I maintained a dignified and
resolute position.

"Of course, if they had provoked it I should have engaged
their nine ships without hesitation, and the chances would

not have favoured my getting the Yorktown out of their harbour. I am glad also that I got away from Valparaiso just when I did, for I am sure that if we had been there when the President's ultimatum came I should have had to open on them, the feeling was so intense. They would have insulted me again, and I should have attacked them. If the Government is going to demand a salute to our flag, and will send a lot of ships, I should like to be in command of one of them. But it is useless to send a single ship; it would only be insulted, as the Chileans respect nothing but force."

The excitement and worry of Valparaiso had told severely on the officers of the Yorktown, especially on me. I was therefore much pleased when the railroad officials at Lima tendered us a trip over the Andes on the Arroyo road,[1] which was a real pleasure and recreation. They were good enough to give me a special car and engine for the use of the party, which consisted of sixteen officers of the Boston and Yorktown. The car was just large enough to hold us, and the engine was in proportion, so that the train looked like a toy concern; but the speed was sufficient for my taste. I had, of course, heard of the splendid work Meigs[2] and his fellow-Americans had done on this road, but I had no conception of its wonderful details, nor do I believe any one can have until he sees them. It dwarfed all the railroad work I had ever seen; indeed, all the work of any kind. The road was completed to a point thirteen thousand two hundred feet above sea level, which left only about two thousand feet more to climb before

1. The famous Oroya Railroad leaves the port of Callao and passes through Lima, some nine miles away. It ascends the valley of the Rimac River, then zigzags up interminable slopes to an altitude of 15,640 feet in a trajectory of only 105 miles.
2. Evans is possibly referring to John F. Meigs, who graduated from the U.S. Naval Academy in June 1867. After attaining the rank of lieutenant on 21 March 1871, Meigs was placed on the retired list on 3 August 1891 and resigned on 22 December 1896.

Harbour of Valparaiso, Chile

crossing the divide, after which it was intended to descend the eastern slope of the mountains to the head waters of the Amazon.

The wild flowers along the roadside were beautiful. Up to an elevation of ten thousand feet the sides of the track were covered with wild heliotrope. All the way to the top of the mountain daisies of several varieties were in abundance. The scenery was grand beyond description. In many places the engineers making the surveys had been suspended over the face of the cliffs thousands of feet from anywhere. The location of such a road seemed to me more wonderful than the construction which followed, though the latter was certainly a monument to American genius and pluck.

When we reached the station at the highest point of the road, I got out and walked a short distance to test the theory that the heart's action is much weakened at such elevation. I was quickly satisfied; the distress was immediate, and I was ready to sit down again when I had walked a hundred feet or less. I found the men in charge and the drivers of the llama trains there were strong and hearty, but it had required many months to accustom them to breathing the rarefied air. These llama trains deserve a mention. The curious, long-necked, delicate-looking animals were used to transport silver ore from the mines in the mountains to the railroad on its way to the smelters. The ore was placed on their backs in bags, and so long as you put one hundred pounds or less on each one they would climb the mountain trails in a wonderful way; but if you put more than a hundred pounds on them, they would lie down quietly and stay there until you removed the extra weight.

On the run down from Chicla,[3] steam was cut off and all brakes put on; but even then we tore around curves and

3. A small Peruvian seaport near Lima. Evans's account is confusing here because there is no Chicle along the railroad route. Perhaps he was referring to Ticlio or Chosica.

through tunnels in a way to make one's hair stand on end. At Lima I dined with our minister[4] and retired early to my hotel, hoping for a restful night, but I was sadly disappointed. Fleas and mosquitoes bit me, foul smells attacked my nostrils, and cats and dogs, which seemed to abound, squalled and barked all night. About five in the morning I heard the most extraordinary noise, something between the squeal of a pig and the cackle of a hen, and, on looking for the cause from my window, found a little, dried-up, old she-devil of a Peruvian woman, who seemed to be in charge of all the servants, and was berating them for everything she could lay her tongue to. She never drew breath until eight o'clock or after.

The English flagship Warspite arrived at Callao about this time from Valparaiso, and her crew, to show their good feeling for us, invited forty men from the Yorktown and one hundred from the Boston to dine on board with them, and afterward gave them a minstrel performance. The admiral at the same time entertained six American officers, and had to meet them five of his own, which, with himself at the head of the table, made a jovial party of twelve. The Warspite was off in the early morning, so that we could do nothing to show our appreciation of their courtesy.

During our stay at Callao the weather was very damp, with constant fogs, and the effect on a steel ship was enough to break an executive officer's heart. The plates wept rust from every joint and rivet, and with constant care and attention it was almost impossible to keep the ship looking her best. Injury was unavoidable from the rust in places where neither scraper nor paint brush could reach. We had a fair sample of what all seafaring men known as a "Callao painter," which turned all our beautiful paint work black as a pot, hence its name. It also offended our nostrils and affected our stomachs

4. John Hicks served as minister to Peru from 30 March 1889 to 24 June 1893.

unpleasantly. The vile odours which arise from the water during the "Painters" have been attributed to various causes, but on this occasion they were immediately followed by a very severe earthquake, which led me to think that possibly the gases escaping from the earth had caused the phenomenon. Many people believed that the accumulated sewage of centuries in the bottom of the harbour had something to do with it. Whatever the cause might be, I was constantly dreading an epidemic of typhoid. I fortunately escaped with one case only.

The mail on February 28th brought home newspapers as late as February 10th. I find in my journal the following:

"The correspondence between Blaine and Montt is published, and certainly the Chilean ought to go home after the skinning Blaine has given him. It amuses me to see that Montt objects to my cablegram of January 18th. The cable was addressed to the Secretary of the Navy, and he and the President evidently did not consider it objectionable, or they would not have given it out for publication. Or if they did disapprove, they have never said so to me.

"*February 29th.*—The good ship Boston got off on time Saturday, crowing over the poor little Yorktown for having been left 'in the soup,' as it were; but I am sure the Secretary will look after us and not let us suffer. To-day our repairs are finished, and I have wired the Secretary that we are ready for sea, and I hope for orders soon. The weather here is very trying, not only to officers and men, but also to the ship.

"Some of the home papers seem rabid on the subject of Mr. Egan; but his course has been dignified and just, and certainly his letters show great ability. His appointment was the most extraordinary thing in diplomatic history, but his conduct at Santiago has justified it. Harrison's message is splendid, and if it does not make him the next President I shall be surprised.

"*March 2d.*—Our orders have come—to 'Frisco in my own time and way. The men are cheering like mad all over the ship. We shall sail on the morning of the 4th, and be in 'Frisco April 2d or 3d. Needless to say, I am delighted with my orders."

After leaving Callao one of my officers developed typhoid fever, and in order to insure his recovery I ran into Acapulco [5] and bought a goat, so that he might have the advantage of fresh milk. Here I again met Admiral Hotham in the War-spite, and the moment he learned that I had a case of serious illness he sent his boat to me with the only piece of ice in the harbour. His courtesy and kindness to me were unfailing whenever we met. I wired the Department from Acapulco, and went to sea at once. I was in the port less than two hours.

When off the Galapagos Islands [6] the water was covered with turtles. I counted five hundred in sight at one time. Many of them were asleep, and as I had to swing ship for compass deviations, I took occasion at the same time to supply the crew with plenty of fresh meat. Two whale boats were lowered and manned for the purpose. They pulled up quietly to the turtles one after another, and before they were fairly awake the men had yanked them into the boats by their flippers. In less than an hour both boats had been filled and were alongside, when the catch was distributed among the different messes and the boats hoisted in their places.

North of the Galapagos Islands I had a curious experience. I had for days noticed a large number of what I supposed to be fish breaking the water at some distance from the ship. I took them to be skip-jacks, a species of mackerel family, as their motions much resembled those of this fish, which I had often caught in the Atlantic. I broke out my trolling lines, and with the most seductive baits fished zealously for several

5. A port in southern Mexico that dates to Spanish colonial days, when goods from the Orient were unloaded for further transport to either the Caribbean coast or across the Atlantic to Spain.
6. An island group in the Pacific about 650 miles west of the Ecuadorian mainland.

days, but entirely without success. Not a scale could I capture. It was only after many months in the arctic later on that I discovered that I had been fishing for young fur seals.

I felt sure that the Yorktown could steam from Callao to San Francisco without recoaling, a distance of about forty-five hundred miles, and meant to give her the reputation of having done it; but when off San Diego we struck a streak of bad coal, and as I only had fifty tons remaining on board I deemed it prudent to run in there and replenish my supply, which I did. I only remained overnight and then hurried on my way, arriving in San Francisco March 26, 1892. On the way up from San Diego[7] after passing Santa Barbara[8] we had a succession of gales with biting cold weather, which caused us much suffering, fresh as we were from the heat of the tropics. My typhoid fever patient was a plucky youngster, and fought hard for his life, but I could see that he was growing weaker day by day, owing to the unavoidable discomforts of the pitching, rolling ship. However, I landed him the moment we arrived, and sent him to the Mare Island Hospital, where he rapidly recovered.

7. A southern California city on the Pacific Coast near the Mexican border.
8. A southern California city north of Los Angeles.

CHAPTER 24

From Chile to Bering Sea

THE people of San Francisco gave me and the crew of the Yorktown a very hearty welcome. They made it plain to us that they considered the treatment of the Baltimore men an outrage which they were quite ready to fight about. The general feeling seemed to be that if I had brought on a war they would have considered that I was right, and would have backed me up for doing so. As soon as I landed I was recognised, though in plain clothes, and the outspoken commendation of the people was most embarrassing to me. I consoled myself, however, with the thought that their condemnation would have been impossible to bear.

After one day at San Francisco I docked the Yorktown at Mare Island, and, being anxious to get ready for service at the first possible moment, put my men to work scraping the outside of the ship as the dock was pumped out. When the last water had disappeared we were ready for the paint, and in forty-eight hours again ready to go to sea. This action led to a bitter attack being made on me by some of the local labour unions, who claimed that I was taking the bread out of the mouths of the poor workmen when I ordered my crew to scrape the bottom of the ship. I contended that it was as much my duty to clean the bottom of the ship as it was the top, and that they had no more right to paint the outside of her than they had the inside. In any case I had done what I considered my duty, and the ship was ready for sea in a very short space of time.

"*Mare Island, California, April 8, 1892.*—We have been two weeks waiting to know what we were to do, but no word came. The men were working hard all the time, hoping for liberty, money, etc., when the work was done, but no money was sent for them, and the yard people would not do the few repairs necessary, nor would they put stores and coal on board. To-day came telegraphic orders, and every man and boy is up to his eyes in coal dust; and at the same time we are taking in provisions and stores of all kinds, and I shall go to sea on Monday most uncomfortable. This sort of thing is anything but good for the navy. My men had every right to expect leave here, as they have not put foot ashore in the United States since we left New York, and while of course they do their work, they do it without heart. Our orders are to proceed to Port Townsend, Washington,[1] and there await instructions.

"*April 10th.*—Another telegram came yesterday to delay departure until a general court-martial could try three of the Yorktown's men, which will delay us probably a week. The court is ordered for next Monday, April 18th, and we shall probably sail for Port Townsend on Thursday or Friday,

---

1. A picturesque Victorian seaport whose settlement predated both Seattle and Tacoma in the Pacific Northwest. At the time of Evans's visit in May 1892, Port Townsend boasted 7,500 inhabitants and was a bustling lumber shipping point, although it had lost out to Tacoma as the great pacific railroad terminus on Puget Sound. Its original hopes for a population of 20,000 and metropolis status dashed, it settled down to remain the port of entry for the Puget Sound district. Today it remains a tourist attraction, replete with numerous residences and buildings dating from its heyday.

where we shall arrive four or five days after sailing. The present programme is for us to wait there until time to stop the sealers and then go to Bering Sea,[2] where we shall spend most of the summer. It will be interesting to see that part of the world; but having fried us in the tropics for months, they are now going to cool us off near the Arctic Circle.

"*Mare Island, April 14th.*—I am informed, unofficially, to-day that I am to be senior officer in Bering Sea, and have five ships to do the work. Of course it is a compliment, and it is good to be so well thought of by the Secretary, but it will give me no end of work and care. If one is to serve, it is best so. To-morrow I go to 'Frisco again to complete my sea outfit for arctic weather, and at the same time make arrangements to have fresh provisions sent north each month for the crew; it seems that we can get nothing of that kind up there.

"*Mare Island, April 18th.*—The people out here are awfully good to me; I never knew anything like the feeling they show. They are now talking about the marvellous way in which I brought the Yorktown up to the yard and took my buoy. There's nothing in it; we only came fast and made a nice turn in a narrow space. If they had seen us come through the English Narrows they would probably have had a fit. I have been in command of the Yorktown nine months today. This summer will be anxious work for me, but at the same time interesting.

"*Mare Island, April 23d.*—I was in the commandant's office day before yesterday when the second terrible earthquake came, and I was never so frightened in my life. The first movement was light, but then came the dreadful twisting, and the building creaked and groaned as if it must surely come down, and I don't see now why it did not. The general court-martial, sitting in the next room, promptly adjourned, and, as I heard all hands making for the open, I asked the

2. A part of the Pacific Ocean between Siberia and Alaska, joined to the Arctic Ocean by the 50-mile-wide Bering Strait.

admiral to excuse me, and it was surprising to see how my old game leg got down the stairs. After it was over I examined the building, and found every arch broken through and the plaster ready to fall in every room. The poor women and children all over the island spent most of the day afterward on the sidewalks—some of them were made ill from it; and I learn from the newspapers that the northern part of the State suffered great damage and loss. At seven in the evening another shock came, but not so severe. Of course, it is only a question of time, if this sort of thing goes on, when the buildings will fall and cause great loss of life.

"A telegram came from the Department yesterday, asking when I could be ready for sea. I requested the admiral to reply that I had been ready ever since I arrived, but I don't believe he did it. I have the idea that a vessel of war should always be ready to do service.

"*Mare Island, April 25th.*—The latest telegram to the admiral about us reads, 'Have the Yorktown ready for sea at the earliest possible moment, but do not allow her to leave without further instructions.' I wonder if the Department is afraid I will run away with the little frigate and turn pirate. Young Jackson[3] was walking about yesterday, and will be well of his typhoid fever in a month or two.

"*Mare Island, April 26th.*—At last the orders have come, and I am directed to proceed to Port Townsend, collect all the information I can about the sealing fleet, and carry out the instructions which will reach me there. Of course, that means that I am to spend the summer chasing sealers.

"*Port Townsend, April 30th.*—We certainly do have bad luck sometimes, and this is one of the times. We left Mare Island on Wednesday at noon, and have made steamer time

3. This reference may be to Richard H. Jackson, who graduated from the U.S. Naval Academy on 10 June 1887. Honorably discharged on 30 June 1889, he was restored to service and commissioned an Ensign on 1 July 1890, lieutenant (junior grade) on 3 July 1889, and lieutenant on 3 March 1899.

up here, but with such a nasty gale behind us that the little ship has rolled more than at any time since we left New York. Thursday I was on deck all day and most of the night, and the strain on my wounded foot was so bad that it gave way, and I am now on my back. Rheumatism followed the strain, and I have suffered very much, but am now 'on the mend.' It is plain that I am to have a pretty hard summer with the fogs, gales, sealers, and other 'varmints.' I am now in command of five ships, but without orders from the Department, and hence at a loss to know what they expect me to do. My instructions will, no doubt, come at the last moment, and give no end of trouble. This morning the shore people have been off to welcome me, and the newspapers are most complimentary. Too much 'Fighting Bob' business.

"*Port Townsend, May 3d.*—My orders have come, and they seem endless, and the telegrams are dropping in by the dozen. The people block up the decks, they are so thick; and, in addition to it all, my cabin table and chairs are piled up with printed documents and charts until I am distracted. My orders are confidential: I am to prepare the fleet, which I am ordered to command, for a six months' cruise in the North Pacific and Bering Sea—the second largest fleet in commission, and the most active and important work of our navy at present. The Yorktown, Mohican,[4] Adams,[5]

---

4. A wooden sail and steam screw-sloop of 1,900 tons, ten guns, a top speed of 10 knots, and a 212–230-man complement, the USS *Mohican* was laid down at the Mare Island Navy Yard on 4 September 1872. Launched on 27 December 1883 and commissioned on 25 May 1885, she became a training ship 1898–1904, then a station ship at Olongapo. From 1910 to 1921 the *Mohican* was a receiving ship at Cavite, serving also as a stationary submarine tender to the end of 1914.

5. The USS *Adams* was a wooden sail and steam screw-sloop of 1,375 tons, a top speed of 11 knots, six guns, and a 178–93-man complement. Laid down in 1874 at the Boston Navy Yard, she was commissioned on 21 July 1876, and ultimately converted to a training and station ship after 1907. The sloop was sold in 1920.

Ranger,[6] and Rush[7] compose the fleet, and if I can do half what my orders call for I shall consider that I have done well. The orders are certainly ironclad, and make me complete boss in the North Pacific and Bering Sea. I shall make a stab at it, and only hope that I succeed and make no blunders. Commanding a fleet without clerks or a staff of any kind is hard work.

"My old bones are better, and if the clear, bracing weather continues I shall pull up to my average in a few days. The view from the ship is finer than anything I ever saw in Italy. Snow-clad mountains, one hundred and thirty miles away, standing out clear as crystal against the most perfect sky and looking as if one could walk to them in two hours, and air that feels as brittle as spun glass as I breathe it.

"*Port Townsend, May 5th.*—The grind still goes on, and playing admiral with no staff is not an easy thing. However, I shall make out somehow, and have the fleet ready for sea next Tuesday or Wednesday, and then wait the word from Washington to sail. I have a serious work ahead of me and appreciate that much depends on the way it is done. It has been much delayed here by the crowds and jams of people, who flock to the ship until we can scarcely move for them.

6. A wooden sail and steam screw sloop of 1,020 tons, a top speed of 10 knots, four guns, and a 148-man complement. Built by Harlan and Hollingsworth, launched in 1876, and commissioned on 27 November 1876, the USS *Ranger* served as a surveying ship from 1880 to 1891, and as a training ship for the state of Massachusetts from 1909 until 1940.
7. A Revenue Cutter that was built by the Atlantic Iron Works at East Boston, Massachusetts, for a cost of $79,000. The *Richard Rush* was launched on 14 March 1874 and commissioned on 21 July 1874. Largely involved with patrolling Alaskan waters in 1878 and 1879, she was then stationed at Port Townsend, Washington, until February 1885, when she sailed to San Francisco for rebuilding. Hull Brothers of San Francisco rebuilt her at a cost of $74,000. She again engaged in the Alaska patrol, as well as cruising in Californian and Hawaiian waters from 1885 to 1893. The *Richard Rush* remained on the Alaskan station until being sold to the Alaska Junk Company for $8,500 on 22 January 1913.

But I know they mean to be kind; they say they admire and like me, and it would be ungracious not to see them. Even more—they would be offended and could not understand if they were told that my official duties were so pressing that I could not see them; so I work along as best I can. Of course, I can only do a very small part of what is expected of me socially. Some of these people came on board with a band to welcome us; it made me feel like a fool. Last night was the first occasion of my appearance in the 'social whirl' here. I attended a reception where I was placed in a parlour, and then each person was formally presented to me—all kind and friendly, some charming. To-morrow I am to go to two receptions of the Governor and Mrs. Ferry.[8]

"*Port Townsend, May 7th.*—Yesterday and to-day have been great days for this place, and very hard on me because of all the work I have had in addition to the functions in connection with the centennial of the discovery of Puget Sound[9] by Captain Vancouver.[10] For days the committees have been running after me constantly to help them out with all sorts of details, which I have done, and yesterday active work began on the arrival of his Excellency the Governor. I went, with all the other officers, in full dress, to pay our respects at a reception given by the President of the First National Bank.

8. Surveyor general and territorial governor of Washington from 1869–80, Elisha P. Ferry became the first state governor. Previously a lawyer and a banker, he guided the new state in its transition from territory to statehood. Ferry presided over the growth in population, state institutions, industry, and commerce from 1889 to 1893, and during his tenure he persuaded the U.S. Navy to establish the Puget Sound Navy Yard on Port Orchard.
9. A 100-mile-long inlet of the Pacific in northwest Washington.
10. George Vancouver (1757–98) was an English navigator who discovered the Pacific Northwest.

"As there are some revenue marine vessels in my command, their officers came as well, and we made a good show, in a long line of carriages, much observed by the people. At the residence of Colonel Landes [11] a company of State troops was drawn up who gave me a salute as I marched by them. I was escorted to the parlour where were the Governor and Mrs. Ferry surrounded by the wealth and fashion of Port Townsend. Colonel Landes introduced me with a most kind speech, which concluded by saying that 'the American people were proud of' me. Then Governor Ferry said many more flattering things, and then they introduced me to every one in the room, and each one said something kind and cordial. To-day we have fired three salutes, twenty-one guns each, dressed ships with flags, and otherwise disported ourselves, to the great gratification of the Port Townsendites. Early in the day I was caught and put as the chief support of the Governor, and something happened to me which really touched me. I was standing on the sidewalk near the grand stand when quite a crowd of plain-looking people—men, women, and children—came up, and one said, 'Governor Ferry, we want to speak to the captain of the Yorktown and introduce our wives.' Of course, I spoke to them all, and

11. A quartermaster and paymaster general of the Washington National Guard, Henry Landes (1843–1926) reflected the burst of energy and activity that attended the transition of Washington from territory to statehood. A native of Floss, Bavaria, Germany, Landes emigrated with his family to Kentucky, and he served with the 20th Kentucky during the Civil War. Turning westward to the British Columbian gold mines in 1870, he failed in that endeavor and became an Indian agent for the Makah Tribe in the Washington Territory. Moving to Port Townsend in 1876, he cofounded the First National Bank and was its largest stockholder and president. Successful in business and as a town father, he became prominent in state and territorial affairs and the local national guard. During Evans's visit, Landes was obviously part of the effort to secure prominence and economic development to Port Townsend via national recognition.

every one had a kind word for me. Then a lot of miners, hard-looking chaps, came and sized me up, and each one said, 'Cap, shake,' and I shook till my hand was almost disabled. After the review we drove to the beach to a mammoth clambake, and there the ladies embarrassed me with their kindness—saying and doing things to me that they might have done to Admiral Farragut.

"*Port Townsend, May 10th.*—Eastern papers have come, some saying that Mr. Blaine admits that my telegram from Valparaiso was 'improper.' Mr. Tracy, my superior and commanding officer, has not said to me that he approved of my course in Chile, but he gives me the most important command in the navy, and I shall go on just the same, and do as I did in Chile, what I feel to be my duty to my country. They are heaping the work on me now. Yesterday I took the Rush and went over to Esquimault [12] to spend the day with Admiral Hotham, and get from him and his officers their plans for the summer. My visit was most successful and delightful, and I am glad I went. The admiral kept me to luncheon and dinner; we had a most satisfactory time, and made all arrangements for co-operation during the summer. They will send the Melpomene and Daphne, [13] and their commanding officers will be practically under my orders, so I am really to have a big command.

"I left here at seven in the morning, and returned at 2 A.M. to-day, but could not get to bed until 3.30, as my desk was full of letters and telegrams, the answers to which had to go at seven. I was up again at eight, and have scarcely had the pen out of my hand since, except for an official interview with the commanding officers of the Mohican and Adams,

12. A small town on Vancouver Island, British Columbia, slightly west of Victoria on the Strait of Juan de Fuca.
13. A composite-hull, sail and steam sloop of 1,100 tons, a top speed of 13.5 knots, sixteen guns, and a 138-man complement, HMS *Daphne* was laid down on 20 June 1887 at Sheerness Dockyard. Launched on 29 May 1888, she was completed in May 1889, and sold in 1904.

and I see no chance for a let-up until we go to sea. I have wired to-day that four vessels of the fleet are ready to sail, and that I am anxious to get away. The other four vessels can join us later at Unalaska.[14] I now have eight under my command—quite a showing for a commander. But Chilean refugees and arctic outfits have hardly left me money to pay my bills.

"*Port Townsend, May 11th.*—The final orders have come, and we are off day after to-morrow (13th) early in the morning with the Yorktown, Adams, Mohican, and Rush, leaving orders for the Ranger, Corwin,[15] Bear,[16] and Albatross[17] to join me at Unalaska. I have written, with my own hands, detailed instructions for each of them, besides many letters of all kinds. Surely I shall have no end of work this trip. We sail under sealed orders, not to be opened until we are outside the straits. It seems a curious thing to do in time of profound peace, and I wonder what it can mean. Until some letters came to-day I had not realized what an amount of talk the

14. An island off southwestern Alaska in the eastern Aleutians.
15. The USRC *Corwin* was a wooden cutter of 424 tons constructed by the Oregon Iron Works of Portland, Oregon, in 1876. She mounted four guns and was transferred to the Navy for temporary service in 1898. A Bering Sea Patrol Force of four or five cutters under a force commander was thus inaugurated in the mid-1890s and thereafter patrolled the Bering Sea and Aleutian chain from April to November each year.
16. The USRC *Bear* was arguably the most famous vessel of the Coast Guard (Revenue Marine), comparable to the Navy's USS *Constitution.* Built of wood in 1874 at Greenock, Scotland (and later sheathed in steel), this 703-ton barkentine with auxiliary steam power could make 8 knots under sail, 9 with steam. She was transferred to the Revenue Marine from the Navy at New York under an act of 3 March 1885, having served the previous year with the Greely relief expedition under the command of Navy Lieutenant W.H. Emory. Thereafter, until 1927, she cruised annually to Arctic waters. Later berthed at Oakland, California, as a museum, the *Bear* subsequently took part in Richard Byrd's expedition to Antarctica and in World War II on the Greenland patrol.
17. A U.S. Fish Commission vessel later transferred to the Navy for service in the Spanish-American War.

papers had made about my work in Chile. I was not aware
that my cables to the Department had been published. It is
bearable to have the papers call me 'Fighting Bob' when I see
that my friends approve of me and are pleased and proud of
the notoriety."

CHAPTER 25

The Navy Among the Sealers

T HE preparation of the fleet for service had been hard
work, but the prospect of doing something braced all
hands up wonderfully. At first it looked as if we would surely
have a collision with the British navy over the seal question,
and I knew, of course, that that meant a bitter and destructive war. The long struggle over the *modus vivendi* [1] was not
concluded when my instructions were sent me, and I knew
the moment I read them that if I carried them out we would
have war on our hands within a week. Hence I was much
relieved when the terms of that instrument had been agreed
upon, and the whole contents wired me for my guidance. My
first orders contemplated the seizure of all sealing vessels
found within certain limits, and the orders of the British
admiral were to protect the Canadian sealers in the same limits. It is easy to see what any action on my part would have
led to. Fortunately, wise counsels prevailed, and united action between the two navies was decided upon.

While these sea preparations were being made I used my

1. A temporary agreement between diplomats pending a final settlement.

best endeavours to find out where the sealing fleet would rendezvous, in order that I might be on hand to seize the supply steamer, which would much simplify my work during the summer. With the assistance of detectives, sent us from Washington, I interviewed the men most likely to give the secret away; but I found that they were absolutely in the dark, as all the vessels of the fleet were to go to sea with sealed orders, which were to be delivered to them only on the eve of their departure.

To make the situation clearer, it may be well to give here, in a few words, the course pursued by these sealers, of whom so much has been written. The fleet was composed entirely of schooners, large and small, and numbered about one hundred and ten. They were not owned, as many people supposed, entirely by British subjects. Many of them had American owners, but, sailed under the English flag. Many others sailed under the American flag. All were controlled by the Sealers' Association. Each vessel had its regular crew for working her, and in addition from ten to forty men, according to her size, who were known as hunters, and who did the killing. They were armed with double-barrelled No. 10 shotguns for the seals, and a good outfit of Winchester rifles for revenue officers or others who interfered with them. Each schooner carried a number of dories or small boats to be used in sneaking on the sleeping seals; and each of these boats had one or two long gaff-hooks, or poles with several hooks on the sides, for the purpose of catching, if possible, the bodies which sank rapidly after being shot.

When the seal herd appeared off San Francisco, usually early in February, from its winter quarters in the south, the fleet joined it, and remained with it until it entered the Bering Sea through one of the passes. During all this long trip of the herd around and across the North Pacific the work of destruction went on. The great majority of the seals were females with young, hurrying on to the Pribilof Islands to their breeding ground, and therefore each one killed represented two lives—mother and pup. In almost any kind of weather, the schooner would heave to in the morning and hoist out her boats, and, drifting away, leave them to their deadly work until a full boat or darkness compelled them to stop. Many boats were lost in the fog, and their crews lost their lives either from drowning or starvation. Yet the profits were so large that men willingly took these chances. Less than half the seals killed in this way were recovered, as their bodies sank very quickly. It is easily seen what was to be the fate of a herd of animals where the females, bearing only one offspring at a time, were being thus destroyed. As the herd approached the Aleutian Islands,[2] and the time for giving birth to the young drew near, the females moved through the water with great rapidity, hurrying on to their breeding grounds, and very few of them, comparatively speaking, were killed. The slaughter in the North Pacific proper was fearful.

Before leaving Port Townsend I had been supplied with printed notices warning sealers not to enter Bering Sea, and these the Department expected me to serve on every vessel in the fleet, no matter of what nationality. The number of vessels was one hundred and ten, and as a matter of fact I found at the end of the season that the force under my command had boarded and served notice on one hundred and seven of them. Some of them had been boarded so often that their log books were veritable collections of autographs of American commanders. It had leaked out before sailing that the Canadian vessels would refuse to obey a warning served by an American officer, and, as I did not wish to make trouble when it could be avoided, I took a sufficient number of notices to Admiral Hotham, who indorsed them in his official capacity, which effectually spiked the guns of these would-be sea lawyers.

When finally ready I sent all but two vessels to the North

2. A volcanic island chain off southwestern Alaska that curves 1,200 miles west from the Alaskan peninsula.

Pacific to follow and serve notice on the sealers. With the Yorktown and one revenue cutter I ran direct to Unalaska, where I arrived after a very rough passage, with much fog to contend with about the passes. As soon as coaled I ran north and skirted the ice all the way around the Pribilof Islands,[3] to make sure that no sealers were lurking about the sea. Then, with the assistance of the cutter, I guarded the passes to prevent any one from entering, while the rest of my force continued its work to the north. My men suffered from exposure and the lack of fresh provisions, but we were always able to give them all the fresh fish they wanted. We had only to stop the engines and get the lines overboard, and in a few hours catch three or four hundred pounds of beautiful codfish. Sometimes I gave them salmon, but I soon found that they could not eat this many days in succession—it was too rich. Codfish was our mainstay. The following from my journal may be of interest:

"*At Sea, June 4, 1892.*—Had a good breakfast today— broiled king salmon, potatoes, cold reindeer roast, onion salad, and a slice of cold English ham—Delmonico[4] could hardly beat it. But yesterday I tried to eat a piece of bear-meat—well, a Chinese baby dead of the smallpox, or a mangy dog that had lived on fish and the little bugs we sometimes find on berries, might be something like it. A kind skipper gave me the meat before I left Unalaska, and my steward let his skill out on it. I afterward let out almost my eternal soul on account of it. Such is life in the arctic, and I am not enjoying it. But as I write this I am surrounded by such beauty and grandeur and calmness as one sees rarely in a lifetime. We are anchored in the open Bering Sea, five

3. Islands off southwestern Alaska in the Bering Sea.
4. The famous New York City restaurant that introduced *haut cuisine* to America under the family dynasty founded by John Delmonico in 1828. Delmonico's French cuisine, served in a Parisian atmosphere, was seriously challenged by Louis Sherry's restaurant, but Delmonico retained undisputed "sovereignty" until after the turn of the century.

miles from the chain of the Aleutian Islands, and from the deck one can count over a dozen of the most graceful, beautiful snow-covered peaks in the world, all dazzling, blinding white. Then I can see two active volcanoes, puffing out smoke and steam as the devil snorts and roars inside the crust, and three extinct ones—all strange to look at but most beautiful and curious. The rim of the crater of one of them is surmounted by what looks, from this distance—sixty miles—like a huge frill of lace, the snow on the contorted lava giving the effect. Add to this that the day has been the first clear one we have had, and warm, and one would think I might be content, and so I am after a fashion. There is nothing for me but duty, and, contrary to much 'guff' given me in my youth on that subject, it does not fill the bill entirely.

"We came down here yesterday—or rather we started yesterday—from Unalaska, to see if we could catch some sealers who have for several years made this vicinity a sort of headquarters for their work. We passed the fishing fleet on the way down, hard at work packing codfish, but nothing in the shape of a sealer. Indeed, I can not see what they would come here for, as I have not laid eyes on a single seal or even a pup. I wonder why seals were made, anyhow. And if I had my way with the curious old idiots who went about the world discovering places—Straits of Magellan, North Pacific Ocean, Bering Sea, etc., etc.—I would feed them on bear-meat and then chuck them down one of these lovely volcanoes. We are here to-day owing to these idiots, and as I wished for a quiet Sunday, I found a place to anchor; and here we are, where I shall stay until day after to-morrow, when I hope to do some target-firing—using a sealer for a target if I can find one—and then clear out for the western end of the islands and so back to the beautiful Unalaska.

"*Sunday, June 5th.*—The little blow of last night was the breaking out of a southeast gale, and now the weather is as nasty as usual in these waters—blowing a gale, cold as charity, thick as mud, and raining in torrents. We are snug, however, and shall hold on until to-morrow, and then run to the west. Every day that passes is so much gain for us on our way somewhere—it may be 'Frisco, it may be China, or it may be some Atlantic port. One can imagine how low we have fallen when we look upon Unalaska as quite a metropolis.

"The men to-day have caught more than two thousand pounds of codfish from the vessel in less than three hours' fishing. It is blowing a gale, and in spite of it and the pouring rain they would fish all the time if I would permit it; but if they were ordered to do so they would consider it a great hardship, and growl accordingly. The life here is more monotonous and isolated than I could have thought possible.

"*Iluiluik, Unalaska, June 8th.*—Here we are, back again, but no target practice and no sealers so far. Yesterday morning the weather was so bad that we got under way and came back here. At midnight I put the ship's head off shore until the fog lifted, and we saw land for a moment, which was all I wanted, and at 6 A.M. we were anchored in this snug little hole. An hour later the Corwin was in, and we had our first mail since leaving Port Townsend. I have a peck of letters, of course, and the newspapers seem to have begun on me again.

"My work here is really beginning to crowd now, and I have a matter of vital importance on hand, in which I hope to succeed; but the chances are dreadfully against me. Every year the British sealing fleet has chartered a large steamer to meet it at some out-of-the-way place in the Aleutian Islands, where all the skins are transferred and so sent back to Victoria,[5] British Columbia, and a fresh supply of provisions laid in. Such action in American waters is, of course, illegal, and I am straining every nerve to find their place of rendezvous for this year. The steamer is supposed by the Navy Depart-

5. The capital of British Columbia, Canada, is located on southeastern Vancouver Island and Juan de Fuca Strait.

ment to be the Danube, and if I can find her I shall seize her and her cargo and all the schooners that have transferred to her, and take them to Sitka[6]—I hope between the 15th and 25th of June. Last year thirty-eight sealers transferred to the steamer in one day twenty-five thousand skins, and received from her a large supply of provisions. Our patrol fleet was then very small and composed of slow vessels. I hope to convince them that we are not up here this year for our health."

6. A town in southwestern Alaska on the west coast of Baranof Island.

CHAPTER 26

Striking at the Source of Supplies

THE problem of how to catch the supply steamer was a very interesting one, and many people have asked me how I did it. The Navy Department had been misled by information purposely sent them from Victoria, and they in turn tried unintentionally to deceive me by sending me this false information, saying that it came from a reliable source. The rendezvous, as given by them, was over eighteen hundred miles from where I caught her. The case I had to deal with was similar to that of an enemy's cruiser on your coast in time of war. What was her objective? I knew that her intention was to take skins from the fleet and give it provisions, and therefore if I kept touch with the fleet I should eventually find the steamer; and I did. Several vessels were detailed to watch the schooners and see which way they were heading, and as soon as I had this information I felt sure that in that direction somewhere I would find the steamer I was looking for.

It is sometimes an officer's duty to do a thing that his Government must afterward disavow and punish him for having done. Such a case was the capture of the Confederate cruiser Florida in Bahia, Brazil, by the United States steamer Wachusett during the civil war. I felt that I might have to do the same sort of thing and face the music. If I found the steamer I was after in one of our ports, having violated our revenue laws, it would be all plain sailing; but suppose I found her at sea? What then? I read plainly between the lines of my orders that the Washington authorities considered it of vital importance that she should be captured, and I made up my mind to get her legally if I could, illegally if I must. If I took her at sea, the Department could disavow my act and punish me; but in the meantime my mission in the North would be accomplished and sealing broken up, at least for that year. The schooners would have to go back to Victoria for provisions, and it would then be too late for them to return to Bering Sea and do any real harm. I again quote from my journal:

"*Iluiluik*,[1] *June 11, 1892*.—We are off to-morrow, and I am sending the Albatross to Port Townsend on Tuesday. Yesterday I spent in bed with neuralgia in the muscles of my wounded leg—very painful, but I am up to-day.

"The two British ships, Melpomene and Daphne, are in, and their captains are fine chaps and seem ready to help me to knock these sealers out in every way. Of course, they don't know that I intend to seize the Danube, if I can find her, but I think they suspect me.

"*Karluk*,[2] *Kodiak Island, June 15th*.—On Sunday we left Iluiluik in a dense fog, and worked our way up here, six hundred miles, where we are suddenly in a mess. We have caught two American schooners violating the law, and may have to seize them both, which will greatly embarrass me in

1. A village (later called Unalaska) on the southern shore of Unalaska Bay, Unalaska Island, in the Aleutian chain.
2. A town on the east coast of Kodiak Island, on Shelikof Strait, which separates Kodiak Island from the Alaskan peninsula off the southern coast of Alaska.

my efforts to catch the English chaps. Johnson,[3] in the Mohican, has seized five, and I hear his ship is damaged by
grounding. We are off as soon as we can get our anchor up.

"This afternoon I saw a wonderful thing in the fishing
way—a haul of the seine in which they caught fifteen thousand salmon. It was a beautiful sight, and they gave me all
the king salmon my gig could carry. Afterward our men borrowed the seine and caught over two thousand, which they
are now salting down. The Kodiak is the greatest salmon
river in the world, supporting seven canneries, each of which
puts up over six hundred thousand fish per year. The water
is absolutely alive with them; my cockswain caught one with
a boathook while we were waiting at the beach.

"*Alitak,*[4] *Kodiak Island, June 16th.*—Just before leaving
Karluk we caught a fool of a schooner captain who had been
violating the law; he thought I did not know it, and gave us
some trouble. He started to get under way in the afternoon
before I had settled his case, but I sent a boat with orders for
him to anchor his schooner and come on board. Before he
got to our gangway he took his hat off and came over the
side with it in his hand and shaking as if he were going to
have a fit. I never saw a man so scared in my life. After
getting some information from him he was allowed to go on
his way.

"The people up here seem to think I am some kind of a
military governor, or something, and come to me with the
most absurd complaints. I don't mind any of them until it
comes to the missionary-school teachers. They nauseate me.
The conditions up here, as I see them, are about as bad as
they could be, and the whole business is a disgrace to our
Government; but I am a policeman this trip for sealers only.

3. Starting his naval career as an acting midshipman on 2 December
1859, Mortimer L. Johnson was promoted to commander on 25 April
1878, and captain on 9 May 1893.
4. Cape Alitak lies at the southwestern corner of Kodiak Island, where
Alitak Bay cuts into the island. Alitak is the principal hamlet.

"The northeast gale is still raging, but we have found the sealers' snug harbour, I think, and are as comfortable as possible, anchored in a sort of lagoon which can not be seen from the outside. Six sealers have run in out of the gale, and we have them anchored under our guns, where they will stay until I am through with them. As we came up the coast this forenoon we made out three schooners, and, as it was blowing half a gale, they tried to get away from us; but it was no use. I let this little frigate out a link or two and just drove the schooners as one would drive geese.

"We found the Corwin in here, and as I am satisfied the transfer of skins will be made in Prince William Sound,[5] I have sent her there to catch the gang, if possible.

"*Friday, June 17th.*—Still the northeaster howls, and the little Yorktown tugs and quivers at her anchors; but the land keeps the sea off, and we are snug and cosy. Three more sealers ran in last night in the blow, and were much surprised to find themselves in my clutches. One of them gave away the place of rendezvous of the English fleet—Port Etches,[6] Prince William Sound, where I have two vessels waiting for them; but I shall run up there myself to-morrow afternoon, I think. It is only three hundred miles, and I want to make sure of that capture if I can.

"*Port Etches, Prince William Sound, 1 A.M., June 21st.*— There is no night here at this season. We left Alitak Sunday morning, after the gale had blown out, and I have been on my feet almost ever since. There are practically no charts of this region, and running full speed, as we do most of the time, is anything but funny. We got here at midnight, just after sunset, and now, at 1 A.M., it is almost sunrise.

"We found the Mohican here, she having captured three American schooners and sent them to Sitka, and having been

5. An arm of the Gulf of Alaska east of the Kenai peninsula in southern Alaska.
6. A bay, ten miles long, on the southwest coast of Hinchinbrook Island.

herself on the rocks and knocked about somewhat. But she will do for service in the Bering Sea this summer. The steamer to receive the skins is expected to-morrow or the day after, and I still hope to capture her."

I had made all plans for the capture of the steamer, and was confident of success. The vessels of the force were gathering for the final move when, on June 21st, I ran into Port Etches, and to my dismay found that the United States steamer Mohican had been lying there for five days, doing just the thing I had cautioned her commanding officer not to do—alarming the sealers so that they would neither transfer skins nor provisions, but seek another port for that purpose. I jumped the Mohican out in short order, and then arranged with the commanding officer of the Corwin to make the seizure. I directed him to run off to the south for a certain distance, and then change his course so as to bring up behind the end of Montague Island,[7] about twelve miles from Port Etches, haul his vessel close inshore, send down his topmasts and cover his lower masts with bushes, so that he would be well hidden from inquisitive eyes. He was to remain in that position twenty-four hours, and then run over to Port Etches and see what he would find. The captain was an able, fearless man, and I knew he would carry out my orders. He said to me that the twenty-seven schooners then in port were well armed and would fight to a finish when the time came. I replied that he had several guns of his own, and that he might rely on the Yorktown to be somewhere near when the shooting began.

After the Corwin and Mohican had gone I visited what seemed to be the flagship of the sailing fleet, a handsome

7. A 50-mile-long island in southern Alaska, on the west side of the entrance to Prince William Sound, some sixty miles east of Seward. It was named "Montague" by Captain James Cook, on 18 May 1778 for John Montague, Earl of Sandwich, the son of Viscount Hinchinbrook. It was called *Isla de Queros* by the Spaniards in the late 1700s.

Burgess schooner of one hundred and fifty tons, having on board a number of gentlemen who were cruising during the summer as a matter of recreation. I told them that I was bound south to look after matters at Unalaska, and asked that they would warn all arrivals to keep out of the Bering Sea during the summer, as I should certainly capture them if they went in. Then I cleared out at top speed, perfectly satisfied that a few days would settle the fate of the chap who had caused me so much thought and trouble. The Corwin waited a few hours, when the fog shut in as thick as pea soup. The captain, fearing that the steamer might get away in the fog, decided after twelve hours that the time had come to act, and proceeded cautiously to carry out my orders. He found the British steamer Coquitlan[8] in Port Etches, and seized her. She had received about thirty thousand skins, and at the time of the seizure, in a dense fog, had her hatches open and was transplanting cargo in violation of law. The case against her was so plain that there was no room for resistance, and she was towed to Sitka as a prize, where she was bonded for six hundred thousand dollars, which all went into the United States Treasury, and, I suspect, paid most of the expenses of our summer's work.

I again quote from my journal:

"*Unalaska, June 25th.*—Back again to this metropolis. On the way out and down the coast from Port Etches the sealers were thick, all standing for Port Etches. We were kept busy, day and night, boarding them, and the work was severe on officers and men, as it blew hard most of the time and the sea was nasty. It was funny to see them try to get away from us—in which none succeeded—and several had to be shot at

8. This 165-ton freighter was acquired by the Union Steamship Company in 1892, having been shipped by sections from Scotland and assembled under the supervision of H. Darling at Vancouver. It was sent north as a tender to the sealing fleet.

to bring them to. Yesterday morning at daylight we were in Uniak Pass,[9] on our way here, and as the fog lifted we made out a schooner in Bering Sea and went for her at full speed. She made sail and tried to get away; but three shots from one of the rapid-fire guns stopped her, the third one striking within a few feet of her. We took her in tow and brought her here, but after a careful search let her go, as she was a whaler bound for the arctic. If the people we sometimes hear of who think the navy has nothing to do could come up among these islands and see the work the navy is doing here and hear the things that are said of it, they would change their minds—if they possess such a thing.

"We have warned nearly every one of the one hundred vessels at sea when we left Port Townsend less than six weeks ago, and the navy is respected hereabouts as it has never been before; all hands have a very wholesome regard for us. I don't know what the Department and Secretary Tracy will think of the work we have done; but there can be but one opinion among people who know of it.

"*Bering Sea, July 5th.*—We have had the fog so thick for two days that it seemed as if one could make a hole in it with the finger, and the finger would pop, like a cork out of a bottle, when it came out. But we must go, all the same, sleep or no sleep.

"We left Unalaska on the 3d, after a week of very hard work coaling, cleaning engines, etc., after our driving trip to the north. I bundled the Adams off on the 1st, the Rush on the 2d, and we followed on the 3d. Captain Parr,[10] of the

9. Or Unimak Pass, a sea passage in southwestern Alaska variously declared to be from thirteen to thirty miles wide. It lies in the northwestern Aleutian Islands between Unimak Island on the northeast and Krenitzin Island in the southwest. Lying between the north Pacific and the Bering Sea, it provides the easternmost navigation channel through the Aleutian chain.

10. Alfred A.C. Parr became a captain in the Royal Navy in 1887, rear admiral in 1901, and vice admiral in 1903.

Melpomene, says he thinks I am interested in the coal contract, as I seem disposed to burn up all there is in Bering Sea. He does not propose to trouble himself over Canadian sealers, and will take things easy, which I can't do; it isn't my way. Unalaska was at its best when we left—plenty of fish and flowers; the mountains covered with snow, and long arms of it running down into the valleys and right into the grass and flowers. No one would credit a picture of it. In five days after the snow has melted the grass is knee-high, and the ground covered with violets, lupines, anemones, and beautiful orchids, but no perfume to any of them. The Alaskan lily is also abundant, a very beautiful, almost black flower. Salmon and trout and salmon-trout in profusion, and such line-fishing as I never heard of before; but I had no time for an hour of it—too busy to think of it. All the returns for the quarter, not only for my own ship, but for all the vessels of the fleet, must pass through my hands and receive my approval, with no one to help me but an officer who has a watch to stand. I have very little time to amuse myself.

"On the afternoon of the 3d we passed close to the island of Bogosloff,[11] an arctic volcano which came up in 1874 and has not yet cooled off, to judge from the clouds of smoke constantly rising from its surface—not from one particular spot, like Vesuvius or Etna, but from the entire surface of the island, making a cone of steam, wafted by the wind this way or that, and reaching many hundreds of feet into the air. We saw it from a distance of forty miles, and soon after we passed it the fog shut down on us and here we are—a sorry sight to see. The coal sent us is cheap, dirty stuff from Nanaimo, British Columbia,[12] and makes a dense black smoke

11. An island, one mile long, in the Bering Sea northwest of Unalaska Sound and Dutch Harbor. Its name stems from the Russian name meaning "Theologian," given because the island "rose from the sea on 18 May 1796, St. John's Day."
12. A city of southwestern British Columbia, on Vancouver Island and the Strait of Georgia.

which unites with the fog and spatters the little ship until she looks like a chimney-sweep. Officers and men are constantly black and clothes ruined.

"*July 6th.*—A gray day, or rather night; everything is gray—sky slate-gray, water blue-gray, air smoke-gray—all most depressing. We are working a traverse up to St. Paul's Island [13] and covering as much ground as possible, but as yet no sign of sealers. It is very like old blockade days—every one on the look-out, lights screened, and no fog whistle. Very unlike the White Squadron picnic.

"The papers say that Congress is going to give admiral's full pay to two officers who have been commanding squadrons. I wonder if they will give me any additional pay? I command more vessels than both these captains together, and do more work in a month than they do in a year. No commander ever had such a command before, either in our service or any other that I know of, but I hear of no more pay for me."

13. Saint Paul Island is the Pribilof island that lies northernmost in the Bering Sea. It was originally called Saint Peter and Saint Paul Island because G.G. Pribilov sighted the island on 29 June 1787, the dedicated day of those two Holy Apostles.

CHAPTER 27

The Home of the Seals

"ST. *Paul Island, July 8th.*—I spent last night on deck in a dense fog looking for this blessed island and listening to the seals jump and play around us. As soon as we came within seventy-five miles of the land we found them thick, and I don't wonder the sealers want to get in here, for they could fill a schooner in a short time. The fog was too much for us all night, but this morning early we made the land and anchored at ten. As soon as I had had my breakfast I went on shore with most of the officers and visited one of the 'rookeries.' We lay down flat in the grass, and, peering over the edge of the bluff, found ourselves within twenty feet of thousands of the beautiful and much-protected animals. The bulls were savage, and from their constant fights much scarred and cut up, and hence not so handsome as earlier in the season, but still very impressive and dignified. Each had his harem of thirty or forty females, and woe unto the male who ventured near! If any wife tried to escape she was viciously torn and hauled back to her place. The two-year-olds, male and female, are not permitted on the breeding ground, and it was most amusing to watch them form into parties of eight or ten and try to slip past the old bulls. As soon as one discovered them, the old chap nearest to them would rise on his hind legs, bellow viciously, and make a start toward them, when the whole gang would tumble over the rocks into the sea and go frolicking away like a lot of children. The young ones—I saw one born while watching them—were thick all over and among the rocks, and it was most curious to watch the mother, as she came from the water, pick out and suckle her own pup. There were thousands of them, all bleating like lambs, and making enough noise to deafen one; yet the mother always recognised the voice of her own pup, and dragged herself through the lot until she got to it. The pups did not know the mother, and many would try to get to her, but she snapped and bit until she got the right one. It was certainly one of the most interesting sights of my rather varied experience.

"We walked back to the killing grounds over a carpet of such beautiful wild flowers as I have never before seen; my cabin is full of them, but all odourless.

"At the killing grounds the natives had just driven out and killed five hundred seals, and as a three-year-old was being skinned a spear head was found completely inclosed and healed up in his flesh. It is the kind used by the Alaska Indians, [1] and must have been in the seal two years.

"When I had returned on board and had my dinner, the officer of the deck reported a schooner in sight at sea. The boats were down, lower booms out, and fires banked; but just ten minutes after I gave the order we were under way and humming out after her. It was most gratifying to see how quickly and quietly everything was done. As we neared the schooner I was surprised to see her lower her mainsail

---

1. Evans is probably referring to what today are called Northwest coastal peoples, including the Tlingitt tribes, for example. The Tlingitt looked more to the sea than land for food; they should not be confused with the Eskimos, however.

and heave to, but it was explained when we passed under her stern and found she was our old friend Jane Gray, which we had seized, towed into Unalaska, and afterward released. Her captain said he did not want any more of our rapid-fire practice at him.

"*Saturday Night.*—More fog and a nasty blow from the southeast which gives us all the comforts of a sea life while at anchor. I have, however, managed to get the whole crew ashore to have a look at the seal rookeries, and they are back on board with a message from the agent that they have behaved so well that he would not object to any number of the same kind coming whenever they please. I am glad the boys were good.

"*Sunday, July 10th.*—It cleared for just two hours to-day, and during that time the Melpomene came in, rolling and wallowing like a tub, and anchored near us. I begin now to understand why the seals selected these islands for their home: they felt that nothing but a seal could stand such a climate.

"*Unalaska, July 15th.*—I am perfectly swamped with work. The letters are piled up until I can see no end to them, and I feel dead beat. We came in late on the 12th, and when I saw the boat-load of mail-bags come off I knew what was ahead of me, and have struggled with pen and ink ever since, and yet do not see the end of it. I have seized the British steamer Coquitlan and sent her to Sitka. I have no doubt the newspapers will make all sorts of a row about it, but that won't save her and her thirty thousand seal skins. The value of the prize is about six hundred thousand dollars, and will help the Government to pay damages if the arbitration goes against us. Captain Hooper,[2] of the Corwin, carried out my instructions carefully and intelligently, and the result is a

2. Revenue Marine officer Calvin L. Hooper was appointed to the service from California and commissioned in 1866. He was promoted to captain in 1879.

A fur-seal family on St. Paul Island, Bering Sea
From a photograph by D. W. Thompson and A. W. Marrett.

happy one. He found the Coquitlan at Port Etches, surrounded by thirty English sealers, and when he made the seizure all the Indians on the different schooners made for the shore, swearing that they were done with the sealing business. After a time they were induced to return on board, and the vessels put out for Victoria; so we are done with that lot, and the rest are so scared that I doubt if one of them will come into the sea. The Coquitlan had supplies for all the sealing fleet, and as they were captured with the vessel, of course the sealers must go home for more before they can go on with their work, and before they can get back the season will be over. I am quite satisfied with it all, and hope the Secretary may be the same.

"There has not been a sealer in the Bering Sea this season, and I am inclined to think they won't come.

"It is amusing to know the ferocious reputation I am getting up here. They seem to think I am going to eat all the sealers I catch, and I am held up as a terror to the crews of all whalers and other merchant ships. The effect is good, but it makes me laugh when I hear about it. There is one coal ship here with a union crew, and I am afraid I shall have trouble with them. The captain has appealed to me, and, on looking into the matter, I find that they won't work unless they have coffee at nine in the morning. I asked if they did not want tea and toast in the afternoon, and told them that I would double iron the whole gang and put them on bread and water where the dogs wouldn't bite them, and if I heard another word from them I would stop the bread. The effect was good, and they are working very well.

"*Saturday, July 16th.*—I gave myself a holiday to-day and spent it in the open air catching trout. It has been a gloriously clear day—a thing seldom seen in this country, but now I have to face double work to make up for it. I am run down and can not sleep, and the doctor urged me to take a rest.

"*July 18th.*—The Danube has come in from Victoria with

coal and stores for the English ships, and I see, from the
Canadian papers she brought, that they are giving me a scor-
ing for the capture of the Coquitlan. Well, we have the
steamer, and Uncle Samuel is well ahead of the game. The
idea of any one daring to execute our laws seems more than
the Canucks can stand.

"*July 19th.*—Something has happened, I don't know just
what; but the English captain is sending a ship at once to
Victoria, and I have news that a sealer or two has come into
the sea, and I am off after them. I don't know what may
happen in the next month, but I shall keep my end up as
well as I can.

"*At Sea, July 21st,* 10 P.M.—Night before last, when the
news was confirmed that a British sealer had come into the
sea, I hurried out after her with two cutters, as soon as we
could get steam, just at midnight, in the blackest fog I ever
saw. One officer swears it was so dense that it slowed the
vessel down running against it. All yesterday and part of to-
day I have been searching for the sealer, but without success.
This afternoon we landed an officer and a dozen men, armed
and rationed for twelve days, with a good sailing launch, to
guard the only pass he can get out of, and later on we shall
probably catch him. Now we are on our way to the Seal
Islands to look up matters there—so we go, always on the
jump.

"*Friday Night, Island of St. George.*[3]—This has been the
devil's own day. I was called at half past three this morning
by a message that a schooner was in sight, but when I
reached the deck found that it was a whaling bark. But once
awake I stayed up, having had about four hours' sleep. By
noon it was blowing hard, and as thick as pea soup again,

3. The southernmost Pribilof island, in the heart of the fur seal area.
Twelve miles long, it was discovered and named after the vessel *Svete
Georgiv* by G.G. Pribilov in June 1786.

and in such weather we spent the day until 6 P.M., when we
found this island and anchored with the sea breaking on the
shore so heavily that no boat could land, and so we shall have
to hang on here until morning to see what we can do. Just
now the orderly comes to report that the officer of the deck
says we are dragging anchor. The ship is most uneasy, and
the seals are bellowing until I can't hear myself think. I must
go on deck, where I shall probably spend most of the night
looking after the ship.

"*Saturday Night, July 23d.*—I did spend most of last night
on deck, and early this morning the sea ran down so that we
could get a boat ashore with some mail; then we pulled out
in another dense fog, and a fine day we had of it. However,
one day up here is much like another—all fog and lookout.
We certainly sha'n't get a foul bottom from lying still during
these six months.

"*Sunday, July 24th.*—We have seen the land occasionally
to-day, or, rather, we have seen a white line of angry surf
breaking on the rocks. No end of seals playing around and
near the ship. They remind me more of a frolicking lot of
school children than of anything else. I wish Russia had them
all back again, and these blessed islands with their beastly
fogs, too. We should probably have other nasty work to do,
but nothing to equal this. Chile was worse, but there we had
the possibility of a fight every day to make the time pass.

"*Unalaska, July 27th.*—Just out of a very bad gale, which
has lasted since Sunday. Now I suppose I have raised the
devil sure enough. The Rush found the British schooner
Winifred,[4] and I have seized her under our revenue laws,
instead of under the *modus vivendi,* and shall send her to Sitka
on Monday. Of course, the Canadians will raise a howl, and
it may be that our own people won't sustain me. But I am
right, all the same, and shall stand to my guns. The reason

4. A schooner commanded by Captain C.E. Hansen.

I have done this is because the captain of the Winifred commanded the Borealis[5] last year and raided the rookeries on St. Paul Island, killing four hundred seals. The year before he commanded the Adele, raided the island, and killed three hundred and fifty seals. This year he transferred cargo in one of our ports without license, which renders him liable to imprisonment and forfeiture of his vessel. For raiding he is liable to ten years in prison. If I turn him over to the English, nothing will be done to him for raiding, so I determined to send him in and let our courts have a shy at him. The British finally yielded, and the sealer Winifred is mine. Her captain, the most noted pirate in Bering Sea, will go to Sitka in her, and I shall be surprised if he does not spend the next ten years of his life in the penitentiary.

"We have also seized and sent to Sitka the Jane Gray, the American schooner we have seen before. In fact, we are raising considerable of a row, I am afraid, but we are stopping sealing in Bering Sea, which is what I was sent up here to do.

"*Friday Night, July 29th.*—No one who has not seized an English sealer under the guns of the English navy can know just how much writing that calls for—not to speak of the bluff—nor can guess what yesterday and to-day have been to me. I have convinced the senior English officer in Bering Sea that my course was the proper one, and he has so stated to me in his official letter on the subject; and now that it is all done with, I have fits of the shakes when I think of the volcano that was under us, and how close it was to the surface. A few more gray hairs in my head tell the story, and to-morrow I am taking the English officers out on a fishing picnic to show how friendly we are. 'Tis a funny world we live in, and I seem to strike many of the sensational snags. Of course, I have had to write some sort of an account of all the business to the Secretary of the Navy; but I have made it

5. The *Borealis* was launched on 19 March 1891 at Victoria, British Columbia.

very short, for the amount of writing and work has been greater than could be imagined, and in addition I have taken in four hundred tons of coal since we came in here. But I shall go fishing to-morrow, and be ready for more work the day after. The Albatross will leave for Sitka on Monday or Tuesday, towing the sealer, and then we shall put to sea and try to find some more of the gang who have boasted in Victoria that 'no Yankee cruiser should ever overhaul them, for they had a strong Government back of them.'

"We all play a pretty strong hand sometimes. It may be that we shall come to grief for it. I hope not.

"*July 31st.*—We had a glorious picnic yesterday, and such fishing as I had never dreamed of; but on returning I found that I had been stung on the hand by some sort of a beast which had given me a fist as large as Sullivan's.

"Before leaving yesterday morning I had ordered the search of the American whaling bark Lydia, of San Francisco, suspecting that she had seal skins on board. On my return, the searching officer reported a barrel found marked 'Salmon,' and on opening it discovered fourteen salted fur-seal skins. The captain had tried to put them on board the whaling bark Northern Light, for 'Frisco, at midnight the night before, but our men were too much for him. Of course, we seized the Lydia, and have sent her to Sitka, which will raise a howl in the 'Frisco papers, and cause me to be called all the scoundrels on earth; but I don't care a sou. These whalers are a set of infernal pirates, and I shall run in some more of them if they give me the chance.

"The Adams came in this morning and reports the capture of the English schooner Mountain Chief, of Victoria, caught sealing in Bering Sea. Nelson put an officer and men on board of her, and she will be in to-morrow, when I shall turn her over to the senior British officer and ask him to keep her out of the sea in future, or we will blow the stuffing out of her.

"*At Sea, Two Hundred Miles Northwest of St. Paul Island,*

August 6th.—As soon as our last mail closed we put to sea in a dense fog for the False Pass,[6] to pick up the landing party, which had been on shore thirteen days. The distance was one hundred and forty-seven miles, and we ran it up without seeing anything but the fog, slowed the engines, got a cast of the lead, and in a few minutes made out breakers ahead and close aboard. I rang her full speed astern, and let go the anchor, and when the fog cleared in the night we were just one mile out of position, which I call the best piece of navigating I ever heard of, and I give the full credit for it to Conway,[7] our navigating officer.

"At 10 A.M. day before yesterday the landing party got off the beach, through the heavy surf, and reported on board in excellent condition and having done good service. They had captured a number of small native boats engaged in sea-otter hunting against the law, taken from them their skins and guns, and released them with a warning. On the day of our arrival they had had a brush with a small steamer, which got away from them in the fog after they had fired five hundred rounds into her from their rifles and thought they surely had her. The whole place is a perfect nest of pirates; but I have not the time to treat them as they deserve, as we must keep constantly moving in order to prevent our Canadian friends from poaching in Bering Sea. The whole condition of Alaska, so far as the execution of the law is concerned, is a disgrace to our Government, and I shall so report; but it will not do any good.

"We are now on a trip of two thousand miles, covering the sea as perfectly as I can, but so far have seen nothing like a sealer. To-day we have seen more seals than during all the

6. The English name for Isanotski Strait in Unimah Island, one of the Fox Island chain of the Aleutians, considered to be impassable.
7. William P. Conway was warranted a midshipman on 1 October 1866, and graduated from the Naval Academy on 7 June 1870. He rose to ensign on 13 July 1871, master on 9 August 1874, and lieutenant on 12 March 1881. Conway died on 14 September 1893.

rest of our cruising away from the islands. They all seem to be feeding, and are probably the cows who have young on the islands. The water has been covered with a peculiar white, greasy-looking substance, and birds of all kinds are about in thousands—all of which may or may not have to do with the presence of the seals. There is much yet to be learned about these animals, and we are not going about it in the best way. The Government should send some hard-headed chap, with good common sense and no theories, to study them. One day, some time ago, a naturalist, sent by the Government, came to me and reported two dead cow seals on the beach. This looked as if there had been a raid on the rookeries, and I felt dreadfully. The man was closely questioned, and said he had examined them for sex, etc. Stanley Brown[8] found the two animals, dead as reported, but they proved to be sea-lion pups—about as much like a seal as a black lamb is like a pig. So goes the Government money.

"*August 7th.*—I seem to do nothing these days but cruise around in the fog, which is black to-day. Even the seals seem to have had enough of it, and have disappeared. We shall get down to Attu[9] in a couple of days, and if we find no sealers there I shall feel perfectly satisfied that there are none in Bering Sea; in fact, I am satisfied now that there are not enough to kill to any extent."

8. Warranted a midshipman on 22 July 1864, and graduating from the Naval Academy on 2 June 1868, Brown was promoted to lieutenant on 13 April 1872, and lieutenant commander on 27 April 1893. His name was placed on the retired list on 5 December 1894.
9. Westernmost of the Aleutian Islands chain lying off of southwestern Alaska.

CHAPTER 28

Cruising in High Latitudes

"*AUGUST 11th.*—We have to-day been to Uncle Sam's western limit, and I do not think much of it as a garden spot, though it was very pretty—what we could see of it through fog and clouds—beautiful green mountains above the nasty, rocky coast, streaked with snow and blurred over with fleecy clouds, and half veiled in fog. For the last three days we have had better weather—not a gale of wind in all that time, and no really bad fogs—most of the time rather clear, with smooth water.

"At daylight this morning we made Attu in a bank of fog, and had to lay off and on for two hours before we could make out anything to run for. About eight o'clock we 'caught on,' as the boys say, and soon had a boat on shore to learn if any sealers had been about. None had been seen, so we kept away to the east again and are now running for Unalaska, where we should be on the 13th. Up to to-day we have made, on this trip, thirteen hundred miles, and not a sign of a poacher, which leads to the conclusion that they are pretty scarce hereabouts. I shall be powerful glad when it is all over and we can see some blue sky and water again in place of this everlasting gray, which I am sure is hurting the eyes of all hands as well as our spirits. The little ship begins to show the effects of her twenty-five thousand miles since last October in the way of leaky tubes, and we shall have to lay up ten days to get things in first-class shape again before our next trip. If we had good coal we could do the work without the least bother, but the Department in its wisdom (?) has sent out cheap, nasty Nanaimo coal, which hurts everything—including my temper.

"*Friday, August 12th.*—We have been spinning along to-day, without the least trouble, at a good fast rate, and if nothing unforeseen happens we shall be at Iluiluik to-morrow before noon. We have to-day seen the sun set for the first time in Bering Sea, and it was a strange and beautiful sight. Maybe the sky was the same blue it used to be, but I had not seen it for so long it was very delightful to look at. Such a relief from the gray we have had for three months! Just before the sun set the fog lifted, and we saw a beautiful snow-streaked peak eighty-five miles away. It has been a wonderful day for this sea, and I fear we shall not have many more such. The orderly just comes to say it is very thick on deck, and that the officer of the watch wants me, so I will go and take my Scotch-mist bath.

"*Dutch Harbour,*[1] *Unalaska, August 16th.*—I have had no time to write since we came in here, because of the vast amount of work on my hands; but now I begin to see daylight through it, and also see an end to our stay in Bering Sea. We came in here at noon on the 13th, and found no ships except the two Englishmen, who are always in port. The vessel that our landing party fired on at False Pass proves to be the American steam schooner Polar Bear, which put in

1. Dutch Harbor is a major Aleutian port—only 0.7 miles in breadth—situated on the north coast of Unalaska Island. So named by the Russians because they believed a Dutch vessel had been the first to enter the area. This major fishing port was bombed by Japanese aircraft in 1942.

here for medical aid, her chief engineer having a bullet through his forearm. The vessel was riddled with bullets fore and aft, showing that our boys shot pretty straight. The captain, of course, vows that he was fired on without provocation, and I have no doubt the newspapers will give me no end of a blackguarding about it. None of the Polar Bear's crew can explain why they neither showed their colours, nor answered the hail, nor stopped when fired on, except that they had a proper 'funk' on, and ran below and hid themselves.

"On the morning of the 14th, the Danube came in, bringing a large mail, and I have been so full of official reports that I can not think coherently of anything else. The Secretary sends me two long telegrams, neither of which has one word of reference to my actions up here, approval or otherwise.

"*August 17th.*—To-day Captain Parr, of the Melpomene, came for me to go fishing. The sport was such as one will only see in this region, I imagine—salmon-trout by the hundred, and the salmon so thick that every few minutes we had one hooked, sometimes in the mouth, but more often in the fins or stomach. The river was so crowded with them that we could have crossed on the fishes' backs if they had not been so slippery. I have often heard the stories of how these creatures crowd themselves to death in the shoal waters, and now I have seen it for myself. There were thousands of them pushing and wriggling up stream, where the water was only a few inches deep, until they were absolutely forced out on the dry ground, and there lay dead in heaps until the air was foul with the stench. When I cam home the Ranger and the Mohican had arrived, and now, near midnight, I am just through with their captains and their numerous reports. All have been busily cruising, and no one has seen a sealer. I am convinced that we have captured the only ones that have come in to the sea.

"Friday, August 19th.—We had a jolly dinner in the wardroom last night—pork and beans the *pièce de résistance.* It blew a nasty southeast gale all day, and rained in true Alaska style, but the lads were glad to have me at their table, and the 'manner of them' took away all the discomfort of the southeaster. Captain Hooper, of the Corwin, was in the party, and proved a jolly companion. As we sat over our coffee and cigars, with the wind roaring and the rain pelting down, there came the flash of a signal outside; presently the Adams came pounding in against the sea, and, as Nelson came over the side in his dripping sou'wester, our wardroom party broke up, and we three commanding officers retired to my cabin to learn the news. 'Nothing in the shape of a sealer,' said Nelson, 'but plenty of wind, and as thick as pea soup.' The old chap was much cut up when I told him the orders had come that he had to stay in Bering Sea until December 1st, but he took it like the good seaman he is, and, after talking matters over, went to his ship apparently content. Hooper remained with me all night rather than face the gale for a mile or so.

"The Adams has something wrong with one of her bottom valves, and to-day our divers have been under her and made it right; but we are all more or less lame ducks from the miserable coal we have had to use. The Mohican and Ranger will not be able to cruise for four or five days, and I doubt if the Yorktown can get away for a week; but it fortunately makes little difference—there are no sealers to catch. They are scared stiff and couldn't be paid to come in—that is, not one of any size or value. Of course, small things, like those we have taken, will or may take the chance, because the vessels are not worth a thousand dollars, and, if they are lucky, they make six or eight thousand in as many days.

"To-day I have spent among the ships, hurrying the work and getting things in order as fast as I can. To-night I have spent several hours working on my reports to the Secretary,[2] of which I have three in hand—all interesting and full of information. I hope he may publish them in full, for they show what we have been really doing.

"*August 20th.*—A cold, raw day, most of it spent over my reports and looking after our engines. The other ships are coaling as fast as they can, and in a few days we shall all be cruising again. The summer, if it can be so called, is over for us, and from now on it will grow colder and more boisterous. Berries and mosquitoes are now at their best. The salmon berries are only a large, watery kind of raspberry, but better than nothing, which is more than can be said of the whortleberries—they are blue and sour and full of seeds, and taste like a pinch of sour sand. This country produces nothing else in the way of fruit, but grows lettuce and radishes and very good turnips. I think they could grow a lot of things, but the natives only care for seal meat and dried, half-rotted fish. The few white people live on canned food almost entirely.

"*Sunday, August 21st.*—I have a very bad foot to-day, but must go on with my work, sick or well. The weather begins to tell on the men in the way of rheumatism, and some are pretty bad. The ships have been kept so 'on the jump' that all hands are getting tired; the duty is not so easy as it was, and the engines have a way of protesting that the severest orders will not affect. The Adams got out to-day, and I am driving the Mohican and the Ranger all they will stand. The Yorktown will be ready as soon as we can get to the coal pile, and in the meantime we are doing our target work as well as we can.

"*Tuesday, August 23d.*—A howling gale to-night, with much cold rain, and no doubt the Adams and Ranger are catching it in good shape. The coaling facilities are so misera-

---

2. Evans's reports to Secretary of the Navy Benjamin Tracy are noted in the latter's published report for 1892. See U.S. Navy Department, *Annual Report, 1892* (Washington: 1893), 39–40.

ble here that we can coal but one ship at a time, and that very slowly; otherwise the little white ship would be fighting the short chop-sea to-night instead of surging at her chains as she is doing. We shall be off before many days, and as gales are the rule now, I have no doubt we shall be sufficiently amused.

"*Unalaska, August 26th.*—Here we are, still in port when we should be at sea, but I am glad we are not, for the usual August gale has us in its grip, and we should be very wet outside. We are tied up to a coal wharf in Dutch Harbour, perfectly landlocked, and yet the sea finds its way in, and we are jumping and charging, to the great danger of the wharf. The Adams is dragging around the harbour in fine style, but as she has steam up I do not worry about her. In fact, I have learned not to worry about anything; but I shall be powerful glad when we are through with Bering Sea. The Adams came in two days ago, after picking up her landing party at the False Pass (where our men had been), and reports that the natives refuse to shoot any more sea otter for fear the Yorktown will come back and catch them. So we really did some good up there. It is a nest of pirates, and needs a firm hand and a lot of ball cartridge before the law will be respected.

"A schooner came running in before the gale yesterday, showing American colours, and I was afraid we had another prize on our hands; but she proved to be a fisherman from the outside in search of medical aid for one of her men, who had accidentally fired a charge of shot into his instep. The accident happened eight days ago, and the man is in a deplorable condition. Of course, the foot had to come off, and the chances are he will die. Day before yesterday our doctor was called on shore to attend a man who had shot his hand to pieces. He was going to shoot a sheep, and found the cartridge stuck in his Winchester. As he could not force it home he struck it with a hammer to drive it in. They have not found the hammer yet, nor some portions of his hand.

"The coaling arrangements here are causing us much delay

and annoyance. When the coal was taken from ships we did very well; but now it has all been landed and piled in the open, so that it is soaking wet. I stopped taking it in this morning, as the rain was coming down in torrents and the coal bunkers were being flooded. I shall hold on here until the rain ceases before I take any more. The coal is of the poorest kind, and absorbs moisture like a sponge, so that in its present condition we are paying for over ten per cent of water. Of course, this pleases the contractor to death, and it would serve the Equipment Bureau rightly if I went on and paid for a hundred or two tons of water. But I don't want the bother of taking it in and pumping it out.

"The Daphne is ordered to Esquimault on her way home— sails on Monday; the Melpomene starts on a cruise as soon as this gale lets up, and will go to Victoria on September 14th, after which I shall have to look after the whole business. There is really no reason why we should not all clear out now, for there are no sealers in Bering Sea and it is too late for any more to come, and we are spending two thousand dollars per day for nothing; but our orders say we must stay, and stay it is. As I have the finest command in the navy at present, I ought to be satisfied.

"The wardroom of the Mohican gave me a dinner day before yesterday, which I enjoyed very much. There is a fine body of young officers aboard her. We had a good dinner for any place—soup, Little Neck clams, salmon trout, and roast ptarmigan are some of the things I remember. Everything except the soup was provided by the sportsmen of the mess.

"*August 28th.*—I dined yesterday on board her Majesty's steamer Daphne with Captain Wood, R.N.,[3] for whom I have great respect and esteem, and did not get home until midnight. The gale let up yesterday, and to-morrow I shall

3. Charles R. Wood is listed only as a Commander (1884) on the British Navy list.

finish coaling and put to sea for a short cruise only, as we must be back here for the mails due after the 1st of September, and get the Corwin off on the 10th for Sitka.

"*Unalaska, September 6th.*—We started to sea on August 28th, but had only got outside when we made out the mail steamer coming in, so we returned for the night.

"After we had our mail we put to sea again the following morning, for a cruise to the westward, and by night were driving into a head sea that made things wet on board. We were in a nasty southwest gale, with a bad, heavy, breaking sea, and continued in it until we ran in here last night, and found the 'Frisco mail steamer in. The Department wires me that it approves of my doings up here, and also that the State Department commends me for something—I don't make out just what. This is the first word of approval or disapproval I have had from them since I left New York.

"*September 7th.*—I did not get over the shaking up we had in the last ten days, until yesterday, and now am pressed with official mail, added to the strain of constant work and worry, without proper assistants to relieve me of details. During the time of this last cruise I could not once write in my cabin; but we did catch a British sealer and brought him in safely, and will send him to Sitka by the Corwin as soon as the gale ceases.

"On Friday, when we were away off to the westward, steering north in a very heavy sea, the feeling suddenly came over me that we must steer east, and the impression was so strong that I sent for the navigator and told him of it, and said unless it left me we would steer east at noon. He was somewhat doubtful of what the sea would do with us on that course, but we steered it all the same. I felt convinced that something would come of it, and the sequel is extraordinary. On Sunday at noon I was on deck, as I usually am at sea, when the lookout aloft reported, 'Sail ho!' and in a few minutes I made out a schooner, which proved to be the Henrietta, of Victoria, British Columbia, with four hundred and twenty seal skins on board. I had not changed the course at all, and yet we ran right up to her. It was curious. When we got near enough to throw a line on board the schooner, the sea was so nasty that her captain evidently thought we would not dare to lower a boat to send men on board of her, so he refused to make the line fast. We did lower the boat, however, much to his surprise, and in fifteen minutes an officer and six armed men had possession of his vessel, and his crew and all the arms were on board the Yorktown. The way the work was done and the boat handled was most gratifying to me—never saw anything better done. For some minutes my heart was in my throat for fear the boat would swamp; but she did her work, came back, and was hoisted without a scratch on her paint. Every man in the ship had his wits about him, and did what was ordered promptly and efficiently.

"Sunday night we kept the schooner in company, and on Monday, the sea having run down somewhat, we took her in tow and brought her here. She will be condemned and sold in Alaska for violating our revenue laws, and the Canadians will note another 'outrage' on their commerce.

Upon our arrival I found the Oscar and Hattie,[4] British schooner of Victoria, British Columbia, had been captured by the Mohican out at Attu Island, and sent in with a prize crew to report to me. She will come under the *modus vivendi,* and soon as Captain Parr comes in with the Melpomene I shall turn her over to his tender mercies. We are really making it hot for the Canadian sealing fraternity. The gale in which we had been cruising calmed down somewhat on Monday, but yesterday the barometer began falling rapidly; last night a fearful southeast storm broke out on us, and to-day I have not been able to get a boat on shore. Of course, sealing is done for this year, as the weather from now on will proba-

---

4. A 90-foot fishing vessel originally out of Swampscott, Massachusetts, and commanded by Captain W.E. Baker at the time of her seizure.

bly be such that no seal can be taken; but we shall keep things on the jump until we start for home, and shall catch any vessel that breaks the law. It is the general opinion hereabouts that we have captured every vessel that has come into the sea.

"*Friday, September 9th.*—I was occupied every minute yesterday, until midnight. I was starting the Corwin home, *via* Sitka, with the Henrietta in tow, as soon as my despatches could be completed, only waiting for the gale to let up. At six I had finished, and went to dine with Captain Hooper before he sailed. Just as dinner was over a vessel was reported coming in, and at 9.30 the Mohican anchored, and Johnson and I talked until midnight. He had struck another rock, out at Attu this time. His ship was not injured, still he was worried over it. All things considered, the Department has been lucky not to lose a ship this summer. We have cruised straight through, night and day, fog or clear, without decent charts, and not a single buoy or light in the entire country.

"The Corwin left at four this morning. I was sorry to see her go, for it is the first break in the fleet I have commanded, and I may never have such a command again. She takes a long report to the Secretary, which I should be glad to have him publish, and one to the State Department, which contains more information on seals and the Seal Islands than has ever been given in one report. I have been working all summer for three Departments—Navy, State, and Treasury—and I have had to make reports to each of them, which has vastly increased my labours; but I am thankful to say it is all now rapidly coming to an end, and in twenty days more we shall be ready to sail for home.

"*Monday Night, September 12th.*—We have improved the time to-day by having target practice; but the water was smooth, and the target has no show against our six-inch guns, two of them being shot to pieces and finally utterly destroyed. The practice was excellent. To-night at eight, dark as a pocket and raining, I suddenly raised the alarm,

'Torpedo boats!' and turned the search lights on a target, which I had previously placed, and in two minutes we had fired sixteen hundred and ninety shots from small arms and machine guns, and the target was a sieve. We must have presented a beautiful sight from the outside, for we were a blaze of fire, fore and aft. If it had been a real torpedo boat coming at us, the man in command would have required a large head not to flinch, and a very small one not to have it shot off. There is not a place on the target as large as a man's hand unmarked by shot.

"To-morrow, weather permitting, we shall go outside and have a try at a target, running past it at high speed.

"*September 13th.*—The Melpomene has come in and is dumping in the coal as fast as she can, and hopes to get off for Esquimault day after to-morrow. Captain Parr will dine with me to-morrow, when he surely won't have much to eat and less to drink, as I am almost entirely out of all sorts of provisions.

"During his cruise he has been over to the Russian coast and back through Bering Sea and saw not a single sealer. The Russians have captured six schooners—one American and five Canadian—all of which have been condemned and burned. They have a good way of treating such chaps over there: the skins were taken out and sent to San Francisco to be sold for the benefit of the Russian Government, and the prisoners released to find their way home as best they could. Next year the Russians mean to have more cruisers and really put a stop to sealing on that side, and then the whole gang will go for Bering Sea, and our commander commanding may have a real lively time of it. It may be that by that time the Department will awake to the fact that this is the command for an admiral or a commodore, at least, and send one up here.

"In a recent letter from Admiral Hotham, he says that the Coquitlan episode amused him very much. First, the Canadians wanted war—demanded that he should go to Sitka with the Warspite and tow the Coquitlan back to Victoria. When he would not do this, they accused him of having given me their place of rendezvous; but about this time, he says, the smallpox came along and the Canadians were so scared that he heard no more about war.

"Now, the smallpox having let up, they are after him again. They certainly are a miserable lot, and the admiral says they surely love me. When they hear of the Henrietta going to Sitka they will probably wish to embrace me. The admiral has been on the rocks with his flagship, which worries him, but he was in no way to blame for it—nor was any one else, except the people who made the charts and neglected to put the rocks on them.

"If I get my ship to 'Frisco without more damage I shall consider myself lucky. I do not expect to be detained here after the 1st of October, unless I hear of sealers being about, in which case I shall stay until I catch them, if I freeze for it; but I don't thing they want to monkey with the Yorktown.

"*Unalaska, September 16th.*—The Melpomene left yesterday morning, the Mohican goes to-morrow, and the Elsie, a small mail steamer, the day after; but I hope to be in 'Frisco before either of them.

"My dinner to Captain Parr and the Canadian commissioners went off well. We had salmon, ptarmigan and wild ducks among other things. Parr wrote me a letter before he left, which is a model of official sweetness, and in reply I applied sugar most artistically. And so Bering Sea has been freed of seal poachers, for one year anyhow, and no war has come of it. The summer has been one of hard work and much anxiety to me, and I hope to have some rest after it.

"*September 22d.*—Since I last wrote I have been 'down to the sea in a ship,' and, like all men who do that in a small ship, I have paid for it. On the 17th we put out in the beginning of a gale, as it proved, and when we came in this evening and dropped anchor I could for the first time sit down to write. When we left the harbour we found a fearful sea running, and it grew steadily worse until we came in to-day, when it blew with hurricane force; but through it all the little white ship grows better and better, and I am proud of her, in spite of the bad name she had when I took command of her. On this last cruise we ran about one hundred and fifty miles to the west of the Seal Islands, toward the Russian coast, when the sea was so tremendous that we were compelled to lay to for twelve hours, and as soon as we could we cruised off and on, looking for schooners, but none came in sight.

"Day before yesterday, still blowing a gale, we started back this way, intending to stop at the islands, but when we came near them the sea was breaking so viciously that we came on, and to-day saw the worst weather we have had since leaving New York. When we were about fifteen miles from Unalaska the wind attained hurricane force, blowing directly from the volcano of Makuslin,[5] and we had a picnic. We were steaming twelve knots at the time, and tried to show some little canvas to steady the ship; but a piece as large as a tablecloth went like smoke, and we had to depend on the steam. The water was picked up in patches of twenty acres and carried off in spray two or three hundred feet, and the force of the wind was so great that the surface of the sea was cut down as level as a floor, and foaming white; but we made it somehow, and here we are safely at anchor, and the Bering Sea work is done, for this season at least.

"I am willing to admit that Bering Sea is the worst patch of water it has ever been my lot to tackle, and I sincerely hope I may never have to do again. I find the Bear is in from the Artic, and as she is to remain until December 1st, we are to give passage to the wife of Captain Healey and one other

5. Makushin volcano is a 6,680-foot peak on Unalaska Island, northwest of Dutch Harbor and Unalaska. Its name probably comes from the Russian word for "the crown (of the head)" or "top," which was applied to the highest point on the island.

person. I shall give up my cabin to them, while I live as best I can. From now until the 1st of October I shall be hard at work getting ready for our trip down, and when once we start I shall make things 'hum' if I can. I hope to sleep tonight for the first time in many nights.

"*Thursday Night.*—I have had a busy day of it, and wound up with dinner on board the Bear, and a very good dinner it was. Captain and Mrs. Healey, Captains Nelson and Nicols,[6] Mr. Ware and son, who, with Mrs. Healey, are to be my guests to 'Frisco, composed the party. Ware and his son have this summer landed a mining party on the Yukon River, and are on their way home to Chicago. The Adams gets off tomorrow, and I shall not see her again, and in a week my command in the Bering Sea will be a thing of the past. The summer seems short to look back at, but how the days drag now as the end approaches! If we get to 'Frisco , as I hope, on October 8th, we shall have steamed a little over twenty-

6. It is unclear from Evans's account whether Captain Healey was the legendary Captain Michael A. Healey, Revenue Marine/Coast Guard. As commander of the USRC *Corwin,* he earned a reputation for his distinguished service and authority in northern waters. *The New York Sun* once stated that he was better known in those parts than any President of the United States or European potentate. Healey's word was law among the native Americans and seal fishermen; for twenty years he had been the recognized legal authority north of Port Townsend. He was blunt and forceful, and knew the Bering Sea, the straits, and even the Arctic better than anyone else. Moreover, Healey's reports to the Treasury Department were almost literary in quality, their style suggesting Jack London, Theodore Roosevelt, and even Evans. (See, for example, his *Report of Cruise of Revenue Marine Steamer Corwin in the Arctic Ocean in the Year 1884,* Washington, 1889.)

Other names cited here by Evans are unidentifiable except possibly Captain A. Nelson, who was born in Sweden in 1855 and sailed the world over until 1883, when he commenced working north of San Francisco. He eventually sailed out of Victoria, British Columbia, in sealing schooners. Captain Melville Nicols was a native of Maine who spent most of his career working ships for the Washington Steamboat Company and the Puget Sound and Alaska Steamboat Company.

eight thousand miles in one year. Certainly no one can say I have not been to sea sure enough.

"*Friday Night.*—One week more of Bering Sea and I am done with it for all time, I hope. It is perhaps this thought that makes these volcanic humps look very beautiful just now in the magnificence of their early winter coloring. This morning the mountains were clearly outlined against a cold steel-blue sky, the line of new-fallen snow, sharp and distinct, about one third of the way down the peaks, and the rest golden-red and green-brown, with here and there in the valleys, sheltered from the cold winds, a bright emerald-green spot. The Adams got away on time at nine o'clock, and one hour after the Rush came in, bringing the first of a southeast gale with her. Later on it came harder, and now it is nasty and cold enough to suit even the bears.

"Captain Coulson reports dreadful weather during the last ten days—just such, in fact, as I have had during our cruising. He is an old hand up here, and says he never knew it so bad before so early in the season, September usually being a fairly good month. No sealers have been seen, and only a few seals away from the islands, where the old ones are now busily engaged teaching the youngsters to swim and get ready for their long sea trip. It is a curious thing in Nature that these animals, which may be said to live entirely in the water, can neither beget nor bear their young except on land, and that the young one would instantly drown if put in the water within several weeks after its birth. A young seal is much more helpless in the water than a young kitten. But this is not more strange than that the mosquito, which is so plainly meant to live by sucking blood through its bill from a thin-skinned, hairless animal, is most abundant in the swamps of the tropics and the frozen regions of the Arctic, where no such animals can exist; nor why the leech, which lives by sucking warm blood, is found only in swamps where Nature forbids warm-blooded life.

"*Saturday Night.*—Finding this morning not too bad, we got under way and went outside for some great-gun target practice, of which we have not had time to do as much as I should have liked this summer. We found a moderate sea with squalls of rain and much wind. The target was soon placed, and running the ship by it at full speed, the six-inch guns opened in a way much to my satisfaction. Every shot was excellent until the eighth, which demolished the target and put an end to the practice.

"I have just now finished my table of distances made by the fleet under my command. The distance covered by all ships since leaving Port Townsend is sixty-one thousand four hundred and twenty-six miles, of which thirty-eight thousand three hundred and ninety-eight miles have been in Bering Sea. Nothing approaching this work has been done since the civil war closed, and I hope the Department may be as well pleased with it as I am.

"*September 30th.*—To-night is the end of this, unless the gale now blowing is too much for us to-morrow morning. Bering Sea has been policed in proper shape, according to my thinking; the job is finished, and to-morrow we are homeward bound. A happy lot we surely are. There is not a drop of anything to drink on board, not even a bottle of beer, so we are all very quiet and subdued in our happiness, and only hoping for a decent day to get well clear of these miserable islands. Yesterday daylight found us smothered in snow and hail, and since then it has snowed in real arctic style. Indeed, I never saw a snowstorm before—had no idea what one was like. I know now, and really don't care for any further knowledge on the subject. I know that I shall have to spend much of the next week on the bridge, but I don't care so long as we can make any way toward 'Frisco.

"*October 10th, 'Frisco.*—Just in, after awful trip down with gales and hurricanes all the way from Unalaska—the worst I have ever known. We were absolutely under water for five days, and I lived in wet clothing. Finally came a hurricane in which we were hove to for twenty hours."

I have made these extracts from my journal at length, since they give a much better idea of my life and doings in Bering Sea than I could possibly write now.

CHAPTER 29

In Command of the New York

THE Secretary of the Navy and the President gave hearty approval for my successful work, and the President was good enough to mention me by name in his message to Congress. Few officers have had this honour in time of peace.

It had seemed to me from the time I first began to study the seal question that the easiest solution was for the United States to declare the seals a herd of domesticated wild animals owned by us and breeding on our territory alone, and after this declaration to state our intention to follow and protect them, no matter where they went. This would, at least, have brought the question to an issue, and a settlement would have had to follow very shortly. The theory of a closed sea did not appear to me consistent with our action in reference to the fisheries on the Eastern coast, where we denied to England the same contention.

A few weeks after my return from the Arctic I was detached from the Yorktown at San Francisco and ordered as naval secretary of the Lighthouse Board. When I reached Washington I found that the zealous watchdogs of the Treasury had checked against my pay the sum of three dollars and sixty-eight cents, because I had taken five days to reach my home instead of four. The checkage was the difference between duty and leave pay for one day. I had turned into the Treasury something over six hundred thousand dollars during the summer, and felt that this last contribution might have been spared me.

When the seal question again came up for consideration the conference was composed of very distinguished men— Secretaries Gresham [1] and Carlisle [2] on our side and Sir Julian

---

1. Born in Lanesville, Indiana, on 17 March 1832, Walter Quintin Gresham attended Indiana University and served in the Indiana legislature in the 1860s. During the Civil War he became a brevet major general; he was U.S. postmaster general, 1882–84; and he served as Secretary of the Treasury in 1884. Gresham was the Populist Party's presidential candidate in 1892; he was appointed Secretary of State, 1893–95, by President Grover Cleveland. Gresham advised against the Hawaiian annexation treaty, and he settled the Nicaraguan boundary dispute and the Allianca affair between the United States and Spain. He died on 28 May 1895.

2. John Griffin Carlisle was born in Campbell (Kenton) County, Kentucky, on 5 September 1835. He served as a member of the Kentucky House of Representatives from 1859 to 1861; in the Senate, 1866–71; as a delegate at large to the New National Congress, 1868; and in the U.S. House of Representatives, 45th–51st Congresses, 1877–91. Carlisle was Speaker of the House, 48th–50th Congresses, 1883 to 1889, but he resigned on 26 May 1890 to become U.S. Senator until 4 February 1893, at which point President Grover Cleveland appointed him Secretary of the Treasury. Affiliated with the gold-standard wing of the Democratic Party, Carlisle resumed practicing law in New York and became vice president of the anti-imperialist league. He died in 1910.

Pauncefote [3] and Sir Charles Tupper [4] representing the Canadian side. I was requested to be present, and was very glad afterward to know that my practical knowledge of the subject had been of value in arranging the rules governing the taking of seals under the Paris award.

My second tour of duty as naval secretary of the Lighthouse Board was made more pleasant by the occasional trips of President Cleveland [5] and members of his Cabinet, in one or the

3. Sir Julian Pauncefote, First Baron Pauncefote of Preston (1828–1902), was the famous lawyer, diplomat, and British envoy to the United States during the closing years of the nineteenth century. Born in Munich, he was called to the bar as a member of the Inner Temple in 1852. He served as chief justice of the Leeward Islands, 1872–74; then, in 1885, on the international commission concerning free navigation of the Suez Canal. He became envoy extraordinary and minister plenipotentiary to the United States in 1889. His patience, urbanity, and impartiality allowed him to make major contributions to relations between the two countries concerning the Bering Sea issue, the Venezuela-Guinea boundary dispute, and Cuban matters prior to the Spanish-American War. Sir Julian was appointed senior British delegate to the first Hague conference on armaments limitations in 1899, but returned as ambassador to the United States from 1899 to 1902.
4. A famous Canadian statesman and politician who was born in Amherst, Nova Scotia, in 1821. He studied medicine at Edinburgh University and returned to practice in his native province. He entered the Nova Scotia legislature in 1855, became provincial secretary in 1859, minister of public works in the federated cabinet of Sir John MacDonald in 1878, and assumed the post as first minister of railways and canals the next year. He served as Canadian high commissioner in London, 1894–96, then as Secretary of State and briefly as Prime Minister of Canada in 1896 before falling prey to the vagaries of Canadian politics of the time. He was noted as a constructive statesman of Canada during very turbulent years, and an instrumental spokesman for Canadian nationalism and the development of the trans-Canadian rail system. He died in 1915.
5. Born in Caldwell, New Jersey, in 1837, Stephen Grover Cleveland later attended Princeton University, where he earned a law degree. He served as mayor of Buffalo, New York, from 1881 to 1884, and was elected for two terms as President of the United States (1884–88,

other of the lighthouse steamers which could be conveniently used for the purpose. I was usually with the President when health or recreation made such trips desirable, and took charge of all preparations and supplies. They were never allowed to interfere in the least with Government work, nor did they involve the expenditure of one cent of public money. They did, however, enable both him and the Secretary of the Treasury, who is President of the Lighthouse Board, to see the practical working of the service by contact with the keepers and inspection of the stations, and in this way were of great benefit. Many desirable changes can be traced to these outings, and it can be safely asserted that no more innocent or enjoyable form of recreation could have been devised.

During the summer of 1894 the fine, new, armoured cruiser New York[6] was in need of a captain, and the Secretary of the Navy did me the honour to give me the command. I had been promoted to the grade of captain after my return from the Yorktown, and was one of the juniors on the list; hence the compliment was all the more marked. I was at Gray Gables[7] making a visit to Mr. Cleveland when the time came for me to report, and he was good enough to take me down to New York with him and put me on board.

1892–96). Cleveland retired to Princeton, New Jersey, where he died in 1908.

6. A steam-powered steel armored cruiser of approximately 9,000 tons, with a top speed of 20 knots, a main battery of thirty guns and three torpedo tubes, and a 566-man complement, the USS *New York* was authorized by an act of 7 September 1888. Laid down on 30 September 1890 at Cramp Shipyard, she was launched on 2 December 1891, and commissioned on 1 August 1893. The *New York* served as Rear Admiral William Sampson's flagship in the Spanish-American War. She was modernized, 1905–09, and renamed the *Saratoga* in 1911 and the *Rochester* in 1917. Decommissioned in 1933, she nevertheless remained at Olongapo in the Philippines, being stricken from the Navy List on 28 October 1938 and scuttled in December 1941 to avoid capture by the Japanese.

7. President Grover Cleveland's two-story clapboard summer home at Buzzards Bay, Massachusetts.

The New York was our only armoured cruiser, and at that time the flagship of Admiral Richard W. Meade,[8] commanding the North Atlantic squadron. A few days after I had relieved Captain "Jack" Philip, the Department gave me additional orders as chief of staff to the admiral, in which capacity I served until he was relieved at his own request and placed on the retired list.

Admiral Meade was an able, courageous officer, and during our winter's cruise with the squadron, consisting of the New York (flagship), Columbia, Minneapolis,[9] Cincinnati,[10] and Raleigh,[11] gave us admirable and systematic drill. Modern methods and appliances were used in a modern way—torpedoes were run under service conditions, and search lights used to their utmost capacity as a means of communicating between vessels at sea at long distances from each other. The tone of the squadron was excellent, owing in a large measure to the personal character and bearing of the admiral. The war

8. Warranted a midshipman on 2 October 1850, Meade was promoted to captain on 13 March 1880, commodore on 5 May 1892, and rear admiral on 7 September 1894. Placed on the retired list on 20 May 1895, he died on 4 May 1899.

9. A sister ship to the USS Columbia, the USS Minneapolis was laid down on 16 December 1891, launched on 8 August 1893, and commissioned on 13 December 1894. She was out of commission from November 1906 to July 1917, possibly because of her high rate of coal consumption. The Minneapolis carried 18-inch torpedoes, compared with the Columbia's 14-inch torpedoes, and she had two stacks, as distinguished from the four-stacker Columbia.

10. The USS Cincinnati was a sail and steam, steel protected cruiser that displaced 3,183 tons, mounted twenty-one guns and four torpedo tubes, had a top speed of 19 knots, and a complement of 322 men. Authorized by an act of 7 September 1888, she was built at the New York Navy Yard: laid down on 29 January 1890, launched on 11 November 1892, and commissioned on 16 June 1894. The Cincinnati was sold in 1921.

11. A sister ship to the Cincinnati constructed at the Norfolk Navy Yard. Laid down on 19 December 1889, launched on 31 March 1892, and commissioned on 17 April 1894, she was sold in 1921.

between Cuba and Spain, or, more properly speaking, the revolution in Cuba, [12] was in its infancy, and the admiral was outspoken in his friendship for the Cubans—so much so that the Department would not allow him to enter a Cuban port for fear that his violent temper might involve us in trouble. This was a source of much concern to him, and was the beginning of the trouble that resulted seriously to him later on. Upon our arrival at New York, early in May, I was directed to fit out for a short cruise to Europe to join in the ceremonies attending the opening of the Kiel Canal. [13]

Probably the most important work of Admiral Meade's squadron during the West India cruise was saving the city of Port-of-Spain [14] in Trinidad. While we were anchored there a fire broke out in the city, which, owing to the strong trade wind blowing, soon made great headway, and would have destroyed the entire place had it not been for the work done by our men. The squadron was anchored five or six miles from the shore, and as the admiral refused to land men until officially asked to do so, much property was lost that otherwise might have been saved. When, however, the request for assistance came, everything was ready, and the fire brigades of the vessels were sent in at once under command of the

12. Abortive attempts to free Cuba from Spanish rule via so-called filibustering expeditions from the southern United States took place in 1848 and 1850. More serious revolutionary outbreaks occurred from 1868 to 1878. In 1873 the former Confederate blockade runner *Virginius* was captured running guns to the rebels, and the American crew was executed. The most serious rebellion took place from 1895 to 1898, with Spanish General Valeriano Weyler instituting the infamous concentration camps that incensed American citizens. The stage was set for Spanish-American confrontation with the destruction of the USS *Maine* in Havana Harbor in 1898, climaxing years of American support for the insurrection.
13. A 61-mile canal in northern Germany that was constructed to connect the North Sea and the Baltic Sea. Elaborate opening ceremonies took place in 1895.
14. The capital of Trinidad and Tobago, on the northwest coast of Trinidad.

executive officer of the New York. After four hours' very hard and dangerous work the city was saved, and the men returned on board. I was sure from the first that the fire was of incendiary origin, and felt that a company of marines with plenty of cartridges would be needed before the job was finished; but the admiral hesitated to land armed men in a foreign state. After some discussion he told me that I might do as I pleased, but advised me not to take the responsibility of doing as I proposed. Without more delay I sent in forty men with two officers and plenty of ammunition. The moment they landed they were deployed through the threatened district, and soon put an end to the looting that was going on. Our men came back at midnight loaded with all sorts of things that had been given them by the people on shore, among others twenty young goats, which I promptly sent back in the morning. The Governor wrote a handsome letter of thanks, commending the excellent conduct of our men under most trying circumstances. He was particularly grateful for the marines, whose bayonets proved just the thing required.

The work of preparing for the Kiel cruise was rapidly done, and by May 18th I was ready for sea. Arrangements had been made for electrically illuminating the ship, and as she was the first of our new vessels to be shown abroad, and the occasion a notable one, it was decided to give as fine a display of fireworks as possible. I sent for the expert who attends to such matters in and about New York, and with him arranged the scheme that afterward astonished Kiel and the ships there assembled. When the various set pieces and the supply of bombs and rockets began to arrive I was at a loss to know what to do with them. After we had filled every available space below, there still remained a lot to be looked after. I had the boxes, which were very large, securely lashed on deck, covered with canvas, and painted. They were a source of great uneasiness to me until they were finally burned. If they got wet, of course they would not go off when the time came, and if some careless man dropped a spark from his pipe on them they would go off much too soon. Fortunately, I had no accident with them, and was well pleased when I saw the last of them.

The U. S. S. Columbia [15] was also fitting out for Kiel, and was expected to beat us badly in the race across. My journal has the following:

"*May 22, 1895, at Sea, off the Banks.*—We got away on the stroke of twelve on Saturday in a most successful way, and apparently to the entire satisfaction of the navy-yard officials, who waved cordially to me as we straightened down the river. The mud bank tried to stop us, but I had said we would go at noon, and so we went. That is about the easiest way to manage: say you are going to do a thing, and then simply go ahead and do it. The ship behaved most beautifully, and the evolution was perfectly performed. Even the chaplain, dear soul! came and congratulated me, and said I must have a wonderful eye for distances, and no end of nerve.

"We came over the bar just behind the Lucania, and the way she ran us out of sight was amusing. If we had been using full power of steam we should probably be in sight of her now, but we had only three boilers, and were making but twelve knots and a half.

"Ice was reported well south of the Banks before we left New York, and not wishing any of that in mine, we came out on a course to keep us south of 40°; but the third day out, Monday, the temperature of the water suddenly fell 24° and the air 5°, so I knew who our neighbour was, and kept

15. A steam-powered steel protected cruiser of 7,375 tons, a top speed of 21 knots, mounting twenty-seven guns and four torpedo tubes, with a 477-man complement, the USS *Columbia* was authorized by an act of June 1890. Laid down on 30 December 1890 at Cramp Shipyard, she was launched on 26 July 1892, commissioned on 23 April 1894, and sold in 1922. Designed as a commerce raider, the *Columbia* was out of commission from May 1907 to June 1915, presumably because of her high coal consumption.

a bright lookout for icebergs. After an hour of most anxious watching the temperature again went up and all danger was past. Up to yesterday afternoon the weather was blowing, with rain and fog, but to-day is clear and beautiful and warm. To-night we shall be halfway over, and I shall treat the ship to another boiler, which should give us fifteen knots. I don't want the Columbia to catch us, and I do want to get in, take my coal and be cleaned up, when Admiral Kirkland [16] puts in, in the San Francisco.

"Everything is quiet and lovely in the ship, but this morning, about four o'clock, I was nearly thrown out of my bed, by the engines reversing at full speed, and no end of a row lowering the lifeboat. A new landsman we had recently acquired has pulled the knob of the life buoy, just to see what would happen. He won't be so curious again, I think.

"*May 23d.*—After I wrote yesterday we came pretty near finding the ice again. The temperature of the water fell suddenly from 65° to 49°, and the air was bitter. I found on examining the last pilot chart that we were almost in the exact spot where a berg four hundred feet high had been seen less than a week ago. After half an hour we ran out of the cold into beautiful, clear, warm weather, which has continued ever since.

"Our extra boiler is helping, and we have been making over fifteen knots since eight last night. We shall be halfway across some time to-night, and the Columbia will have to 'hump herself' to sight us before we anchor. The doctor tells me to-day that, after carefully measuring the quantity of air pumped into the New York per hour, he finds that she is better ventilated out here on the sea than most of the large buildings in New York. Careful analysis shows that

16. William A. Kirkland was warranted a midshipman on 2 July 1850. He was promoted to captain on 1 April 1888, commodore on 27 July 1893, and rear admiral on 1 March 1895. Retiring on 3 July 1898, Kirkland died on 12 August 1898.

the quality of the air in the ship is as fine as the quantity is abundant.

"*May 27th, Two Hundred Miles West of Land's End.* [17]—We are drawing up to the entrance of the Channel. We have made a lovely run—probably the quickest ever made by a man-of-war. The weather has been fairly good—a long swell from the northwest, which has cut our speed down somewhat, and a strong, steady southwest wind all the way. Today is clear, and, if it continues so, we shall make the Bishop's Rock Light [18] without trouble and be anchored off Netley Abbey [19] to-morrow evening. We left New York in company with a large four-masted steamer, and for two days had her in sight all the time. Then she steered more to the north and we lost her. This morning at daylight she was in sight on our port beam, and it looks now as if we should run up the Channel side by side.

"*Off Netley, Southhampton, May 29th*—I stopped writing off the Scilly Islands, [20] and yesterday afternoon the blessed fog caught us about two hundred miles off Land's End, but fortunately cleared as we came by Bishop's Rock, and so I entered the Channel knowing our position accurately. After passing Eddystone [21] it shut in as thick as pea soup and I saw nothing up to Portland, [22] when it cleared, and we ran for the entrance to the Solent, [23] which we made night before last at

17. A cape of southwestern England, it is the westernmost extremity of the country.

18. A lighthouse atop Bishop's Rock off the west coast of the Isles of Scilly.

19. Located on the eastern shore of Southampton Water (Harbor).

20. Islands of southwestern England at the entrance to the English Channel. They lie to the west/southwest of Lands End.

21. A famous lighthouse in the English Channel, directly south of Plymouth.

22. Portland Bill lies south of Weymouth, in Dorset County.

23. A 15-mile-long channel between the Isle of Wight and the English mainland.

ten, but no pilot could we get, so we had to anchor until six yesterday morning, thus losing valuable time. The run up past the Isle of Wight[24] was exceedingly beautiful, as was the view of Cowes Roads;[25] but the ship took most of my time and attention, and I could only glance at things as we ran by them.

"We found the San Francisco,[26] Marblehead,[27] and Alliance[28] here, but not the Columbia. Admiral Kirkland will not take the squadron to Kiel, but orders us to meet him at Copenhagen June 12th, and from there we will go to Kiel for the show. After that is over, we are to be cut loose, as it were, to go where we please, and find our way back to New York when ordered.

"The Columbia came in last night at 9.30, having burned

24. An island in the English Channel off south-central England.
25. Cowes is a town on the north coast of the Isle of Wight.
26. The USS *San Francisco* was a sail and steam, steel protected cruiser that displaced 4,088 tons, had a top speed of 19 knots, mounted twenty-two guns, and had a 384-man complement. Authorized under an act of 3 March 1887, she was laid down on 14 August 1888, launched on 26 October 1889, and commissioned on 15 November 1890. Converted to a minelayer at the Norfolk Navy Yard, 1910–11, she took part in the Northern Mine Barrage during World War I, was decommissioned in 1921 at Philadelphia, and renamed the *Tahoe*, then the *Yosemite*, 1930–31. The cruiser was sold in 1939.
27. A sail and steam, steel protected cruiser, the USS *Marblehead* displaced 2,094 tons, mounted seventeen guns and three torpedo tubes, had a top speed of 17 knots, and a complement of 274 men. Authorized under an act of 7 September 1888, she was laid down in October 1890, launched on 11 August 1892, and commissioned on 2 April 1894. A sister ship of the *Montgomery* and *Detroit,* the *Marblehead* was sold in 1921.
28. The USS *Alliance* was a sail and steam, wooden screw-sloop constructed at the Norfolk Navy Yard. Laid down in 1874, launched on 3 March 1875, she was commissioned on 18 January 1877. The sloop's engines were removed in 1904 and this sister ship of the *Adams* was converted to a store ship and sold in 1911.

fourteen hundred tons of coal on the way over, as against eight hundred for us. We ran at half power, she at two thirds, so the New York is not a very slow ship.

"The admiral is to leave on the 5th, and we shall follow on the ninth; so we must hurry up the coaling that we may get cleaned up and ready. Yesterday afternoon I 'struck the beach' and had a delightful hour in the ruins of Netley Abbey, certainly one of the most beautiful spots I have ever seen. The light and shadows were exquisite, and the air was filled with the songs of birds. Afterward I dined at the club for the sum of five shillings. I had soup, grilled mackerel, devilled kidney, three vegetables, cold roast beef and salad, cherry tart, cheese, a cup of coffee, and a pint of good red wine. No club in the United States can do anything like it for the money.

"Two Italian ships have come in to-day and more are expected to-morrow. I hear they are sending a fleet of ten vessels.

"*May 30th.*—Our flag was at half-mast yesterday, and the same to-day, for poor Mr. Gresham.

"*Off Netley, June 5, 1895.*—I came back from London last night at midnight, after a most delightful visit. Met many friends there who gave me dinners, luncheons, drives, and made as much fuss over me as if I were named Mahan.[29]

29. Alfred Thayer Mahan (1840–1914) began his naval career as an acting midshipman on 30 September 1856. The intellectual godfather of the New Steel Navy, he served in customary assignments, including blockade duty, before being summoned in 1885 to lecture at the Naval War College. Mahan succeeded Stephen Luce to the college's presidency, 1886–89 and 1892–93. In 1890 he published *The Influence of Seapower Upon History, 1660–1783,* which vaulted him to worldwide fame; Captain Mahan was forced to sea duty in command of the flagship USS *Chicago* from 1893 to 1895. Following retirement, he was recalled to sit on the Spanish War Board in 1898, and the following year he served as a delegate to the Hague Peace Conference. In 1906 he was promoted to rear admiral and placed on the retired list. At first better recognized abroad than in the United States, Mahan was

Sunday we went into the park to see 'Church Parade,'[30] and surely it was a sight. The Duke of Cambridge[31] was walking slowly through the park and eying the dresses with apparent interest. After the park we drove to the zoo, where the Afghanistan prince was having an outing. All the royal carriages were out, and the Prince and Princess of Wales[32] were showing him about. They call him a 'nigger' and at the same time bow down to him and make much of him, for fear of what he may do in the East. Funny people! The nigger prince at a dinner party last week refused to enter the drawing-room because of the low dresses of the ladies, saying it was not decent. When he had to take out the lady of the house, he walked two yards ahead of her, and wouldn't look at her during the dinner. Funny nigger!

"This morning the admiral signalled for all commanding officers to repair on board. There he told us that we would have to be at Copenhagen on the 11th, and that he would then transfer his flag to the New York. Orders have come from Washington that we are to assemble at Kiel on the 15th—four days before we are wanted—and that the admiral, captains, and as many officers as the ship can hold, are to go by rail to Hamburg,[33] and thence through the canal on board the Marblehead.

"*Copenhagen,*[34] *Denmark, June 10th.* Here we are, and if I am to do much of this sort of work I shall need new eyes and new legs. We got under way from Southhampton at 3 A.M.

---

not especially popular among traditionalist sea dogs of the Navy Department.

30. A compulsory formation in the Victorian-era British Army that required half of Sunday for preparation. It was a distinctly unpopular part of military life, apparently prejudicing the enlisted man's outlook toward organized religion and churches.

31. Commander in chief of the British Army in 1895.

32. The eldest son of Queen Victoria, the Prince of Wales ascended the throne in 1907 as Edward VII; his wife, Princess Alexandra.

33. A port city in northwestern Germany on the Elbe River.

34. The capital of Denmark on the east coast of Sjaeland Island.

Saturday, after I had slept just two hours. Friday night I thought I would get some sleep, but, as I was removing my coat, four English officers came on board to say good-bye, and it was midnight when they left. At 3 A.M. I was on the bridge, my clothes have not been off since, and my poor legs and feet are very bad. When we got under way, Saturday, the Columbia followed immediately, and we had it 'nip and tuck' up the Channel. After three hours we passed her, both of us going very fast, and as we entered the Dover Strait [35] we were leading about two ships' lengths. Off the South Foreland [36] we passed the Spanish squadron—the Columbia on one side and we on the other. It was coming on foggy, and at first the Dons could not make us out, but as we ranged up abreast of their rear ship they 'caught on,' and their admiral, not wishing to exchange salutes, I suppose, hauled down his flag until we had passed him. At the same time he made signal for full speed, and it was funny to see his efforts. We raced by them as if they had been tied to a wharf. It was a beautiful sight—what we could see of it for the fog. Shortly afterward I slowed to half speed, as it grew so thick one could 'cut it with a knife.' The Columbia passed under our stern, going full speed, and we saw nothing more of her until we found her anchored here at noon to-day.

"*June 11th.*—Night before last, as we ran out of the North Sea, the sun set at nine o'clock exactly, and at half past eleven it was still light enough to read on the bridge. The twilight gradually moved around to northeast and the moon rose in the south. At 2 A.M. the sun came up over the Swedish mountains, and the scene was worth coming all this way to look at. About 3 A.M. we passed a fleet of battle ships heading for Kiel, and soon after entered Skaw

35. A twenty-one-mile-wide strait at the east end of the English Channel, between southeastern England and northern France.
36. The shoreline cliff area south of Dover.

Sound[37] without a pilot, and from there on I was kept busy."

The harbour is, comparatively speaking, a small one, and the channels narrow and very crooked; but we managed after a while to get a good berth near the San Francisco. Admiral Kirkland transferred his flag to me the following day with his staff and all their belongings, but, as he was only to remain on board a short time, concluded to mess with me rather than start his own mess.

37. The Skaw is a cape on the northern extremity of Jutland, Denmark, that extends into the Skagerrak.

CHAPTER 30

The Kiel Celebration

TWO days later we started for Kiel[1] through the intricate waters of the Little Belt[2] and arrived without accident. On the way we passed vessels of almost every nation, most of them at anchor putting the last touch of paint on before entering the harbour. When off the entrance to the port we were met by a torpedo boat, which put a German naval officer on board of each ship to show us where our buoys were. The one who came to us was from the Naval College in Berlin and was detailed for duty on the admiral's staff during our stay. He spoke English well and was a most accomplished man.

As we entered the harbour we found the German fleet drawn up in two long lines, and as we passed them each ship

---

1. A city in northwestern Germany on Kiel Bay, an inlet of the Baltic Sea.
2. A body of water north of Kiel Bay. It is unclear why passage occurred through this body of water unless Evans confused it with the Store Belt, a wider passage also in Danish waters.

manned her rigging and cheered us. The cheering and the noise of the saluting guns made quite a Fourth-of-July effect. Before we reached our buoy the New York had fired one hundred and fifty guns in saluting the various notable persons in the harbour, though the Austrian fleet was the only one ahead of us. We took our buoys in a way to elicit the admiration of all who saw the evolution. As soon as we were fast to them, the telephone from shore was connected to our pilot house, and from that day until the day of our departure we had only to 'phone for anything that we wanted from a keg of beer to a brownstone front and it was furnished free of cost. The perfect way in which everything was arranged was a great credit to the emperor, who personally had his eye on every detail. Eighty-five buoys were laid down in the harbour, each one with the number of the ship that was to take it painted on it, and on top the flag of the nation to which she belonged. Each ship, as she took her buoy, was connected with the shore by telephone, as in the case of the New York.

In the space of two days all the fleets had arrived and were composed of the finest ships in the navies of the world. The question of the exchange of official visits under such circumstances was a most puzzling one, and here the good sense of the emperor showed out strongly. He designated one of his own vessels, a very large and roomy one, and invited all admirals and captains to meet him there at breakfast. With the invitation came a request that each would bring his orderly provided with a mail bag. After the breakfast was over, the orderlies were drawn up in line, and each admiral and captain dropped his card in all the bags except his own, and thus in a few minutes cards had been exchanged with all hands. After that, if one had the time, he could call on such officers as he had known before, or those whose acquaintance he cared to make. The New York was about the newest thing in the way of a cruiser, and everybody wanted to see her. She was also neutral ground, so to speak, where all could meet with a freedom not possible on other ships. We were not hunting for alliances with other nations nor they with us, and we could be and were as independent as was our far-away country.

The French and Russian fleets met outside the harbour of Kiel and came in together, showing in this, as in other actions, their strong desire to have the recent alliance between the two countries noticed. Both admirals declined the invitation of the emperor to land their crews and be entertained by the German naval contingent, and both fleets put to sea at the earliest possible moment permitted by the strictest etiquette.

The English squadron of four battle ships and two armoured cruisers seemed to me the most businesslike-looking outfit of the whole gathering. The ships were in perfect condition, and it was evident at a glance that they were not made so for the occasion, but that it was their usual condition, while in the case of the ships of some other powers the practiced eye could see that "paint and putty covered a multitude of sins." I was particularly interested in the English cruiser from which the New York was supposed by many to have been copied. She was lying very near us, and her officers, as well as the British admiral in command, after looking us over carefully, admitted that the New York was far the better ship of the two. The admiral finally asked if I would object to the chief constructor of the British navy coming on board and having a look at us, and when I assured him that it would give me the greatest pleasure to show my ship to so distinguished a guest, he wired the admiralty, and I afterward, at Gravesend, had the pleasure of having Mr. White[3] on board for many hours.

The ceremonies attendant upon the opening of the Kiel

3. Sir John William White was the director of naval construction for the British Admiralty.

Canal began at Hamburg, where the burgomasters gave a banquet to the emperor and his guests. Twelve hundred sat down to dinner, among them the most distinguished men in Europe. All military officers were in special full dress and the burgomasters wore their state robes. The emperor wore a gorgeous military dress with many brilliant decorations. After the banquet there was a fine display of fireworks on an island in the lake, which had been made for the occasion. Several thousand persons walked about on this island listening to the bands and enjoying the beer and other refreshments which were in abundance everywhere, and I doubt if any, except those familiar with the place, knew that they were on made ground, so perfectly had the work been done. In the midst of the banquet, which was most elaborate, schooners of beer were served. The idea of drinking mine was more than I could face, but the German officer who was looking after my comfort promptly disposed of it as well as his own. I had great admiration for his capacity.

Before this time the admiral commanding each fleet had sent a small vessel to Hamburg to convey the minister and other officials through the canal. After the fireworks display, we all got under way at 2 A.M. and started down the river according to rank, the emperor leading in the Hohenzollern. We, having the baby admiral, were No. 20, being near the tail end of the procession instead of near its head, where the importance of our country should have placed us. We ran down the Elbe sixty miles to Brunsbüttel,[4] where we entered the canal, steamed through it a distance of about seventy-eight miles, and came out two miles below Kiel. At intervals along the line of the canal the emperor had massed bodies of troops, who were paraded and saluted the colours as each vessel passed. As the Hohenzollern, showing the emperor's

4. Located where the Elbe River flows into the Kiel Canal, quite near the confluence of that river with the North Sea.

flag, entered the harbour, there was a great outburst of cheering with the roar of salutes as the assembled fleets welcomed him.

For the purpose of entertaining his naval guests, the emperor had built on the land, near Holtnau,[5] almost at the Kiel entrance to the canal, a large ship of the line. She was full ship-rigged, had all her yards across, and her gun deck was beautifully decorated for the diner, which was given on the day following our arrival from Hamburg. When the banquet was over, souvenir medals were presented to all of us and we retired to the upper deck for our cigars, where all were presented personally to his Majesty and exchanged a few pleasant words with him. I stood near him during the time he conversed with the French admiral[6] and his officers, waiting my turn to be presented, and could not help being impressed by his manner as well as by that of the Frenchmen. They were all ideally polite, but there was, in the bearing of the emperor, a hearty feeling of success which I did not observe in the manner of the distinguished officers who were saying good-bye to him. They were to sail in the early morning in company with the Russian fleet. When I was presented to him the emperor gave me a cordial hand-shake and kept others waiting quite five minutes while he talked to me in the most pleasant way. He had many questions to ask me, which he said he would expect me to answer before I left

5. This island lies north of Kiel, just as the harbor opens into Kiel Bay.
6. Admiral François Maire Maxime Menard (1837–1902), commander in 1895 of the 2d Division of the Squadron of the North. He entered the service in 1852, rising to the rank of vice admiral in 1896 and commanding the northern squadron from 1899–1901. His commands included: *L'Antilope* (1875–77); *Le Hugon* (1881–83); *La Minerve* (1886–87); *L'Amiral Duperré* (1889–91); 2d Division *de l'Escadre du Nord* (1894–96); and commandant en chef *l'Escadre du Nord* (1899–1901). He led the French battleships *Dupuy de Lôme* and *le Hache* to Kiel, and because of this successful mission, Menard was promoted to vice admiral.

Kiel. His whole manner to the American officers was most pleasing and cordial.

I had arranged with the chief of staff to get rid of my fireworks on this occasion, that the emperor might witness them on his way back to the Hohenzollern from dinner. Certain signals had been agreed upon, and when these were made, indicating that his Majesty was in position to see, the New York cut loose. All the ships had been doing something in the way of fireworks, but it had leaked out somehow that the Yankees had something up their sleeve, and when we began, all the rest stopped to see what would happen. We started off with a set piece eighty feet long suspended between our military masts, a portrait of President Cleveland at one end and of the emperor at the other, and between them the legend in German script, "America sends heartfelt congratulations to Germany on the opening of the North Sea Canal." As this blazed out, the thousands of people massed on the shore only three hundred yards away broke into a great roar of cheers, which was taken up by the different ships, and gradually died out in the distance. Then the show went on with such bursts of rockets and bombs and mines as had never before been seen on a ship, and finally wound up with another set piece, the American shield at one end, the German double eagle at the other, and "Good-night" between them. The upper deck of the New York had been carefully covered with six inches of wet sand, but, notwithstanding many streams of water were constantly playing, I found that we were badly marked in many places. The carpenters were busy with their planes for several days before they were all removed. The German papers, as well as all the officers who witnessed the display, were unstinted in their praise. The feeling uppermost in my mind was one of thankfulness that it was all over without an accident.

At a reception given on board one of the German battle ships on the Sunday after our arrival I had an interesting experience. When I went over the side I found a large company, most of them dancing. As I was not a dancing man, I stood to one side to be out of the way, and entered into conversation with a young clean-cut-looking German captain who spoke English perfectly. It was soon evident to me that he was brilliant in his profession, and we engaged in a rather sharp professional talk. I did not agree with the captain, whose name I had not caught, and did not hesitate to speak my mind—nor did he. After a time he said he would be glad to present me to his wife, which he did, and I found her a very charming and attractive woman. Of course I had not caught her name either, and, after talking with her half an hour, I noticed that a good many people seemed to be waiting to speak to her, so I took myself off to the smoking apartment to enjoy a cigar. When I entered, Admiral Knorr [7] greeted me and said, "Evans, the prince says you are a good fellow, and he wants the emperor to know you." I replied, "My dear admiral, I haven't seen the prince and don't know him." "Well," he said, "you ought to know him; you have been talking ship with him for half an hour, and I don't know what you have been saying to the princess during your conversation with her."

I had been talking with two of the most delightful people I ever met, Prince Henry [8] and the Princess Irene, [9] without knowing in the least who they were, and I certainly told

7. Vice Admiral Eduard von Knorr was chief of the (Naval) High Command, May 1895–March 1899. He had previously commanded the German East Asia Squadron.
8. Prince Henry of Prussia (1862–1929) was the only brother of Kaiser Wilhelm II, and a grand admiral in the Imperial German Navy. He was a handsome man of physical and moral strength, simple decency, and modesty, and many observers thought he would have made a better ruler than his brother. He also took up flying during his mature years.
9. Princess Irene of Prussia (née Princess of Hesse-Darmstadt) was the sister of Empress Alexandria Feodorovna of Russia.

them both exactly what I thought about the different things we discussed. The prince was in his uniform as a captain in the navy, and commanded the vessel on which the reception was given. I afterward saw much of both of them and was indebted to them for much courtesy, and the better I knew them the more I saw in them to admire. It was no doubt owing to the courtesy of Prince Henry that his brother, the emperor, gave me such marks of his distinguished consideration. The Princess Irene came several times to the New York, and seemed always interested and pleased with her visits.

CHAPTER 31

The German Emperor

THE racing spirit was rife at Kiel, and our men were delighted to have a hand in anything in that line. The San Francisco held the championship of the navy for twelve-oared cutters, and had on board the boat with which she had won it. We of the New York had a boat as yet untried and unnamed, which we thought well of, and I had given much time and care to the training of a crew, with the intention of winning the coveted prize if possible. When we met at Kiel we raced in the presence of all the foreign ships, and my men won by a good margin. This led to an interesting incident, which I shall record later on. We also entered our sailing launch for the regatta, which was arranged by the emperor for man-of-war boats under sail, and won the fifth prize, competing with thirty-six German boats of the same kind. It was generally admitted that we would have taken the first prize if there had been a bit more wind. When the race started, the breeze was very light and all German boats were well ahead of us, but later on it freshened up, and it was glorious to see the way our boat walked out to windward of them. At the finish we had done up all but five, and were so close to them that ten minutes more would have given us the lead. We were the only outsiders in the race, and brought away two silver cups as our trophies.

In return for all the hospitality we had received we gave two entertainments of note. The officers of all the ships combined, and gave a dancing reception on board the New York, and I a dinner to the emperor and a party of his ranking officers. Of course, all the ships were constantly entertaining officers of various nationalities, and I doubt if there was a meal served in any mess of our fleet during our stay at Kiel, not even a breakfast, without the presence of guests. I can not do better than quote the following from my journal written at the time:

"*Kiel, June 28, 1895.*—The Kiel spree is a thing of the past, and we are now only waiting the arrival of our orders to be off. The whole business has been the most complete success possible, and when the last one of our nine hundred guests left, yesterday evening, I was gratified to think that we had not had a mishap of any kind except the explosion of the San Francisco's launch boiler, which was nothing. In order to wind up in proper shape, we gave a dancing reception on board the New York. All ships combined, and it was a magnificent success. All Kiel was invited, and all Kiel is talking of it to-day.

"Unfortunately, the empress was too ill to come, and the Princess Henry could not leave her, which was a disappointment to all hands. We had two bands and no end of dancing on both decks from three o'clock to 7.30. The flowers were beautiful, the women more so, and the food excellent—they drank nineteen kegs of beer and thirty gallons of punch.

"On the 26th Prince and Princess Henry came in the afternoon with a party of ladies and spent two hours on the ship, really enjoying themselves. When they were about to go, the princess presented me with her photograph, and I was

ashamed to have to say that I had not one of mine to give
her in return. They are lovely, refined, kindly people, and I
am glad to have known them.

"The evening of the 26th was the crucial test. I had invited the emperor and Prince Henry and ten admirals to
dine, and they all accepted. When the emperor came on
board I had the men and officers massed aft on the superstructure and in the gangways, and as soon as Admiral Kirkland had welcomed him I made him a short speech, reciting
that we had the champion twelve-oared cutter of the American navy, and asked on the part of my crew the honour of
naming her after his daughter Victoria Louisa.[1] He was really
touched by the compliment, and, taking my hand, granted
my request most graciously. As soon as I could, I turned to
the crew and called for three cheers for the Victoria Louisa,
and then three cheers and a tiger for the emperor. I don't
think he ever heard such cheers before. It was a very pretty
episode and gave our dinner a good start.

"As soon as we sat down the emperor said: 'How pleased
the empress will be when she hears of this! You must have
your boat and crew photographed and send the empress one.'
(This I did on my return to New York.)

"The dinner was one of the most delightful I have ever
seen, a perfect success, and George, my steward, who bossed
the entire affair, is as proud as a peacock.

"At 1 A.M. the emperor expressed a desire to visit and
inspect the engine room. And so we did. He looked into
every hole and corner, and even had us disconnect one of the
engines, marking time on us himself. Then we went through
the gun deck and out on to the forecastle, where he asked
how long it would take to close all water-tight doors. I replied that in the daytime we could do it in thirty seconds,

1. Princess Victoria Louisa of Prussia (Viktoria Luise) was the only
daughter of Kaiser Wilhelm II; later the Duchess of Brunswick.

Visit of the German Emperor to the cruiser New York

but at night it required about two minutes. Much to my surprise, he asked if I would mind doing it for him. Of course I had to say yes, but when I tried to blow the siren, the signal to close water-tight doors, there was not steam enough, and the blessed thing would not blow. The emperor thought he had me, and said, 'Now you see, captain, you can't close your bulkheads.' But he did not know everything. I said, 'You will see in a moment, sir,' and I touched one of the general alarm buttons, which calls all hands to quarters, and in a few seconds the men were swarming up like rats.

"The emperor took the time himself, and in one minute and a half the entire ship was ready for action with all water-tight doors closed. It was 2 A.M., the royal standard at our

main and the search light of the Columbia turned on it, the
ship ready for action, and the emperor complimenting the
captain on the forecastle. I find myself in some funny positions.

"When we went aft, where every one could hear him, he
said, 'Captain Evans, I can not imagine that a ship could be
in better condition'—very nice for all of us. He left the ship
just at 2 A.M., and all Germany has been reading accounts of
it since."

I can recall very vividly how surprised I was when at five
o'clock the same morning my orderly called me out of a
sound sleep to report that the officer of the deck said the
emperor was just then passing the ship, steering his own
yacht. My only reply was, "For Heaven's sake don't stop
him!" I managed to get one eye open, and looking out of an
air port in my cabin, discovered him, dressed in white flan-
nels, steering the Meteor bound for an ocean race, and looking as if he had never taken a drink or smoked a cigar in
his life.

People often ask me to tell them what impression the emperor made on me, and I always find it very difficult to answer the question. To say that he made a pleasant impression
is simple and easy, but it means nothing. I found him one
of the most magnetic and companionable of men—I should
say, with one or two exceptions, the most magnetic. He
knows more about more different things than any man I have
ever met. When I was in Kiel my band was playing music
composed by him, and on my cabin table was a book of
poems written by him. He was the head and front of the
finest army in the world, and at the same time giving his
personal attention to what must some day be reckoned one of
the leading navies. The Kiel Canal was of his creation, and
his engineers told me that he was familiar with all its details,
as well as with those of bridge-building in a large sense. The
farmers informed me that he could instruct them in their
business, and I personally saw him manœuvre a fleet at sea

in the most creditable way. After luncheon at the palace one day, during a very interesting conversation, he described to me our first battle ship, the Indiana, [2] which I afterward commanded, and his knowledge of her construction and details of armour and guns was perfect. He seemed to have the same knowledge of all foreign ships. When I gave him a Smithfield ham [3] for dinner he even knew where Smithfield was.

On one occasion the emperor turned on me suddenly and said: "Captain, I understand you think I ought to have a strong navy. Will you tell me why you think so?" I replied that many of us who were interested in such matters had observed that the Jews had at one time made serious encroachments on English trade, but having no navy, of course they made no efforts to control the carrying trade; that then we had observed that the Germans had taken a hand in the game and had beaten the Jews, as they had the English, and that if I read the signs correctly, he, the emperor, meant with his cheaply built merchant ships to follow up this advantage of the German merchants and control the carrying trade of the world. I pointed out to him that a powerful navy was necessary to this scheme to protect his merchant fleet against the navies of those who might be disposed to contest this supremacy with him. He listened very attentively, and when I had finished he said, "Captain, unfortunately, my Parliament does not entertain the same view of the question."

2. A steam-powered steel battleship that displaced 10,788 tons, mounted forty-two guns and six torpedo tubes, had a top speed of 15 knots, and a maximum complement of 636 men, the USS *Indiana* was authorized under an act of 30 June 1890. Built at Cramp Shipyard, she was laid down on 7 May 1891, launched on 28 February 1893, and completed on 20 November 1895. She incorporated Harvey and nickel steel in her construction. The *Indiana* and her sister ships *Massachusetts* and *Oregon* were the prototype first-class battleships of the New Steel Navy. She was reclassified a coastal battleship in 1919 and sunk the next year as a target ship.
3. The famous smoke-cured, extremely salty ham indigenous to the Smithfield, Virginia, region.

To which I replied, "If your Majesty will permit me to say so, I think you will eventually bring your Parliament to think as you do." I had many opportunities to see him among his people, and if he was not their idol, then they were certainly well up in the art of deception, for they seemed to worship him. To us, as representatives of our country, he was most cordial and considerate, and took no pains to conceal from others his strong friendship for the United States. I shall always remember him as I last saw him. He had given a splendid banquet in Kiel as a finish to his wonderfully successful opening of the canal. On one side of him sat the Grand Duke Alexis,[4] on the other the Duke of York,[5] while the lesser lights were seated according to rank. At the proper moment the emperor rose from his chair and, with a full glass of champagne in his extended hand, in clear, ringing tones that could be heard in every part of the room, said, in perfect English, "I drink to all the great sea nations who have sent their magnificent fleets to Kiel to join in the opening ceremonies of the North Sea Canal." He was to me the picturesque figure among all the ruling heads of Europe.

4. The third son of Czar Alexander III, Alexis was the uncle of Czar Nicholas II of Russia, and commander of that nation's armed forces.
5. George V (1865–1936) was the second child of the Prince and Princess of Wales, who as Prince George was pronounced the Duke of York on Queen Victoria's birthday in 1892. He came in succession to the throne that same year upon the death of his older brother, the Duke of Clarence. His early life was spent in naval service. He ascended the throne upon the death of Edward VII on 6 May 1910.

CHAPTER 32

Back to Home Waters

On June 30th I left Kiel with much regret and started on my return trip to New York, *via* England. The following extract from my journal is of interest.

"*North Sea, July 1, 1895.*—We left Kiel at 2 A.M. yesterday and had a beautiful run through the intricate channels of the Great Belt [1] and out of the Skager Rack. [2] The Columbia started with us and was in company until seven in the evening, when we ran her out of sight. The wind was fresh from the northwest, which was ahead, and the fleet of sailing craft beating out of the Baltic was beautiful to see, but I was glad when we were clear of them. We shall probably be in Gravesend at 8 A.M. to-morrow, weather permitting.

"*July 2d.*—An awful night! Up all night and most anxious. North Sea full of vessels, and the rain and fog nasty. Made the coast of England at 2 A.M. and found a pilot, but

---

1. The Danish Store Belt is a strait—forty miles long and ten miles wide—that connects the Kattegat with the Baltic Sea.
2. A 150-mile-long strait that is 85 miles wide, the Skagerrak lies between Norway and Denmark and links the North Sea and the Kattegat.

he was afraid to take us in, so away I went to Ramsgate,[3] where we arrived three hours later, and soon had another pilot on board who brought us to this anchorage, six miles below Gravesend.[4] Blowing a living gale all the way up, and my eyes fairly cut out of my head. As soon as the tide serves I shall go up to the town, make fast to a buoy, coal ship, and get ready for the trip to New York.

"*At Sea, Six Hundred Miles off New York, July 22d.*—We have had a real old-fashioned 'North Atlantic passage'—one gale following another in rapid succession. Until yesterday the shaking of the ship was so bad that writing was practically impossible, but now it has calmed down somewhat.

"Our last days at Gravesend were well filled with visits. Mr. White, chief constructor, came down from London, bringing some of his staff, to make notes on the ship, and the same day Admiral Morant came up from Chatham to spend the day, so we had a merry lunch party. On Sunday, Admiral Hotham and Captain Lambton came down from the city, and we had a long yarn over old times. In the meantime the ship was so crowded with all sorts of people that we had to stop them from coming on board. Everybody, from the member of Parliament for the district down to the servant maids, wanted to see the ship, and were, one and all, most enthusiastic over her condition. I never knew more hospitable people in my life—they wanted to do all sorts of things for us, from four-in-hand drives to dinner parties.

"On Monday, at 4 A.M., we left, and once being clear of the river and down as far as Dover, I let her go on her semi-annual full-speed trial. We had a straight run in the Channel for it, and I was gratified to find that the engines and all their dependencies were in better condition than when we made our trial in January last. We had half a gale on our nose all day and all night, and when we cleared the Scilly

3. A borough in southeast England on the Isle of Thanet.
4. A borough in southeast England on the Thames River near London.

Islands, at four the next morning, it turned into a whole gale from northwest with a nasty sea, and that state of things continued until yesterday afternoon, when it broke, and only the long, heavy sea remains. We should have made New York to-morrow evening if the weather had been halfway decent, but as it is we shall go in on Thursday—not a bad run, everything considered. Through it all the ship has proved herself wonderfully able and seaworthy, and I wish we had more like her, instead of the Columbia and Raleigh classes."

Upon my arrival in New York, July 25th, I was ordered to report to Admiral Bunce [5] for duty as flagship of the North Atlantic squadron, which I did at the navy yard on the following day. I had carried the flag of two admirals, and now had the third, which was a rare experience for any captain, and one I imagine few captains would ever care to have. Flagship duty is not considered desirable as a general rule.

When the New York had had some small repairs made, we began cruising, and Admiral Bunce inaugurated the system of fleet drills which did so much to prepare the navy for its success in the Spanish War which came a few years later. I am sure that the feeling is general, among officers at least, that no officer ever did more conscientious work—work that led to more splendid results—than Admiral Bunce. He established two drill grounds, as they were called—one off New York and one off Cape Henry, Virginia—and when not coaling, the fleet could be found on one or the other of these grounds or cruising between them for months. We had constant torpedo drill, until each torpedo on board could be made to run with all the accuracy it was capable of. The firing was systematic and continued until the gun captains

5. Francis M. Bunce was warranted an acting midshipman on 28 May 1852. He was promoted to captain on 11 January 1883, commodore on 1 March 1895, and rear admiral on 6 February 1898. His name was placed on the retired list on 25 December 1898.

could hit the target with reasonable certainty; and the ships were kept under way in all kinds of fleet manœuvres at different speeds, until those in charge of them could handle them with confidence and without fear of collision. I am sure no such persistent work was ever before done by any fleet, and the good effects were most marked.

CHAPTER 33

On the Indiana

IN October following my return from Kiel, I was detached
from command of the New York and ordered to Philadelphia to fit out and command the Indiana, our first battle
ship. She had been built at Cramp's shipyard, and was the
heaviest armed and armoured ship in the world. The New
York had seemed to me a complicated mass of machinery,
but this new thing was a real machine shop from top to
bottom. It required weeks of hard work and study after I
joined her before I felt reasonably sure that I would not get
lost, if I attempted to inspect her throughout; but when I
did get the hang of her she certainly was a magnificent command. The Department has selected a fine set of officers for
her, and to them, particularly to the able executive officer,
Lieutenant-Commander Swift,[1] I owe all the reputation I
made in her. After two months of constant work we got away

1. William Swift began his naval service as a midshipman on 25 September 1863. Having graduated from the Naval Academy in June 1867,
he attained the rank of lieutenant commander on 24 October 1889 and
commander on 6 April 1897.

from League Island, and, having taken in our torpedoes at Newport, joined the admiral at Fortress Monroe. Before reporting to him, however, the Inspection Board, presided over by Commodore George Dewey,[2] took us to sea and gave us a thorough overhauling. Their report was very favourable, considering the short time we had been in commission and the few opportunities we had had for working the enormous guns of her battery. She carried the first thirteen-inch breechloading rifles ever put afloat in our service; she had four of them mounted in pairs in turrets, one forward and the other aft.

During the winter it became necessary to clean the bottom of the Indiana, and the so-called dock at Port Royal, South Carolina, was the only one ready to receive her. I was ordered to proceed to that point for the purpose, and then return to my station with the fleet. I sailed from Hampton Roads with coal enough to leave me with only two hundred tons on board when I should reach my destination, hoping in this way to reduce the draught of the ship as much as possible. Everything went well with me until I had passed Cape Hatteras, when I ran into a sudden terrific gale, which soon produced a very ugly heavy sea. I was naturally desirous of testing the ship in such weather, as none of us knew what a battle ship would do under such conditions, so I kept her going at full speed and drove her hard into the seas. We were

2. George Dewey's illustrious naval career began on 23 September 1854, when he became an acting midshipman. Graduating from the Naval Academy in 1858, he was promoted to commodore on 28 February 1896, rear admiral on 11 May 1898 and admiral on 2 March 1899. He saw action in the Civil War, then commanded the USS *Pensacola* (1886–88), was chief of the Bureau of Equipment (1888–93), and headed the Board of Inspection and Survey (1896–98). Dewey commanded the Asiatic Squadron that defeated the Spanish fleet at Manila Bay on 1 May 1898. Congress created the rank of Admiral of the Navy especially for him in 1899. He served as president of the General Board from 1900–1917. His success at Manila Bay enabled Dewey to exercise great influence over naval policy making for many years.

From a copyrighted photograph by Enrique Muller.

Battleship Indiana

soon battened down fore and aft, and, despite our best efforts, much water found its way below. The waves were going clear over us forward, at times completely covering our
thirteen-inch gun turret with solid green water and throwing
heavy spray over the upper bridge. Having satisfied myself
that the Indiana could stand any amount of sea, so long as
she was kept head on to it, I changed the course and brought
the sea abeam, when to my surprise she rolled very little and
was entirely comfortable, except for the water sweeping over
her spar deck. I then slowed her down to good steerage way,
when she was as dry as a cork and looked like a small island
surrounded by seething white breakers.

When the fury of the gale had passed I steamed on to the
Port Royal lightship, and there waited for high water to help
me over the dangerous bar. With a lighthouse tender sounding ahead of me I passed in on the very top of high water,
and at the worst point in the channel had just one foot of
water to spare. The least bit of a sea would have caused us to
take the bottom, which is of hard sand. The risk was very
great and the sensation anything but pleasant. Once inside,
however, we were comparatively safe, and I steamed on to the
so-called dockyard, hoping to dock the ship at once. When I
arrived there, however, I found that nothing was ready for
me. There was not sufficient water even if the dock had been
ready. In the meantime the tide had begun to fall, and I was
caught like a rat in a trap. It was impossible to take the ship
to the lower bay again on that tide, so I had to remain where
I was. The commanding officer of the station and the pilots
came on board and pointed out to me a berth where the
largest ship in the world could safely swing to her anchors.
Indeed, according to their accounts, the only trouble with
the place was that they had too much water and too much
swinging room. However, I had my own views about all this;
but as I could not get away, I had to make the best of it.

Half of South Carolina was on hand to see the first great

battle ship placed in their beautiful dock, and as soon as I had anchored in the selected spot they crowded on board of me by thousands. The ship filled to suffocation with them, when at half tide she sat down on the hard bottom and remained there, much to my discomfort. I soon hustled the visitors out and then waited quietly to see what harm would be done before I could get out of the trap in which I was caught. It was impossible to move until daylight the following morning, when I hoped that Divine Providence would send in a tide sufficient for me to go into dock. As the flood made, it lifted the ship from her uncomfortable and dangerous berth and she swung with her stern up stream, in which position I attempted to hold her with heavy stern anchors, but it was no use. There was so little water under her that she practically formed a dam, and no power on earth could hold her. As the ebb tide again made, she swung to it, and I found myself with a wire hawser wound around our propellers to add to my comfort. The moment there was water enough I cleared out and anchored in the bay eight miles away from the bothersome dock.

Each high tide for a week I got under way and came up only to find that there was not water enough. Then I settled down to drill and target practice, determined to wait until an easterly gale or some other convulsion of Nature should send in the desired quantity of water. I waited, as I now recall it, nearly two weeks before I succeeded, and then only got into the dock by driving my engines at full speed. As we passed over the sill we had just five inches of water to spare. Once in and the gates closed, we were safe until such time as we wanted to get out again; but as there was no immediate prospect of water enough for that, I gave myself no concern about it. As the dock was being emptied, the powerful pumps gradually slowed down and finally stopped, choked up with shrimp. Cart loads of the finest shrimp I ever saw were taken out before the pumps were cleared and fit to run again. When the water was all out, I fed my crew of five hundred men on fresh shellfish the like of which they had never before seen. We had found one good thing at least in the Port Royal naval station, but I could not help thinking that it was a costly and dangerous way of getting shrimp.

Two days was all we required to do the necessary work, and after that we waited for water enough to escape. For nine days we watched the gauge, and then an easterly wind swelled the tide to the necessary point and we started. When about half of the ship was clear of the entrance the flood tide caught her stern and she started in the direction of a heavy stone structure, which was sure to crush her side in if she struck it. There was but one thing to do, and I did that as promptly as I could. I rang both engines full speed astern, and called out for all hands to stand clear of the lines and hawsers by which we were held. The engines responded promptly, the ship gathered way quickly, and, after a second or two of snapping lines, she shot out of the dock into the stream. For a few minutes it looked as if she must be seriously damaged, but she escaped the threatening stone structure by exactly eleven inches. We had a cork fender hanging over the side which was twelve inches in diameter, and she squeezed this against the blocks of granite as she passed. I lost no time in making my way to a safe anchorage, firmly resolved that if any more battle ships were to be docked at Port Royal some other captain would have to command them.

The Indiana was soon again with the fleet, and when the Massachusetts[3] had been fitted out and commissioned, the two of them formed an excellent unit in the long months of drill which followed. Admiral Bunce kept us at it night and day, until the officers had become as familiar with handling battle ships as they had previously been with smaller vessels.

3. Sister ship to the *Indiana* and *Oregon*, the USS *Massachusetts* was also built by Cramp Shipyard. Laid down on 25 June 1891 and launched on

We took them to the navy yard and berthed them without even the assistance of tugs, and the way we handled them in the narrow parts of crowded New York Harbour showed that some of us had mastered our job. And we had mastered it in the only way possible to seamen—by constant work and practice out on blue water. We all owe much to Admiral Bunce.

In the fall of 1896 the squadron started from Fortress Monroe for New York. It had been blowing hard for several days, and the admiral considered it a fit opportunity to test the sea-going qualities of the Indiana, and particularly the strength of the securing devices on her turrets. We found a heavy sea running before we were out of Chesapeake Bay, and when Cape Henry light was abeam I signalled that all my eight-inch turrets, four in number, were adrift, thinking that the admiral would direct me to return to port and secure them. On the contrary, we held on our course, and when the sun went down these turrets were securely lashed so that they could give no further trouble; but the sea in the meantime had increased very much, and the thirteen-inch turrets, each weighing five hundred tons, began to work loose, and by ten o'clock had destroyed their controlling devices and were free to do as they pleased. The after-turret was secured by lashing the muzzles of the guns to the towing bitts on the quarter-deck with hawsers. There was no great danger in this work, as I kept the ship as nearly head to sea as possible, but several times the men were almost swept overboard.

At midnight the gale was very bad and the sea coming on board in every direction. The night was as black as a pocket and the rest of the squadron out of sight ahead. I had been forced to slow down to protect the men and officers who were working on the forecastle in a desperate effort to secure the forward thirteen-inch turret, which was thrashing from side to side as the ship rolled and pitched. I stood by the wheel

---

10 June 1893, she was completed three years later. Made a coastal battle-ship in 1919, the *Massachusetts* was scuttled in 1921 as a target ship.

on the upper bridge, and frequently the whole forward end of her would go under water, men and all, and the sea would come up until I could easily have put my foot into it. At such times I held my breath as the water rolled off and the black heads of the officers and men, one after another, came in sight; I fully expected to see them swept overboard by the dozen. She was rolling forty degrees, and nothing I could do seemed to ease her. The sea was so irregular that I could not keep her bows on to it, and the night so pitch dark that I could not see where the heavy seas were coming from.

At 1 A.M. the ash-chutes on the gun deck had their covers torn off and the deck was flooded, and there was no way to get the water out except by bailing with buckets. The carpenter, who was in a great funk, came to me on the bridge, white in the face, and reported in a trembling voice, "Sir, the gun deck is full of water, and I can't see how we are ever going to get it out!" I replied, "Go down and drink some of it out, sir, and don't bother me again with your whining!" which sent him on his way and I saw no more of him. By the almost super-human efforts of the executive officer and the officer of the forward turret, assisted by one hundred or more men, the thirteen-inch guns were finally lashed securely to the eight-inch turret on the upper deck, and the forward turret thus secured. The work required four hours, and most of the time all hands engaged in it were under water. In the meantime the lifeboats, which were hoisted on the upper deck of all, were smashed by the sea, which came up under them and stove them against the davit heads. By four o'clock in the morning we had everything well secured and the water all cleared out, so that I felt no apprehension for the safety of the ship. Indeed, I had felt none after the first few heavy rolls she made with her gun deck flooded; then I did feel some doubt as to the result. I was soon satisfied that she would not capsize, and, later on, I made up my mind that she could do anything but climb a tree, and I thought she would do that if I gave her half a chance.

Between midnight and four in the morning one of the young officers lost his leg by having it caught by an armoured door weighing two tons, which, unfortunately, carried away its fastenings at the wrong moment and closed just when the young man was thrown out of his bunk across the doorsill. This was the only serious accident we had, though many of the men were somewhat bruised. I was glad when daylight put an end to one of the worst nights I ever spent at sea, and thankful that I had escaped a serious disaster. The officers behaved, as they always do, perfectly, and the crew, many of them very young and new at the business, excited my warmest admiration. Not a soul on board, except the man who was advised to drink salt water, showed the least sign of fear or hesitation. I certainly had a crew full of sand up to their necks, and I felt like hugging every man Jack of them.

We landed our wounded officer in New York the following day, and then went to the navy yard for repairs. I was told that the ship had not rolled as badly as I thought she had by those who imagined that they knew many things which they really only guessed at. The fragments of the various gimcracks which had been intended to hold her turrets were taken out, in many cases with a dustpan and broom, and new and better things put in. We were getting experience in battle-ship fittings, but, like the shrimp-catching, it was costly and dangerous.

In fitting out the Indiana I was careful to see that she had, among other necessary things, a twelve-oared cutter, which I hoped some day might win from the cutter of the New York, which had done such good work at Kiel. I was careful in selecting the crew for her, and, after many months of faithful training, the race took place at Fortress Monroe. The distance pulled was six miles, in a rough sea, and the Victoria Louisa had to lower her colours to Uncle Sam, the name of our new boat. I think the same boats pulled several races after I gave up command, and honours were about even between them.

While refitting in New York, Mr. Rudyard Kipling[4] breakfasted on board with me and seemed much interested, particularly in the machinery, which he examined very closely. Some weeks afterward he was good enough to send me a set of his books. On the titlepage of Plain Tales from the Hills, facing a beautiful picture of Sergeant Mulvaney, done by my dear friend R.F. Zogbaum,[5] he had written the following graceful lines, which I had hoped would always remain my personal property. But some one stole them and gave them publicity. For that reason I allow myself to put them in this book.

> "Zogbaum draws with a pencil,
> And I do things with a pen;
> And you sit up in a conning tower
> Bossing eight hundred men.
>
> "Zogbaum takes care of his business,
> And I take care of mine;
> And you take care of ten thousand tons
> Sky-hooting through the brine.
>
> "Zogbaum can handle his shadows,
> And I can handle my style;
> And you can handle a ten-inch gun
> To carry seven mile.
>
> "'To him that hath shall be given,'
> And that's why these books are sent
> To the man who has lived more stories
> Than Zogbaum or I could invent."

4. English author, poet, and winner of the Nobel Prize for Literature in 1907.
5. Rufus Fairchild Zogbaum was born on 28 August 1849 in Charleston, South Carolina. He became a well-known illustrator of military and naval subjects. He wrote *Horses, Foot and Dragoons, or Sketches of Army Life*; *All Hands*; and *Ships and Sailors: the Junior Officer of the Watch*. Zogbaum died on 22 October 1925.

During the fall of 1896 I was detached from the Indiana and once more ordered to duty on the Lighthouse Board, but this time as a member and not as naval secretary, where I had previously served. While on this duty I was detailed in addition as a member of the Personnel Board, which Secretary Long,[6] of the navy, had ordered to consider some remedy for the controversy which existed between the line and engineer officers of the service. The board was composed of leading officers of the two corps, and ably presided over by Mr. Theodore Roosevelt,[7] Assistant Secretary, to whom more than any other man belongs the credit for the remedy applied later in the shape of the Naval Personnel Bill. The scheme of amalgamation embodied in that bill was first proposed by me, and I wish to assume the responsibility which attached to my act. The entire board, of course, voted on the proposition and approved it as a body.

6. Secretary of the Navy John Long (1839–1915) was a Harvard-educated lawyer who was elected governor of Massachusetts (1880–82); served in Congress (1883–89); and was Secretary of the Navy (1897–1902) in William McKinley's administration. Long wrote extensively on naval affairs and in support of social and political reforms. He was an unspectacular official who ably guided the Navy through the Spanish-American War and into the postwar period of expansion.

7. Assistant Secretary Theodore Roosevelt (1858–1919) was a wealthy Harvard graduate, a civil service reformer in early 1890, and a police commissioner in New York City. He was an aggressive assistant under Secretary Long (1897–98), and the famous leader of Rough Riders in the Spanish-American War. Roosevelt was governor of New York, 1899–1901, and vice president under William McKinley in 1901. The President's assassination vaulted him to the Presidency, which he held until 1909. Roosevelt personally dominated the Navy Department. He was an arch navalist and internationalist who sponsored the worldwide cruise of battleships, 1907–09, to flex American might.

CHAPTER 34

The Approach of War

IN the early winter of 1897 I was honoured with the confidence of Mr. Roosevelt, and was frequently consulted by him about various naval matters. He saw clearly the approaching storm of war, and knew well how unprepared we were in many ways to meet it, and it was owing to his strong will and earnest recommendations to Mr. Long that many most important steps were taken. In making this statement I detract nothing from the wonderful ability shown by Mr. Long. He had a most patriotic and painstaking assistant in solving a problem, the solution of which has reflected great credit on the country for all time to come.

I left Washington in December, 1897, to make a trip of inspection of all the light stations on the South Atlantic and Gulf coasts in the lighthouse steamer Armeria.[1] At Key West, Florida, I found the North Atlantic fleet under com-

---

1. The lighthouse tender *Armenia* displaced 1,600 tons and mounted two guns. She was transferred to naval service in 1898.

mand of Admiral Sicard,[2] and it was plain to me that that able officer expected war with Spain and was doing all he could to be ready for it when it came. The day before we sailed from the port the Maine was coaling preparatory to her visit to Havana. A large lighter was hauling out from the coal dock and on her deck were a number of her men who had been loading the coal, and it seemed to me that I had never before seen a finer-looking lot of men. Among them was an old shipmate of mine, William Fuer, a boatswain's mate, who had served with me in the Yorktown, and as he stood on the bows of the lighter, directing her movements, he was the picture of a man-of-war's-man—strong, handsome, and fearless. I found his name in the list of those killed that awful night in Havana, when, whether by accident or design, Spain sealed her fate in the Western world.

A few weeks later I was in New Orleans, Louisiana, where I had been enjoying the festivities of the carnival season, when the news of the destruction of the Maine shocked the civilized world. Men of all classes talked to me on the subject and asked my opinion, and, though I had a very decided one, I expressed none. It seemed to me the time of all others for a man in my position to hold his tongue and prepare for the serious work I felt was in store for all of us. I begged them all to await quietly the finding of the board that had been ordered to investigate the whole matter, which I felt sure

2. William Sicard was warranted an acting midshipman on 1 October 1851. Promoted to lieutenant commander on 16 July 1862, he commanded a gunboat in the Civil War and afterwards became the leading expert on ordnance. He co-authored a book on ordnance in 1880, and became chief of ordnance in 1881, the same year he made captain. Rear Admiral Sicard commanded the North Atlantic Squadron, 1897–98, going ashore on the eve of the Spanish-American War, during which he served on the Naval War Board created to advise the Secretary of the Navy. Some view him as the prime architect of New Steel Navy ordnance. Sicard retired on 30 September 1898 and died on 14 September 1900.

would be painstaking and thorough. But I could see, from the set faces of those Southern chaps, and the quiet, determined way in which they spoke, that somebody was going to get whipped because the Maine[3] had been blown up. When I had visited Galveston and found the same smouldering volcano there, I was strengthened in my conviction that if the authorities then in power did not declare war, they would be turned out and others put in who would. I felt that if the action of our admiral had been different—and it probably would have been had he been younger and not so sick—time at least would have been saved. If he had gone into Havana the morning after the disaster with his whole fleet and said to General Blanco[4] that he had come to find out why these American officers and men, the guests of Spain, had been foully murdered, it would, in my opinion, have produced immediate results and saved much time.

About the middle of March I again arrived at Key West on my way back to Washington, and was struck with the weakness of our fleet in the way of torpedo-boat destroyers and guard boats.[5] If war should suddenly come, and it looked

3. Probably the most famous of the Spanish-American warships due to her controversial destruction in Havana Harbor on 15 February 1898. A second-class, steam-powered steel battleship of 6,682 tons, a top speed of 17 knots, mounting twenty-five guns and four torpedo tubes, the USS Maine was protected with Harvey and nickel-steel armor plate, and carried a 374-man complement. Authorized under an act of 3 August 1886, she was laid down at the New York Navy Yard on 17 October 1888, launched on 18 November 1889, and commissioned on 17 September 1895.
4. Ramon Blanco was the governor-general of Cuba who succeeded the infamous General Valeriano Weyler and attempted to ameliorate conditions in the Spanish colony.
5. The U.S. Navy had six torpedo boats but no torpedo-boat destroyers in commission at the outbreak of war with Spain. This led to a rushed authorization on 4 May 1898 to construct sixteen of the craft, but none were commissioned before 1902.

as if it might at any moment, an enterprising enemy, with the Spanish torpedo vessels known to be in and about Cuba, could seriously damage if not destroy our entire force in a single night. I hurried on to Washington, determined to give Mr. Long my views on the subject. Fortunately, he sent for me the day of my arrival, and, having heard patiently and with deep interest what I had to say to him, at once, with the assistance of Mr. Roosevelt, proceeded to apply the only possible remedy. He ordered the purchase of a number of fast yachts and tugs in New York and other ports and directed that they be armed with all despatch and hurried off to Key West.

While I stood talking with him he gave directions to detach Admiral Sicard, who was condemned by medical survey, from command of the squadron, and order Captain Sampson to relieve him. Then, turning to me, he said, in his quiet, forcible way: "Now, captain, I have a surprise for you. I am going to order you to relieve Sampson in command of the Iowa.[6] How soon can you start?" I had only arrived in the city five hours before, but feeling as I did the importance of not losing time, replied that I could leave for Key West at 4 P.M. that day, which I did. When trouble with Spain first threatened I had asked that if war came I might be ordered to command the St. Paul[7] in case she was taken into the

6. The steam-powered steel battleship USS *Iowa* displaced 11,410 tons, mounted forty-two guns, had a top speed of 16 knots, and a complement of 486–654 men. Authorized under an act of 19 July 1892, she was laid down on 5 August 1893 at the Cramp Shipyard, launched on 28 March 1896, and commissioned on 16 June 1897. The *Iowa* became a coastal battleship in 1919 and the first radio-controlled target ship to be used in fleet exercises. She was sunk by a salvo of 14-inch shells in 1923.

7. The USS *St. Paul* was an armed merchant cruiser that belonged to the International Navigation Company. She was taken up for the Spanish War emergency and returned to her owners on 2 September 1898. Built at the Cramp Shipyard, she displaced 14,910 tons, mounted eighteen guns, and had a 381-man complement. The *St. Paul* engaged and drove

service. I was therefore much gratified to command the finest
battle ship in the navy.

I arrived at Key West as soon as steam could get me there,
and went at once to the Iowa, then lying with the other large
vessels off Sand Key light,[8] about eight miles from the town.
It was a time of intense excitement. We all felt that war was
sure to come, and we were anxious to have it done with, and
therefore the sooner it came the better. That we were not as
ready for it as we should have been was not our fault; what
the navy itself could do we had done, and we felt confident
that we could do the Spanish fleet up in an hour if it would
come out in the open sea and give us a chance, but we knew
it would never do that. It was borne in upon me that the
worse use you could put a navy to was fighting, and the best,
keeping the peace, yet we were about to be driven to the
former because our naval force was and had been too small
for the latter.

Admiral Sampson spared neither himself nor his officers
and men in his preparations for the coming struggle—work
was incessant day and night. Drills of all kinds were indulged
in, but target firing was considered the most important one
of all. Day by day we wasted Government ammunition, as
some of the yellow newspapers had it, and no end of targets
were destroyed. Night after night the torpedo boats had their
try at us, that our men might know what the real thing
would look like when it came. Coal bunkers and magazines
were kept constantly full, as well as bread rooms and store-

---

off the Spanish destroyer *Terror* at San Juan on 22 June 1898. Later she
was used as a transport, and rammed and sank the British cruiser *Gladia-
tor* in a collision in The Solent on 25 April 1908. She served as a transport
in World War I, but capsized in North River, New York, when being
towed to the dock on 28 April 1918. Raised and reconstructed, the *St.
Paul* was sold in 1923.

8. A lighthouse on the northern end of Sand Key, which lies on the
southern side of Biscayne Bay, Florida.

rooms. In the meantime the admiral constantly conferred with his commanding officers, and with their assistance drew up a complete plan for the attack and capture of the city and defences of Havana. Our officers who had been in Cuba recently knew every fort about the city and the number and calibre of guns in each, and with this information in our hands, we knew just what we had to meet.

Sampson believed, and we agreed with him, that the thing to do, as soon as war was declared, was to strike quick and strike hard; but such was not to be our good fortune. The Secretary thought highly of the plans which were submitted to him, but, for reasons which he no doubt considered convincing, decided against them, in favour of a close blockade. I have always thought that we could have captured or destroyed Havana two days after the declaration of war, and it is my belief that this of itself would have ended the struggle in a very short time, and that Cervera's [9] fleet would not have

9. Pascual Cervera y Topete (1839–1909) was the Spanish admiral whose fleet was destroyed in the battle off Santiago de Cuba in the Spanish-American War (1898). A graduate of a naval cadet school, he engaged in operations off Morocco and in the Sulu Islands and the Philippines. Afterward he was in the West Indies during the early part of the first Cuban War (1868–78), returning to Spain in 1873 to serve on the Basque coast against the Carlists. Over the years he rose to flag rank, and in 1892 became the minister of marine in the cabinet of Praxedes Mateo Sagesta. Cervera soon resigned, however, when he was unable to receive backing and funding for naval reforms.

In April 1898, when the Spanish-American War broke out, he was chosen to command a squadron comprising four cruisers and several destroyers stationed in the Cape Verde Islands. This ill-fated force started upon its reckless dash across the Atlantic only after its commander had repeatedly warned both the Spanish minister of marine and the prime minister that the ships were insufficiently provided with coal and ammunition. In compliance with government instructions, Cervera made for the landlocked harbor of Santiago de Cuba, where he cooperated in the defense by landing some guns and a naval brigade.

In spite of his energetic protests, Cervera received orders from Madrid, crossed the Atlantic. I make this statement with a full knowledge of what we had to encounter and after close study of the situation, which afterward changed very rapidly and was entirely different when General Blanco had strongly fortified the entrance.

In the early days of April the newly purchased yachts and tugs began to arrive at Key West, and it would have been amusing, if the matter had been less serious, to see the value placed on these improvised guard boats. It was simply because we had no torpedo-boat destroyers, and officers of experience knew the danger of attack from the coast of Cuba. So these new arrivals were put to work at once, some of them on guard duty at night and others towing stores and coal from Key West, eight miles away, to the fighting ships, which were anchored in the open sea off Sand Key light. As a base of supplies, in a military sense, Key West was at this time an absolute and utter failure, because we had no supplies for war, either there or anywhere else, and the necessary shops and machines were not on hand. A few officers were working their hearts out over the same old impossible scheme of boring a two-inch hole with a one-inch auger, only in this case the auger seemed to all of us like a very small gimlet. However, we did manage somehow to keep the ships in a fair state of preparation, and as the days went by we felt that the important thing of all—our men—was most satisfactory. They were as fit and ready as men ever were, or could be, and only waited the chance to prove it to the country and the world.

---

dictated by political considerations, to sally forth against the American blockaders. The squadron met forces trebly superior to it and was totally destroyed. The admiral, three of his captains, and 1,800 sailors and marines were taken by the victors to Portsmouth, New Hampshire, after the war. Cervera and his captains were tried before the supreme naval and military court of Spain, which honorably acquitted them all. In 1901 he became vice-admiral, in 1902 was appointed chief of staff of the Spanish Navy, and in 1903 was made a life senator.

CHAPTER 35

The Havana Blockade

T HE tension grew greater and the excitement and strain
harder to bear as the month advanced, until the 20th of
April came, when we knew from the Washington despatches
that the critical moment had arrived. During the evening of
the 21st all the commanding officers of the outside fleet were
summoned on board the flagship for consultation, and there
we remained until nearly midnight, waiting for the message
we felt sure must come before daylight. Some of us prepared
to return to our vessels about ten o'clock, but Sampson requested us to remain. So over our fresh cigars we sat and
listened to the quiet words of our clear-headed commander,
while the wind howled and the ship pitched and rolled in
the choppy sea. Just before midnight a naval cadet came to
the cabin and reported a torpedo boat coming out at high
speed, and in a few minutes a staff officer handed the admiral
a telegram from President McKinley,[1] which he immediately

1. Born in Niles, Ohio, on 29 January 1843, William McKinley was
educated at Allegheny College. During the Civil War he rose from private to major. After that service he became a lawyer, and served in the

read to his assembled commanders. It said: "War declared; proceed to blockade the coast of Cuba," etc., etc.—Then, with serious, thoughtful faces, we said good-night to the admiral and each other, and returned to our ships. The expected had happened this time at least.

When I reached the Iowa, about midnight, all of the officers and most of the crew were on deck waiting to hear the news. I told them in a few words, and for half an hour I could hear the low hum of conversation among the men, then perfect silence fore and aft. The signal lights of the New York glinted and winked as the signal officers transmitted the order to be ready to get under way at daylight. The assistant chief of staff was sent into the inner harbour with orders for the vessels assembled there to come out as fast as possible, and by one o'clock they began to appear. I say they began to appear, but in reality we could only see the long, ghostlike beams of their search lights as they felt about for the buoys of the difficult channel. Before daylight every vessel of the fleet was under way, formed in double column, and headed for the coast of Cuba. In less than four hours from the receipt of the order the navy showed its state of readiness by actually starting for the enemy's coast. Fortunately for the country, we were in much better shape than the people thought we were.

Everything was done to the ships in the way of protection that careful thought and long experience could suggest. Those of us who had been in battle before were aware of the idiosyncrasies of shot and shell—how they were apt to strike just in the spot where they were most unwelcome—and we therefore protected the soft places with such material as came

---

House of Representatives from 1876 to 1891. He was chairman of the Committee on Ways and Means, and sponsored the protective McKinley Tariff Act of 1890. Elected Governor of Ohio in 1891 and again in 1893, McKinley had been boomed for President as early as 1884. He was elected in 1896, defeating William Jennings Bryan, but was assassinated in 1901.

to hand. I had taken on board the Iowa many tons of sand in bags, and these I had used where I thought they would do the most good. I had also unshackled our heavy sheet-anchor chains and wound them carefully around the exposed ammunition hoists, a job that took over a week of as hard work as I ever saw men do. In a word, everything had been done to make the ships ready for the ordeal they had to face.

At seven o'clock on the morning of April 22d, as we were standing on our course for Havana, a steamer was made out to the westward heading toward us with the Spanish flag flying. The Nashville[2] was signalled to capture her, and in a few minutes that vessel had fired the first gun of the war and had taken the first prize. In the late afternoon the land about Havana was made out in the distance, and every preparation was made for battle in case the enemy fired on us. Shortly after we sighted the land, a vessel was seen well inshore attempting to escape to the eastward, and the New York left her place in column and gave chase, at the same time flying the signal, "Disregard movements of the commander in chief."

I, as next in rank to Sampson, hoisted the guide flag, and, as senior officer present, held the fleet to its course direct for the Morro Castle[3] at the entrance to the harbour of Havana. The New York soon ran out of sight, and I saw nothing more of her until about two o'clock the next morning, when she rejoined, having in the meantime captured the Spanish steamer Pedro and sent her into Key West with a prize crew. When we could make out clearly the lighthouse on the

2. The USS Nashville was a steam-powered, steel patrol gunboat that displaced 1,371 tons, mounted fourteen guns, had a 180-man complement, and a top speed of 16.3 knots. Authorized by an act of 3 March 1893, she was constructed by the Newport News Shipbuilding Company: laid down on 9 August 1894, launched on 19 October 1895, and completed on 19 August 1897. The Nashville was sold in 1921.
3. Castillo del Morro was an old Spanish fort that guarded the entrance to Havana Harbor at the Straits of Florida.

Morro, I formed the fleet in double column, with the lighter vessel double distance to the left, in order to bring them closer to the shore after I had established the blockade, and in this order continued on my course with all hands at the guns ready to return any fire that we might receive. We had orders not to bring on an engagement, but I did not consider that this order would apply in case the Spaniards fired on us. When the Iowa was about five miles from the Morro Castle, I made signal, "Head of columns right!" and, as the signal went up, I saw the flash of a gun on shore, and then others, until five had been fired. I gave the order to stand by to fire, and cautioned those about me to watch carefully for the splash of a shot; but, unfortunately, none came; they were only signal guns to announce our arrival. I continued on my way and established the blockade, and night settled down. General Blanco and the city of Havana were in a grip that was to make them very tired and hungry before it relaxed.

Our first night on the blockade was very exciting work. I had made up my mind that the Spaniards would attempt something in the way of a torpedo attack that night. It was the logical thing for them to do, and it is possible that they might have met with some success if they had been bold and daring. I was on the bridge during the entire night, and if I saw one torpedo boat I saw a thousand! Every breaking sea was to my imagination a torpedo boat. I had the fleet standing to the westward toward Mariel,[4] and at one o'clock in the morning it became necessary to turn about and cruise slowly back toward the Morro. The night was intensely dark, and not a sound could be heard or a ship seen in any direction. As I made the preparatory signal from the bridge of the Iowa the answering lights flashed out, and there they were, the whole fleet in two long lines, as if tied on strings. They

4. A town in western Cuba in the agricultural province of Penar de Rio. It lies on a sheltered bay about twenty-seven miles west-southwest of Havana.

Battleship Iowa

turned promptly at the signal and stood back in the direction indicated. Between two and three o'clock in the morning the New York rejoined, and the responsibility of command passed to the able shoulders where it belonged.

For ten days the Iowa, in common with the others, rolled and pitched in the trade-wind seas, watching the Spanish army, while new forts were built and new guns placed in position. At night we hauled off a few miles, so that our torpedo boats and guard vessels could have a fair chance at anything that came out. About daylight in the morning I steamed in and took my place in plain sight of the city and within easy range of the batteries, if any one wanted to try a shot at me; but the shot never came. It would not have been wise on the part of General Blanco to provoke the fire of the battle ships with their twelve- and thirteen-inch guns.

One afternoon, just before sundown, I saw with my glass two very trim-looking Spanish gunboats coming out of the harbour. They turned to the east and steamed along close to the shore, evidently much admired by the great mass of people I could see crowding the docks on the water front. After a short time the little chaps turned and steamed to the west toward Mariel. I signalled Mackenzie, who was near me in the Mayflower,[5] to stand by to chase and at the same time gave orders to bottle up steam on the Iowa. When I thought there was a chance to cut them off, I made the signal to chase, and headed straight for the entrance at full speed. Mackenzie dashed in like a shot off a shovel, and for a few moments it looked as if we might nab them, but they saw us the moment we started and put for home with all the speed they could make. When they entered the harbour I could no doubt have reached them with my heavy guns, but

5. The USS *Mayflower* was an armed yacht of 2,690 tons, a top speed of 16.8 knots, a battery of fourteen guns, and a 171-man complement. Built by J. & G. Thompson, she was launched in 1896, commissioned on 24 March 1898, and served as the presidential yacht from 1905 to 1929. The *Mayflower* was sold 1931.

they were not of much consequence, and I did not fancy the idea of sending a shell into the mass of women and children on shore. We were within easy range of the forts, and I did hope that they would give us a chance to pay our respects to them, but they remained quiet, though we could see the men about the guns. The gunboats never came out again while I remained on the Havana blockade.

During the early days of May I ran over to Key West, filled up with coal, and was back at my station during the night. The following morning at daylight I made out a tug-boat coming out from the land with the signal flying, "Send a boat!" which was unusual if not cheeky. I examined her carefully with my glasses and discovered an officer on board in cavalry uniform. It turned out to be Colonel Dorst,[6] of the United States army. He had landed some Cubans and a company of our men during the night, but the Spaniards had surrounded them, and the colonel explained to me that unless I went to their assistance his men would probably be killed or captured. While I was talking with him, the New York came in sight, steaming very fast, with the signal flying, "Iowa steer east by south, speed eleven knots!" I told Dorst that Sampson would no doubt send a gunboat to look after his party, which he did, and I started immediately in obedience to the signal, which I knew meant business of some sort. It was the starting of the expedition to San Juan, Puerto Rico.[7]

6. Joseph H. Dorst was born in Kentucky in 1852, and appointed to the U.S. Military Academy from Indiana, graduating in 1869. He was posted to the cavalry and rose to the rank of major of the 2d Cavalry in 1898. Following the war Dorst was posted as colonel of the 45th Infantry. He retired as colonel of the 2d Cavalry in 1903.
7. The capital of Puerto Rico in the northeastern part of the island, on the Atlantic Ocean.

CHAPTER 36

The Cruise to San Juan

THE Iowa, Indiana, and New York ran all day to the eastward, and at sundown that evening met the other vessels that had been directed to rendezvous off Cruz del Padre light[1] on the north coast of Cuba. News had come from Washington that Admiral Cervera had sailed with the Spanish fleet from the Cape de Verde Islands,[2] and it was plain to all of us that Sampson's fleet should be well to the eastward to meet him if he attempted to pass through the West Indies, either to threaten our coast or enter a port on the north side of Cuba. The natural place for him to go to recoal and repair his ships was San Juan, Puerto Rico, where there were stores and machine shops, and Sampson had every reason to expect to find him there. It turned out afterward that Cervera was bound for San Juan, and had it not been for the unexpectedly low speed of his torpedo boats we should have found him there on May 12th. As it was, he received the news of

1. A lighthouse at the entrance to the Bay of Puerto Padre, on the north coast of Cuba.
2. Islands in the north Atlantic that lie west of Senegal.

the bombardment of San Juan when off Martinique[3] and shaped his course for Curaçoa,[4] and thus escaped. We all thought that we had given him ample time to reach his destination. Twelve hours more and we should have trapped him at San Juan instead of at Santiago.

When we reached the appointed rendezvous, late in the evening, we found there, among other ships, two monitors—the Terror[5] and the Amphitrite.[6] As they could not carry coal enough to steam to our destination, they were taken in tow. I was directed to tow the Amphitrite with the Iowa. The sea was very smooth, and we were soon pulling her along at nine knots, but before the job was finished I wished I had never seen a monitor. When once out from under the protection of the shoals the sea began to rise, and soon everything in the way of towlines had been parted, and it was only when we slowed down to seven knots or less that we could make

3. A French island in the West Indies.
4. An island in the Dutch Antilles in the southern Caribbean, off the northwest coast of Venezuela.
5. An iron monitor of the *Miantonomoh* class, the USS *Terror* displaced 3,900 tons, was protected with a 7.5-inch side armor, had a top speed of 10.5 knots, mounted twelve guns, and had a 171-man complement. Laid down circa 1874 and partially constructed by William Cramp and Sons, she was launched on 24 March 1883, completed at the New York Navy Yard, and commissioned on 15 April 1896. The *Terror* was stricken from the Navy List on 15 December 1915 and thereafter was employed as a gunnery target. Her hulk was sold on 10 March 1921.
6. One of the four *Miantonomoh*-class wooden-hulled monitors designed by the Bureau of Construction and Repair, this vessel, originally named *Towanda,* was laid down in 1862 and commissioned in 1865. She was renamed the *Amphitrite* on 15 June 1869 and broken up in 1874–75. With their wooden hulls decaying, all four ships were rebuilt into iron-hulled "New Navy" monitors as a subterfuge to circumvent Congressional refusal to allocate funds for new construction. The *Amphitrite* was rebuilt by Harlan and Hollingsworth and the Norfolk Navy Yard. She displaced 3,390 tons, mounted twelve guns and had a complement of 113–91 men. Laid down in 1874, launched on 7 June 1883, and commissioned on 23 April 1895, the iron monitor was sold in 1920.

anything hold. We found ourselves in the open sea looking
for an enemy who could steam at the speed of sixteen to
eighteen knots while we could barely maintain seven. The
prospect of catching him was not very bright. However, we
were doing our best with the tools the Government had given
us to work with. After many vexatious delays, we arrived off
the north coast of Puerto Rico on the afternoon of May 11th,
and at sundown Admiral Sampson transferred his flag to the
Iowa and notified me that I should have the honour of leading in the battle which we hoped would be fought the following day.

At daylight on May 12th the high land and forts about
San Juan could be dimly seen. The fleet was in battle order
and every ship ready to open fire. Slowly the Iowa steamed
in until she was fairly within range of all the guns, when I
stopped the engines and waited until we could see clearly
everything in the harbour. The forts, as well as the city,
seemed to be sleeping soundly, and there was nothing to
indicate that the Spaniards expected or suspected our un-
friendly visit. Our glasses soon disclosed the fact that Cervera
was not there.

To give our men practice and season them a bit for what
was to come, Admiral Sampson decided to bombard the batteries. I was standing by him on the bridge when he gave
me permission to open fire. I stepped to the nearest six-
pounder and ordered the captain of the gun to fire at the
lighthouse tower with an elevation of twenty-six hundred
yards, which he did, and I saw the shell explode near the
base of the tower. I then gave the range to the whole battery
as twenty-five hundred yards, with directions to fire at the
Morro fort, and immediately ordered the bugler at my elbow
to sound "Commence firing!" In a few seconds the whole
starboard battery was firing rapidly, and, as the Indiana and
other ships astern of us took it up, the roar became deafen-
ing. It was fully five minutes after we opened before any
reply came from the shore, and during this time I could see

the shells bursting and kicking up great clouds of dust and smoke as they struck or exploded in and about the batteries. Finally, when we were about one thousand yards from the Morro fort, a battery well back on the hill opened fire and several shells passed over us. I at once directed our guns on this battery, which did not respond so long as we were firing at them. In the meantime many other guns had opened on us, but those of the Morro fort remained silent, until two hours later, when we were hauling off. Our fire had been so severe that this particular fort could not respond.

In order to define our firing line, the admiral had ordered a boat anchored off the entrance to the harbour on the edge of the shoal to mark the point where we were to begin, and the Detroit [7] was sent in to a point about eight hundred yards from the batteries to mark the edge of the shoal at that point, and between these two we were to steam, turning out as we passed close to the latter and coming on to the firing line again as we approached the former. Thus the fleet was to move in an ellipse until the signal to draw off was given. As we approached the Detroit for the first time the smoke was blinding, as there was no wind to blow it away. I ordered the rapid-fire guns to cease firing and continue to use the guns of the main battery, which eased the situation at once, and, as the smoke cleared, the sight was one long to be re-membered. The Spanish batteries were all paying more or less attention to the Detroit, and the shells were cutting the water up all about her and bursting over her. Captain Day-ton, who commanded her, was handling her beautifully, and

---

7. Together with sister ships the *Montgomery* and *Marblehead,* the USS *Detroit* was judged to be slow and weak, with no effective deck protec-tion. She displaced 2,094 tons, had a top speed of 17 knots, mounted seventeen guns and three torpedo tubes, and had a 224-man complement. Authorized under an act of 7 September 1888, she was built by Colum-bian Iron Works. The *Detroit* was laid down in February 1890, launched on 28 October 1891, and commissioned on 20 July 1893. She was sold in 1910.

her crew was making her five-inch rapid-fire guns roar and blaze. She was simply magnificent, a veritable spitfire. After we had passed over the firing line the second time she was signalled to change her position and draw off somewhat, but Dayton took a long time to answer the signal, and withdrew with great reluctance. We were much relieved when he signalled that he had escaped without injury. If I had had the power I would have changed the name of the Detroit that morning; I would have painted "Gamecock" on her stern, and kept it there as long as she remained afloat.

When the Iowa turned from the firing line for the second time, the Spanish fire became very steady and accurate. For a few minutes, until the Indiana and New York got to work on them, it was the best shooting I saw the Spanish artillery do during the war. Just after we turned and were steaming away from them I heard a shell coming, and an instant afterward it came into our upper deck and exploded with a sharp ringing report. The projectile, a Krupp[8] armour piercer, passed through a steal beam and exploded under the boats, knocking the bottoms out of two of them and badly wrecking the third. The deck was filled with smoke, and I expected to find serious loss of life when it cleared up. The men to the number of one hundred or more were standing about in groups watching the fight when the smoke hid them from view. Many of them had their caps blown off by the explosion, and, as the smoke blew away, they were laughing and joking while they brushed the dust from their clothes. Everything about the deck was ripped and torn by fragments of the shell, but not a man was even scratched. The bottom of the sailing launch was badly wrecked, and a large fragment of shell completely destroyed the boat box, which contained

8. The Krupp family of steel manufacturers from Essen, Germany, supplied steel armor and ordnance to navies across the world. They were largely instrumental in the birth of the Imperial German Navy as a force in European politics.

an outfit of various articles. The small American flag belonging to the boat was blown out of the box and spread on the rail, it being the only thing left. It was not damaged in the least. I afterward gave it to President McKinley as a souvenir of the fight. Two more shells came in rapid succession, and both exploded in the superstructure. They were perfectly placed and showed that the enemy had our range accurately. Three men were wounded by the second, these being my only casualties during the day. We were much cut up and marked about the upper works, but no serious damage was done. The escape of our men was simply marvellous.

As we made the third round on the firing line, the return fire from the batteries was very weak, and it was plain to me that the city could be captured if we continued our bombardment a few hours longer. I counted nine places where fire had broken out on shore as the result of our exploding shells, and I felt sure that if we turned our guns on the city we could compel its surrender or destroy it in a short time. So far the only damage to the town was caused by a few wild shots due to the rolling of the ships in the trade swell. There had been no orders to fire at anything except the batteries, but, as they were very close to the town, some damage was unavoidably done to it. After we had been in action about two hours and a half, signal was made to withdraw; and as the fleet passed out of and beyond the range of the enemy's guns, Spanish flags were hoisted on all the forts and a furious but harmless fire kept up as long as we could see them.

Our men had received just what they most needed—practical demonstration of the fact that it required a great many shots to seriously injure a modern ship, and that every shell fired was not going to kill each individual man who heard it screaming over his head. Our experience that morning was of immense value to all hands, but particularly to those who were under fire for the first time. If we had had sufficient force to hold San Juan, it would undoubtedly have been taken that day; but such was not the case, and we could not wait for the arrival of troops, even if they had been available for the purpose. Admiral Cervera was somewhere in the West Indies, and it was our business to get between him and our base of supplies at Key West as soon as possible. We knew that we had no time to spare, and I, as well as other commanding officers, advised Admiral Sampson to get to the westward with all possible despatch.

CHAPTER 37

With the Flying Squadron

AFTER dark on the 12th of May I took my monitor in tow and we began our vexatious return trip to the Gulf of Mexico. Admiral Sampson was convinced that the Spanish fleet would make for Santiago or Havana, with chances in favour of the former place. When we arrived off the north coast of Hayti a torpedo boat brought the news that they were at Curaçoa, and shortly afterward I was left in command of the fleet, with orders to get the ships to their various stations on the blockade as rapidly as possible, while the flagship hurried on to Key West with all speed. Had it not been for the monitors the problem would have been easy to solve, but with them to tow, and all hands short of coal, it was most difficult.

During the afternoon of May 17th, as we were passing in sight of Manzanillo [1] lighthouse, I discovered two Spanish gunboats close inshore, evidently making for Nuevitas. [2] As I

1. A city in southeast Cuba on the Golfo de Guacanayabo.
2. A town about 25 miles east of Minas, situated on the north coast of Cuba in Camaguey province.

could not go after them myself without casting off my monitor, and thus losing valuable time, I made signal to the Montgomery,[3] Commander Converse[4] commanding, to give chase. The way he made those two gunboats hunt a hole was beautiful to see. They disappeared behind the land, and to my great concern Converse did the same in hot pursuit. After a few minutes I saw him open fire with one battery and then with both, firing very rapidly. Fearing that he was in trouble, I signalled the Indiana, Captain Taylor, to go to his assistance. As the battle ship turned out of column to obey the signal, the Montgomery came out of the narrow channel stern first at full speed, having been handled from first to last in the most gallant and seamanlike way. I called Converse within hail and told him what I thought of him and his crew.

At eight o'clock in the evening, as we were entering the Bahama Channel,[5] during a vicious black rain squall, the keen-eyed lookouts of the Iowa made out a torpedo boat coming toward us at top speed. She soon made her night signal and proved to be the Dupont,[6] with Commander Kimball,[7]

3. The USS *Montgomery* was a sister ship to the *Detroit* and *Marblehead*. Built by Columbia Iron Works and laid down in February 1890, she was launched on 5 December 1891 and commissioned on 21 June 1894. The *Montgomery* served as a torpedo experimental ship from 1908 to 1914, and was renamed the *Anniston* in March 1918. She was sold the following year.

4. George Albert Converse graduated from the Naval Academy in September 1865. He was promoted to lieutenant commander on 12 July 1878, commander on 23 March 1889, and captain on 3 March 1899.

5. Lies off the north coast of Cuba at Archipelago de Camaguey.

6. The USS *DuPont* was a steel, steam-powered torpedo boat of 165 tons, a top speed of 27.5 knots, four guns, three torpedo tubes, and a 24-man complement. Authorized under an act of 2 March 1895, she was constructed by Herreshoff. Laid down in February 1896, launched on 30 March 1897, and commissioned on 23 September 1897, she was restyled a coastal torpedo boat in 1918 and sold in 1920.

7. William W. Kimball graduated from the Naval Academy in 1869. He attained the following ranks during his career: lieutenant, 18 Decem-

commanding the torpedo flotilla. He had orders for me to cast off my monitor and get to Key West as soon as steam could take me there, as there was important work for my ship to do. I cast off the Amphitrite, signalled the Montgomery to take her in tow, and Captain Taylor to assume command of the squadron, and went below to my cabin with Kimball to read the despatches which he had in his hand.

We seated ourselves at the cabin table and I was deeply interested in Cervera's movements, when I heard a startled voice exclaim, "Look-out, captain!" I threw my head to one side to see what I was to look out for, when there was a tremendous crash and I was aware that I was hurt and more or less dazed. My first impression was that one of the Spanish gunboats had sneaked up on us and put a shell into my cabin. I had been thinking all the afternoon what a fine chance it would be for them that night; but when I was really conscious I saw that that was not the trouble. My cabin was full of men, all staring at me, their eyes fairly sticking out of their heads. They thought I was killed, and wanted to see the last of the "old man." I was soon aware that one of the doctors was feeling and twisting my right arm and that my right shoulder was in pretty bad shape. Through it all I was very sorry for Kimball, who, I thought, was surely killed, and I was greatly relieved when I heard his voice, which sounded a mile away.

The accident was soon explained. The men were running in the steel hawser, which we had been using to tow the monitor, and it had picked up the steel battle hatch, weighing something over four hundred pounds, which was lying on deck ready to be put on the cabin hatch when needed. The line had carried it along until it came directly over the hatch under which I was sitting, when it slipped off, came down edge first, and caught me on the shoulder

---

ber 1874; lieutenant commander, 6 December 1896; and commander, 8 December 1899.

instead of the head. The man who called to me to look out held on to it in his effort to stop it, and came down with it. My shoulder was badly mashed and dislocated, but the excellent medical men soon wiped the blood off, reduced the dislocation, bandaged my arm to my side, and turned me in with a stiff glass of grog under my belt. The only serious damage was to the cabin table, which was no longer fit for use. If my head had been four inches farther forward, I should never have had the pleasure of writing this book.

The Iowa arrived at Key West after sundown May 18th and anchored near the flagship New York. The flying squadron,[8] Commodore Schley commanding, was at anchor in the immediately vicinity. Coal and ammunition lighters were brought alongside at once, and all night long my willing men shovelled away and stowed bread and powder. Sampson came on board to see me and urged me to my best efforts, as he wished the Iowa ready at the first possible moment to join Schley. Early on the 19th the flying squadron sailed for Cienfuegos[9] and my men tugged away at the coal whips, scarcely taking time to eat. During the night of the 19th it was very rough, and by daylight officers and men were about worn out, but with a rest of only an hour we went at it again, determined to do all that men could do to carry out the wishes of our commander in chief.

At eleven o'clock Sampson signalled me, "You must go now, cast off lighters, show yourself off Havana before sundown, and then proceed with all possible despatch to Cienfuegos and report to Commodore Schley." At the same time he sent my written orders and official mail for the commander of the flying squadron. In ten minutes I was under

8. The Flying Squadron comprised the battleships USS *Massachusetts* and *Texas* and the armored cruiser *Brooklyn*. It was later augmented by the auxiliary cruiser *New Orleans* and the protected cruisers *Columbia* and *Minneapolis,* under the command of Commodore Winfield Scott Schley.
9. A city of south-central Cuba on Cienfuegos Bay, a narrow-necked inlet of the Caribbean.

way and standing out to sea with my decks piled waist-high with boxes of provisions and ammunition, while the whole ship was black with coal dust, and the officers and men looked like a gang of chimney-sweeps. Just as the sun was setting I slowed and stopped my engines about two miles from the Morro lighthouse, and remained in that position until it was fairly dark, when I rang the engines full speed ahead, and at twelve knots speed steered my course for Cape San Antonio at the west end of Cuba.

In the forenoon of the following day, when nearly up with the cape, I found the torpedo boat Dupont thrashing about in the heavy sea and her commanding officer unable to make out his position. I gave him his bearings, and he was off at once to deliver his orders to Commodore Schley. We had no despatch boats, properly speaking, and these delicate torpedo boats had to be used for the purpose. It was like ploughing a stumpy field with a carefully groomed and trained thoroughbred horse. On Sunday, May 22d, at 1.30 P.M., I stopped my engines two hundred yards astern of the Brooklyn,[10] off Cienfuegos, Cuba, and, as my arm was still bandaged to my side, sent my executive officer on board to report the ship to Commodore Schley for duty in his squadron, and at the same time deliver him the official mail I had received from Admiral Sampson for him. I had, about 1.15 P.M., saluted the flag of the commodore. It was thus that I became a part of the much-talked-of and discussed flying squadron.

On May 23d I took in two hundred and fifty-five tons of coal from a collier between the hours of 10 A.M. and 6.30

10. A Harvey and nickel-steel, steam-powered armored cruiser that displaced 9,215 tons, had a top speed of 20 knots, mounted thirty-six guns and five torpedo tubes, and carried a maximum complement of 581 men, the USS *Brooklyn* was authorized under an act of 19 July 1892. Built at the Cramp Shipyard, laid down on 2 August 1893, launched on 2 October 1895, and commissioned on 1 December 1896, she was Commodore Winfield Schley's flagship at the Battle of Santiago, and later served as the flagship of Pacific Fleet destroyers. The *Brooklyn* was sold in 1921.

P.M., besides giving coal to a torpedo boat. During the night
it was reported to me that there were three white lights in
line on shore, which I knew was the signal from the insurgents that they wished to communicate. I, of course, took it
for granted that the commodore understood this signal as
well as I did, otherwise I should have informed him of its
significance. It appeared afterward that he did not; and thus
much valuable time was lost. On the morning of the 24th
the Marblehead [11] arrived, and the moment Commander
McCalla [12] heard of the three lights he went in and communicated, and in a few hours Schley knew that the Spanish fleet
was not in Cienfuegos.

In the meantime I had received a draft of thirty-seven men

11. The USS *Marblehead* was a sister ship of the *Montgomery* and *Detroit*.
Built by City Point Iron Works, she was laid down on 11 August 1892,
commissioned on 2 April 1894, and sold in 1921.
12. Born in Camden, New Jersey on 19 June 1844, Bowman Henry
McCalla graduated from the Naval Academy in 1864. He advanced
through the grades to attain the rank of rear admiral on 11 October
1903. He served in the yacht *America* in pursuit of the Confederate steamers: *Florida* and *Tallahassee*; *Susquehanna*, 1865–66; *Brooklyn*, 1866–67;
Sabine, 1867–68; *Tuscarora*, 1868–71; *Wabash*, 1871–74; *Wachusett*,
1874. Returning to the Naval Academy from 1874 to 1878, he became
executive officer of the *Powhatan*, 1878–81. McCalla was assigned to the
Bureau of Navigation, 1882–87; commanded the *Enterprise*, 1887–90;
and was in charge of the Mare Island Navy Yard, 1893–97. After a brief
tour at the Naval War College (1897), he commanded the *Marblehead* in
the North Atlantic Squadron during the war with Spain. For "eminent
and conspicuous gallantry in battle during Spanish War," he was advanced six numbers in rank. McCalla was on duty at the Norfolk Navy
Yard, 1898–99, and commanded the *Newark* of the Asiatic Squadron,
1899–1901. During the Boxer Rebellion in June 1900, he commanded
the landing party from the Asiatic Fleet that formed part of the column
under Vice Admiral Sir Edward Seymour, RN, in an attempt to relieve
the legations in Peking. For this service McCalla was advanced three
numbers in rank. He commanded the *Kearsarge*, 1901–2; was commandant of the Naval Training Station, San Francisco, 1902–3; and of the
Mare Island Navy Yard, 1903–6. Retiring on 19 June 1906, he died
in 1910.

from the Marblehead, most of them recruits from Detroit,[13] Michigan. At 7.55 that evening the squadron got under way and went to sea, bound for Santiago. During the 25th and 26th we steamed along slowly, at times making as low as five knots in order to allow the Eagle,[14] a small converted yacht, to keep company with us. She was bothered by the roughness of the sea, which did not trouble the larger vessels. The Brooklyn or Iowa could have towed her ten knots or more without difficulty. At times we steamed eight or nine knots, which was the greatest speed we made during the trip. At 5.25 P.M., May 26, we stopped our engines at a point twenty-six to thirty miles to the south of Santiago, and there remained four hours or more in communication with the St. Paul, the Yale,[15] and the Minneapolis. The air was very clear and the high mountains back of Santiago could be seen, but nothing else. No attempt was made, so far as I know, to determine whether the Spanish fleet was in the harbour or not. At 7.50 P.M. the commodore made the following general signal to the squadron: "Destination Key West, *via* south side of Cuba and Yucatan channel,[16] as soon as collier is ready; speed nine knots." At 9.10 we went ahead at nine knots' speed, heading west, bound, as I supposed from the signal, for Key West.

All hands on the Iowa were greatly surprised at this unexpected retreat, and I for one was absolutely in the dark as to

13. A major city in southeast Michigan on the Detroit River.
14. The USS *Eagle* was a yacht of 434 tons, a top speed of 15.5 knots, a battery of four guns, and a 64-man complement. Built by Harlan and Hollingsworth, she was launched in 1890, commissioned on 5 April 1898, and sold in 1920.
15. An armed merchant steamer built by J. & G. Thompson for the Inman Line as the *City of Paris*, the USS *Yale* was launched in 1888 and commissioned on 2 May 1898. Returned to her owners on 9 September 1898, she was used as a scout and transport in the Spanish-American War and World War I. The *Yale* was eventually sold and scrapped in 1923.
16. A body of water that links the Caribbean Sea and Gulf of Mexico between the west coast of Cuba and the Yucatán prominence of Mexico.

its meaning. I felt reasonably sure that Cervera was in Santiago, but concluded that the commodore had better information than I on that point. My natural inference was that the Spanish ships had left Santiago and gone to the westward, and that we were going after them. This inference was completely wrong, for after two hours we stopped again and drifted about until noon of the following day, while some of the vessels took coal from the collier. Then we stood on to the west again, occasionally stopping, until 1.25 P.M., May 28th, when we were signalled to steer east, one half north, and steam six knots per hour. Thus we headed back in the direction of Santiago.

As there had been no conference of commanding officers, we were all completely bewildered as to what this peculiar manœuvring might mean. Some of us, remembering the fate of Admiral Byng,[17] felt that if Cervera was really in Santiago and got one of his ships away and on to the coast of the United States, while we were tinkering at the machinery of a collier, the world might be startled by another dreadful court-martial sentence.

17. John Byng (1704–57) was a British admiral shot for his neglect of duty. In 1756, just before the Seven Years War, Byng was sent to protect Great Britain's island base on Minorca in the Mediterranean. Failing to drive off an attacking French fleet, and believing himself seriously out-gunned and outmanned, he withdrew to Gilbraltar. He was court-martialed, found guilty, and given a mandatory death sentence. Despite a recommendation for mercy, Byng was shot to appease an enraged public.

CHAPTER 38

Fighting at Long Range

A T 7.40 P.M., May 28th, the squadron stopped off the entrance to the harbour of Santiago, distant therefrom about nine miles. During the night we steamed slowly back and forth, closing in somewhat before daylight. At early dawn I was standing on the bridge with the executive officer, Lieutenant-Commander Rodgers,[1] who had been our naval *attaché* at Madrid[2] and who knew every vessel in the Spanish navy. As we stood straining our eyes for what we hoped we might see, he suddenly turned on me and said, "Captain, there's the Cristóbal Colón!"[3] In a moment I caught her with my glasses lying moored in front of the Punta Gorda battery[4]

1. Raymond P. Rodgers graduated from the Naval Academy in June 1868. He was promoted to lieutenant on 10 October 1872, lieutenant commander on 4 July 1893, and commander on 3 March 1899.
2. The capital of Spain, on the central plateau of the country.
3. HSM *Cristóbal Colón* was an unprotected, iron-hulled, steam and sail cruiser that displaced 1,152 tons, had a top speed of 13 knots, mounted nine guns and two torpedo tubes, and carried a 193-man complement. She was built by Carraca and launched in 1887.
4. A Spanish harbor battery located to the rear and on the east side of the harbor entrance. It contained four heavy guns, including two 15-cm.

in a position to command the channel. The information was quickly flagged to the Brooklyn, and in a second or two the answer came back, "I understand." Then we made out another Spanish ship and a torpedo boat and flagged this information at once. Again the answer came back, "I understand."

In the meantime I had gone to general quarters and loaded the heavy guns, hoping that we might have a chance to use them on the Colón as she lay helpless and at our mercy, but such was not to be our luck. We steamed about in front of the harbour until a signal was made during the forenoon for commanding officers to repair on board the flagship. Then the fleet stopped while the commodore and his commanders discussed the situation. The details of this conference I am not at liberty to give, but I may say without impropriety that Commodore Schley was at last satisfied that Cervera's fleet was in Santiago Harbour and not in Cienfuegos. We continued to steam about in front of the place during Sunday, Monday, and Tuesday, while the Colón, with fires hauled and awnings spread, lay in plain sight, quietly watching us.

At 11.20 A.M., May 31st, Commodore Schley made this signal to the squadron: "The Massachusetts, New Orleans, and Iowa will go in after dinner to a distance of seven thousand yards and fire at Cristóbal Colón with eight- and twelve- and thirteen-inch guns. Speed about ten knots." At 1.25 P.M. the three ships mentioned formed column, the Massachusetts leading, showing the broad pennant of Commodore Schley; the New Orleans,[5] a vessel purchased in England and

---

Mato howitzers and two 9-cm. breech-loading Krupp guns; under the command of artillery captain Seijas.

5. A steel and steam-powered cruiser of 3,769 tons, a top speed of 20 knots, and a battery of thirty-three guns and three torpedo tubes. The USS *New Orleans* was purchased from Brazil as the *Amazonos* under an act of 3 September 1888. Built by Armstrong, she was laid down in 1895,

with a new crew came second; and the Iowa last. The second-class battle-ship Texas,[6] the splendid armoured cruiser Brooklyn, and the gunboat Marblehead, were spectators of the fight that followed.

The Massachusetts opened fire at 1.50, her first thirteen-inch shell striking the water outside the Morro, as I judged about two thousand yards short of the Colón. I therefore set my gun sights at eighty-five hundred yards and at 1.56 opened fire as soon as the Colón could be seen. All the projectiles fell short, though our guns were elevated to nine thousand yards. The harbour entrance was so narrow and our speed so great we could only fire a few shots before the Spanish ship was shut out by the land. At 2.01 I ceased firing. The Massachusetts in the meantime had turned with port helm away from the land, and thus materially increased the distance from the Colón. She opened fire again at 2.05, and the commodore made this signal: "Do not go in any closer." When I had turned the Iowa and could see the Colón, I decreased my speed and opened fire at 2.08, range ninety-five hundred yards, which I gradually increased to eleven thousand as I saw the shells falling short. At 2.16 the commodore signalled, "Cease firing," and the battle was over. Nobody had been struck, Spaniard or American. Two battle ships and a cruiser on our side had engaged one cruiser and

launched on 4 December 1896, commissioned on 18 March 1898, and decommissioned in 1922. She was sold in 1930.

6. The USS Texas was a Harvey and nickel-steel, steam-powered battleship that displaced 6,135 tons, had a top speed of 17 knots, mounted twenty-six guns and four torpedo tubes, and carried a maximum complement of 508 men. Authorized under an act of 3 August 1886, she was the first of the second-class battleships designed by John of the Barrow Shipbuilding Co., selected from thirteen designers. Built at the Norfolk Navy Yard, she was laid down on 1 June 1889, launched 28 June 1892, and commissioned on 15 August 1895. The Texas was engaged at the Battle of Santiago. Renamed the San Marcos on 16 February 1911, she was used as a target ship, 1911–12.

a few guns mounted on shore on the Spanish side for about fifteen minutes and then drew off. The only cause we had for congratulation was the fact that nobody was hurt. I had all four of my twelve-inch guns disabled by damage to the dash pots from high-angle fire, but they were repaired long before we had any real necessity to use them.

Commodore Schley transferred his flag back to the Brooklyn at 2.50 P.M., the enemy ceased firing at 3.10, and we resumed our peaceful cruising up and down in front of the entrance to the harbour. Captain Moreau[7] of the Colón told me weeks afterward that the last large shell from the Iowa struck about forty feet short of him, and when it exploded a small piece of it found its way into his cabin, and that he retained it as a souvenir of the day. This he said was the nearest any projectile came to striking his ship.

On June 1st Admiral Sampson arrived early in the morning, and after steaming well in toward the Morro made signal, "Come closer." From that hour the blockade of Santiago was so maintained that it was not possible for any vessel to escape. Orders were issued that if the enemy's ships attempted to escape we should close in at once and force them ashore or sink them; and these orders were posted on the bridge of the Iowa, and, I assume, on other ships also, so that even the signal boys knew what was to be done when we sighted them.

Preparations were at once begun for sinking the Merrimac[8] in the channel, which was done in the most gallant and daring manner by Assistant Naval Constructor Hobson[9] on the morning of June 3d, about half an hour before daylight. Dur-

7. Captain Emilio Diaz Moreu and Commodore José de Parades were both on board the *Cristóbal Colón* in the battle.
8. A collier used in an attempt to block Santiago channel.
9. A naval cadet as of 21 May 1885, Richard P. Hobson (1870–1937) was a top graduate of the Naval Academy's Class of 1889. Promoted to assistant naval constructor on 1 July 1891, and naval constructor on 23 June 1898, he failed in his attempt to scuttle the *Merrimac* in the channel

ing the afternoon of June 2d Sampson had signalled me, "I want volunteers to sink the Merrimac." I gave the signal to the executive officer, with directions to read it to the crew and give me the names of those who wished to go. In a short time he came to me and said that all the officers had volunteered, and also the entire crew of six hundred men. It was something of a job to write down all their names, and, as I was sure only a few could be required, I signalled: "My entire crew has volunteered. How many men do you want?" The answer came back promptly, "I want one seaman from the Iowa." The question then was how to select one man out of six hundred good ones. I was naturally anxious to send a man who would die reflecting credit on the ship. I had no idea that any one would ever come out of the scrape alive.

Two men were selected, one by me and one by the executive officer. I took a petty officer named McLean, who had served with me in the Yorktown, a first-class man in every respect; the executive took a young seaman named Murphy, a native of the State of Maine, also first-class in every way. When told that I was going to sentence one of them to death in a few minutes, and being asked if they still wanted to go in the Merrimac, they both smiled and said "Yes." McLean offered Murphy fifty dollars for his chance, which was promptly declined, and the toss of a penny decided the case in Murphy's favour. Then McLean offered him one hundred and fifty dollars for his chance, which was also promptly declined, and the poor fellow went forward with the tears streaming out of his eyes because he had lost a chance to have his head shot off! They were fine fellows to tie to, those blue-shirted chaps of mine.

The position of the Iowa on the blockading line was di-

leading to Santiago Harbor, and he and his men were captured but returned home heroes. He was promoted directly to captain, and resigned in 1903 to promote the causes of naval supremacy and prohibition of alcohol. Congressman from Alabama, 1907–15, Hobson was awarded the Medal of Honor in 1933 for his Spanish-American War exploits.

rectly off the entrance of the harbour, so that we could look straight up the channel as far as the Punta Gorda battery, and in this position I and my men lived from June 1st until July 3d. I was absent but one day, when I ran up to Guantanamo Bay [10] for coal, and was back at my station at night. We took coal and food and ammunition on the blockading line, and, as I have said, did not leave it until the necessity for a blockade ceased to exist. The infernal place got to look like home to us; we almost knew the sharks and fishes that swam around us. Certainly we knew the batteries and just when we might expect to hear from them.

It was from this position that I watched the Merrimac make her last trip on the morning of June 3d. During the night of the 2d I caught sight of her several times, but it was nearly daylight when I saw her distinctly as she made for the entrance of the harbour. The Spaniards were on the alert, and just as the Merrimac turned into the channel I saw the flash of a small gun, and immediately afterward the firefly sparks along the shore indicated that the infantry had opened on her with their Mausers.[11] Then the guns on Socapa[12] began to blaze and were followed by those on the Morro[13] and Esmeralda batteries[14] and the Punta Gorda fort. Within

10. An inlet of the Caribbean on the south coast of Cuba, east of Santiago. It later became the site of a U.S. naval base.
11. Spain adopted its first Mauser rifle in 1891. Chambered for the 7.65 Mauser cartridge, this bolt-action five-round magazine firearm saw extensive use in the Spanish-American War—with deadly effect.
12. A Spanish battery of three old 21-cm. howitzers, located on the western side of the entrance to Santiago Harbor.
13. A Spanish battery of five old 16-cm. guns and two old 21-cm. howitzers, located on the eastern side of the entrance to Santiago Harbor. Morro was commanded by artillery lieutenant Leon.
14. Evans undoubtedly meant the Estrella Battery at Estrella Cove, comprising two old 21-cm. howitzers, two 8-cm. modern Plasencia guns, and two old 12-cm. bronze guns. All these were commanded by artillery lieutenant Sanchez.

three minutes the Reina Mercedes [15] and other ships opened up, and, as their heavy guns flashed, the doomed ship stood out clear and distinct in the accumulating clouds of smoke. Finally the whole entrance to the harbour was a roaring blaze of powder smoke, and the Merrimac was shut out from our view. It was a dreadful sight—to my mind what hell might look like with the lid off! I had seen all I cared to look at, and, convinced that the gallant Hobson and his equally gallant men had gone aloft forever, I retired to the pilot house, where I consoled myself with a pipe. Slowly the clouds of smoke lifted and daylight disclosed the smokestack and masts of the sunken ship sticking out of the water.

As soon as it was fairly light I received a signal to stand in close and prevent any interference with the wreck of the Merrimac. I understood at once that Sampson wished me to see that dynamite was not used on her, and, having reached a point where I could command the channel with my guns, I stopped the engines and waited for something to happen. All was as still as death, and there was no living thing in sight. I could see something swinging to a line from the mast of the Merrimac that looked like a life raft, but my strongest glasses failed to show anything like a man on or about it. Just at sunrise, as I stood on the end of the bridge watching intently, a white-covered navy steam launch came in sight steering down the channel, and, as she approached the wreck, the executive officer, who was by my side, said, "Captain, shall I open fire?" "No," I replied, "not yet." I meant to sink the boat, of course, if she showed any inclination to disturb the quiet of the scene. She stopped near the

15. HSM *Reina Mercedes* was an unprotected, steam and sail light cruiser of 3,042 tons, twenty guns, five torpedo tubes, a top speed of 17 knots, and a 370-man complement. Laid down in August 1881, her construction was delayed for five years due to shortage of materials. The *Reina* was finally launched on 9 September 1897, the sister ship of *Alfonso XII* and *Reina Cristina*.

wreck for ten minutes or more and I could see a few men moving about on her rail, then she turned and went back up the harbour. I never knew until Hobson told me, weeks afterward, that Admiral Cervera was himself in the launch and that he (Hobson) was under the raft with his seven men, and that he surrendered to the Spanish admiral and was by him taken to the flagship. If I had opened fire on the boat, I should probably have destroyed her and killed the whole party, and two of the most picturesque figures in the Spanish war would have disappeared—Cervera and Hobson.

About three o'clock on the afternoon of June 3d Admiral Cervera did a thing that stamped him as the gallant Spanish gentleman we afterward found him to be. He sent out a vessel under a flag of truce with his chief of staff, Captain Bustamente, [16] to communicate with Admiral Sampson and to say to him that Hobson and his men were well, had behaved most gallantly, and that he personally would see to their welfare; also that he would be glad to have us send in clothing or other things that would add to their comfort. There was never a more courteous thing done in war, and I am sure that every man in the American fleet appreciated it. That they afterward showed their appreciation and in a very substantial way is now a matter of history.

During the early days of June the bay of Guantanamo was seized, and, after a sharp engagement, the battalion of marines under Colonel Huntington [17] and the force under Captain McCalla controlled the entrance to the harbour. The American flag was hoisted on the captured Spanish fort, and for the first time it flew over Cuban soil supported by American men. I, for one, hope it may never be hauled down. The

16. Joaquin Bustamente was the captain of Admiral Pascual Cervera's flagship, the *Infanta Maria Teresa*.
17. R.W. Huntington's Marine Corps career was marked by the following promotions: captain, 21 June 1864; major, 24 October 1889; lieutenant colonel, 2 February 1897; and colonel, 10 August 1898. He retired on 10 January 1899.

possession of this beautiful landlocked water gave us a secure base where small vessels would be safe in storms, and all hands could coal in any kind of weather. A great load was lifted from the minds of all commanding officers, but the relief to the commander-in-chief was the greatest of all.

There had been rumours of the approach of the American army under General Shafter,[18] and while we maintained our strict blockade we prayed that they would come soon, for the heat and strain of the work were hard to bear. We fired on the batteries frequently, more to give our men practice than for any other reason, for we all knew that it was impossible for any naval force to destroy them because of their location and commanding positions. We could and did drive the men away from the guns and keep them away from them whenever we opened on them, but the entire destruction of the works was beyond our power. The harbour and the ships it contained were inaccessible to a naval force, owing to the character of the channel and the mines planted in it. The capture of the forts was an army job, and we of the navy

18. Born in 1835 in Galesburg, Michigan, William Rufus Shafter lived on a farm and attended common schools. He taught school for three years prior to the Civil War, and upon its outbreak enlisted as 1st Lieutenant, 7th Michigan, on 22 August 1861. Promoted to the ranks of major and lieutenant colonel in the early years of the war, he rose to colonel, 17th U.S. Colored Troops, on 19 April 1864, and brevet brigadier general on 13 March 1865. He mustered out of volunteer service on 2 November 1865, and entered the regular army as lieutenant colonel on 26 January 1867. Shafter became a breveted colonel on 2 March 1867, and was given the Medal of Honor for gallant and meritorious services at the battle of Fair Oaks, Virginia. Assigned to the 24th Infantry on 14 August 1869, he made full colonel ten years later, and was promoted to brigadier general on 3 May 1897, in charge of Department of California. As major general in May 1898, he went to Tampa, Florida, to take command of the Cuban expeditionary force and conducted operations leading to the capitulation of Santiago de Cuba and forces defending the city in July 1898. Shafter commanded the departments of California and Columbia, 1899–1901. He retired on 30 June 1901, and lived in Bakersfield, California, until his death in 1906.

waited with absolute faith and such patience as we could command for the time when our brother arm of the service would come and do it.

At last the rumors took positive shape and we knew that General Shafter was on the way to Santiago with seventeen thousand of the best men in the world. On the afternoon of June 20th the great forest of masts and smokestacks off to the south of Santiago showed that the transport fleet had arrived. In a few hours orders came to send our boats, properly officered and manned, to a rendezvous off Baiquiri at a stated time to land the army and their belongings. This was a great surprise to us all, as we had been notified that this duty would not be required of us and we had left nearly all our boats at Key West. However, we were only too glad to do all and everything in our power to assist those who had come to help us to capture Santiago and its Spanish garrison. Our only regret was that they found us so badly prepared to do the work in the shortest possible time. Our officers and men were constantly employed night and day for three days landing the troops, and many of them for over a week more landing provisions and stores. In a word, we did everything that it was possible for us to do, and in return received the warmest thanks and the commendation of General Shafter expressed in official form.

From my position off the Morro I saw little of the work of the army. Occasionally I could see small parties of men on the hills back of Siboney,[19] and when the troops were seriously engaged I could judge their position by the clouds of smoke from the field guns, but of the actual fighting I saw nothing.

As time passed and the lines were established on the land side, Admiral Sampson drew in closer his blockading lines,

19. A village in eastern Cuba, on the Caribbean, nine miles east-southeast of Santiago de Cuba. It was a disembarkation point for American troops in July 1898.

so that we were always within easy range of the Spanish guns. At first our distance from the harbour entrance during the daytime had been four or five miles; now it was three, and during the night two miles and even nearer.

The plan of using search lights was perfectly carried out and originated, no doubt, with Sampson himself. I was the first one to carry out his orders in this respect, and I shall never forget my sensations as I did it. The Iowa was well in toward the land when the New York steamed in near me and the admiral hailed and said, "At dark, I wish you to go in and turn a search light on the channel." "How near shall I go, sir?" I replied. "Go in until you can detect a small boat crossing in front of the Punta Gorda battery," came back through the megaphone. "How long shall I remain there, sir?" I asked. "All night, sir." "Ay, ay, sir." The admiral certainly had given me a new sensation. The idea of deliberately placing a battle ship within a mile of two of the fastest torpedo boats in the world, and then turning on a search light to mark her position, was novel at least. All writers on the subject had advised sending such valuable ships to sea at night to keep the torpedo boats away from them; but Sampson had thought rapidly and accurately, and had gauged the features of this special case most admirably, as the result showed.

At dark that night I steamed the Iowa in for this new duty, and, when I reached what I supposed to be the proper position, turned on the search light and stopped the engines. All hands were at quarters, guns loaded, and everything ready to return the fire I felt sure would be opened on us. As the ship lost way and came to a standstill in the water, I examined carefully the channel with my glasses and concluded that I was not yet near enough to insure the work I was ordered to do. I therefore shut off the light and again steamed in, and when I stopped the second time, the beam of the search light showed up everything very distinctly. The sentries on the Morro could be seen plainly as they pulled their hats down over their eyes as a protection against the glare. The infantry fired spitefully with their Mausers without doing any harm, but the batteries remained silent, which has always been a great surprise and puzzle to all of us. They could have shot the search light out of us without doubt if they knew the first principles of pointing guns. Maybe they knew there were a lot of search lights in that fleet and it would be a hard job to put them all out.

After the first night, three battle ships—the Iowa, Oregon, and Massachusetts—were detailed to do search-light duty, and there was never a minute at night, until the Spanish fleet was destroyed, when the channel was not so lighted that it was impossible for anything to move on the water without being seen. The duty was well done, and only those who did it know how hard it was or how great the strain. As a rule the darkness was intense, and between the battle ships and the shore were guard boats and picket launches which would be endangered if their position were disclosed, and as a consequence the beam of the search light had to be accurately held on the channel. To do this when the heavy swell and the strong tide were cutting the ship about was more difficult than the average person would imagine. It was beautiful to see the accuracy with which these great ships were handled as they came in or went out of position with twenty-five or thirty vessels crowded about them and not a light on any of them. During all the time we were there the paint was not even scratched on one of them by collision.

On July 2d the long-looked-for attack on the shore batteries about Santiago was made, and the Spanish resistance found more stubborn than was anticipated. The fleet was much disheartened by the report that General Shafter intended to retire and fortify in a stronger position; but we all felt that, whatever he did, the Spanish fleet was doomed. None of us imagined for a moment that Admiral Cervera would attempt anything in the nature of a sortie, for that would be courting certain destruction. What we thought he might at any moment do would be to destroy his ships, land his men, and attempt to cut his way through our weakened lines. Toward evening on the 2nd we discovered that several of the Spanish blockhouses to the west and northwest of Santiago were on fire, which indicated that the outposts on the mountains were being forced in by the insurgents and that they were destroying everything before retiring. Just at sunset Lieutenant F.K. Hill,[20] who was the officer of the deck on board the Iowa, sent for me, and when I reached the bridge pointed out to me these fires, which presented a beautiful sight. He also called my attention to six columns of smoke near the entrance to the harbour which rose straight in the calm evening air. His opinion was that this indicated some movement on the part of the enemy's fleet, which was correct. It showed beyond a doubt that they had moved down from in front of the city; but, as they had often moved about the harbour, I did not consider it a matter of importance. I only said to Lieutenant Hill that we had the first search-light duty that night, and if they came out we should have a good chance at them, dismissed the subject from my mind, and went about my business. The incident, however, made a more serious impression on the mind of the signal quartermaster who was looking after the flags, and he, without orders to do so, bent on signal 250—"Enemy's ships coming out"—and had it ready to hoist. The flags remained bent on to the halliards all night, and were therefore ready to hoist on the morning of the 3d, when the fleet came out.

20. Warranted a cadet engineer on 1 October 1880, Hill became an ensign on 1 July 1886, a lieutenant (junior grade) on 15 June 1895, and a lieutenant on 7 June 1898.

CHAPTER 39

The Naval Battle off Santiago

ABOUT daylight on the morning of Sunday, July 3d, my son, Franck Taylor Evans,[1] a naval cadet serving on the battle ship Massachusetts, came on board the Iowa. He had been on picket duty during the night of the 2d, and as his ship had gone to Guantanamo for coal, he brought his boat to my ship to remain until his own vessel returned. It was this lucky chance that enabled him to take part in the battle of that memorable day. The officers and men were about to be sent to quarters for Sunday inspection, all dressed in clean white uniforms, and I and my son were just finishing our cigars after breakfast when the alarm for battle sounded all over the ship. Both of us sprang to our feet and started for the deck, and as my head came above the hatch a gun was fired from the lower bridge of the Iowa, aimed in the direction of the Maria Teresa[2] by Lieutenant Hill, who was again

1. Evans was warranted a naval cadet on 6 September 1894, and an ensign on 4 April 1900.
2. HSM *Infanta Maria Teresa* was a steam-powered, steel armored cruiser that displaced 6,890 tons, had a top speed of 20.2 knots, a main battery of forty guns and eight torpedo tubes, and a 484-man complement. Or-

officer of the deck. Before this gun was fired, and immediately upon discovering the bows of the leading Spanish ship, the signal 250, which had been bent on the night before, was run up, and thus the Iowa had the honour of firing the first gun of the action, and first making signal that the enemy's ships were attempting to escape. When I reached the bridge I found the engines set full speed ahead and the ship pointing straight for the entrance of the harbour. In about two minutes the guns of the starboard battery began firing— that is to say, the eight- and four-inch guns of the starboard battery and the forward twelve-inch guns. The crews of the rapid-fire guns were held in reserve until we should get to closer quarters.

As soon as I had a chance to look about me, I saw the New York about seven miles away off Siboney with her helm to port and turning rapidly in the direction of the fleet, and, judging from the great volume of smoke pouring from her smokestacks, her fires were being forced as much as possible. I could see distinctly the admiral's flag at her masthead, and with my glasses could have read any signal she had hoisted. She had started to the eastward a short time before, flying the signal, "Disregard the movements of the commander in chief," a signal that had been made whenever the admiral had for any reason been compelled to leave the blockading line. This signal indicated that we were not to follow the motions of the flagship, but, instead, close up somewhat so as to cover the interval caused by her absence, all of which was perfectly understood by the fleet. Before the firing began, my son asked me where he should take station, and I directed him to report to the officer commanding the division that corresponded to the one he served in on board of his own ship. I also directed that the men of his boat's crew should be stationed where they could render good service.

---

dered in June 1889 and launched 4 October 1891, she was sunk on 3 July 1898 off Santiago de Cuba.

As the leading Spanish ship, the flagship Maria Teresa, swung into the channel leading out from the Punta Gorda, she presented a magnificent appearance with her splendid new battle flags and her polished brass work. Her bright new coat of paint was in marked contrast to the lead-coloured, iron-rusted ships that were rushing full speed at her. As she passed the Diamond Shoal at the entrance to the harbour she swung off to the westward and opened fire smartly with her port broadside and turret guns. From this moment the battle may be said to have been on, and the roaring of the guns was incessant. The Vizcaya[3] came second, about six hundred yards astern of the flagship, followed by the Colón and then the Oquendo,[4] bringing up the rear; the torpedo boats Furor[5] and Pluton[6] were not yet in sight. The speed I judged to be about eight knots as the ships came down the channel, which was increased to thirteen or more as they kept away to the westward in the open sea. They came at us like mad bulls, and presented a fine appearance as I caught sight of them occasionally through the dense smoke of our battery.

It had been my intention from the first to ram or torpedo the flagship if I could reach her, and to insure this, I remained, as much as I could, in the conning tower at the side of the quartermaster, who was steering, watching carefully every move of the wheel and directing the man just where to head. I kept the Maria Teresa open on my starboard bow, so that the guns could have a chance at her, until it became

3. A sister ship of the *Infanta Maria Teresa* and *Almirante Oquendo* in every respect except that the HSM *Vizcaya* was launched 8 July 1891. She too was sunk on 3 July 1898.
4. A sister ship of the *Infanta Maria Teresa* and *Vizcaya* in each aspect except her launch date; namely, 4 October 1891.
5. HSM *Furor* was a steam-driven, steel torpedo craft of 370 tons, a top speed of twenty-eight knots, six guns, two torpedo tubes, three funnels, and a 67-man complement. Built in 1896 by Clydebank, she was sunk at the Battle of Santiago.
6. An improved version of the *Furor* class, HSM *Pluton* displaced 400 tons and had a top speed of 30 knots. She was built in 1897.

evident that I could not ram her or even get within torpedo range, when I swung off to port, gave her the full benefit of my starboard broadside, and then swung back quickly and headed across the bows of the second ship, hoping to be able to reach her with my ram. The Maria Teresa passed me at a distance of about twenty-six hundred yards, and, as she crossed my bows, our forward twelve-inch guns were fired and I was confident that I saw both shells strike the Spanish ship. As I swung back for the second ship, my port battery opened on the Maria Teresa and the starboard guns continued to play on the Vizcaya and Colón, which were approaching us at great speed. The fire of the first ship had been very rapid and accurate when she opened, but it grew ragged and inaccurate as the range decreased. I soon found that the Vizcaya would also pass ahead of me, and that I could not reach her with ram or torpedo. I accordingly swung to port, gave her my broadside, and, as she passed at nineteen hundred yards, put my helm to port and headed in again to try for the next ship.

At this time the Colón came with a great show of speed, passing between the leading ships and the shore and much protected by their smoke. As she passed she struck me twice—two as beautiful shots as I ever saw made by any ship. I had been doing my best to fight the Iowa from the conning tower, but the temptation to see the fight was more than I could resist, and I frequently found myself on the bridge, deeply interested in the magnificent spectacle about me. It thus happened that I was on the end of the bridge when the Colón paid her respects to us. The first shell she fired at us, through a rent in the smoke, struck on the starboard side a little forward of the bridge, about four feet above the water line, passed through the cellulose belt, and exploded on the berth deck, demolishing the dispensary, breaking almost every medicine bottle in it, and doing great damage otherwise. The smells that came up in consequence of this explosion were variegated and intense, a mixture of medicine and mellinite. The second shell, of the same size as the first—about six and a half inches in diameter—struck just at the water line and about six to ten feet farther forward, passed through the side and into the cellulose belt, where it broke up without exploding. It however, made an ugly, jagged hole, eighteen inches long and eight inches wide, through which the water poured with great rapidity. The cellulose in the coffer dam, which was supposed to swell up and stop the shot hole, washed out and floated astern in a broad, brown streak. I think the Colón fired only twice at me, and, as I have stated, she did excellent shooting as far as I could see.

When the Oquendo approached me, I found that if I held on my course she would pass ahead of me, so I changed and ran parallel with her at a distance of about sixteen to fourteen hundred yards and opened on her my entire battery, including the rapid-fire and machine guns. At this time she was under the concentrated fire of several of our ships and the effect was most destructive. She rolled and staggered like a drunken thing, and finally seemed to stop her engines. I thought she was going to strike her colours, and was on the point of ordering the battery to cease firing, when she started ahead again and we redoubled our efforts to sink her. As I looked at her I could see the shot holes come in her sides and our shells explode inside of her, but she pluckily held on her course and fairly smothered us with a shower of shells and machine-gun shots.

In the meantime the Spanish flagship headed for the shore, in flames, fore and aft, and soon took the ground about seven miles to the west of the entrance to Santiago Harbour, and a few minutes later the Oquendo followed her, the flames bursting out through the shot holes in her sides and leaping up from the deck as high as the military tops. It was a magnificent, sad sight to see these beautiful ships in their death agonies; but we were doing the work we had been educated for, and we cheered and yelled until our throats were sore.

When we were hotly engaged with the last ship, two dense

spots of black smoke and two long white streaks on the water
indicated the positions of the Spanish torpedo boats as they
made their gallant dash for liberty. We turned our rapid-fire
guns and the after guns of the main battery on them, and at
the same time other ships concentrated on the little game-
cocks. In a very short time—not more than five minutes, I
should say—a splendid column of steam mixed with coal
dust sprang hundreds of feet in the air, and I knew that the
boiler of one of them had blown up. A few minutes later the
second one blew up, and the torpedo boats that had caused
so much worry to friends and foes alike were things of the
past. They had given us many sleepless nights, but when it
came to the test of battle they had done just what many of
us thought they would do. They had been disabled and destroyed in the shortest possible time. It was almost wicked
to waste the lives of brave men in such an attempt.

About this time the flagship New York came racing back
to join in the fight. As she passed the batteries they concentrated a heavy fire on her, to which she paid no attention,
but fired three shots at one of the Spanish torpedo boats and
then hurried on, coming up directly astern of the Iowa. She
had the Vizcaya within range of her eight-inch guns for some
time before that vessel ran ashore, but in order to hit her,
would have had to fire over the Iowa, which I suppose was
the reason why Captain Chadwick held his fire. Afterward,
when she passed between me and the wreck of the Vizcaya,
as I was hoisting out my boats to go to her relief, my men
broke into cheers as they made out Admiral Sampson on the
bridge.

The course of the Iowa had carried her inside of the rest of
the American fleet, and, as I drew up abreast of the two
burning Spanish ships on the beach, I could see their crews
struggling in the water where the shells of our ships seemed
to be bursting among them. The Maria Teresa had a white
flag flying forward, which I was sure could not be seen by
the vessels firing on them, so I hoisted the signal, "Enemy's

ships have surrendered!" and the fire was at once concentrated on the fleeing Vizcaya. She was soon on fire, and off Accerraderos[7] turned and headed for the shore, smoke and flames pouring from her ports and hatches. The Colón, the last ship of the splendid squadron, was standing to the westward, hotly pursued by the Oregon,[8] Brooklyn, Texas, and New York. All the rest were shapeless wrecks on the Cuban shore, and nearly six hundred of their gallant officers and men had fought their last fight. God and the gunners had had their day.

At this point the battle of Santiago may be said to have terminated; at any rate I took no further part in it. I felt that I should be of no use in the chase of the Colón, as my speed was low, owing to the foul condition of the ship's bottom. She had been in the water seventeen months without docking, and her cylinder heads had not been off for six months. There was a duty for me, however, which I felt to be an imperative one, and that was the rescue of the brave but unfortunate men who had fought us so gallantly. Their wounded were in danger of burning to death, and those who had been fortunate enough to escape from the ships were in danger of death at the hands of the Cuban insurgents, who were willing, and I must say with ample provocation, to take the life of any Spanish officer or man. They were our prisoners, however, and I made up my mind that no harm should come to them if I could prevent it. I therefore ran in close to

7. According to American naval officer Winfield Scott Schley, Asserrados is a point approximately 15 miles west of Santiago Harbor.
8. The third of the Indiana-class battleships, the USS Oregon was constructed by Union Iron Works, having been laid down on 19 November 1891 and launched on 26 October 1893. She was commissioned on 15 July 1896, served as a coastal battleship, and was eventually moored at Portland as a floating monument from 1925 to 1942, at which point she was sold for scrap. Converted to ammunition hulk for the reconquest of Guam, the Oregon was again sold for scrap in 1956.

the burning wreck of the Vizcaya, hoisted out what boats I had and sent them to the rescue as rapidly as possible. I also directed the torpedo boat Ericsson[9] and the converted yacht Hist[10] to join in the work. The danger to our men and officers from exploding magazines was imminent, but they faced it with a courage and coolness that were habitual to them.

It was only a short time before the boat loads of dead and wounded began to arrive alongside, and then the ghastly, horrible results of our Sunday morning's work were apparent. I had made every possible preparation for the comfort of the wounded, and as the poor chaps were tenderly lifted over the side and handled by the men who, half an hour before, were anxious to kill them all, I could but be struck with this splendid phase of war. The beautiful white quarter-deck of the Iowa was soon stained with the blood dripping from the wet clothing of the wounded, and she looked as if she had been used as a slaughter pen.

9. The USS *Ericsson* was built of steel and powered by steam. She was a 120-ton torpedo boat, with a top speed of 24 knots, a battery of four guns and three torpedo tubes, and a complement of twenty-two men. Authorized under an act of 30 June 1890, she was laid down at the Iowa Iron Works on 21 July 1892, launched 12 May 1894, and commissioned on February 18, 1897. The *Ericsson* was used as a target ship and sunk in 1912.

10. The USS *Hist* was a screw-steamer that mounted five guns and had a complement of fifty-six men. Built in 1895, she was purchased from David Dows, Jr., on 22 April 1898 for Spanish-American War service. She was commissioned on 13 May 1898, with Lieutenant Lucien Young in command. In June and July she undertook patrol duty off Cuba, where she captured several Spanish schooners and sank a Spanish gunboat on 30 June. Together with the USS *Hornet* and *Wompatuck,* she engaged shore batteries and a Spanish flotilla at Manzanillo Bay, returning twice more in July and August for further such success. She was engaged in the Battle of Santiago, where she helped rescue Spanish sailors from the *Vizcaya,* and during the subsequent period of the war served as a patrol and dispatch boat between Santiago and Guantánamo. Decommissioned in February 1899, she was recommissioned to serve in similar capacities in 1902 and 1903. The *Hist* served with submarines as a tender from 1903 until being sold in 1911.

Presently a boat came alongside bearing Captain Eulaté, commander of the Vizcaya. That was a sight I shall never forget as long as I live. In the stern, supported by one of our naval cadets, sat the captain, covered with blood from three wounds, with a blood-stained handkerchief about his bare head. Around him sat or lay a dozen or more wounded men. In the bottom of the boat, which was leaking, was a foot or so of blood-stained water and the body of a dead Spanish sailor which rolled from side to side as the water swashed about. The captain was tenderly placed in a chair and then hoisted to the deck, where he was received with the honours due his rank. As the chair was placed on the quarter-deck he slowly raised himself to his feet, unbuckled his sword belt, kissed the hilt of his sword, and, bowing low, gracefully presented it to me as a token of surrender. I never felt so sorry for a man in all my life. Of course I declined to receive the sword, or rather I instantly handed it back to Captain Eulaté,[11] but accepted the surrender of his officers and men in the name of Admiral Sampson, our commander in chief. My men were all crowded aft about the deck and superstructure, and when I declined the sword the brave hearts under the blue shirts appreciated my feelings and they cheered until I felt ashamed of myself.

As I supported the captain toward my cabin, he stopped for a moment just as we reached the hatch, and drawing himself up to his full height, with his right arm extended above his head, exclaimed, "Adios, Vizcaya!" Just as the words passed his lips the forward magazine of his late command, as if arranged for the purpose, exploded with magnificent effect. Captain Eulaté, a sensitive, passionate man, conducted himself in a way to elicit the admiration of all who saw him. After he had been attended to by the surgeons he occupied a part of my cabin, and did all in his power to aid me in making his officers and men comfortable.

11. D. Eulate was a captain in the Spanish Navy.

The work of rescue was progressing rapidly; nearly three hundred prisoners—officers and men—had been received on board when the U. S. S. Resolute,[12] Commander Eaton[13] commanding, hove in sight, blowing her steam whistle, and with this signal at her yardarm, "Enemy's battle ship to the eastward." At first I thought that she had dressed ship in honour of our victory, and that the combination of signal flags was an accident, but as she drew nearer I knew this was not the case. A signal man was signalling that a Spanish battle ship was off Siboney, and Captain Eaton soon confirmed the news through a megaphone larger than any I had ever before seen. In reply to my inquiries, I was informed that the Resolute had been close enough to the newcomer to distinguish her colours, and that she was undoubtedly a Spanish battle ship, and probably at that moment was engaged in destroying our transport fleet at Siboney. After giving me this information, Captain Eaton continued his course to the westward in search of the admiral, who was out of sight, in chase of the Colón.

I felt absolutely confident that there was no Spanish battle ship anywhere to the eastward short of the coast of Spain, but after a while I saw the Harvard,[14] Captain Charles Cotton[15] commanding, coming my way at top speed with a tremendous bone in her mouth and followed by a dozen or more

12. A naval auxiliary craft transport purchased for Spanish-American War service.
13. Joseph Giles Eaton was warranted a midshipman on 24 September 1863. He was promoted to lieutenant on 21 March 1871, lieutenant commander on 19 June 1888, and commander on 10 November 1896.
14. The USS Harvard was a sister ship to the USS Yale (originally City of New York). She mounted sixteen guns, had a top speed of 21.8 knots, and carried a 407-man complement. Commissioned on 26 April 1898, the Harvard was returned to her owners on 2 September 1898, and renamed the Plattsburg for use in World War I.
15. Charles S. Cotton became an acting midshipman on 23 September 1858. He rose to the rank of commander on 25 April 1877, captain on 28 May 1892, and rear admiral on 27 March 1900.

army transports, all making the best speed they were capable of. Captain Cotton flew the signal, "Enemy's battle ship in sight to the eastward." The Harvard slowed and stopped quite close to me, while I hoisted in my boats and made ready to engage the new enemy. I asked Captain Cotton, who had assured me that he had been near enough to the stranger to make her out beyond doubt as a Spanish battle ship, why Captain Taylor in the Indiana was not knocking the roof off her. I could see the Indiana's smokestacks as she lay at her station off Santiago, where Sampson had sent her to prevent some Spanish gun vessels from doing the very thing this new battle ship was supposed to be engaged in. The answer to my question came back very promptly from Cotton: "Bob, he has fooled Taylor; don't let him fool you."

I could see the vessel referred to well out to sea, but standing in toward us, and I at once shaped a course to intercept her. My ship was cleared for action, the guns all loaded, and the men cheering wildly at the prospect of having a Spanish battle ship all to themselves; but the three hundred Spanish prisoners were a source of anxiety to me. To expose them to the fire of their own people would be barbarous, and to allow them to mix in with my men and go below in my ship during a fight would be tempting Providence. I decided at once on the only way out of the difficulty. I went to Captain Eulaté, explained the position to him in a few words, and placed him, his officers, and men on parole not to commit any act of violence against the authority of the United States. Then I put all his people where they would be reasonably safe, and, with the Harvard and a score of transports following me, stood rapidly out to sink the approaching ship. Most of the troop ships had stopped near me for protection, but some of them continued, I believe, as far as Jamaica, ninety miles away. The stranger was now in plain sight and my officers and best signal men declared her colours to be Spanish. I gave orders to open fire at five thousand yards, and was rapidly approaching the distance when she made signal, "I am an Austrian," and a few moments later hoisted her number. She proved to be the Austrian armoured cruiser Infanta Maria Teresa. One of that name was a wreck on the beach a few miles away, and the second would have gone to the bottom of the sea if she had delayed her signal a few minutes longer. The Spanish and Austrian flags were dangerously alike for such manœuvering on that particular day.

A number of dead Spanish sailors had been brought on board the Iowa from the Vizcaya while we were rescuing her crew. They had either been taken dead from the water or had died in the boats. I had had them placed well aft on the quarter-deck and covered with the Spanish flag. The time had now come to bury them, and I therefore stopped my engines and lowered my colours to half mast, and my motions were followed by the Harvard and the troop ships. Then all hands were called to bury the dead; the service was read by their own padre in the presence of their own officers and men, and the bodies were committed to the deep while my marines presented arms and my officers and men stood uncovered and silent as if we were burying our own people. I doubt if a more impressive funeral ever took place from the deck of a vessel of war, certainly not on the conclusion of a great naval battle before the combatants had had time to remove the powder stains.

As soon as the prisoners were received on board they were given all the coffee they could drink and all the hard bread and corned beef they could eat. Then they were scrubbed and fitted out with clean new uniforms, and it was hard to distinguish them from our own men. They were a fine, muscular lot of well-disciplined people. The officers, as well as the men, had lost everything except the clothing they wore, and this in many cases was very scant. Indeed, many came on board entirely naked, having removed all their clothing before attempting to swim ashore from their burning ships. The officers of the Iowa, from the captain down, gave up their quarters to the Spanish officers and supplied each one with a complete suit of clothing and as much champagne as they could be induced to swallow. We did all we could to make them forget their unfortunate surroundings, and their gratitude was what we expected from gentlemen of their profession.

When I had satisfied myself that the Resolute and Harvard had not seen a real Spanish battle ship, I directed the course of the Iowa to the eastward and resumed my station off Santiago, where I found the Indiana and Gloucester [16] on guard. The latter was about to transfer Admiral Cervera and some of his officers to the Indiana, but, as I knew that Captain Taylor had little if any spare room in his cabin, and I had plenty, I offered to take them on board the Iowa, which offer was at once accepted, and Captain Wainwright, [17] who had that day made a name for himself worthy the stock from which he comes, brought them alongside in his boat. The full marine guard was drawn up on the quarter-deck while the Spanish prisoners were lined up on the opposite side and the crew of the Iowa, just as they came out of the fight, were massed on the superstructure and after-turrets. I and my officers stood near the gangway. As the brave old admiral came over the side scantily clad, without shirt or hat, yet an admiral every inch of him, the officers saluted, the marines presented arms, and the buglers sounded the salute for an officer of his rank. As he bowed and extended his hand to me, my men burst

16. Originally the *Corsair*—a steel armed yacht owned by Pierpont Morgan—the USS *Gloucester* displaced 786 tons, had a top speed of 17 knots, mounted eight guns, and carried a complement of ninety-four men. Launched in 1891, she was commissioned on 23 April 1898. The *Gloucester* effectively destroyed HSM *Pluton* at Santiago. The yacht was sold in 1919.
17. Warranted a midshipman on 28 September 1864, Richard Wainwright graduated from the Naval Academy in June 1868. He was promoted to lieutenant on 25 September 1873, lieutenant commander on 16 September 1894, and commander on 3 March 1899. Superintendent of the Naval Academy from 1900 to 1902, Wainwright retired as a rear admiral in 1911.

Admiral Cervera's reception on board the Iowa

into cheers. For an instant it seemed to me that Admiral Cervera misunderstood the demonstration; but then he realized its meaning, that it was the tribute of brave men for a brave and gallant foe, and he stood bowing his acknowledgment while the men behind the guns made him understand what they thought of him.

The meeting between the late commander in chief, who had with him his son, acting as his flag lieutenant, and the commanding officers of the torpedo boats, and Captain Eulaté and his men, was touching and pathetic. After I had made him as comfortable as possible, he asked to see the wounded Spanish sailors who were crowded into our sick-bay. He had a word of comfort and encouragement for each of them and they appreciated his visit. I gave him my cabin, where he lived until after sundown on the following day, when I transferred him to the St. Louis[18] for passage North in company with the other captured Spanish officers. During the evening of the 3d of July he sat on deck under a small awning I had arranged for him, smoking and receiving the various officers who called to pay their respects. While he was somewhat depressed over the disaster that had befallen his fleet and his country, it seemed to me that he had anticipated it and bore himself with great dignity and courtesy. His conversation was most interesting, and I listened to him with great interest until he retired about eleven o'clock.

By that time Admiral Sampson had returned from the wreck of the Colón and we all knew of the complete annihilation of the Spanish fleet. There was a death-like silence over

18. The USS *St. Louis* was a sister ship to the *St. Paul*. An armed merchant cruiser, she displaced 14,910 tons, had a top speed of 22 knots, mounted 12 guns, and carried a 377-man complement. Built by Cramp & Sons, she was launched on 12 November 1894, commissioned on 24 April 1898, and returned to her owner on 2 September 1898. The *St. Louis* was used as a transport under the name *Louisville* at the end of World War I. Having been burned out while undergoing reconditioning in 1920, she was sold in 1925.

our fleet as the tired officers and men sought such rest as they could obtain. For me there was no rest, and I spent the night walking the deck, keeping a keen watch on the prisoners and occasionally visiting the wounded officers in my cabin to do what I could to add to their comfort. I felt that we had done a good, clean piece of work during the day, and was glad for the people at home who would be much relieved by our victory.

On July 4th we dressed ship, fired salutes, and conducted ourselves generally in a way befitting the day. When we had transferred our prisoners, we took our former blockading stations and fell again into our watchful routine. Toward midnight the Massachusetts, on search-light duty, discovered the Reina Mercedes, a Spanish cruiser of thirty-five hundred tons, coming out of the harbour. The Massachusetts opened on her at once and the Texas joined in the fight. The rest of us held our fire and watched one of the most beautiful engagements ever fought. The beams of the search lights showed up the Spaniard until she looked like a ship in a picture, and we could see the shells tearing through her and exploding all about her. Gradually she began to turn, then listed over to one side, and soon joined the Merrimac on the bottom and only a few hundred yards away from her. The batteries in the meantime opened up and for half an hour mortar shells and six-inch projectiles whizzed and roared over our heads. The Indiana received a mortar shell through her quarter-deck, and was the only ship struck. At midnight everything was quiet. The sea power of Spain had been destroyed in a manner which must bring great credit to the navy of the United States, and give us a standing as a naval power which we had never before enjoyed. And, beyond this, the war must speedily end.

During the evening of July 4th I wrote and submitted to Admiral Sampson my report of the engagement of July 3d. When I had about concluded it and was thinking of something good enough to say of the brave men who had fought under my command, my pen, without conscious effort on my part, wrote the following words: "I can not express my admiration for my magnificent crew. So long as the enemy showed his flag they fought like American seamen, but when the flag came down they were as gentle and tender as American women." I didn't know whether it was the memory of the gentle American women, or the presence about me of the gallant American seamen that influenced my pen, but it certainly wrote exactly what I felt.

The blockage of Santiago was strictly maintained until the Spanish army surrendered, when we retired to Guantanamo, and a squadron of twelve ships, the Iowa one of them, was made ready to sail for the coast of Spain and call the bluff of Admiral Camara [19] in passing his fleet through the Suez Canal [20] ostensibly on his way to Manila to annoy Admiral Dewey. For several days we lay with steam up and everything ready to get under way on the receipt of telegraphic orders, but the orders never came. Spain was vanquished, Sampson at Santiago had completed the work so brilliantly begun by Dewey at Manila, and she sued for peace. When the protocol had been signed we received orders to proceed to New York.

19. Manuel de la Camara was the Spanish admiral who commanded the Spanish reserve fleet in home waters.
20. The 107-mile-long canal from the Mediterranean Sea to the Gulf of Suez. This British-controlled waterway was essential prior to 1956 in maintaining the lifeline to British colonial possessions in India and the Far East.

CHAPTER 40

CONCLUSION

WITH men cheering and the bands playing "Homeward bound," we sailed from the island of Cuba, having wrested it from the nation that discovered it four hundred years before.

We reached New York August 20th, and there received a welcome which will never be forgotten by any one who witnessed it. The squadron, fresh from the enemy's coast and just as they had fought, steamed up the beautiful harbour, fired a salute of twenty-one guns off the tomb of General Grant,[1] and returned to the anchorage at Tompkinsville.[2] The hearts of officers and men were full to overflowing because of the kindly, patriotic welcome of their fellow-countrymen. The hardships we had endured were forgotten in the satisfaction we felt in having pleased our employers. There had been no time to advertise our coming or prepare for us a

1. Grant's Tomb is located in the northern part of New York City's borough of Manhattan.
2. Tompkinsville, New York, is located in the northeastern part of Staten Island, between Upper Bay and The Narrows of New York Harbor.

formal welcome; nevertheless New York city was one blaze of American flags, and every vessel that could steam or sail was crowded to suffocation with men and women and children from all parts of the republic to welcome our homecoming. It was a spontaneous outburst of patriotism and affection the like of which this country had never before seen.

Late in October the Iowa was ordered to be ready to sail for San Francisco and I was detached from her. I left her with great regret, much touched by the kindly feeling of her officers and crew.

From the day of my return I was generously treated by the people of all sections of the country. They showered invitations upon me for banquets and entertainments of all kinds. I could not accept many of them, but was, and am still, heartily grateful for the feeling that prompted them.

Some time after I left the Iowa I received a beautiful sword, which I value above all my earthly possessions, and the following letter:

"U.S.S. IOWA, FIRST RATE,
SAN FRANCISCO, CALIFORNIA, *February 14, 1899.*
"*Captain* ROBLEY D. EVANS, *U. S. N., Washington, D. C.*

"SIR: The members of this ship's company, who had the high honour of serving you from San Juan to Santiago, beg leave to present this sword as a token of our affection and reverence.

"It had been our intention to make this presentation when you relinquished command, but owing to the disintegration of the crew following our arrival at New York in August last, and our hurried departure, it was not done. Coming at this late day, it will show you, sir, that this action is not from momentary impulse, but that the affection and respect of this crew for you is deep-rooted and lasting, and that the men of the battle ship Iowa will ever cherish the memory of their beloved commander.

"And with this sword we send our wishes for your health

and happiness always. It is an assurance from us that you are
more than a hero to a *nation—you are a hero to your men.*
"Very respectfully,
"F. ZULCH,
"A. E. MOORE,
"J. COLLINS, *Chief M.A.A.,*
"E. McCORMACK
"H. ENELS HOLT
"Committee."

My yarn of forty years of naval life is spun. I think I can
not close it more appropriately than by repeating a remark
made to me in Cincinnati.[3] I was attending a reception in the
Chamber of Commerce, where many people had assembled to
greet me. A white-haired old gentleman stopped in front of
me and, taking my hand, said, "Captain, I want to know
how it feels when you are sure that there are seventy millions
of people each of whom would like to look into your eyes
and say, 'God bless you!' " I could have told the kindly old
man that it made me feel that fighting by day and watching
by night, that danger in storm and suffering in tropic calm,
were but "reasonable service" to such a country, and such
fellow-countrymen as I am bound to by every feeling of my
heart.

3. Located in the southwestern corner of Ohio on the Ohio River, Cincinnati was a bustling commercial center.

ABOUT THE EDITOR

Chief Historian of the Department of Energy, Dr. Benjamin Franklin Cooling also serves as Professorial Lecturer in History at George Washington University. Previously associated with the historical programs of the Army, Air Force, and National Park Service—as well as serving as curator of the Cruiser *Olympia* Association—Dr. Cooling taught at Weidner University, the U.S. Army War College, and the University of Pennsylvania. He is immediate past Executive Director of the Society of Military History.

Among Dr. Cooling's publications are *Benjamin Franklin Tracy: Father of the Modern American Fighting Navy* (Hamden, CT: The Shoe String Press, 1973); *Gray Steel and Bluewater Navy: The Formative Years of America's Military Industrial Complex* (Hamden, CT: The Shoe String Press, 1979); *Forts Henry and Donelson: The Key to the Confederate Heartland* (Knoxville: University of Tennessee Press, 1988); and editor of *Case Studies in the Development of Close Air Support* (Washington, DC: Office of Air Force History, U.S. Air Force, 1990). He has published more than sixty articles on military and naval history.

CLASSICS OF NAVAL LITERATURE

JACK SWEETMAN, SERIES EDITOR

Herman Melville, *White-Jacket; or, The World in a Man-of-War.* Introduction by Stanton B. Garner

Edward P. Stafford, *The Big E.* Introduction by Paul Stillwell

Nicholas Monsarrat, *The Cruel Sea.* Introduction by Edward L. Beach

Arthur W. Sinclair, *Two Years on the* Alabama. Introduction and notes by William N. Still, Jr.

James Fenimore Cooper, *Ned Myers; or, A Life Before the Mast.* Introduction and notes by William S. Dudley

C.S. Forester, *The Good Shepherd.* Introduction by J.D.P. Hodapp, Jr.

Samuel Eliot Morison, *John Paul Jones: A Sailor's Biography.* Introduction by James C. Bradford

Frederick Marryat, *Mr. Midshipman Easy.* Introduction and notes by Evan R.L. Davies

Harold and Margaret Sprout, *The Rise of American Naval Power, 1775–1918.* Introduction by Kenneth J. Hagan and Charles Conrad Campbell

Robert Southey, *The Life of Nelson.* Introduction and notes by Robert D. Madison

Erskine Childers, *The Riddle of the Sands.* Introduction and notes by Eric J. Grove

Saburo Sakai and Martin Caiden, with Fred Saito, *Samurai!* Introduction by Barrett Tillman

Thomas Heggen, *Mister Roberts.* Introduction by David P. Smith

Mitsuo Fuchida and Masatake Okumiya, *Midway: The Battle That Doomed Japan.* Introduction by Thomas B. Buell

Alexander O. Exquemelin, *The Buccaneers of America.* Introduction and notes by Robert C. Ritchie